P9-AFO-990

The Other Europe

The Other Europe

A Complete Guide to
Business Opportunities in
Eastern Europe

Christopher Engholm

McGraw-Hill, Inc.

New York San Francisco Washington, D.C. Auckland Bogotá
Caracas Lisbon London Madrid Mexico City Milan
Montreal New Delhi San Juan Singapore
Sydney Tokyo Toronto

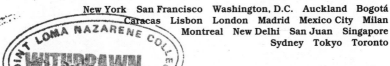

Library of Congress Cataloging-in-Publication Data

Engholm, Christopher.
    The other Europe : a complete guide to business opportunities in
Eastern Europe / Christopher Engholm.
        p.   cm.
    Includes bibliographical references and index.
    ISBN 0-07-019434-3
    1. Investments, American—Europe, Eastern.   2. International
business enterprises—United States—Management.   3. International
business enterprises—Europe, Eastern—Management.   4. Corporations,
American—Europe, Eastern.   5. Europe, Eastern—Economic policy.
I. Title.
HG5430. 7. A3E53,   1993
332. 6' 73' 0947—dc20   93-26167
                                                                              CIP

1 2 3 4 5 6 7 8 9 0   DOC/DOC   9 9 8 7 6 5 4 3

ISBN 0-07-019434-3

*The sponsoring editor for this book was Caroline Carney, the editing
supervisor was Olive H. Collen, and the production supervisor was Suzanne
W. Babeuf. This book was set in Palatino by McGraw-Hill's Professional Book
Group composition unit.*

Printed and bound by R. R. Donnelley & Sons Company.

To Bernard A. Engholm

Contents

4. Successful Selling: Researching the Market, Distributing a Product   88

5. Why Invest in Eastern Europe? Smart Strategies for Investors   111

6. Deciding Where to Invest: Weighing the Potential and the Pitfalls   130

7. Riding the Waves of "Transition": Managing Business Risk   160

8. Finding the Perfect Partner: Qualifying People and Enterprises   182

Preface

In the months following the fall of the Berlin Wall, I became increasingly awed by the human commercial energy unleashed by the opening of markets in Central-Eastern Europe and the former Soviet Union. During that time, throughout my home state of California, business groups and associations intent on profiting in the "New East" proliferated, and many of my business associates packed their bags and headed off to Warsaw, Budapest, and Prague. While attending Eastern European business conferences that seemed to spring up everywhere, I was moved by the eloquent pleas of Eastern European officials for foreign investors to come to their countries and by the commercial daring of American business people who were taking the plunge. It was then that I committed myself to chronicle firsthand what I had witnessed once already in the People's Republic of China five years before—the opening of a new megamarket.

This time, though, I would issue a clarion call in a book beckoning U.S. firms to move into the former Eastern bloc as fast as possible, since I remembered well the opportunities missed by corporate America in Asia because of a lack of initiative. Experience had also taught me that the "gold rush in Eastern Europe" would not last and that disillusionment with both the markets and the investment climates would surface as soon as foreign executives experienced the frustration and uncertainty of dealing with unempowered bureaucrats, buyers without foreign exchange, and a legal and political atmosphere that made business forecasting impossible. I recognized that many American firms might enter Eastern Europe without caution, not having learned from the past mistakes of their brethren, and get burned. I decided to write a book about our corporate pioneers in the region, who, in many cases, have found profits across the Rhine—people who had reinvented themselves to operate in transitioning economies and whose insights could help others do the same.

Time was of the essence as business suitors headed East en masse. But alas, in the course of fifteen months of research, travel in the region, and interviewing people who had started up businesses there, I found that the countries I would include grew in number from eight to twenty-five. Deadlines passed as Yugoslavia exploded and Mikhail Gorbachev braced the world for the dissolution of the U.S.S.R. into fifteen new countries. To my great surprise, corporate America did not sleepwalk through Eastern Europe's opening or turn tail and run when the going got tough. In 1992, American investment in the region topped that of all other countries, even surpassing neighboring Germany. This book is about the people responsible for this bright statistic—those out there on the front line whose experience can educate others aiming to venture into "the Other Europe."

Christopher Engholm

Acknowledgments

Many people have contributed their time, knowledge, and humor to help make this book a reality. The scope of this book is wide; indeed, I can hardly claim expertise in all the areas it covers. I am therefore deeply grateful to all those who responded to my questions, assisted in research, or remained at my side during the hard times. I extend thanks to the following people (in alphabetical order): researcher Kari Abraham; the folks at the American Graduate School of International Management in Arizona; interpreter Pat Austin; consultant Kim Barnes of Barnes & Conti; Dr. James Baur of Science Solutions; Chuck and Annie Benson; consultant Bonnie Best of Best Communications; John Betchkel of General Electric; entrepreneur Nigel Bonny; typist Helen Bloomfield; Dr. Dennis Briscoe at the University of San Biego; Caroline Carney at McGraw-Hill; my agent, Julie Castiglia; Andre O. Chmielewski of AmexpoCo.; commercial officer James Joy at the American embassy in Berlin; Russian expert   Barbara Chronowski; Mike Cloud at Kodak; Robert W. Courtney, vice president of King International; entrepreneur Anne Devero; Jim Devoss of Amway Corporation; entrepreneur Hoff Doerr in Vienna; Barney, Yvonne, and Jeanie Engholm; all the helpful people at the Eastern European Business Information Center; Lyn Fabrizio at the Department of Commerce; Carsten Finke of Arthur D. Little in Berlin; Richard Fischer of General Electric Aircraft Engines in Warsaw; Andrea Freedman and Jaimie Sanford of the Center for Citizen Initiatives (formerly the Center for U.S.–U.S.S.R. Initiatives) in San Francisco; Gale George of Emergency

Packs, Inc.; William Gladstone of Waterside Productions, Inc.; Jan Glinski, Ph.D., of Bell Northern Telecom in Ontario; Czechoslovakia expert Martina Spifiak; management consultant Sue Gould; former U.S. senator Gary Hart of International Strategies in Denver; Robert Hecht-Nielsen, chairman of the board of HNC, Inc.; Tracy Hightower; Ewald Hiltenkamp of the Treuhandanstalt in Koln; Dr. Csilla Hunyadi of the newsletter *Hungary Today*; Romanian entrepreneur Albert Jacmin; Richard Jenner, Ph.D., at the Bureau of Business Research at San Francisco State University; Jeremy Keller at the Department of Commerce; consultant and entrepreneur Boris I. Khersonski; Hanno Kirk, Ph.D.; John Kiser, Peter Walsh, and Barney O'Meara of KRI Research, Inc.; Andrew L. Kozlowski of Jennings, Engstrand, & Henrikson in San Diego; David A. Kruest of the Poland-California Chamber of Commerce; international marketing consultant Ruth Langhorst; Susan Lewenz at the Office of Independent States and Commonwealth Affairs; Dariusz Linert of the Daro Trade Company in Poland; Mark Malry at the Department of Commerce; Ed Mattix of USWest; Amway distributors Lawrence and Ruby Maxham; Vivian Miller at Price Waterhouse in Los Angeles; Jo Murray and George Nikolaieff of the firm Jo Murray & Nikolaieff in Oakland; Jan Myslivac of Intertrade Associates; the folks at Paul Ray & Carre Orban International; David Kern Peteler of Peat, Marwick in Los Angeles; international marketing consultant John Pfieffer; entrepreneur Ron Plunkett; Piotr Puchala of M.P.P. World Trade Company; entrepreneur Larry Rabbi; Dieter Riechel at Signet Armorlite, Inc.; Olga Ringo of ZOV, Inc., in San Francisco; Jerry Rohan of Price Waterhouse in Moscow; Hubert Romanowski at the Embassy of the Republic of Poland in Washington, D.C.; Diana Rowland of Rowland & Associates in San Diego; Sandra Rowland of Appropriate Technology in Washington, D.C.; Ray Schonholtz of Partners for Democratic Change in San Francisco; Russia expert and consultant Sairan A. Schuman; author Gini Graham Scott, Ph.D.; Stephen Seng of Grand United, Inc.; Inga Sertic; Zbigniew "Zbig" Skiba of the U.S. Polish Chamber of Commerce in Chicago and Skiba Consulting; Francis Skrobiszewski of the Polish Enterprise Fund; Tadeusz Slawek in Cyssyn, Poland; Michael A. Pappan at Ward Howell in New York; John Turco of Technologies West; Martin Janak and Renee Wenrick of Wenrick and Associates in San Diego and Plzen, Czechoslovakia; Donald Wesling, Ph.D., at the University of California at San Diego; Tom and Nancy Woolsey; and Shelley Zeiger of Shalmar in New Jersey.

Introduction

Cosmonaut Sergei K. Krikalev* had orbited planet Earth in the Mir Space Station for five months longer than planned. He thought he would never get to come home. Orbiting the Earth for 306 days starting in October 1991, he had been delayed in space because his country didn't have the money to bring him home. Finally, a German-Russian mission was sent up, funded by German private interests, to fetch Sergei back to Earth. During his 10 months in space, as the space station passed repeatedly overhead, 250 miles above Eurasia, much had happened down below.

What was Sergei Krikalev returning home to?

Earth Life had Changed

"A lot of things have happened without me," he said in a radio transmission to reporters. "I will have to restore my normal physical condition and return to normal, everyday Earth life." Indeed, he would. He had hailed from Leningrad. It was now called St. Petersburg. His return flight would touch down in Kazakhstan, which was now an independent republic, no longer a part of the Soviet Union. In fact, the Union of Soviet Socialist Republics had ceased to exist.

That wasn't all. The Cold War had ended, and the Soviet Communist party had met its demise in the aftermath of the August putsch. Yugoslavia had endured a civil war that resulted in its division into five independent states. Nationalism in Czechoslovakia threatened to divide the country into two independent republics—one controlled by Czechs, and the other by Slovaks. The members of the Warsaw Pact had dissolved their political union and their trading organization, Comecon, orienting their trade away from the East and toward the West. And market economics had come to replace state-controlled socialism for 400 million people in Eastern-Central Europe and the former Soviet Union. Moreover, the countries of what was known as "the

*Pronounced *sur'-gay kreek'-uh-lawf*.

Other Europe" were vying to become part of the European Economic Community!

Russian television announced: "Krikalev's return after almost one year's absence is like a favorite story out of Soviet science fiction, in which cosmonauts who have spent a short time in space return to Earth, where ages have gone by and everything—everything—has changed."

By radio, however, Sergei told Western reporters gathered at the once-off-limits Flight Control Center north of Moscow: "Before, the republics were united in the Union of Soviet Socialist Republics; now they join the Commonwealth of Independent States. Therefore, the changes might not be so dramatic as they appear at first glance." In reality, the changes were dramatic; after forging 53 cross-border agreements, almost none of which had been implemented, the three-month-old commonwealth was teetering like a monolithic political Humpty Dumpty, threatening to fall apart completely. Cosmonaut Krikalev was lucky to be making it home at all.

While he had floated in orbit, capitalism had taken root and grown in the East. West and East had "Come Together," as the ubiquitous Philip-Morris cigarette-advertising billboards now commanded passersby from Warsaw to Bucharest. Western advertising had been plastered grotesquely across the gray facades of former government buildings, train stations, and airports. The corporate logo of the American computer giant Digital Electronics now stood atop the spire of the Stalinesque Palace of Culture in the heart of Warsaw. The Warsaw Stock Exchange now occupied the building that once contained the headquarters of Poland's Communist Party! East and West now groped for common ground in "mutually profitable business deals."

For the West, a new market frontier (representing 430 million consumers—including the former U.S.S.R.—with half the buying power of Western Europe) had been laid open for exploration and exploitation. Over half of all the factories in Eastern Europe needed technological upgrading, and it was no secret that Eastern Europeans produced 15 percent of the world's gross national product (GNP) and that Hungary, Czechoslovakia, and Eastern Germany had a combined GNP greater than China. If current trends continued, the pundits predicted, the European market (including Eastern and Western Europe) would be bigger than the U.S. market by 1993. Moreover, the U.S. government had embarked on a concerted effort to vigorously support U.S. business activity in the region as part of its strategy to strengthen the region's embryonic democracies. Corporate America hit the ground in the New East sprinting.

In early 1991, a survey conducted jointly by *The Wall Street Journal*, Booz-Allen & Hamilton, and *Nihon Keizai Shimbun* (Japan's leading business newspaper) found that one of every three corporate CEOs in North America, Asia, and Western Europe planned "to build or buy factories in Eastern Europe during the next four years." That meant *one out of every three* CEOs around the world! A survey conducted only two years before had reported that *only one CEO out of 20* had such plans to expand into Eastern Europe. Of 1,500 American CEOs surveyed in early 1991, 35 percent of them indicated that their companies intended to initiate business ties in East Europe within 12 months, as reported in *The Wall Street Journal*. A survey conducted a few months later indicated that *67 percent* of American executives believe that the Eastern European market would become a "major world market comparable to Western Europe" within two decades.

With a speculative enthusiasm of the sort and degree that must have fueled the California gold rush, Western business declared open season on the markets of the East. When I spoke to former U.S. senator Gary Hart about the phenomenon, he compared it to the opening of the Klondike—a new frontier ripe for exploitation by enterprising traders and investors. Senator Hart had practiced what he preached: He hitched his fortunes to the region by becoming an international business-development consultant focusing on Eastern Europe and Russia. The big four U.S. accounting companies rode into the region on the coattails of their clients; not to do so would have been left in a cloud of Fortune 500 entrepreneurial dust. Nearly every multinational corporation headquartered in the United States was formulating plans to expand in the New East. Overnight, PepsiCo set up 60 bottling plants in the region. Honeywell sold $50 million worth of goods there in 1990 alone. Japanese companies ogled the region, too. Ten of Japan's largest *soga sosha* trading companies set up offices in *each* of the countries of the former Eastern bloc. While Cosmonaut Krikalev had drifted aloft, Eastern Europe had become a lava-hot landscape of commercial opportunity; and interest among international executives and entrepreneurs was growing despite sporadic social unrest and growing political uncertainty throughout the region.

Meanwhile, a new business mentality surfaced in the East—Get Rich Quick. Ex-Communist officials were among the first to learn the ways of capitalist enterprise. Like sharks, they snapped up pieces of their state-owned command economies and sold them for dollars and deutsche marks. Even Lenin's corpse was put up for sale—for foreign exchange only, mind you. A competition had begun between the newly market-oriented countries of the region. Their objective: To attract Western investment. Western-style preferential-investment laws were hastily enacted. Austerity measures were implemented and tightly enforced in order to gain favor with the International Monetary Fund (IMF) and the World Bank and thus win desperately needed development loans.

Within the investment pipeline there began a trickle, and then a flow. The numbers made the outside investment in the China market of the early 1980s look miniscule in comparison. America's trade with Eastern European countries increased 275 percent between 1987 and 1989, *before* the Berlin Wall came down. United States exports to Hungary increased 80 percent in 1991, even as recession began to squeeze the region. By the end of 1990, over 9,700 foreign ventures had been established in Poland, Hungary, and Czechoslovakia, representing over $1.2 billion in foreign investment. PlanEcon, a Washington database company, predicted that by 1993 Hungary, Czechoslovakia, and Poland would be attracting $3.5 billion a year in foreign corporate investment.

But the social costs had been staggering. Unemployment in the East had rocketed as plants shut down or were auctioned off to management or foreigners. In Poland, 1.3 million workers, and in Romania 10 percent of the working population lost their jobs. Some observers predicted that joblessness in Eastern Germany would climb to 50 percent of the working population! Inflation soared with the loss of sources of cheap energy and raw materials from the Soviet Union; it ranged from 30 percent in Poland to 316 percent in Bulgaria in the first quarter of 1991. Higher prices, loss of jobs, and curtailed welfare subsidies ripped a widening gash in social safety nets. Economic austerity measures encouraged by the IMF meant loans were withheld and interest rates were raised. Hundreds of thousands of people found themselves unable to deal with the rough transition to capitalism.

Massive new investment was needed. Western companies wanted to help, but a U.S. recession put plans on hold. Germany plowed money into Eastern Germany but had little to donate to other countries. That didn't imply, however, that German companies were not active in the New East. One could not help but overhear the incessant panicked refrain: "The Germans are everywhere!" German companies had moved with lightning speed in Eastern-Central Europe, capturing a 30–45-percent share of the markets and accounting for 26 percent of the joint-venture deals signed in the region. (The United States has signed only 11 percent of these deals; Austria has penned 25 percent.) Czechoslovakia's president, Vaclav Havel, even agreed to return to Germans their holdings in the Sudetenland (northern

Czechoslovakia), a move hardly thinkable when Sergei's spacecraft blasted off 10 months earlier. German companies had moved into the former Soviet republics, too, utilizing associates in the former East Germany and Poland who maintained contacts with trading officials in the former Soviet Union.

But where were the Americans?

Most of the "Other Europeans" want to meet and do business with Americans. Not Germans. And certainly not the culturally unfamiliar Koreans and Japanese. Although the somewhat-idealized view of the United States is being revised by the arrival of MTV and CNN, Americans enjoy a wonderful cultural advantage in these markets. Easterners associate American goods with quality and want to "be like Americans" more than any other people.

But American companies had run into problems. International-trade development programs were not properly funded. Enterprise funds may have been awarded start-up grants, but financing was hard to qualify for without prior in-country experience. Eastern Europe, it turned out, was far away. And expensive. Large U.S. firms, of course, could hire the best expertise available, and avoid the pitfalls that lie in any newly opened overseas market. Small and medium-sized companies, however, often floundered, and turned away in frustration.

The problems they encountered and continue to experience are manifold. They lack the personal connections in the markets that can save time and resources. Often they lack language capability. Or they can't "understand the mentality" of Eastern Europeans, who may want to initiate private enterprise and set up joint ventures with foreign companies but often lack the know-how or a concrete incentive to do so. Moreover, investment laws keep changing, and retaining a lawyer to keep up with them is expensive. Market research is virtually nonexistent, and the markets are small. [Total U.S. sales to the former East bloc equaled $1.68 billion in 1990. Together with the U.S.S.R., these countries bought only 2.6 percent of Organization for Economic Cooperation and Development (OECD) exports in 1988, worth $51.6 billion; the U.S. captured only a 4.5 percent market share.] Business information is hard to find and harder to make sense of. There are ownership questions. Political uncertainty pervades the entire region; political violence erupts continuously. Some companies have been burned by overzealous business people in Eastern Europe who failed to pay for goods received. Moreover, small companies are in no position to take fish meal, lumber, or vodka in lieu of cash. Some currencies have become internally convertible; others, including the ruble and the dinar, have not. And then there was the Asia syndrome: "The growth is in Asia," one heard frustrated executives cry. America's competitive edge, however, exists in the New East, not the Far East. The competition is notably less intense in East Europe than in Korea or Japan or Singapore.

If there had been inflated optimism among American businesses, it fell away. For companies that set up shop in the region, worker wages began to rise, cutting into margins. Devalued local currencies made purchasing raw materials more expensive for start-up joint ventures than had been forecast. Indeed, the economic makeover of the region's former socialist economies would take years, not months, to carry out. Thousands of enterprises—hundreds employing over 10,000 workers—came on the auction block, making the privatization of the region's factories the largest such undertaking ever attempted. Large, sprawling enterprises have been slow to move into private hands, even in the former East Germany, where the Treudhandanstalt has managed the sell-off of enterprises comparatively quickly. Negative press reports in the West focused on the "slow pace of privatization in the East," concluding falsely that doing business in the region wasn't worth the effort. (Most commentators failed to mention that an immense amount of business was being done *outside* the still-state-owned sector.) Pessimism crept into the boardrooms of corporate America. The Eastern European rush was over. *Wait and See* became the watchwords for corporate America, which would watch from afar for a while, and await developments.

Sergei Krikalev did the same.

Japanese companies held off, too, because of a recession at home and trade friction with the European Economic Community (EC). The Japanese government also was seeking to recover territory lost to Russia after World War II before it sanctioned large-scale investment in the former Soviet Union. The Germans and the Italians and the Austrians, however, continued to storm in, selling consumer and capital goods and locking down deals with the cream of the private sector—the lean and hungry new capitalists of the East.

"Where are the Americans?" asked Eastern Europe's investment officials, many of whom bristle at the pervasive German business presence in the region. Lech Walesa publicly scolded the United States for moving slowly to invest. Former president Nixon spoke out about the risks of not supporting the East's fledgling democracies, claiming correctly that ignoring the region's dire need for aid could cost the United States dearly in the future. Meanwhile, U.S. companies were in a wait-and-see mode, thus risking the loss of a golden opportunity to stake a claim in the new markets of the East. It was not without symbolism that a Germany-funded mission was instrumental rescuing Sergei Krikalev. But Americans would not ignore Eastern Europe for long. In 1992, the year of European unity would bring another "rush" of deals by American companies—especially medium-sized companies—that could see the prudence of taking the East Europe plunge before their competition.

This book was written with two objectives in mind: (1) To encourage U.S. business people to become involved in the emergent markets of the East before German companies monopolize them and (2) to explain *how* to enter these markets and acquire the know-how necessary to prosper in them.

The book provides detailed corporate accounts of doing business in the region. It offers checklists of tips and advice garnered during discussions with lawyers, consultants, Eastern European officials and business people, and American executives with ground-level experience in the region. It is written to help you in the process of preparing to enter these markets, to acquaint you with the numerous distinct and diverse markets of Eastern Europe (both extant and just emerging), and to suggest proven techniques and methods for investing in the region with the objective of gaining a market presence there. The trade systems and governmental decision-making culture pertaining to business transactions throughout the region are described, as are the management and operating problems faced by foreigners running Eastern European ventures. This book offers advice about how best an American business person can anticipate (and respond to) Eastern European styles and strategies of negotiating. It describes how one can conduct oneself gracefully whether toasting a Hungarian counterpart at an official banquet, visiting a mosque in Albania, or hosting an eastern German delegation in the United States.

The central idea is that you, as a Western business person venturing into Eastern Europe, must *reinvent* yourself as a business person in order to succeed. You must learn to cross into non-Western business cultures and bureaucracies, collect your own information about markets, make your own connections, put together creative financing, initiate government-to-business relationships, gauge political risk, and conduct yourself according to local business standards of etiquette. Competing companies have not yet achieved real momentum in the East because it is difficult to line up lending institutions to fund projects. To do so is one of the keys to success. You have to be an authentic international dealmaker to succeed in this rapidly changing part of the world. You have to reinvent yourself to deal with unorthodox requisites of these markets, becoming skilled in banking internationally, bidding on international aid projects, dealing with the IMF and the World Bank, and navigating the smoky halls of Eastern bureaucracies, in which members of the Communist *nomenklatura* of yesterday have all too often become part of a new breed of reformer-capitalists today. People who I believe have "reinvented" themselves to do business in Eastern Europe and the former Soviet Union have shared their personal stories in this book: Like Shelly Zeiger, who courted Russian dignitaries for five years before signing a U.S.-U.S.S.R. joint-venture deal in 1973; Renee Wenrick, whose marketing and advertising company, Wenrick Communications, has signed an exclusive advertising deal with the only media organization in Czechoslovakia to advertise and distribute Western goods and services; James Baur, owner of Science Solutions, who has scoured the research institutes of Russia in search of high-tech-product prototypes that his company can market to Western markets; George Nikolaieff and Pat Murray, who started out providing public relations for the mayor of Nakhodka, on the Pacific coast of Russia, and now have deals with Aeroflot and a Russian free-trade zone; Anne Devero, who has assembled a network of jewelers and craftspeople throughout Poland who make jewelry based on her designs, which she sells to boutiques in the United States; and Ron Plunkett, whose company has worked to locate and purchase rare World War II aircraft in the region, with the help of Boris Yeltsin and a famous Russian cosmonaut. Of course, this list does not include the forward-looking U.S. corporations that we'll discuss as well, such as General Electric, General Motors, and Amway Corporation.

I have tried to combine firsthand reportage, corporate surveys, and fully cited academic research to offer the international-business practitioner a manual for marketing and managing in Eastern Europe, as well as a road map for building long-term business relationships in the region adroitly and without blunder. The book is designed to be a fast and enjoyable read for the business executive with little time to waste before entering Eastern Europe as an entrepreneur.

1
Rushing to the "New East"

The Myths and the Realities

Events in Eastern Europe have created a new world without walls, facilitating the West-East movement of ideas, capital, technology, and people across once-closed borders. An irresistible course of change has replaced the inflexible Communist five-year plans of the past. New business opportunities have emerged and multiply each new day. All companies in all countries crouch on a brand-new starting line, together facing the same opportunities and the same challenges; no contender can claim that this playing field is not level. The starter's gun has fired—the rush to the East has begun.

Go East, Young Man!

For me the symbol of the return to capitalism in Eastern Europe is the Palace of Culture in the center of Warsaw, a past gift from the Soviet Union. The gray and dismal 38-story "wedding cake"-style palace features two dozen Corinthian porticoes and pseudo-Renaissance finials; the 3,300 former propaganda offices inside have been transformed into boutiques filled with Levi jeans, Samsonite luggage, and displays of Bic pens. Not long ago I strolled through the cavernous structure and watched upper-crust Poles, many of whom probably worked as party officials, peruse the Georgio Armani and Yves St. Laurent apparel. In the shadow of the Palace of Culture in Warsaw, Russians and gypsies from the former Soviet Union hawked wares at a never-closing swap meet of gargantuan proportions where they earn convertible zlotys with which to buy foreign goods to be sold for rubles home. The outdoor bazaar is such a complex microeconomy that a Polish university recently assembled a gaggle of Ph.D.'s to conduct a case study of it.

The same sudden and inexorable changes have occurred everywhere in Eastern Europe. On the Vaci Utca in the heart of Budapest foreign tourists now buy specially packaged Hungarian paprika and red salami in boutiquelike grocery stores, while street musicians and money changers, gypsy women and merchants crowd around the foreigners heading for McDonald's, pleading with them to buy colorful tablecloths at triple the price offered just around the corner. You'd think everyone in Eastern Europe had become a vendor desperate to make a ruble, a kroner, or a dinar, bartering goods of infinite variety and infinite uselessness in swap meets and in front of glistening new foreign-funded hotels. Many of the goods had been stolen from the former socialist infrastructure—doorknobs, broken tools, a set of screws, a plastic camera, an old pair of shoes.

In eastern Germany, I bought a piece of the Berlin Wall for five bucks, and in Hungary, a hawker peddled me a sealed can of air with a label that read The Last Breath of Communism. A year after the coup attempt, Moscow, as described by David Remnick in *The New Yorker*, had become "a post-communist world as it might have been painted by Hieronymus Bosch....In the subway stations and kiosks, you could buy a lace tablecloth, a bottle of Curaçao, Wrigley's spearmint gum, Mars bars, a Public Enemy tape, Swiss chocolate, plastic "marital toys," a Mercedes Benz hood ornament, American cigarettes, and Estonian pornography....The city is awash with twenty-five-year-old men wearing slick suits and black shirts and announcing their occupation as "a little buying, a little selling."

"Everything will sell here," Andezej Kita proclaimed. The president of Akita Electronics, a new private enterprise in Poland, added (quoted in *Business Week*), "Everything is in demand." Market-starved Americans were ecstatic. About the opening of the 290-million-strong Russian consumer market, telecommunication guru Kenny Schaffer, who has set up a communications venture in Russia, exulted to *The New Yorker*, "A dozen time zones that never heard of Phil Spector!"

The Rush Across the Rhine

Deal making in the East really began with a blunder. Gunter Schabowski, a spokesperson for the East German Central Committee, misspoke in a fashion that led East Germans to believe that the Berlin

Wall had been permanently opened. The citizens stormed the wall. Shortly thereafter Saatchi & Saatchi placed an advertising billboard on the wall. Then business suitors from around the world filled hotel lobbies in Prague, Budapest, and Warsaw, ready to ink the perfect deal.

Deals were struck at an amazing clip given how recently the wall had come down, and how intransigent the infrastructural problems were that awaited foreigners in these larval markets. The former U.S. ambassador to Hungary, who had become a venture capitalist, told the American Chamber of Commerce in Budapest, "If you stand in the lobby of the Forum Hotel, you are lucky not to get knocked down. The gold rush is on in Hungary. Budapest is a boom town." As were Moscow and Kiev and Leningrad (now St. Petersburg). "This is like the Wild West," declared Jeff Ostrovsky, a Russian immigrant who founded Atlantic J&S Corporation in Staten Island to set up joint ventures with the Soviet Union. The demand for products in the Soviet Union is "absolutely tremendous," he told the *Los Angeles Times*. Even before the Berlin Wall came down, Coca-Cola had started handing out free Cokes to dazed and confused East Germans crossing over the border. Not long after, the company followed up by injecting $140 million into eastern Germany to set up bottling plants and provide trucks and vending machines. East Germans yelled to one another as they raced through the widening gap in the Berlin Wall, on November 9, 1989, "Hurry, McDonald's is still open!" The West Germans gave them roses, and giveaway crews gave them Camels and Marlboros. Coca-Cola people tossed six-packs into buses filled with Easterners heading West. "The Easterners laughed," observed Peter Laufer, author of *Iron Curtain Rising*. "They looked dizzy. This was the West. This was capitalism. Free flowers, cigarettes, and soda. Free money."

Action in the "Evil Empire." Meanwhile, in the "evil empire," the capitalist West got pummeled in the media less and less. "Suddenly, instead of reports about homeless people in New York, they were showing feature stories about the glories of Fifth Avenue," Kenny Schaffer observed. "And the stars of the morning exercise show were doing aerobics instead of marching in place." Advertisements for Lego sets appeared, even though you could not yet buy Lego sets in stores. Foreign business people, lured by the seductive rhetoric of glasnost and perestroika, were cooking deals so fast even the plethora of new business newsletters couldn't keep up. "There were California entrepreneurs wanting to sell the Soviets swimming pool tarpaulins," writes A. Craig Copetas in his wry book *Bear Hunting with the Politburo*. "Texas entrepreneurs pushing bull semen. Florida entrepreneurs extolling the virtues of prefabricated houses, and North Carolina entrepreneurs pedaling sod....Jane Fonda jogged around the Kremlin peddling her exercise video tapes, Ronald McDonald pranced down Gorky Street marketing Big Macs, and Vermont ice-cream magnates Ben & Jerry wandered through rusted Soviet ice-cream plants with dreams of Raisa Raspberry and Mickey-Mocha Gorbachev."

Everything Is in Demand! Everything Is for Sale! I left the Palace of Culture in Warsaw and ran straight into the ubiquitous crowds of Russians that operate a 24-hour-a-day flea market in the grassy area between the palace and the central train station. Traditionally, the Soviets sold their wares to Poles for zloty, which they could resell in Russia on the black market. But now, with Russians feeling the painful pinch of capitalism's offspring—inflation and joblessness—the market was more intense than usual. "Everybody's selling out in Russia," Ukrainian émigré Larry Rabbi told me later. "They're selling grandpa's *samovar* just to survive! This is called private enterprise—selling everything you own, *to survive.*" Nothing was sacred. The Kremlin walls were up for sale as advertising space; even Lenin's corpse, for up to $50 million. "I wonder if I could middle a deal to sell Lenin to Michael Jackson?" a marketing friend of mine wondered.

What Lay Beyond the Crumbling Wall?

The shotgun marriage of West and East meant different things to each side. The West saw in the East a new source of cheap labor, a virgin bevy of consumers long deprived of Western products, and a brand-new site to invest in factories that could serve both the European Community and the former Soviet Union. Most Easterners were simply dumbfounded; they hadn't a clue how to deal with the West's eager, ingratiating, and market-ravenous multinational firms. A rising tide of Western consumer products had broken through to the East, and many locals felt not only engulfed but uneasy. "Philip Morris is sending us billions of cigarettes," remarked Gennadi Gerasimov, then Soviet Foreign Ministry spokesperson, "so some people suggest our new name should be Marlboro Country."

For many Westerners the attraction to the burgeoning markets of the former Eastern bloc was fueled by a compulsion to become part of the profound social and economic transformation suddenly under way in the region. They saw themselves playing a part in history, sowers of democracy and freedom, preachers of the capitalist gospel. Was there an element of cultural condescension in this? A little, but the impetus seems to have been more a sense of cultural identification. "I am Hungarian myself, and I owe it to my brothers who have suffered under the Russians for forty years to help out," is the sort of declaration one hears incessantly at trade conferences. I asked David Kreust about the phenomenal interest that California business people had shown in doing business in Poland, and in becoming members of the Poland-California Chamber of Commerce, which David cofounded. He snapped back, in his inimitable style: "Haven't you read the news lately? The Japanese think we're stupid and lazy!" I thought to myself about the negative comments emanating from Japan in the wake of President Bush's visit there in 1992. Maybe Kreust was right. It was a dynamic that I would see again.

Unfortunately, many market-hungry Westerners had plunged into the New East somewhat blinded by the potential for instant profit. Some of these people were the very same who had trampled into the People's Republic of China in the early eighties, mesmerized by the "market of one billion," only to learn the hard way about China's Byzantine bureaucracy and the lack of consumer buying power. Many companies that had rushed into Eastern Europe were unprepared to deal with the realities of the region's embryonic commercial infrastructure.

Separating the Pitfalls from the Potential

As in all business environments around the globe, there are pitfalls to doing business in Eastern Europe markets that you must consider before spending money and resources—especially since these countries are just emerging from the oppressive tutelage of Soviet state socialism. However, when talking about the pitfalls of the region, many pessimists forget to mention that, although the region's warts and weaknesses represent obstacles to fast and easy business intercourse, they also represent opportunities for profit to firms that can help solve the problems. A bad communications infrastructure, for example, may make it difficult to call the home office, but it also means that the country will be a likely customer for telecommunications equipment. The same goes for bad roads (an opportunity for civil engineering firms), incomplete business law (a boom for lawyers and consultants), and lung-singeing air pollution (a target market for pollution-control equipment suppliers). I asked senator-turned-consultant Gary Hart about the real or perceived pitfalls of the Eastern Europe and former-Soviet market. "The most immediate one is political instability. The second is the nonconvertibility of the ruble. The third is [a lack of] business stability, in the sense of whether the people you deal with today will be the people running the enterprise tomorrow." But Hart went on to say that there are ways to deal with *every one of these* drawbacks: you master the art of bartering noncash items instead of dollars, you buy business insurance to protect your interests in a risky investment climate, or you deal with a new private enterprise rather than an inefficient state-owned company recently placed on the privatization auction block. The point is that one can manufacture objections to entering *any* overseas investment climate.

Let's look more closely at some of the oft-stated objections to entering Eastern Europe and spend a moment checking our (possibly false) assumptions about the viability of doing business in the region.

Assumption 1: The Eastern European market is too small to get involved with

In fact: When combined with the European Community (EC), the Eastern European market is the largest geographically integrated market in the world. The EC's population of 320 million plus Eastern Europe's 400 million population (including the former U.S.S.R.) brings the total population for the region to 720 million people, roughly one seventh of the world's population. Eastern-Central Europe is home to 105 million people who have been shut out of Western markets and who literally *need everything.* American marketers often ask Gary Hart whether their company's products are needed in Eastern Europe. Over and over, Hart tells them: "the Eastern Europeans need everything, not only in goods, but also in services. They need pollution control equipment, they need technology, they need training, food, fuel, medicine....You name it, they need it. It's a wide-open, brand-new market, and the same can be said in spades for the former Soviet Union."

"Russia possesses the largest forest in the world and they don't have toilet paper," remarks Larry Rabbi. "That's the reality of the market. They need everything." In short, the Eastern European market can hardly be characterized as small or insignificant.

Assumption 2: Mostly, Eastern Europeans work on the farm and thus lack sophistication as a consumer group

In fact: Only one in five Eastern Europeans works on the farm, and the region is uncharacteristically urbanized relative to its stage of economic development; it is hardly a region of traditional agrarian societies, as is Southeast Asia, for example. Seventy-five percent of the Czech people live in cities. Sixty-one percent of the Poles do, and so does 66 percent of the population of the former Soviet Union. Only in Albania, where 35 percent of the population lives in cities, does the region's urban population drop below 45 percent of the total for a country. Moreover, because of their proximity to Western Europe and exposure to Western media, Eastern Europeans have been exposed to Western products and lifestyle for decades. They own more consumer items than one might expect, too. One out of four eastern Germans, for instance, owns a car; roughly one out of two owns a television, a washing machine, and a refrigerator. One third of all former Soviet citizens watch their own televisions, whereas one out of two Czechs and Hungarians do. Nearly half of all Czechs and Hungarians own both a washing machine and a refrigerator. A small, backward, and unsophisticated market of rusticated farmers? Not by a long shot. Figure 1-1 illustrates the extent of urbanization in Eastern Europe.

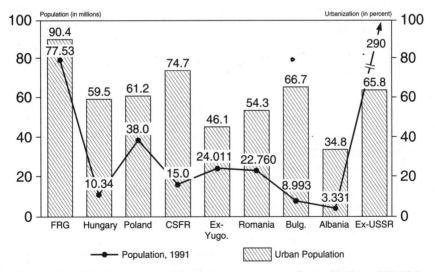

Figure 1-1. Population and urbanization—a region of city dwellers. (*PC Globe; U.S. Department of Commerce International Trade Administration; Europa World Yearbook, 1992.*)

Assumption 3: Eastern Europe lacks the buying power and hard currency to be a viable market for western goods

In fact: It is true that a child's Lego set costs the equivalent of a year's wages in the Commonwealth of Independent States, it is also true that during the years of Communist rule, Eastern Europeans stashed away *$25 billion* in their mattresses, which they are now investing in private enterprises and Western consumer products. As of mid-1991, Hungarian private citizens held $1.4 billion in hard currency. Polish citizens had in pocket $5.0 billion, Czechs and Slovaks $300 million, Romanians $120 million, and Bulgarians $100 million. And all the countries of former Communist Europe have achieved internal currency convertibility except for Bulgaria and (because of political upheaval) the former Yugoslavia.

Moreover, many companies have successfully surmounted the convertibility dilemma in the former U.S.S.R by accepting payment in kind. PepsiCo's $3 billion barter deal with the Russians is the most famous. The company provides bottling plants capable of producing 75 million cases of its soft drinks a year in exchange for Stolichnaya vodka and Soviet-built ocean-going freighters and tankers. Let there be no illusions, however. Tradeable products in the former U.S.S.R are, indeed, difficult to obtain and even tougher to maintain in steady supply. "They'll *all* offer you vodka," complains Ron Plunkett, an international lawyer-turned-international-businessman in California. "And even Pepsi can't move enough Russian vodka to make a profit." In short, countertrade and barter arrangements are no panaceas to the convertibility conundrum when doing deals in the region's 15 ruble-based economies. Yet, with the International Monetary Fund (IMF) now ready to set up a stabilizing fund to make the ruble convertible, the entire issue may eventually become a business obstacle of the past.

Assumption 4: Eastern Europe lacks importance strategically

In fact: Eastern Europe, including the former Soviet Union, occupies an enormous geopolitically and geoeconomically strategic area and is a natural bridge between the European Community (EC) and the former Soviet Union. "The Other Europe" has increasingly become integrated with Western Europe, both politically and in terms of division of labor. Central Europe enjoys close proximity and past trading ties with the European republics of the former Soviet Union. The untapped natural resources in these former Soviet republics are vast, and the productive synergy that will be generated by Central Europe and these adjacent republics working in unison will be incredible. Central Europe also enjoys access to ports in the Adriatic Sea, the Black Sea, and the Baltic Sea, and Russia's Far East has fast become a Pacific Rim export zone and bustling port.

Assumption 5: Eastern Europe will take decades to make the transition from communism to capitalism

In fact: Although it is true that state-owned factories in the region suffer from outdated production machinery, outmoded technology, inefficiency in management operations, and low levels of automation, the region has already experienced an astounding rate of privatization, both in terms of newly formed private companies and in terms of the percentage of gross national product (GNP) now generated by private enterprise in these economies. Accelerated growth in the number of financial institutions and the number of strategic alliances with foreign firms are evidence that command-oriented economic habits are fading quickly. The pace of change and the momentum that has gathered guarantee the region's ultimate success in reengaging with the world's capitalist economies. "Progressive liberalization has wrought substantial change," notes John Doohan, senior editor for *World Link*. "The potential scope of reform is so vast and comprehensive that once the problems of ownership legislation and infrastructure are sorted out, parts of East-Central Europe could rank among the best business environments in the world." That endorsement should not be taken lightly by international corporate strategists.

Assumption 6: Eastern Europeans don't know how to manufacture anything

In fact: These are highly industrialized economies; engineering ranks as the dominant industry in every Eastern European country. Machine building and metallurgy make up 29 percent of total industry in the former East Germany; the figure is 26 percent in Hungary, 26 percent in Poland, 31 percent in Czechoslovakia, and 28 percent in the former Soviet Union (see Fig. 1-2). Eastern Europe produces 20 percent of the world's chemical products; the region's chemical producers rank

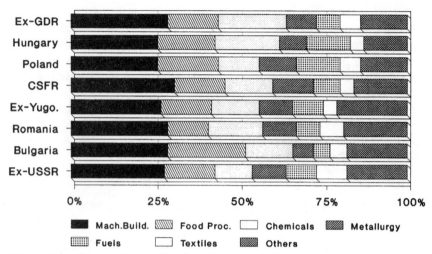

Figure 1-2. The structure of Eastern European industry—an emphasis on engineering. (*PlanEcon.*)

among the world's biggest as suppliers of butadiene, synthetic rubbers, and fibers. Eastern Germany and Hungary have especially large chemical industries; they account for 20 and 19 percent of the total industry in those countries, respectively. In short, workers and managers in Eastern Europe are experienced line-production manufacturers who can achieve first-rate performance if we assume some training and technological upgrading of their factories.

Assumption 7: Eastern Europe's former Communist managers can't be retrained

In fact: Managers in some Eastern European countries have been more exposed to Western business practice than others. Hungary, for example, permitted limited private enterprise for decades, whereas Czechoslovakia allowed none. The "typical" factory in Eastern Europe traditionally employed one manager for every three workers, but some "atypical" enterprises managed in a more Western style (and thrived as well, though small in number, especially in Poland and Hungary). The innovative managers of these companies have now become innovative owners, and they seek innovative business partners from the West. Although all foreign joint-venture managers in Eastern Europe have had to grapple with raising worker productivity, *within one year* of starting up production in Hungary, a Levi Strauss factory was as productive as the company's 50 other worldwide operations. Among its innovations, the company piped American music into the factory, which helped heighten morale.

Assumption 8: Eastern Europe was an economic mess before the Berlin Wall came down and it will remain so indefinitely

In fact: The region appears poised for renewed economic growth. Industrial production did dive in concert with a predicted regional recession, but by 1992, Central European countries were turning the corner, their negative rates of economic growth slowing down significantly. Poland, for instance, suffered an 11.6 percent contraction of growth in gross domestic product (GDP) in 1990 but achieved zero growth in 1992 and was expected to achieve positive growth by the end of 1993. Throughout the region, a contruction of outmoded state industry is occurring, and current economic indicators reflect this. What indicators do not show, however, is the enormous underlying surge of entrepreneurial activity in the private sectors of these countries—"hidden" growth that will shape the future growth cycles in the region.

Sustained growth will be further ensured by international funding. *Business Eastern Europe* forecasts "that by 1995, real aid flows, excluding balance-of-payments and export guarantees, will reach $30 billion. The World Bank will lead the way with up to $10 billion; $7.5 billion has already been earmarked for the region....The European Community, through its PHARE program and the autonomous European Investment Bank (EIB), will be the second biggest donor, providing additional billions in loans and grants. No serious marketer or provider of managerial or technical assistance can afford to ignore the economic growth that this lending will generate.

Assumption 9: Eastern Europe lacks technically skilled people

In fact: Workers in the region are quite skilled and highly educated. Because of the superior quality of, and priority placed upon, secondary education, the average blue-collar worker in the region possesses a high school education which may be equal to, or better, than that of a person with a junior college degree in the United States.

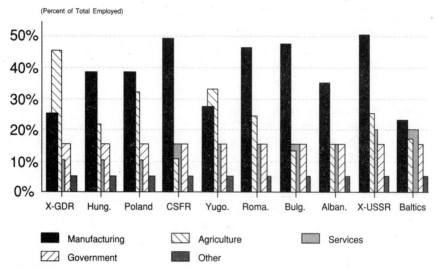

(Percent of Total Employed)

Figure 1-3. Employment by economic sector—industrial workers predominate. (*PlanEcon.*)

Literacy rates throughout the region would humble any "education president" in the United States. Because work experience and skill level outmatch Third World production sites such as Mexico and Malaysia, Eastern Europe is not simply a sight for "maquiladora"-style manufacturing. In Poland, for example, in numerous industries such as shipbuilding, steel, and electronics, you can hire people who have 10 to 20 years of solid work experience. Again, these people don't just farm the land. In the former Soviet Union alone, 103 million people work in industry—80 percent of the population. More than half of the Czech population works in industry; 45 percent of the Romanians and Bulgarians do (Fig. 1-3).

Assumption 10: Eastern European countries lack the necessary business regulations and laws to make business possible

In fact: Eastern Europe's investment ministries have ratified thousands of laws and regulations seemingly overnight, compared to how long other "transitioning" countries like Chile, Mexico, and China have taken. Granted, the Eastern European business bureaucracy may seem like a morass, in which a purchase order can require 23 separate signatures. But just in terms of making their currencies internally convertible and ratifying privatization and foreign-investment law, the government officials coordinating the effort in the region have performed extremely well. In 1990 new laws were being ratified in the region at a rate of one every 30 minutes by my nonscientific calculation.

Foreign complaints focus on vagueness in property-ownership laws. Although the former East Germany and Hungary have ratified laws that will compensate property owners who lost land and property after 1939, in other countries, questions still loom. The problem vexes Eastern European business people as much as it does foreigners. Listen to a Polish private business person, Krzysztof Mikulski, president of Polmicon, vent his frustration over the ownership dilemma. "We started to reconstruct the premises in Jerozolimskie Avenue and signed an agreement for a long-term lease with the Splem cooperative, which has, for the last thirty years, been using the site and the building on it. But that does not, unfortunately, mean that it has right of ownership. Who, then, is the owner? Nobody knows. It could be the state, district, borough, or city. With whom should we renegotiate the lease agreement? We submitted what seemed to be a compromise plan, namely that the money we pay for the lease should be deposited with a public notary. With the problem resolved, we would then pay whoever is the rightful owner. But our offer was rejected." The problem of ownership remains the most intransigent obstacle to smooth business dealings in the East; yet the former East Germany, Hungary, and Czechoslovakia have shown that it can be overcome. Happily, foreign business people will have to deal with this issue less and less as restitution arrangements are worked out and new owners obtain irrefutable title to their land and assets.

Assumption 11: Eastern Europe is just too far away

In fact: The United States is closer to Eastern Europe than to Japan, Hong Kong, Singapore, and, certainly, the Middle East. From Los Angeles, Berlin is about 10 hours away by jet, and 8 hours from New York. Tokyo is 11 hours from Los Angeles and 15 hours from New York. Indeed, it costs less to fly round trip from Los Angeles to Budapest ($525) than from L.A. to Hong Kong ($610).

Assumption 12: Doing business in Eastern Europe would require me to be there all the time

In fact: With the widespread use of the fax machine in the region, you don't have to be there to sell there. In terms of telecommunication infrastructure, Central European countries match countries such as the Philippines, Thailand, and Brazil; they far surpass China, Burma, and Vietnam. International calls can be placed at any international hotel, and the connection may be clearer than if one were calling across town.

Assumption 13: American products and services can't compete with those of Germany, which is right next door

In fact: American companies have experienced great success in many sectors. Curtis Construction has been involved in Poland for close to a decade and has invested $40 million there with an annual return of 10 to 15 percent. The company's diversified investments in Poland include a joint-venture pharmaceutical factory managed through Curtis Health Care; the manufacture of coat hangers, television repair and manufacture; import and manufacture of consumer electronics (the largest such factory in Poland); production of animated films and commercials in a joint venture with Hanna Barbara; a Baltic fishing joint-venture operation called Schooner; developing real estate and constructing residential housing; and developing commercial office space in Warsaw. While only *one* of the 1,300 Soviet joint ventures with the West was turning a profit as of January 31, 1990, that company was, indeed, *American owned:* Combustion Engineering. American advisers have been instrumental in writing Eastern Europe's "Marshall plan" for rebuilding after decades of Communist rule. American companies maintain a competitive edge in the region in research and development activities, software sales and development, financial services, information system management, communications and computing, entertainment and leisure, as well as franchising.

Ironically, while American manufacturers trail Germany and Japan in terms of market share in Eastern Europe, the region remains one of the few places on earth where there still exists a *perception* of the high quality of American-made products. Older Hungarians will tell you they learned to respect the quality of American products during the Allied bombing raids in their country during World War II. They quickly learned that bombs dropped on their cities by the Russians often failed to explode, but the American ones always did. It is encouraging for our long-term potential success in these markets that Eastern Europeans sincerely *want* to do business with Americans based purely on their cultural and historical identification with—if not idealization of—the United States. Just ask Sall Berisha, the physician with the Elvis haircut recently elected president of Albania. "It's no accident," he recently told *The Wall Street Journal,* that "the largest opposition parties [in Albania] are called the Democrats and the Republicans. Many Albanians became rich in the U.S.A., and the admiration for all things American here is immense." Later I spoke to the desk officer for the Commonwealth of Independent States (CIS) at the Department of Commerce in Washington, D.C., about this phenomenon. "There are 280 million former Soviets *begging* for American goods. Not Japanese or German, but American goods. That says to me, if you're farsighted, you ought to be looking at this market *now.*"

Welcome to a Seller's Paradise

Where are the *emerging* market opportunities in Eastern Europe? What are some workable business ideas? I sat down with a successful young Polish entrepreneur, Dariusz Linert (whom you'll meet again later), and asked about the business ideas he was currently pursuing. His current projects included sending raw materials to the region to be manufactured into finished products, to be sold in the United States and the former Soviet Union; setting up a joint venture in Poland for packaging food to be sold in Poland; manufacturing and packaging detergent that would cost less than imported brands; and buying natural-resource products in Poland and the former Soviet Union (like amber, wood, silver, and crystal) and selling them in the United States or trading them for U.S. products such as T-shirts, wine, and artwork. Moral of the story: Don't limit yourself when approaching these markets. Keep a wide-open perspective.

And *go there.* I spoke to a Department of Commerce commercial attaché about how Eastern Europeans perceive American companies. "The Eastern Europeans say that American companies, relatively speaking, are less educated about Eastern European countries and their culture. I'm not talking about speaking the language—that's not as critical—but what the system there is like. I keep telling companies that as things decentralize, they're going to be dealing with people who may be completely new to foreign trade, and they're going to turn to the American company to come up with the creative solutions to make a deal work." In short, *being there* during the early stages of transition in the East is itself a comparative advantage. Go there, walk around, keep your eyes open, and maintain an open perspective. Winning business ideas are usually staring you right in the face. But you must spend some time wandering around in the market with your eyes open if you are going to stumble upon them. The best I can do for you in assisting your search is to broaden your idea of what type of opportunities exist that you should include in your "principled perspective."

Let's begin our tour of the markets by taking a look at the numbers in the next chapter.

2

The Eastern European Market

A Diamond in the Rust

Central European countries obtained most of their imports from the U.S.S.R. until the fall of the Berlin Wall, purchasing only 2.6 percent ($51.6 billion in 1988) of their imports from Western countries each year. Of total Comecon* purchases, the U.S.S.R. bought 47 percent of the total, Yugoslavia 16.8 percent, Poland 9.3 percent, and Romania 2.2 percent. Until 1989, the U.S.S.R. purchased 40 to 55 percent of Eastern European exports; when the Soviet Union collapsed, so did inter-Eastern Europe trade. Total trade for Poland, for example, fell by 41 percent from March 1990 to March 1991—a decline brought on both by the sudden end of trade in raw materials purchased with rubles inexpensively from the U.S.S.R. and by the sudden inability of Russian buyers to purchase Polish goods with foreign currency.

Eastern Europe's Massive Trade Shift

Former Comecon members sought desperately to shift 80 to 90 percent of their trade to the West overnight. The West, however, did not

---

*Comecon (or CMEA) stands for the Commission for Mutual Economic Assistance; it was a group of countries, disbanded in February 1992, that included Czechoslovakia, Hungary, Poland, the U.S.S.R., Bulgaria, Romania, East Germany, and Yugoslavia (as an associate member).

immediately begin to buy Eastern European goods. Total trade between OECD countries of the West and former Comecon countries reached only $100 billion in 1990; Western countries enjoyed an approximately $1.8 billion trade surplus. During the Communist era, Eastern Europe mainly sold mineral fuels (42.3 percent of exports) and a few manufactured goods (15.5 percent) to the West. The composition of exports to Western countries must change before increasingly balanced trade will be achieved.

United States Trade with Eastern Europe

The United States ran a $19 billion trade surplus with the European Community in 1991, almost three times the surplus the year before. Not including the former Soviet Union, the United States sold approximately $1.68 billion worth of goods to former-Communist Europe in 1990. American sales to Central European countries in 1991 were as follows: $157 million to Hungary, $406 million to Poland, $89 million to Czechoslovakia, $566 million to Yugoslavia, and $369 million to Romania (Fig. 2-1).

The United States sells roughly 12 percent of its total exports to Eastern Europe each year, more than Italy, France, Finland, and Japan, but not as much as Germany, which annually sells more than 20 per-

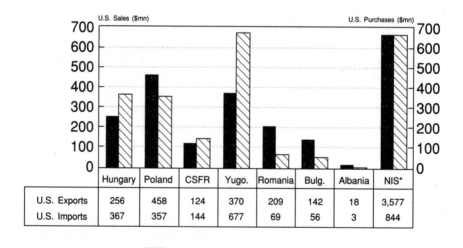

	Hungary	Poland	CSFR	Yugo.	Romania	Bulg.	Albania	NIS*
U.S. Exports	256	458	124	370	209	142	18	3,577
U.S. Imports	367	357	144	677	69	56	3	844

■ U.S. Exports   ▨ U.S. Imports

Figure 2-1. U.S. trade with Eastern Europe—1991. NIS stands for Newly Independent States of the former Soviet Union, including the Baltics. (*U.S. Department of Commerce.*)

cent of its exports to Eastern Europe. The United States was the second-largest importer of Polish ($107 million) and the third-largest of Yugoslavian ($229 million) manufactured goods. The United States was also the second-largest purchaser of machinery and transport equipment from Hungary ($85 million), and the third-largest buyer of these types of items from Romania ($17 million) and Yugoslavia ($125 million).

Our Lackluster Market Share. In 1988 the United States captured only a 4.5 percent share of Comecon purchases. Meanwhile, Germany maintained a 30.2 percent share, France and England each won roughly 7 percent, and Japan got 4.0 percent. Particularly troublesome is our dismal share of manufactured goods imports—only 1 percent of the East German machinery import market, for example, while West Germany took 57 percent and distant Japan got 7 percent. Even in Bulgaria, West Germany sold 45 percent of machinery imports in 1988, whereas the United States had only 2 percent; Japan captured a formidable 9 percent! The United States was responsible for only 1 percent of manufactured imports in Czechoslovakia; Germany scored a whopping 48 percent. A recent survey of consumer attitudes, buying patterns, brand awareness, and ownership of Western products among a cross section of urbanites in Hungary, Poland, Yugoslavia, Czechoslovakia, eastern Germany, and the U.S.S.R. was chastening for American suppliers of manufactured goods. The survey showed that Eastern Europeans counted on American companies to sell them fast food and apparel but wanted to purchase electronic goods and most other durable goods from vendors in Japan and the European Community (EC). The five brand names of durable goods that Eastern Europeans recognize the most *do not include one American firm*; Phillips, Sony, Panasonic, Hitachi, and Toshiba were the brand names most recognized in the consumer goods category. (This should make EC companies shudder, too, since only one EC company made the list, and the study was conducted in the EC's backyard.) American food, apparel, and household consumer goods companies did not do as badly. In fact, they enjoy what must be considered huge recognition ratings, given the only-recent opening of the East to Western advertising. The figures are evidence that Western products, and their images, have been entering Eastern European markets over the airwaves and through the black market for many years. Unfortunately, American manufacturers of durable products have not enjoyed the market acceptance that Japanese firms have. The figures in the accompanying table indicate the average percentage of people in six countries who recognize each Western brand name in all categories of products.

Brand Recognition in Eastern Europe*

Brand	Recognition, %
Pepsi-Cola	99
Coca-Cola	97
Nescafe	84
Nivea Cream	83
Chanel	75
Levi Jeans	75
Johnnie Walker	75
Hitachi	65
Guinness Book of Records	74
McDonald's	74
Phillips	72
Gillette	70
Palmolive	69
Sony	68
Panasonic	68
Toshiba	63

*The survey was published as "Perestroika: The Consumer Signals" and is available in the United States from Goldring/MIL (820 North Orleans St., Chicago, IL 60610-3051; Tel: [312] 440-5252).

An Armchair Tour of the Markets

The initial phase of selling goods directly to cash-rich former Communists has ended. Disposable cash quickly dried up after a frenzy of buying Panasonic cassette players, Samsung televisions, and IBM computers. A new wave of buying is cresting, however—this one based on acquiring the capital goods and technology necessary to create substitutes for imports and to upgrade infrastructure. At the same time, the consumer market is growing increasingly sophisticated in its tastes and preferences for Western products. The following sections give an overview of "what you can do in Eastern Europe" to exploit the selling opportunities that currently exist and should help you plot your tactics for riding the new wave.

Sell Consumer Products to New Markets

There are 100 million households in Eastern Europe, all starved for modern appliances. The now-liberalized pricing of consumer goods has removed the price gap between foreign and domestic products, making foreign products available to large numbers of Easterners. Among new Western "sensations" are food products such as cereals, coffee, wines, chocolates and other sweets, peanuts, raisins, spices, canned and fresh fruits, all kinds of "fancy" foods, shoes, sporting equipment and apparel, small household appliances, video equipment, cameras and video cameras, personal computers, and toys.

Although the consumer market that flourished during in the months after liberation has dropped off somewhat with the decapitalization that has occurred in Eastern economies, it behooves American marketers to introduce their product lines to Eastern consumers now, since consumer buying power will only increase in the years to come. Hungary has a larger consumer goods industry than most Eastern European countries, with a market size of approximately $10 billion. With the notable exception of a renowned china and glassware industry, most consumer goods do not achieve the quality of Western manufactured products. In 1990 United States exports to Hungary in this sector totaled $120 million. American companies that have responded include Amway, which has launched a multilevel marketing plan in Hungary and has signed 30,000 distributors. In Poland, Levi Strauss has opened the first of 30 planned shops in Gdynia to retail clothing. The company is also investing $16 million in a new plant to produce jeans and sports clothing in Plock, 70 percent of which is to be exported to Scandinavia. Avon has received permission to begin marketing its company's products. It seeks a 5 percent share of Czechoslovakia's $350 million cosmetic market. I recently learned that Cary Harrell, a veteran marketer in Chicago, has set up a store in Tallin, Estonia, called American Style. She buys out-of-season merchandise in the States for 20 cents on the dollar and sells it in her hard-currency store at a 100 percent markup. Her store in Tallin clears $21,000 a month, and Harrell has plans for a chain of new stores all across the former Soviet Union.

Publishing and film making have taken off. Hollywood has shot numerous films in Budapest recently. Producers pay half the production costs of the West and use the city as an "old Europe" set to stand in for expensive cities like Paris and Vienna. *Readers Digest* is now read in Hungary in the form of *Readers Digest Valogatas,* which has a circulation of 80,000. In Czechoslovakia, Time Warner Enterprises is discussing a joint venture to construct amusement parks, a cable television network, and book and magazine publication. Gini Scott, Ph.D., is an American author of 20 books, none of which has sold extremely well in the States. Four of her books, however, were recently snapped up by a Russian publisher and sold outstandingly in Russia compared to her domestic sales. In fact, she quickly accrued 1 million rubles in an account in Russia! At the time, before the ruble was devalued, that translated into roughly $100,000. I consider the region ripe for life-enhancement products such as tapes, videotapes, and books on the subjects of personal enrichment, visualization, achievement, and personal finance. The entire region, for better or worse, hungers for new, healthier, diet-conscious foods; vitamins; hair products; skin products; and the books, tapes, and videotapes that preach the Western way to good looks and longevity.

Provide Health-Care Products. Privatization of many elements of Eastern Europe's health sector has moved rapidly, particularly with respect to manufacturing of pharmaceuticals and medical instruments. Hungary's desire to upgrade its medical facilities and improve its health-care system, for example, has resulted in numerous opportunities for U.S. health-care firms, particularly for smaller, specialized medical service centers. In both Hungary and Poland, there are opportunities for U.S. firms to manufacture pharmaceuticals and medical and optical equipment and distribute health-care products through retail drug stores and medical equipment rental outlets. Disposables and diagnostic equipment are among the most-needed import items. Areas with particularly acute needs include the following: ambulatory surgery, outpatient care, diagnostic capabilities, maternity and prenatal centers, rehabilitation facilities, and small, "Western-style" hospitals.

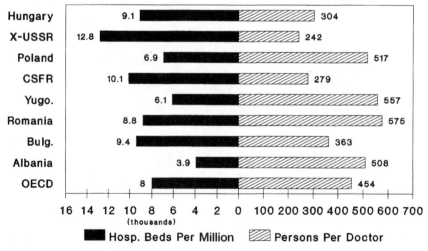

Figure 2-2. Hospitals and doctors—"Don't get sick in the Balkans." (*Population Reference Bureau, 1989; Economist Book of Vital World Statistics; UN Human Development Report, 1991.*)

For example, a new, 100-bed, American-style, acute-care hospital is being planned in Budapest for use as the base for an eventual health-care "campus" of services, including retirement housing. Figure 2-2 shows the distribution of patients among doctors and hospitals by country. In Czechoslovakia, IVAC has sold its disposable syringes through its partner Gama.

Franchising. Franchising as a means of penetrating consumer markets has gained many adherents among Western companies like Shell International (U.K./Netherlands), Coca-Cola, PepsiCo, McDonald's, and Burger King, which have signed franchising agreements. In fact, Burger King's largest franchise in the world is in Eastern Europe: It is a three-level, 15,000-square-foot restaurant in the heart of Budapest.

Sell Services to New Markets

Now is the time for American companies to set up chains and sell franchises offering customer services that are prevalent in the West and absent in the East. When I was in eastern Berlin recently, I counted only a handful of shops skirting the Alexanderplatz, old East Berlin's city square and shopping center. No dry cleaners. No shoe repair. No tax accountant office. The variety of services that urban Americans find within walking distance of their homes simply does not exist in Eastern Europe...yet.

Join the Consultant Invasion. The East's appetite for Western service businesses devoted to law, insurance, travel, freight forwarding, computer repair, waste disposal, management training, marketing of technical innovations, teaching, accounting, and patent protection is enormous. Trained experts in pollution control, packaging, construction engineering, environmental impact, and technical issues in banking find the landscape rich in both private and publicly funded projects. Because of the large number of joint ventures being considered and because of the privatization of state-owned industry, asset evaluation has become especially important. In Hungary, Banker's Trust handles the privatization of Taurus Rubber in conjunction with the State Property Agency; Sheraman & Sterling has helped GE and Tungsram in exchange for a stake in that deal; J. P. Morgan has been hired to manage the privatization of Czechoslovak Airlines (CSA), the country's state airline. Other services needed include a computer bulletin board for barter exchange between East and West, a computerized legal bulletin board with legal updates for each country, a franchise brokering service set up to sell all varieties of Western franchises to Eastern European entrepreneurs, a computer bulletin board listing Eastern European technology and technicians for Western customers and employers, and a chain of repair centers for VCRs, automobiles, tractors, and machinery of all types. A plenitude of skilled engineering and mechanical talent in the East seeks new employment opportunities, and the region's private entrepreneurs have traditionally been offered repair services in the "hidden economy." One shop would quickly grow into a chain of shops as the industrial base expanded.

Set Up Distribution Services.   Another significant, attractive, and largely ignored business opportunity for U.S. firms is distribution, including multilevel marketing, book and magazine distribution, freight forwarding, trucking, and mail-order catalog sales. "In distribution and wholesaling, investors can now buy or lease storage facilities and transport equipment cheaply, and ownership and valuation problems are less problematic," writes Charles Jonscher, managing director of Central Europe Trust Company Ltd. As foreign companies team up with local private enterprises to manufacture import substitutes, distribution will grow in importance. Companies that move in early will be winners, as West German agents and distributors were when, the day the Wall came down, they moved into eastern Germany to tie up distribution partners.

Real Estate Development and Services.   Eastern Europe offers tremendous opportunities in all facets of real estate development. Office space in Warsaw, for example, costs $3 to $4 per foot. Office space in San Diego costs $1.70 to $1.80 per foot. This type of demand translates into opportunities for real estate developers. Investment capital has become more available to this sector with the involvement of European banks and the Overseas Private Investment Corporation (OPIC). Moreover, demand will continue to grow for additional hotel space in Warsaw, Prague, and Budapest, where hotel capacity is normally 95 percent utilized. Business people fill top Eastern European hotels to capacity year round. As property ownership questions are clarified, and foreigners take advantage of loosening regulations concerning the buying and leasing of real estate, the current construction boom will continue to build momentum. Hotels and commercial buildings are desperately needed; they will open the market further to direct foreign investment, as well as to suppliers of building materials and machinery.

Resupply the Region's Manufacturers

Firms in the New East have lost their artificially cheap supply of raw inputs—such as oil, gas, basic food ingredients, and wood products.

Suppliers from the West can now compete in selling raw materials for the production of indigenous products. Some American companies may be capable of resupplying local firms with inputs of upgraded quality, enabling the Eastern European factory to better compete in Western markets. For example, high-quality wood pulp could be supplied to Czechoslovakia, where it could be manufactured into value-added paper products destined for EC markets. The majority of that country's forests have been damaged by acid rain.

Supply Capital Goods. Building materials, food processing equipment, industrial processing equipment, quality control systems, and office equipment are a few of the types of capital goods desperately needed in Eastern Europe. In the textile-equipment sector, there is need for spinning mills, looms, special sewing machines, weaving machines, knitting machines, machines for production of synthetic fibers, fabric dyeing machines, needling machines, and all kinds of finishing machines. There are currently 100,000 copiers on-line in the region, and there is an immediate need for 5 million.

Address Shortages. Spot shortages have occurred in many industry sectors where demand has caused back orders. This is particularly true in areas where the booming West German economy already was experiencing short supplies before reunification. Building materials, construction equipment, medical equipment, and food processing machinery are a few examples. With many items in short supply, it is possible that western German manufacturers may want to purchase products made to specification to replace shortages in their supply chain, or for private labeling.

Eastern Europeans may be willing to consider purchasing used, yet functional, equipment that saves them hard currency, including agricultural machinery, food processing equipment, and medical equipment, to name only a few areas of interest. For example, a magnetic resonance imaging machine (MRI), the next-generation X-ray-like technology now used in hospitals, runs about $4 million in the United States, brand new. But you can buy a used machine for $20,000 to $30,000. Every hospital in the East wants one, but the cost of a new machine is prohibitive. Solution: Sell them used. Recently, I spoke with Piotr Puchula, president of the M.P.P. World Trade Company, about selling used equipment to Eastern Europe. His company markets American products in the region, and he told me that the need for used processing equipment is tremendous. The problem for American companies, he said, is that the cost of shipping the equipment from the States to Eastern Europe escalates the price above what the Germans can offer from next door. For some U.S. companies, the solution might be to sell used equipment currently in use at their locations in Western Europe, trucking it to Eastern Europe when the time comes for upgrading. This equipment shift from Western to Eastern Europe could become an ongoing dynamic for an innovative multinational firm with business activities on both sides of the Rhine.

Serve a Growing Tourist Industry.   More than 16 million tourists visit Hungary each year and 19 million visit Czechoslovakia, yet in 1988 these countries earned only $0.9 billion and $0.3 billion for their trouble, respectively (Fig. 2-3). Things are changing. Budapest and Prague will remain hot spots for EC tourists, but with pricing now more closely aligned with Western destinations, earnings will soar. In fact, tourism is one of the hottest investment opportunities in Eastern Europe. In 1991 American Express opened a 100 percent subsidiary in Hungary, offering traveler's checks and travel services, and it opened a travel agency in Dresden. Even in off-the-tourist-path Albania, Sheraton is conducting talks about managing a hotel, and Hilton International is talking about building one.

American companies could go much further in offering creative and exciting travel and tourism services. With the few big-name hotels filled with foreign business people, the room rates for the typical "Eurail traveler" with a backpack and camera are prohibitive. A chain

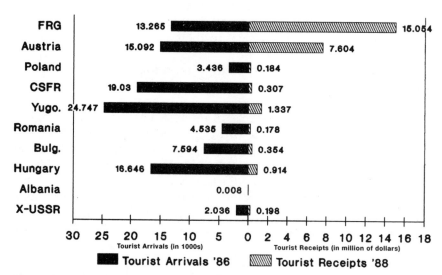

Figure 2-3. Tourism in "the other Europe"—traditionally a hot spot for visitors, but not profit. (*PCGlobe 4.0, 1990, PCGlobe, Inc.*)

of inexpensive tourist pensions and bed-and-breakfast inns seems appropriate. With little overhead, an American company could create a network of small inns by contracting with homeowners in outlying areas and apartment owners in the major cities to serve the swelling horde of "budget" travelers flocking to the East to take part in history. Tours for sophisticated tourists would also be a winner. Throughout Eastern Europe, history and current events offer high potential for "thinking tourist" tours—trips to little-known historical sites and, possibly, meetings with local personalities and folk heroes. You may also want to consider holding international conferences in Eastern Europe; conference facilities are well equipped and available at less than half the cost of facilities in the West.

Refit Eastern Europe's Dilapidated Infrastructure

Eastern Europe will continue to be the recipient of billions of dollars in international aid, and much of this aid will be funneled into infrastructural improvements such as telecommunications, roads, energy, and environmental cleanup. "While forecasting aid flows to Eastern Europe is not easy," reports *Business Eastern Europe*, "all indications are that by 1995, real flows, excluding balance-of-payments and export guarantees, will reach $30 billion." The World Bank is already committed to lending $10 billion during the early 1990s. The European Bank for Reconstruction & Development (EBRD); the EC, through its PHARE program; and the independent European Investment Bank are expected to bring total lending to the region up to roughly $50 billion by 1995. Clearly, these are sums that Western companies, especially vendors of technology and consulting services, cannot ignore. Project decision makers in Eastern Europe have exhibited a willingness to farm out these projects to competent, well-managed consortiums of Western companies rather than pursue a "locals-only" approach. Nimble Western companies will be able to sell their project management expertise on projects that address infrastructural needs in housing, road and bridge construction, power-plant construction and upgrading, and environmental control and cleanup. Such a consortium that can organize big projects and come in under budget stands a chance of winning large state-funded contracts in these countries. What's clear is that you don't have to be Bechtel to win these contracts. You do have to be *there*, pitch your proposals to the appropriate people, and be able to put together the financing. (Many of these deals allow the foreign company to use third-party financing; the anticipated cash flow from fees for industrial end-users of, say, a waste management facility, are used as collateral.)

Expand Power Generation Capacity. Eastern Europe depends heavily on thermal power. The former East Germany, for example, is 83.4 percent dependent on thermal; Czechoslovakia is 79.6 percent; Hungary is 72.1 percent. For this reason, sulfur dioxide emissions per square kilometer in eastern Germany, Czechoslovakia, and Hungary are characteristically over 10 times the level in the West, and nitrous oxide discharge levels are characteristically 3 times higher. American companies can supply the region with state-of-the-art and environmentally sensitive power generation equipment. The introduction of clean coal technology in electric power stations will include the installation of fluidized bed boilers in steam-gas plants, the modernization of thermoelectric power stations, the preparation and improvement of low-quality coal, and the reduction of pollution caused by using old power-generating technology. Priority subsectors include power generation equipment, power transmission equipment, boilers, steam-gas plants, and thermoelectric equipment.

American companies have already made great strides in this lucrative sector. In Czechoslovakia, for example, Westinghouse Electric has agreed with Skoda to construct and upgrade power plants, including two nuclear power stations. In eastern Germany, Bonneville Pacific and Portland General have signed a letter of intent for the construction of a power plant. Eastern European electric power production and consumption are shown in Fig. 2-4.

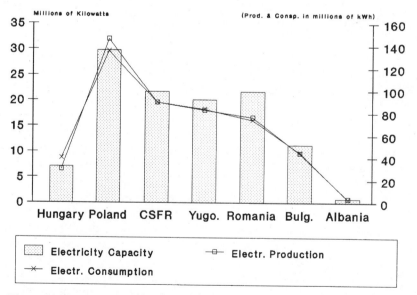

Figure 2-4. Electricity-starved Eastern Europe—electric power produced and consumed. (*CIA Handbook of Economic Statistics, 1990.*)

Upgrade Telecommunications. When the first person in space, Yuri Gagarin, parachuted back to planet earth in 1961, tumbling down in the Samara region of the Volga, he had to trudge around looking for a phone to call mission control to alert search parties where he had landed. He found a girl and her grandmother hunting berries and asked them whether they knew where a telephone would be. Three decades later, telephone service in Russia is so primitive and sparse outside the foreign-owned hotels that in many places Gagarin would still have a hard time finding a working phone. While 91 per 100 people in the United States have telephones, in former East Germany only 23 per 100 people have one. In Czechoslovakia the figure is 24.5, in Hungary 15.2, and in the former Soviet Union 15.7. In 1987, 24 million Eastern Europeans applied for phone installation; the wait for these phones was estimated to be about 10 years. There are only 13,000 public telephones in all of Hungary. Eastern European telephone availability is shown in Fig. 2-5.

Telecommunication companies from around the world have converged in Eastern Europe, and some big deals have been inked. In Poland, Ameritech, with France Telecom, won a $150 million contract for the construction and operation of a cellular telephone system; Chase Enterprises has signed a joint venture to install cable television connections there. AT&T has contracted to modernize inner-city telecommunication centers in several Polish cities (funded by the World Bank and by AT&T). In Czechoslovakia, USWest, in partnership with Bell Atlantic, has invested $80 million with the

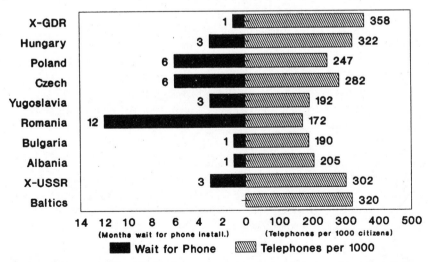

Figure 2-5. Availability of telephones—not easy to reach out and touch someone. (*Euroinfo, 1991*)

Czechoslovak government to manufacture telephones and telephone switches.

Build Up Computer Networks.   Most Eastern European companies are not yet computerized. The list of potential end-users of U.S. hardware and software is long; it includes manufacturers, government agencies, local administrations, foreign trade companies, hospitals, transport, scientific centers, schools, universities, and private individuals. New opportunities in industrial-application computers and computerized controls have resulted from U.S. liberalization of technology export controls concerning Eastern European countries and the former Soviet republics, and much progress has been made by Americans in the industry. The personal computer market is dominated by IBM-compatible clones of Far Eastern origin, and the market is highly price sensitive. Areas of greatest interest exist in establishing modern banking systems based on computer networks with full support services, management and planning software for companies, and process controls for factories. Just in Hungary, Hewlett-Packard has penned a joint-venture agreement to market its computers and electronic measuring devices, Digital has signed a joint-venture agreement to sell and service its computers, and Apple Computer's Hungarian agent sold $1.1 million worth of the company's computers between September 1990 and June 1991.

Upgrade Transportation Networks.   Automobile and auto-parts manufacturing deals have been nearly as numerous as computer-related deals in Eastern Europe. In Hungary, GM has invested $150 million with Raba to build engines and automobiles and Suzuki of Japan has committed $110 million with Autokonzern to build automobiles. United Technologies Automotive (UTA) has started a brand-new wholly owned operation in Hungary to produce auto parts. In the former Soviet Union, GM has opened representative offices in Moscow and Togliatti; in 1990, the company supplied $1 billion worth of engine parts to Volga Automotive Works.

Aircraft and Parts.   Beyond the sale of small and large passenger and cargo planes, other market priorities in aviation include air-traffic control equipment such as radar, ground support equipment, and jetways. Many large contracts have been won by American companies. In Hungary, Rogerson Hiller is supplying helicopters to a venture which will also represent the company at a new civilian air base, Boeing is in the process of selling $300 million worth of its 737s to Poland, and in Czechoslovakia, General Electric has signed a long-term agreement with Motorlet to develop and manufacture aircraft engines and components;

in 1990, the company won a $300 million order for turboprop engines. Cargo services opportunities have grown with the development of the transportation sector. In the former Soviet Union, Evergreen International Aviation has signed a joint venture with Aeroflot to operate cargo flights to commonwealth cities. Northern Air Cargo has done the same. Sea-Land Service is planning to set up a rail-freight cargo service using the Trans-Siberian railroad, and Skidmore Owings & Merrill has designed a new airport for Sakalin Island.

Decentralization of transportation brings new opportunities to Western companies, especially in forwarding and trucking services. Promising subsectors include all sorts of road and building construction equipment. Opportunities to sell railroad equipment focus on track-quality improvement, advanced track equipment, machinery for building turnouts that can stand up to greater wear, automated signaling systems, and rolling-stock repair facilities.

Environmental Cleanup and Pollution Control. The environment scorecard for Eastern Europe contains no winners. Let us note some of the lowlights for each country: In the former East Germany the air is severely polluted from coal burning, the land has suffered severely from acid rain, and half the children living in industrial areas are reported to suffer from bronchitis and eczema. In Poland, a macabre 95 percent of the country's rivers have been fouled with sewage and industrial pollutants, and the Polish Academy of Sciences believes that roughly 13 million of the country's 40 million citizens live in "ecological hazard" areas. Half the country's farmland is damaged by high levels of acid metals and pollution. In the former Soviet Union, the environmental fallout of the Chernobyl nuclear disaster continues to be felt. An estimated 100,000 child fatalities are blamed on radiation exposure linked to the accident. Most of the former Soviet republics must contend with serious industrial plant pollution as well as the nerve-wracking prospect of a repeat of the Chernobyl disaster at one of over 40 similarly unshielded nuclear reactors. In Romania, the capital of Bucharest has no sewage treatment plant, and most of the country's other sewage plants don't work. One third of Bulgaria's forests suffer damage due to acid rain; metals pollution continues to destroy farmland. Sixty-five percent of the country's river water and 70 percent of its farmland have been tainted by industrial waste. In the former Yugoslavia, the Adriatic coastline has been affected by pollutants, and in Hungary, arsenic contaminates the drinking water throughout the entire southern region of the country. In the Czech and Slovak republics, 600,000 acres of woodland have been damaged by acid rain, 70 percent of the rivers are polluted, and half the drinking water fails to meet the country's own water standards. *Moreover,* 40 percent of Czechoslovakia's sewage spews into waterways untreated, and half its forests are damaged or already destroyed. *Moreover,* with energy subsidized by the state, enterprises saw little reason to conserve energy. Consequently, these countries consume as much as 30 percent more energy relative to industrial output than Western countries. Relying on the burning of low-grade brown coal to meet its energy needs, Eastern Europe must now pay the price by managing the ravages of acid rain. Freely elected Eastern European governments are now accountable to their citizenry, whose health has been adversely affected by the low pollution standards of the past. Poland, Czechoslovakia, and Hungary have ratified stringent environmental legislation; major industrial polluters have been identified and told to clean up their act or liquidate their facilities.

With growing international attention on the region's environmental management and cleanup, opportunities have been created for American business. The political stakes are high. Thus governments will be ready to spend hard currency to deal with environmental problems and to offer concessions to investors in environmental projects. Joint ventures in this sector may be able to obtain a special tax holiday of up to six years in some countries. Many environmentally conscious firms have already sought U.S. partners to assist them in upgrading pollution controls. In Poland, for example, United Energy Products has entered a joint venture to reduce pollutant emissions, expand a power plant, and establish long-distance heating systems in Krakow to reduce pollution. Several Western nations, including the United States, established the Regional Environmental Center (REC) in Budapest, Hungary, in 1990; it serves the entire Central and Eastern European region as a clearinghouse on environmental issues. The center maintains an international data and environmental information network, coordinates environmental education and training, and promotes environmental institutions in the region. It also publishes a quarterly called *Information Bulletin,* which reports on the center's programs and activities as well as those of other environmental organizations. To get on the mailing list, contact: Private Sector Information Center, Regional Environmental Center, 1035 Budapest, Miklos ter. 1, Hungary.

Increase Agricultural and Food Processing Productivity

The estimated market size of the food processing sector in Poland alone tops $100 million per year. Future growth of 3 to 4 percent is expected. Prices of farm products have been totally decontrolled; this has helped Polish farmers because prices for their products, which had been kept artificially low, rose to the prices on the world market. Increasingly, Polish farmers have hard currency to spend on upgrading their farms. Although Bulgaria's large food processing industry makes up 23 percent of the country's total industry, because of low productivity in the processed-food sector, a high percentage of agricultural products are currently exported with little or no value-added processing. Modernization of this industry will involve meat processing, milk processing, grain elevators, fruit and vegetable processing, cold storage, and modern packaging. As the younger generation in Eastern Europe adopts more Western-style eating habits, Western trends such as healthy eating, dieting, and concern for the environment are sure to gain popularity. The region's food processing industry is thus expected to put more emphasis on nutritional considerations in food formulation and production; U.S. companies can play a role in the shift. For example, in Hungary, Sarah Lee has set up a joint venture to process, package, and distribute foods such as coffee, tea, and spices. In Poland, Inline Plastic is setting up a plant in Ostrow Wielkopolski to produce plastic packaging for food and medical products. Other projects include purchase of equipment for fruit and vegetable processing, deep freezing, cold storage, and modern packaging. Joint ventures in this area can obtain a special tax holiday of up to six years in some countries. World Bank credits are available in this sector, mainly for the purchase of machines, equipment, and complete production lines.

3

Getting to Know Eastern European Customers

"Country Capsules"

With the emasculation of European communism, diverse countries have reemerged—unique in their histories, cultures, customs, religions, and taboos. The Eastern bloc, laid bare to us by the sudden disappearance of communism, turns out to be no "block" at all. Even in their common Communist experience, Eastern European countries differ greatly. Nearly all books that advise entrepreneurs emphasize one cardinal requisite for success: *Know your customer.* Yet how can we hope to know our potential customers in Eastern Europe when we hardly comprehend the striking contrasts between countries there? But maybe you're an expert already. Here's a chance to appraise yourself.

Eastern European Cultural Literacy Quiz

To measure your general knowledge of European society and culture answer the following questions in writing. When you have completed all the questions, check your answers against those given below and enter the points you've earned in the Score column. Total your points and look up your score in the rating categories at the end of the answers.

1. Which Central European country (not including the former Soviet republics) is the largest both in terms of land mass and population?

2. How many republics did the former Soviet Union contain?

3. What Eastern European country has a Latin-based language?

4. Which country is known for its "velvet revolution" of 1989?

5. Name the former Communist dictator of Romania assassinated with his wife in 1989.

6. Most Hungarians are ethnic Magyars: True or false?

7. Name the three Baltic states.

8. In what country, and city, was Solidarity formed?

9. Czech lands were once part of the German empire. What empire were Slovak lands once part of?

10. What language is spoken in Croatia?

11. What country was famous for "goulash communism"?

12. Which region aligned itself with the Nazis during World War II: Croatia or Serbia?

13. What minority ethnic group in Bulgaria has traditionally been at odds with the government?

14. Which Eastern European people consider themselves descendants of Romans?

15. Serbia's president has been called "the last Stalinist in Europe." What's his name?

16. What did G.D.R stand for?

17. What Eastern European country achieved the highest level of industrialization before World War II?

18. The former East Germany is made up of how many states?

19. What is the traditionally German-controlled land in northern Czechoslovakia called?

20. What country takes its name from a Turkic people called the Bulgars?

21. Which region inside Yugoslavia has a population that is 90 percent Albanian but is considered by the Serbs as the cultural cradle of their civilization?

22. Which Eastern European country is the most ethnically homogeneous?

23. What country is Bohemia located in?

24. What small but rugged country's name means "Eagle's Country"?
25. The Hungarian Revolution occurred in what year?

Answers. 1. Poland. 2. Fifteen. 3. Romania. 4. Czechoslovakia. 5. Nicolae Ceausescu. 6. True. 7. Latvia, Lithuania, and Estonia. 8. Gdansk, Poland. 9. Austro-Hungarian. 10. Serbo-Croatian. 11. Hungary. 12. Croatia. 13. The Turks. 14. Romanians. 15. Slobodan Milosevic. 16. German Democratic Republic. 17. Czechoslovakia. 18. Five. 19. The Sudetenland. 20. Bulgaria. 21. Kosovo. 22. Poland. 23. Czechoslovakia. 24. Albania. 25. 1956.

Scorecard

20–25   Congratulations! You're on your way to becoming an expert in Eastern European business culture.

15–19   You may be prepared to do business like a pro in some Eastern countries, but you'll be handicapped in others.

10–14   You're off to a good start but need to expand and update your Eastern European cultural literacy to interact comfortably and knowledgeably.

1–9   Your hopes for business success in Eastern Europe are at high risk of failure; consider an in-depth study of the East before doing business in the region.

Eastern Europe: A Political (Rather Than Geographic) Entity

The division of Europe into East and West began centuries ago, initially as a division between Rome and Byzantium. Russia, Romania, Bulgaria, Greece, and Serbia all looked east toward the Byzantine capital of Constantinople, while other countries and regions were attached to Rome. Later, when the Turks swept through southern Europe, the region became divided between areas controlled by Turks and those not. With the end of the Ottoman Empire, the East became divided again, Russia on one side and Central Europe and the Balkans on the other.

Because of the unnatural borders drawn through Europe by Russia's Stalin, Britain's Churchill, and America's Roosevelt at the Yalta Conference in 1945, the region became a powder keg of ethnic resentment and political dissatisfaction. What occurred at Yalta is best summarized in Flora Lewis's fine history, *Europe: A Tapestry of Nations.*

Stalin did not hide his expansionist ambitions. To protect Russia, and in compensation for the enormous suffering wreaked by the German invasion, he determined to change the map. East Prussia was to be taken from Germany and divided between Poland and the Soviet Union, which had already absorbed the Baltic states of Latvia, Estonia, and Lithuania. Poland was to be shoved westward, ceding its eastern territories.

Pomerania and Silesia were to be detached from Germany and awarded to Poland in compensation, putting its new frontier along the line of the Oder and Neisse rivers and eliminating the need for the awkward, contentious Polish Corridor to the Baltic invented by post-World War I mapmakers. Ruthenia, or Transcarpathia, was to be detached from Czechoslovakia and incorporated in the Soviet Ukraine. Romania's province of Bessarabia and northern Bukovina were also transferred to the Soviets, as part of the greatly enlarged Ukraine.

Not all of these border realignments were made at Yalta; some came later. Stalin later reneged on all his commitments, eventually severing Eastern Europe from Western Europe in every country that Russian troops occupied after the war. In Fulton, Missouri, the inimitable Churchill summed up the situation dramatically: "From Stettin on the Baltic to Trieste on the Adriatic, an Iron Curtain has descended across the continent." Not until the Russians usurped control of Czechoslovakia in 1948 by coup d'état were Stalin's ambitions finally satiated. Main streets in every major Eastern European city were renamed in honor of him; other streets and monuments of folkloric or historical significance were rededicated to honor Soviet revolutionary events and Bolshevik heroes. Before long, Stalin's affinity for monumental wedding-cake architectural style marred skylines across Central Europe. The best view of Warsaw, the Poles came to joke, was from the Soviet-inspired Palace of Culture, the only place where you could view the city and not see the Palace of Culture. While the Marshall plan revived Western Europe, the countries of Eastern Europe came under the tutelage of the Soviet-imposed economic organization called Comecon, the Council for Mutual Economic Assistance, which cemented economic and production ties between member nations and installed Russia's stringent system of industrial guidance and planning. Eastern European client states produced what Russia needed to fulfill its unrealistically ambitious five-year economic plans.

Eastern Europeans didn't take all this lying down. The well-known uprisings in East Berlin in 1953, in Poland and Hungary in 1956, and in Czechoslovakia in 1968 weren't the only popular revolts in the region. The list of upheavals and rebellions confronted by the

Kremlin in Eastern Europe over the past 35 years lends an ironic twist to the propagandist's label "Fraternal Socialist States of the Warsaw Pact." Since the end of World War II, revolutionary events have also included Albania's defection from the Warsaw Pact in 1960–1961 and Romania's assertion of an independent foreign policy and national independence from 1962 onward. The Russians prevailed with brute force, and the West did little to thwart their intentions, beyond issuing some vitriolic words unenforced by action. The Iron Curtain separated Eastern and Western Europe for over 40 years. Starting in the Baltic Sea, it split prewar Germany into East Germany and West Germany. It ran south to divide West Germany and Czechoslovakia and further south to separate Austria and Hungary—partners in an old empire. Between Italy and Yugoslavia on the Adriatic Sea the curtain finally ended. The only anomaly in the demarcation line was the Berlin Wall, which enclosed the western half of Berlin to keep East Germans from venturing into Berlin's western enclave, where the four winning Allies quibbled over administerial control of defeated Germany. Deep behind the Iron Curtain, Berlin lay like an island in a sea of Soviet influence.

The End of Communism

Communism died a slow death rather than of a sudden overnight seizure. The ailing Soviet leader Konstantin Chernenko personified the denegrated and crippled state of the Communist system in the 1980s. He inspired in the Eastern Europeans a sense of hopelessness, a national shame, and a red-eyed envy of the West. Party corruption in the Soviet Union worked its way into every niche of industry and interlocked with the so-called Soviet mafia, which played an increasingly overt role in the "shadow economy," the black market that accounted for 25–30 percent of the economic activity in the country. Under Chernenko, party members received less and less respect; the party itself inspired less fear and more loathing among a populace that was younger and increasingly exposed to intoxicating images of freedom, democracy, and the comforts of the West. Gorbechev's glasnost and perestroika were only last-ditch, stop-gap attempts to cure a cancer on the Soviet Communist system; they were not revolutionary initiatives. When Ronald Reagan stood at the Brandenberg Gate and intoned, "Mr. Gorbechev, tear down this wall," he was only voicing the inevitable.

The region lying east of the Rhine has bred a beguiling lexicon of vague and often misleading terms. For our purposes the terms "Eastern Europe" (denoting the countries of Central Europe and the

Figure 3-1. (*a*) Ethnic groups in Eastern Europe. (*U.S. Department of Commerce.*)

European republics of the former Soviet Union), "Central Europe" (denoting only the European countries east of the Rhine but not former Soviet republics), and "former Soviet republics" (denoting all forms of Soviet territory) will be used most often (Fig. 3-1*a* and *b*).

Figure 3-1. (*b*) Eastern European countries. (*U.S. Department of Commerce.*)

The "Country Capsules" that follow will orient you to the geographic, ethnic, and political makeup of the countries of Central Europe and the former Soviet Union. They offer a quick reference overview of their market-opening economies, unique histories, and resultant business priorities. Those readers who scored high on the cultural literacy quiz may wish to just skim the capsules and then move on to the following chapter.

Country Capsule: Hungary

Hungarians consider their country the eastern outpost of Western civilization in Europe, the commercial bridge between East and West. Hungary is ethnically homogeneous: 93 percent of Hungary's population is Magyar. Virtually all Hungarians speak Magyar, though many older people speak Russian, which was compulsory in Hungarian schools from 1949 until 1989. Just over 3 percent of the country's people are Gypsy, 2.5 percent are German, and 0.7 percent are Jewish. Sixty-seven percent of Hungarians are Roman Catholics; 20 percent are Protestant Calvinists; 5 percent are Lutheran.

Hungary is flat, temperate, and about the size of Indiana. One in five Hungarians (2.1 million) lives in the capital of Budapest; the country's other major cities have a population of 210,000 people or less. Before World War II, half of all Hungarians worked the land; now only 20 percent do. Figure 3-2 and its accompanying table give a statistical overview of the country.

A Violent Past

Historically, Hungarians have had a knack for fighting on the losing side in conflicts; they have endured a violent past. The country was part of the Austro-Hungarian dual monarchy that ended after World War I. By war's end, Hungary had lost two thirds of its territory and nearly as much of its population. Twenty years later, Hungary entered and fought in World War II as an ally of Germany. Nonetheless it was occupied by German troops and lost its independence under a pro-Nazi dictatorship. Advancing Soviet armies drove out the Germans in a campaign that ended in April 1945. Following nearly two years of parliamentary coalition government, Hungary's Communist minority triumphed—with the support of repeated interventions by Soviet occupation authorities—in seizing power in the summer of 1947. By means of terror, blackmail, and kangaroo courts, the Communists forced opposition parties into the People's Independent Front, and on May 15, 1949, held an election in which Communist-approved candidates, without opposition, received 96 percent of the votes. Hungary was proclaimed a "People's Democracy." With the opposition neutralized and the people terrorized, Hungary came under the de facto dictatorship of Soviet-trained Matyas Rokosi, who carried out purges of the rank and file, potential rivals, and opponents. Worst of all for Hungary's future modernization, private enterprises employing more than 10 workers were nationalized, and industrialization and farm collectivization

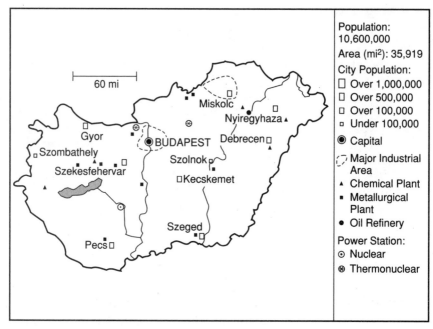

Figure 3-2. Map of Hungary. [*U.S. Department of Commerce and National Geographic, June 1991, p. 47 (for industrial data).*]

Hungary at a Glance

Area:	35,919 square miles
Population:	10.6 million
Labor force:	45.7% of the population
Ethnic groups:	Hungarians 96.6%; Germans 1.6%; Slovaks 1.1%; South Slavs 0.3%; Romanians 0.2%
Religions:	Roman Catholic 69%; Calvinists 20%; Lutherans 5%; Other 8%
Language:	Hungarian; German and English (frequently used in business)
Capital:	Budapest (2.1 million)
Major cities:	Debrecen (219,000)
	Miskolc (208,000)
	Szeged (189,000)
	Pecs (183,000)
	Gyor (132,000)
	Nyiregyhza (119,000)
	Szekesfehervar (114,000)
	Kecskemet (107,000)
Government:	Multiparty parliamentary democracy

SOURCE: U.S. Foreign Commercial Service, Central and Eastern European Trade and Technical Assistance Center, International Division, U.S. Chamber of Commerce.

were mandated by fiat. The result was economic collapse and poverty by 1953.

Hungarian popular revolt exploded in 1956 during a peaceful march in Budapest. The fighting did not abate until Imre Nagy, a moderate who had briefly replaced Rakosi as premier in 1953, was reinstated. He carried out a purge of the Stalinists, and Soviet forces quickly withdrew from Budapest. However, a larger number of them returned shortly. Nagy, upon hearing that a large contingent of Soviet troops was rolling into Hungary, withdrew his country from the Warsaw Pact and issued a plea to the United Nations for protection. World attention, however, was focused on the Suez Canal at the time and Hungary was forsaken. The Soviets invaded on November 3–4, 1956, and subsequently executed Nagy. Janos Kadar, a "moderate" Communist close to the Soviets, emerged after the crackdown and meted out reprisals. Thousands were executed. In the 1960s, Kadar offered a general amnesty to political dissidents, curbed some of the excesses of the secret police, and allowed some liberalization of the economy—which, however, was again forcibly collectivized in 1958–1959.

A Tradition of Private Enterprise

The Hungarians were never completely insulated from Western capitalism. The 1956 uprising had, indeed, prompted the Soviets to allow Hungary to pursue a mixed economy. By mixing market mechanisms into Soviet-imposed socialism the Hungarians created what became known as goulash communism. The Hungarian government owned the large factories and businesses, but local managers were encouraged to start up competitive operations that would respond to the needs of consumers. They were even allowed to profit from their efforts, and small private shops flourished. Outside the state-owned network of enterprises and cooperatives, small private businesses made up 6 percent of the economy.

Enjoying social freedoms that other Central Europeans only dreamed of, Hungarians were allowed to travel abroad starting in 1987. The problem was that they took their money with them, forcing Hungary to enhance its living standards by borrowing from the West. After liberation in 1989, Hungary's post-Communist government inherited the country's $21 billion foreign debt, money that had been spent on sustaining Hungary's living standard (higher than its Socialist neighbors), rather than on the modernization of the country's factories and infrastructure. Added to its debt burden, Hungary then had to face the collapse of CMEA (Warsaw Pact) trade, a cutoff of cheap Soviet oil, and a leap in oil prices from $17 to $29 resulting from the Persian Gulf War. Trade suddenly had to be conducted in foreign exchange rather than barter; this siphoned off reserves. Hungarian firms dependent on Soviet orders fell on desperate times. Prices shot up and Hungarians suddenly found it difficult to make ends meet without working two or three jobs. Unemployment soared; 60,000 were unemployed in October 1990 and 150,000 in March 1991. Eighteen percent of all workers in the iron, steel, and aluminum industries lost their jobs, and no category of worker has been unaffected by the transition to capitalism. On the bright side, the number of joint ventures with foreign companies rose 500 percent in 1991 from 1,000 to 5,000.

The Hungarian living standard is low in comparison to that of its Austrian neighbor. The typical Hungarian family lacks the discretionary income to buy Western luxury goods. However, the rapid growth of the private sector has increased demand for Western products in all categories and is improving Hungary's overall purchasing power.

Country Capsule: **Poland**

On August 31, 1980, workers at the Lenin Shipyard in Gdansk, led by an electrician named Lech Walesa, signed a 21-point agreement with the Soviet-backed Polish government that ended their strike. Ten years later, Lech Walesa became the country's first popularly elected president and a profound influence on all other anti-Communist revolutionary movements around the globe. Poland's revolution as well as its ongoing transition to capitalism continues to be founded on worker power.

Forty-four years of Soviet-imposed Communist rule on the heels of World War II, which obliterated Poland's key industrial cities, crippled Poland's industrial progress. Polish enterprise and infrastructure remain decades behind Western European standards. Poland's foreign debt, accumulated by the Communist government's borrowing during the 1970s, has hindered economic progress as well. Poland is now banking on its population of 40 million people, its large territory, and the richest resource base of any Central European country to guarantee its transition to a market-oriented economy and its inclusion in the family of richer Western European nations. One sign of Poland's importance as a gateway to the Eastern European marketplace is the large number of government- and privately sponsored trade events that take place in Polish cities each year: In 1992 there were 11 major trade events in Poznan, 6 in Lodz, 3 in Gdansk, and 9 in Warsaw.

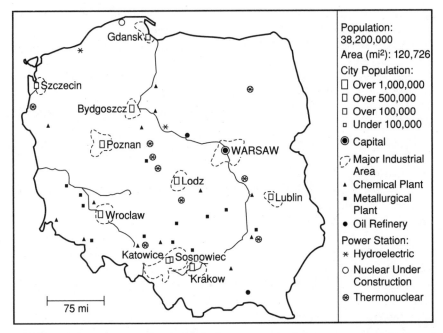

Figure 3-3. Map of Poland. [*U.S. Department of Commerce and National Geographic, June 1991, p. 47 (for industrial data).*]

Poland at a Glance

Area:	120,726 square miles
Population:	38 million
Labor force:	17.3 million
Ethnic groups:	Polish 98.7%; Ukrainian 0.6%; Byelorussian 0.5%; Jewish 0.5%
Language:	Polish
Religion:	Roman Catholic 90%
Capital:	Warsaw (1.6 million)
Major cities:	Lodz (848,500)
	Cracow (735,100)
	Poznan (570,900)
	Gdansk (464,800)

SOURCE: U.S. Foreign Commercial Service, Central and Eastern European Trade and Technical Assistance Center, International Division, U.S. Chamber of Commerce.

Figure 3-3 and the accompanying table summarize Poland today—at a glance. Poland is the largest country in Central Europe, in terms of both land mass and population. Poland is also the most ethnically homogeneous country in Eastern-Central Europe; 99 percent of the population is ethnically Pole. Largely because of the power and political activism of the Catholic church, Poles enjoyed more personal and intellectual freedoms under communism than did citizens in most other Warsaw Pact countries; 95 percent of the population is Roman Catholic. Almost all of Poland's prewar ethnic groups emigrated, including 45 million Ukrainians, 1 million Byelorussians, and 50,000 Germans. Most of Poland's 3 million Jews were killed during the Holocaust.

Poles are Western in philosophy, and although they are going through economic transformation, dealing with the Polish market does not entail waiting for the social standards of Poles to rise to Western European standards. Poland's *economy* may have to rise but its intellectual and cultural standards do not. In many ways, Poland is not a developing country, especially in terms of technical know-how and consumer appetite. The revolution in mindset that may take a generation to change in eastern Germany—weaning people off the Socialist "iron rice bowl"—has already been accomplished in Poland. Poland's population is young; 50 percent of the population is under the age of 28. Thus the Poles may be able to change their Communist mindset and retool themselves to work in a market-driven economy more readily than other peoples of the region. The small business community has grown extremely quickly. The country's younger population is taking to private enterprise much more quickly than older populations that typically desire to revert to the older system rather than retrain for a capitalist future. A significant percentage of the population is just old enough to be entering the job market, and they have never learned another system. They can learn to work in a free market from ground zero rather than spend years working their way out of a command-economy straitjacket.

Plus, Poland has a relatively stable population, ethnically. Provincial border clashes and ethnic strife in Poland will not occur, because Poland is ethnically homogeneous. The world has witnessed what ethnic differences have done in Yugoslavia; the same condition exists in Czechoslovakia, where the country formally split into two republics based purely on ethnicity in 1993. In Hungary, too, ethnic differences play a destabilizing role, though to a lesser degree. Over the long term, this will amount to a substantial benefit for Poland in the competition for foreign investment and modernization.

Economic "Shock Therapy"

Poland's Parliament, called the Sejm, passed legislation in December 1989 to implement "shock therapy" as a treatment for its economy.

The result was a drop in inflation from 79 percent in January 1990 to just 5 percent in January 1991. The fast-devaluating zloty was stabilized. But unforeseen events took Poland by surprise, including the sudden insolvency of Soviet buyers, the drying up of tax revenue, and a bulge in the number of retirees living on pensions (an ironic demographic occurrence in a country that bills its population as "young"). Industrial production plummeted 25 percent; average real incomes dropped more than 20 percent; average real wages shrank 30 percent. By 1990 unemployment had spread from a few thousand to more than 1 million, over 6 percent of the population. In the ensuing months, Solidarity forces split into factions on the Center-Left and Center-Right, other political parties have mushroomed, and the political scene in Poland has become extremely fragmented.

Private Enterprise Takes Root

Small-business retail sales in Poland exploded with the legalization of the former "second economy" in early 1989, which permitted the importation of foreign products. The selloff of thousands of state-owned enterprises has begun, alongside the proliferation of tens of thousands of new private companies. Small Polish private firms successfully sought trading and partnership relationships with similarly small Western businesses, many spurred by the government's emphasis on small-business development. Poland has also been a fortunate relation of the World Bank and the International Monetary Fund (IMF) since 1985; this has helped ensure economic stability even as Poland has destabilized politically, with four changes of goverment in a single year.

A key point for business people entering Poland to keep in mind is the continuing legacy and influence of political groups like Solidarity which find their base of support among politicized, often unionized, workers. The power of workers' congresses inside Polish enterprises, vis-à-vis managers and owners, may be the most distinguishing difference between Poland and its former Socialist neighbors, at least in the eyes of Western business managers and consultants. In Poland, workers remain solidly united.

Country Capsule: Romania

The Romanians, who make up 88 percent of Romania's population, are a group that, unlike the Slavs and Magyars, find their ancestral roots among Latin-speaking Romans and Thracians. Indeed, Romania was a colony of Rome during the second and third centuries. As a result, Romania's language is directly related to French, Italian, Portuguese, and Spanish; it contains only isolated elements of Slavic, Turkish, and other languages. Before World War II, Romania was home to minorities that made up 28 percent of its population. At present, 7.9 percent of the population is Magyar (Hungarian) and 1.6 percent is German; the Magyars reside in Transylvania, and the Germans live in areas to the north and west of Bucharest. Other notable minority groups include Gypsies, Serbs, Croats, Ukrainians, Greeks, Turks, Armenians, and Great Russians. Eighty-eight percent of the population is Greek Orthodox; 6 percent is Roman Catholic—mostly Magyars and Germans.

Survivors of Countless Invasions

Romanians have suffered 2,200 years of invasions and migrations that have left their mark and many scars. Yet the Romanians survive. "The Romanians have survived as a nation not by courage in battle but by outwitting and outlasting their conquerors," wrote Hannah Pakula in a recent article.

> Overrun by the Romans, they were later subjugated to [sic] five hundred years of Turkish suzerainty. To appease the Turks, the local aristocracy kissed the hem of the pasha's robe and carried him from his bed to his chair....Toward the end of the eighteenth century, the Austrian and Russian empires challenged the Turk's claim to the rich farmland, forests, and mineral wealth that were Romania's curse as well as her birthright. Besieged on all sides, this essentially feudal people had a brief, unhappy fling at self-government, then brought in a German dynasty to give their nation legitimacy and autonomy. Two good kings delivered nationhood in 1878 and additional territories, including Transylvania, after World War I. The third, King Carol II [sic] was an abysmal failure who tried to appease Hitler and wound up ceding valuable territory to Russia, Hungary, and Bulgaria. In danger of losing his life, Carol fled in 1940 with $40 million, nine railway cars crammed with El Grecos and other valuables,...

Romania entered World War II on the side of the Axis powers, in part to recover Bessarabia and Bukovina, which had been taken by the Soviet Union in 1940. During the war, Romania's authoritarian military dictatorship was deposed in a coup led by King Michael that was organized by opposition politicians and Soviet intelligence agents and supported by the army. After an armistice was signed in Cairo, later in 1944, Romanian forces went to war against the Germans in Transylvania, Hungary, and Czechoslovakia; having already suffered

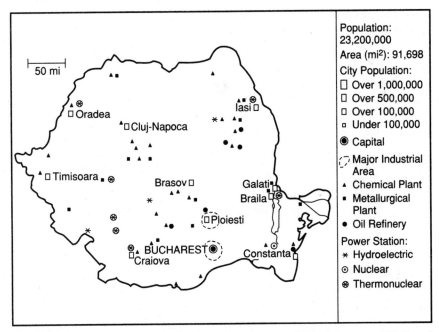

Figure 3-4. Map of Romania. [*U.S. Department of Commerce and National Geographic, June 1991, p. 47 (for industrial data).*]

Romania at a Glance

Area:	230,340 square kilometers
Population:	23.7 million (1992)
Labor force:	11.4 million
Religions:	Orthodox 87%; Roman Catholic 5%: Calvinist, Lutheran, Jewish, Baptist
Languages:	Romanian 90%; Hungarian 7%
Capital:	Bucharest (2 million)
Major cities:	Brasov (346,000)
	Iasi (314,000)
	Timisoara (319,000)
	Constanta (323,000)
Government:	Republic

SOURCE: U.S. Foreign Commercial Service, Central and Eastern European Trade and Technical Assistance Center, International Division, U.S. Chamber of Commerce.

grave losses in the fighting against the Soviet Union, Romania then incurred more casualties in the fight against the Germans. In 1947, the Romanian People's Republic was formed with the help of Soviet occupation forces (Fig. 3-4 and accompanying table).

A Cultural Bridge between East and West

Before the Communists took control of Romania after World War II, the country looked to the West, particularly to France, for cultural, educational, scientific, and social inspiration. Even under Communist rule, since the late 1960s Russian was not compulsory, and German, French, and English were widely taught. Before World War II, less than 20 percent of trade was with nations that became Communist, and half of this was with Czechoslovakia. This figure rose to 86 percent between 1947 and 1959, but in 1973, Romania became the first Warsaw Pact country to conduct less than half of its trade with Communist nations. The country is well equipped to reintegrate with Western Europe since the ouster of its Communist helmsman, Nicolae Ceausescu.

Large in Size, Population, and Industrial Output

In Eastern Europe, Romania is second only to Poland in size and population. It has long been a major European corn- and wheat-growing country as well as an important producer of oil, timber, and natural gas. The rapidly expanded machine-building industry accounts for 30 percent of gross industrial production. Postwar economic programs have emphasized developing power, mining, forestry operations, construction materials, metal production and processing, chemicals, and machine-building. In July 1990, the ban on foreign credits was lifted in order to attract foreign direct investment for agriculture, textiles, and tourism. Few foreigners rushed in, partly because investment law had not been written. The private sector has been legitimized, and the number of small private enterprises has already leapt into the tens of thousands.

Lurching toward Democracy

Romanians lived under the heavy hand of an extensive internal security apparatus that restricted basic freedoms and civil liberties until the assassination of Nicolae Ceausescu on Christmas Day 1989. Sympathy for Romania's new government turned to suspicion when it was discovered that the ruling National Salvation Front was made up of former Communist cronies. Critics feared that these so-called revolutionaries were merely party thugs who all along only wanted to snuff out Ceausescu and his nepotistic rule as part of a scheme to keep the party apparatus intact. In January 1990, three weeks after the revolution, President Ion Iliescu and Prime Minister Petre Roman were nearly lynched by an angry anti-National Salvation Front mob. Other violent incidents followed. No one knew for sure who was behind them— émigré organizations abroad, right-wing parties in Romania, the dreaded Securitate, or Gypsies, who account for 10 percent of the population and might have been bribed to ignite street disturbances. Finally, industrial workers mobilized behind the National Salvation Front and set about harassing and attacking opposition leaders and breaking off their meetings. Protests, often violent, became weekly ritual theater in Bucharest. A hunger strike started in University Square in the center of the capital. When Iliescu garnered 85 percent of the vote in 1990, the opposition shouted fraud. Finally, in June 1990 crowds set fire to the Interior Ministry building and took over Romanian television studios. A train load of coal miners arrived by train the next day, and bashed opposition heads, and beat up anybody who got in their way, all with the encouragement of Iliescu.

The Economic Picture Brightens

Romania's current economic program has set out to bring about a fast transition to a market economy, to catch up to Eastern-Central Europe in the liberalization of its economy, to substitute instruments such as taxes, credits, investments, and legislation for state ownership and management of enterprises, to set up a stock exchange, and to end price controls. The policy has been dubbed "legislative shock therapy" rather than economic shock therapy. Some of the many problems that Romania faces include falsified statistics on enterprise productivity, a lack of energy for industry, the collapse of many enterprises dependent on Soviet trade, a thriving black market, thievery, an inability to sell state-subsidized Romanian-made goods abroad, and declining managerial discipline. A year after the revolution, gross national product (GNP) had declined 15 percent and productivity had fallen 20 percent.

Romania has benefited from most-favored nation (MFN) trading status since 1975. The United States granted Romania additional trade advantages in 1976 under the generalized system of preferences (GSP). Because of human rights violations, however, the United States revoked Romania's MFN trading status in 1988 and had not restored it at the time of this writing. Principal imports include electric energy, coal, natural gas, iron ore, sulfur, cotton fiber, televisions, soy beans, wheat, fish flour, raw sugar, coffee beans, beef, tinned meat, oranges, and olives. Principal exports include steel, aluminum, tractors, cars, bearings, electric motors, refrigerators, petrol, gas and oil, wooden furniture, household glassware, cement, cotton fabric, and footwear.

Country Capsule: **Bulgaria**

Imagine a land the size of Ohio, three quarters covered by mountains, one third lying 1,600 feet above sea level. With Yugoslavia and Albania, Bulgaria lies on the Balkan Peninsula. It has a low population density of only 207 persons per square mile. The Danube River divides Bulgaria from Romania in the north; Greece and Eastern Turkey lie to the south and southeast. Most citizens speak Bulgarian, but the Turkish minority speaks Turkish as well; however, before 1984, the Bulgarian government had, in effect, banned the use of Turkish in public. Other ethnic groups include Gypsies, Greeks, Armenians, Jews, and Russians. Most Bulgarians belong to the Bulgarian Orthodox Church. Other religions practiced in the country include Islam, Roman Catholicism, Protestantism, and Judaism (Fig. 3-5 and accompanying table).

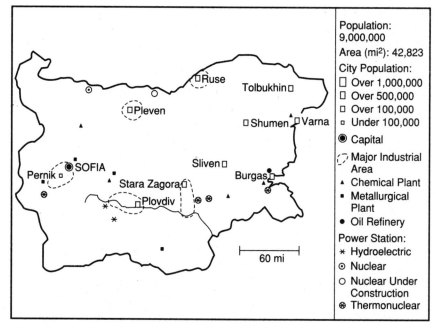

Figure 3-5. Map of Bulgaria. [*U.S. Department of Commerce and National Geographic, June 1991, p. 47 (for industrial data).*]

Bulgaria at a Glance

Area:	111,000 square kilometers
Population:	8.9 million
Labor force:	4 million; 33% industry and 20% agriculture
Ethnic groups:	Bulgarian 85.3%; Turkish 8.5%; Gypsy 2.6%; Macedonian 2.5%; Armenian 0.3%; Russian 0.2%
Religions:	Bulgarian Orthodox 85%; Muslim 13%; Jewish 0.8%; Roman Catholic 0.5%; Protestant 0.5%
Language:	Bulgarian
Capital:	Sofia (1.4 million)
Major cities:	Bourges (200,000)
	Rousse (91,000)
	Varna (306,000)
Government:	Parliamentary democracy

SOURCE: U.S. Foreign Commercial Service, Central and Eastern European Trade and Technical Assistance Center, International Division, U.S. Chamber of Commerce.

Turkish Influence

Bulgaria's name is derived from a Turkic people called the Bulgars; 85.3 percent of the population is Bulgarian; 8.5 percent is Turkish. Although the name "Bulgaria" is not of Slavic origin, the Slavic people who had earlier entered the Balkan Peninsula, absorbed invading Turkic people, and they are the predecessors of present-day Bulgarians. Bulgarian kingdoms existed on the Balkan Peninsula as part of the Byzantine Empire during the Middle Ages, and then independently, until 1396, when the Ottoman Turks conquered. They ruled Bulgaria for 500 years, until 1878. Communist rule in Bulgaria began on September 9, 1944, when a Communist-dominated coalition called the Fatherland Front seized power on behalf of a coalition government that had formed to arrange an armistice with the Allies. Soviet forces marched in without resistance. Bulgaria is the only country in Eastern Europe to have overthrown its Communist leader, only to subsequently reelect a new Communist government. This it did in 1990; the revised name was the Bulgarian Socialist Party. Bulgaria's first non-Communist, democratically elected government in 46 years was put in office in October 1991. The government has set out to liberalize prices, curb inflation, rein in a swollen budget deficit, and seek foreign financial assistance to help pay off the country's $8.2 billion foreign debt.

Privatization Takeoff

Bulgarians formed 178,000 private enterprises during their first two years of freedom from Soviet domination, in a country of only 9 million inhabitants. The overwhelming majority of new enterprises are owned and operated by one person, and the private sector accounts for only 2–3 percent of total economic output, but the pace of privatization is laudable. Bulgaria's commendable industrial output mix includes steel, chemicals, plastics, robots, electronic tools, and automobiles. Machinery and equipment make up 60 percent of exports. Other primary exports include fuels, chemicals, and rubber. Of special note: Bulgaria is the largest exporter of electronics in Eastern Europe.

Country Capsule: **Albania**

Albania is a small, isolationist, self-reliant country (Fig. 3-6). Its 3.2 million inhabitants live on 27,000 square miles of isolated rugged land that inspired the country's name: "Eagle's Country." Albania's Kosovo region lies precariously in southern Serbia, and is 90 percent Albanian. The Serbs regard it as the cradle of their civilization. Kosovo was given autonomous status with the intention that eventually it would become part of a union with Albania, and that then greater Albania would be drawn under the umbrella of Yugoslavian federation. But in

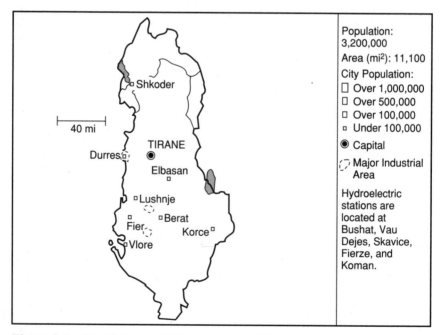

Figure 3-6. Map of Albania. (*U.S. Department of Commerce*)

1948, Yugoslavia broke with Stalin and Albania sided with him. Today, the thought of Kosovo linking up with Albania or declaring independence is considered by the Milosevic government in former Yugoslavia as a reason to carry out a pogrom of Albanians there. The Serbian leader has promulgated the myth that to give up Kosovo would be to desecrate sacred Serbian historical and cultural lands. The Serbs battled the Ottoman Turks there, and lost, in 1389.

Communism's Slow Death in Albania

Albania was under Turkish rule for 400 years, until 1912. After World War II, Albania aligned itself with the U.S.S.R. to counter Yugoslavian expansion. However, when it accepted Chinese Communist ideology, Albania strained its relations with the U.S.S.R., and subsequently it withdrew from Comecon and the Warsaw Pact. Premier Enver Hoxha ruled Albania for 41 years and survived several coup attempts—one, ironically, backed by the Chinese. The Communist government pursued a policy of crisis management after the Berlin Wall came down in 1989. By the end of 1990, however, the government was forced to put an end to a ban on foreign credits, it decentralized enterprise management, it granted Albanians the right to appeal court verdicts, and it approved wage incentives to increase production. (They had been banned in favor of the principle of spontaneous egalitarianism.) President Ramiz Alia even started talking about setting up another Ministry of Justice, which had been abolished during Albania's version of China's "cultural revolution" in the mid-1960s. The number of crimes punishable by death was reduced from 34 to 11; legal leniency became the norm in dealing with political crimes and the exercising of religious faith. Albanians were even given the right to hold a passport. Things looked so good that U.N. Secretary General Javier Perez de Cuellar visited Tirana in May 1991 along with 18 journalists, the most reporters ever admitted into the country at one time.

But as Albanians besieged foreign embassies seeking asylum, Alia stated publicly that he saw no value in allowing political pluralism in the country and declared free-market capitalism a nefarious instrument of imperialist forces. The party's changes did little to quell Albanian popular dissent or international criticism of Alia's government. Demonstrations erupted again in Tirana. Democratic forces, however, had to watch as the Communists, supported by the peasantry, won two thirds of a newly elected assembly. It was not until March 1992—after months of grinding shortages, growing crime, bread riots, and a drop in economic output of 55 percent—that the

Communist night in Albania came to an end, defeated by the Democratic party in a popular election. Little Albania was back on the map as a potential recipient of international aid (Albania has received MFN status) as well as foreign investment.

Woefully Undeveloped

Albania holds the inglorious distinction of being the poorest, least-developed country in all of Europe. There are no business-class hotels in Albania's capital of Tirana. In the entire country, there are only 32,000 telephones, only two sets of traffic lights, and 468 automobiles. Regular air transportation within the country is nonexistent, and as of 1991, U.S. and Soviet nationals were generally refused entry into the country. Visas are still difficult to obtain.

Country Capsule: Former Yugoslavia

The dissolution and destruction in former Yugoslavia, a country with such palpable promise, have been Eastern Europe's greatest commercial letdown. Nonaligned, perfectly positioned geographically, endowed with seaports and resources, bordering the European Community (EC), Yugoslavia appeared to have a bright future in the world economy after the end of communism in Central Europe. Sales to the West were high, and only 14 percent of Yugoslavia's trade was with the Soviet Union. The country had the potential to usurp Spain in the late 1980s as a prime destination for foreign investment. Yugoslavia had been pursuing privatization vigorously and quite successfully under the Milosevic administration. "The Yugoslavians had gone farther with privatization than practically anywhere else in Eastern Europe," observed Jeremy Keller, desk officer on Yugoslavia at the U.S. Department of Commerce. The dinar was convertible. Intellectual property rights had been put in place. Investment law was forward-looking and consistent. "Virtually everything had been done that we deemed necessary for a functioning economy," says Keller. But then, *Poof!* The Yugoslavians were cutting off the fingers of their enemies' children and bashing old ladies' heads with rifle butts. International trade hung on until the end of October 1991, according to Department of Commerce statistics. By February 1992, however, it had tapered off steeply because of a drastic drop in productivity associated with civil war and the imposition of a trade embargo by Western countries. At this juncture, the economy is, to put it bluntly, *gone*. The currency is now worthless, which has ruined internal convertibility. Factory production has been utterly disrupted. The banking sector has vanished.

A Violent Jigsaw

Former Yugoslavia is as big as Wyoming, a jigsaw puzzle of ethnic rivalry and violent animosity made up of six republics and two autonomous provinces. Now, it comprises four independent countries, with a fifth—war-torn Bosnia-Herzogovina—divided into 10 autonomous areas based on ethnicity. The people of the former Yugoslavia have the greatest ethnic and religious diversity in Eastern Europe (not including the former Soviet Union). Formed as a nation after World War I in 1918, Yugoslavia encompasses the principal South Slav ethnic groups and an additional 17 minorities, which are distinguishable to this day. Languages spoken in the region include Serbo-Croatian, Slovenian, Macedonian, Albanian, Hungarian, and Italian. Religion follows ethnic lines for the most part. The 7 million inhabitants of former Yugoslavia who adhere to the Orthodox faith include most Serbs, Montenegrians, and Macedonians. The 5 million Roman Catholics include Croats, Slovenes, and Hungarians. In Bosnia-Herzogovina, the population is 40 percent Muslim.

Before World War I, the area of present-day Yugoslavia comprised the kingdoms of Serbia and Montenegro and parts of the Turkish and Austro-Hungarian empires, a highly attractive and strategic geopolitical locus and the object of intense rivalry among the European powers. The assassination of Archduke Franz Ferdinand in Sarajevo sparked the First World War. With the end of three empires—German, Austro-Hungarian, Ottoman Turk—and the demise of imperial Russia due to the Bolshevik Revolution, the entire map of Europe had to be redrawn. The Balkans and Central Europe were an ethnic collage and could not be reconciled by neatly etched borders. Many minorities, especially on the Balkan Peninsula, were left out in the cold. A multinational state was formed in the south, where many ethnic groups, it was hoped, could live together harmoniously. An independent Yugoslavia was formed on December 1, 1918, with a Serbian king named Peter I at the helm. Peter I tried to keep non-Serb unity at bay by dividing the country into 33 *oblasts,* or administrative provinces, under centralized authority. But in reaction, unrest, political intrigue, and assassination plagued the government.

Between the wars, the Serbs and Croats grew contemptuous of each other as a result of nationalistic issues: In short, the Serbs, and their political allies, the Slovenes, dominated the highly centralized government located in Belgrade. The Croats demanded a federal system that would grant them more regional and ethnic autonomy. Sounds reasonable. Then a Montenegrin Serb (this is getting complicated) shot a Croatian leader, Stjepan Radic, in the parliament because he had insulted the Serbian people. The Croats reacted by withdrawing from parliament. Serbian King Alexander escalated matters by establishing a royal dictatorship, thwarting regionalism and nationalistic yearnings and espousing the historically implausible policy of "Yugoslavism." By 1939 the Croats had won considerable autonomy.

Meanwhile, pro-Serbian military elements became acutely aware of public opposition to the support the Serbian monarchy was giving Germany, Italy, and Japan as the war progressed; so this military group staged a coup and replaced Prince Paul with 17-year-old King Peter. Well, the Axis powers did not care for this move, and beginning in April 1941, the armed forces of Germany, Italy, Hungary, and Bulgaria goose-stepped into Yugoslavia and gave the Serbian royal family and government leaders their walking papers. Then things got ugly. A fascist, pro-Nazi, separatist group of Croatians called the Ustashe seized power in the northern city of Zagreb and established the so-called independent state of Croatia. The new Croatian government allied itself with Hitler. During the war, Croatian Ustachi exterminated about 500,000 Orthodox Serbs. In the end, the war cost 2 million Yugoslavian lives; about half those deaths were the result of Yugoslavians killing each other.

Out of the smoke and ruin and political division rose the Communist party, led by Marshall Josip Broz Tito, which had enjoyed Allied support during the war. Yugoslavia became a "people's republic" in 1946, after which Tito led it down an "independent road to socialism." Yugoslavia became a maverick in the Communist world, which helped it to direct its trade toward the West and broaden its economic contact with the "Free World." Both politically and economically it defined itself as a torch bearer for the nonaligned nations. But the violence continued after the Communists took control. In the five years following Nazi defeat, Communist purges claimed an estimated 300,000 Croatians, 70,000 Germans, 17,000 Slovenes, 6,000 Montenegrins, and 3,000 Serbs. Borders were redrawn again.

Tito experimented with economic reform long before other Communist regimes did so, in part to hold onto power in the face of Stalin's attempts to oust him. Worker self-management programs provided factory incentives. Private business was allowed to thrive. Rapid growth ensued, fueled in part by Yugoslav workers sending foreign exchange home from abroad. Antireligion campaigns abated. Freedom of expression and legal emigration set Yugoslavians apart from their Romanian and Bulgarian neighbors.

Meanwhile, each republic of the country kept its own books and racked up its own foreign debt. When the IMF finally stepped in to unravel Yugoslavia's economic mess, it discovered that the country's total debt ran upward of $20 billion. That was greater even than Poland's on a per capita basis. Worse still, the country's industry, which was built with borrowed money, had been located according to the whims of local party bosses rather than economic reason. The irregularities and imbalances eventually broke the peace. Slovenia, for instance, earned 28 percent of the country's hard currency through exports, although it was home to only 8 percent of the population. It produced 17 percent of total GNP. No wonder the Slovenes believed that the Serbians didn't deserve to control the territory. Croatia's long, thin finger of Adriatic coastline attracts tourist dollars that gave Croatians the clout to vote an end to Communist government in Croatia in 1990. Meanwhile, the Slovenes were making even more money than the Croatians by doing business with Austria and the EC and refusing to deliver tax revenue to Belgrade. In 1990 the Slovenes, like the Croats, ousted their Communist government and declared independence from Belgrade.

Does Former Yugoslavia Have a Commercial Future?

It's difficult to see how, at least in the short term. It was hoped that the presence of the United Nations would reduce the numbers of those killed in battle, but with Serbian attacks in Bosnia-Herzogovina, the possibility of a realistic lasting peace grew dim. As of July 1992 over 25,000 people had perished in that conflict and 1 million had left the region as refugees.

Country Capsule: Eastern Germany

On an autumn day in 1989—October 3 to be exact—the German Democratic Republic, otherwise know as Communist East Germany, merged with the most competitive capitalist country on earth (Fig. 3-7). A convoy of armored vans drove in 460 tons of deutsche marks for the conversion of East Germany's currency. Department store windows filled up, and vendors set up shop everywhere. With reunification of East and West Germany, all the institutions of the former

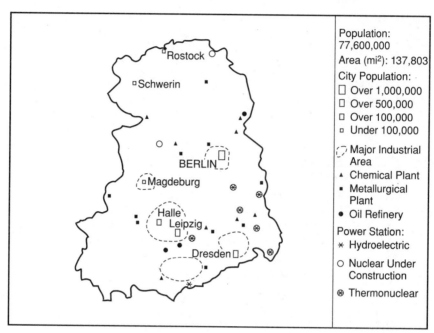

Figure 3-7. Map of united Germany. [U.S. Department of Commerce and National Geographic, June 1991, p. 47 (for industrial data).]

German Democratic Republic were dissolved, and they have been replaced by government ministries in Bonn. Organizations such as the Trust Agency (Treuhandanstalt), which is responsible for the privatization of industry in Germany's five new states, have been created to respond to a responsibility unprecedented in world history—the sale of virtually all former East German companies. In reunifying with the Federal Republic of Germany, the area of the former German Democratic Republic (G.D.R.) was divided into five states, or *lander,* plus the city district of Berlin. When the first blush of unification was over, however, east German companies found that they could no longer sell their once-sought-after products in the Soviet Union and throughout Eastern Europe. While east Germans enjoyed a year of being cash rich after converting their currency into deutsche marks at a ratio of 1:1, the conversion rate saddled their enterprises in increased debt.

Slow Recovery

Economic recovery from 40 years of communism in the G.D.R. has turned out to be a slower and more painful process than predicted. Local eastern German industry is generally in poor condition. Few companies can compete in the world market or be sold to foreign investors. In fact, 30 percent of the enterprises in the East have been deemed unworthy of continued operation. Moreover, an economic Grand Canyon has widened between eastern Germans (known to western Germans as *Ossis*) and western Germans (known to eastern Germans as *Wessis*). Joblessness in the West is 5.8 percent; in the East unemployment has climbed to roughly two thirds of the working population. "The surest way to tell an East Berliner from a West Berliner," said Steve Kroft on the television show "60 Minutes," "is to find out which collects an unemployment check." Eastern Germany's population is one quarter that of western Germany, yet its GNP is only 8 percent of western Germany's. Bonn is pouring money into eastern Germany. One hundred billion deutsche marks were earmarked to be spent from the time of currency conversion to the end of 1991—money allocated to build roads, set up telephone systems, and provide office equipment to new businesses.

The Treuhandanstalt

A freely elected Volkskammer made it the Treuhand's mandate to sell off 8,000 to 9,000 enterprises employing 4 million workers, including chemical plants, power stations, restaurants, and small vendor shops. The Treuhand sold 1,260 enterprises by March 1991; the first to go were all the department stores, an eighth of the industrial enterprises, and three quarters of the shops and restaurants. However, the Treuhand also shut down 300 enterprises, putting thousands of people out of work. At other enterprises it cut the number of employed. On April 1, 1991, Detler Karsten Rohwedder, the head of the Treuhandanstalt, was assassinated, ostensibly murdered by the Red Army Faction, a terrorist group that has been carrying out killings since the 1970s. It seemed the Trehandanstalt was dislocating too many east Germans too quickly. Political pressure eventually forced the Treuhand to consult state and local governments before slashing jobs and to financially help affected enterprises survive. "We get cursed all the time," says the current president of the Treuhandanstalt, Brigit Breunel. "The Treuhand was created to take all the difficult decisions which the politicians could not take." Compared with the privatization of agencies and ministries elsewhere in Eastern Europe (which, however, do not enjoy massive financial support from the West), the Treuhand's performance has been exemplary, a fact that the German press sometimes overlooks. Of the 8,000 companies earmarked to be sold, the Treuhand has successfully sold well over 2,000. By June 1991 the Treuhand was moving 15 to 20 companies a day into private hands.

Country Capsule: The Czech and Slovak Republics

In Czechoslovakia the road from dictatorship to democracy was paved with velvet, the product of a revolution brought on by a profound national desire to uphold human rights. Under Charter 77, signed in January 1977, 250 people (including Vaclav Havel) issued a public criticism of the Communist government's human rights abuses and pleaded for change. The government reacted by taking a series of steps to persecute dissidents that ranged from denying jobs, to detention, to imprisonment, to exile. By 1989, the number of signatories of the charter had grown to 1,500. Peaceful demonstrations erupted in Prague in late 1988 as opposition groups multiplied and then coalesced into the Civic Forum, an umbrella group championing bureaucratic reform and civil liberties. Its Slovak counterpart was called "Public without Violence." In December 1989 the Communist party collapsed and its leaders resigned.

What *Was* Czechoslovakia?

Czechoslovakia is a horizontally oriented land of plains, hills, and plateaus divided into three regions: Bohemia, Moravia, and Slovakia. Bohemia is the western region, the most important part of the country, both politically and economically. Moravia lies between Bohemia and Slovakia; it features important coal and steel industries in the north and agricultural areas in the south. Bohemia and Moravia make up the historic Czech lands and together form the Czech Federal Republic. Slovakia (the Slovak Republic) lies in the east; it is ruggedly mountainous in the north and has important agricultural lowlands in the south. Slovakia has never been comparable to Bohemia and Moravia in terms of economic output or political power—that is, until Czechoslovakian liberalization in 1989, which put the republics on a more equal footing.

Of the 15.6 million people who live in the Czech and Slovak republics, 65 percent are Czech and 30 percent are Slovak. Throw in another 600,000 Hungarians in Slovakia, 25,000 Gypsies, and a large number of Ukrainians, Germans, and Poles for a rich, if not volatile, ethnic mix. Two out of three Czechoslovakians are Roman Catholic, 400,000 are members of the Czechoslovak Hussite Church, 400,000 are members of the Slovak Lutheran Church, and about 10,000 Jews remain of the prewar Jewish population of 360,000. The Czechs are by and large secular, having lived under German and Austrian influence, while the Slovaks are mostly Catholic, having been under the influence of Hungary (Fig. 3-8 and accompanying table).

A History of Division

Czech and Slovak division has roots deep in European history. The Slovaks lived under Hungarian rule for 10 centuries during the Middle Ages, while Bohemia and Moravia were part of the Holy Roman

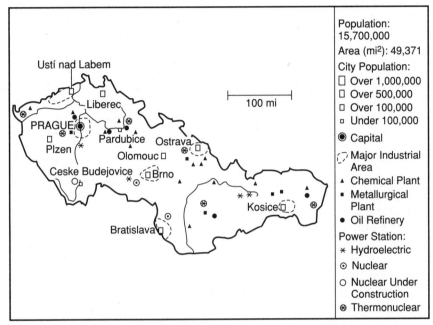

Figure 3-8. Map of Czechoslovakia. [U.S. Department of Commerce and National Geographic, June 1991, p. 47 (for industrial data).]

The Czech and Slovak Republics at a Glance

Area:	128,000 square kilometers
Total population:	15.0 million
Total labor force:	7.8 million
Ethnic groups:	Czechs 64%; Slovaks 31%; Hungarians, Poles, Germans, Romanians, Gypsies 5%
Religions:	50% Roman Catholic, 20% Protestant
Languages:	Czech, Slovak
Capitals:	Prague (1.4 million) and Bratislava (380,000)
Major cities:	Brno (360,000)
	Kosice (190,000)
	Plzen, Ostava (150,000)
Government:	Parliamentary democracy

SOURCE: U.S. Foreign Commercial Service, Central and Eastern European Trade and Technical Assistance Center, International Division, U.S. Chamber of Commerce.

Empire. Slovakia remained under Hungarian control, while Czech territory was under Austrian dominion for 300 years, starting in 1620. Czech and Slovak lands were united in 1918 after the fall of the Austro-Hungarian Empire. Their languages are virtually identical.

In the late 1930s, Czech nationalists, urged on in part by Nazi Germany, encouraged the country's large German population, which made up 22 percent of the entire citizenry and was concentrated in the Bohemian and Moravian border regions (the Sudetenland), to reject Czech-German reconciliation. Eventually, France, Italy, and the United Kingdom acceded to Nazi pressure and agreed to force Czechoslovakia to cede the Sudetenland to Germany in 1938. Hitler invaded the region in 1939 and established a "Protectorate." Remaining Czech lands were carved up by Germany, Hungary, and Poland. An independent fascist puppet state of Slovakia was then formed, also under German domination. Since the country's "Velvet Revolution" in 1989, Czechs living along the German border on land that once belonged to Sudeten Germans who moved to West Germany after the Nazi defeat have feared a new invasion of Germans crossing the border to take back the lands that they had abandoned. In early 1992, in an undreamed-of eventuality, German economic pressure on the Czechoslovakian government resulted in former German-owned land and homes being returned to their original German owners; the current Czech owners would be relocated and compensated by the Czech government.

Czech and Slovak lands were reunited as "Czechoslovakia" in 1945 after the liberation of Europe by American and Soviet troops. The new country's Communist party was victorious in free elections held in 1946, and in 1948 Soviet-based Communists forcibly seized power in a coup. Nationalization of basic industries and retail trade was completed in 1950–1951. Companies began to fail by the early 1960s because of inadequate incentive for labor and management and resulting high labor turnover, low productivity, and low quality. By the 1980s, 80 percent of Czechoslovakia's trade was with Communist countries (45 percent with the U.S.S.R.) and consisted mainly of the exchange of Czechoslovakian machinery for Soviet oil, natural gas, and iron ore. In 1968, the country divided politically into two federal republics: the Czech Socialist Republic (C.S.R.) and the Slovak Socialist Republic (S.S.R.) or Slovakia. Together, the country was called the Czech and Slovak Federal Republic (C.S.F.R.). The national capital, and capital of the Czech republic, is in Prague. Bratislava in the south became the capital of Slovakia.

The Slovaks were not at the same level of economic and technical development as the Czechs, but joining the new Czechoslovak Republic gave them the chance to make rapid strides toward catching up. Slovakia, which occupies one third the land area of the Czech

Republic, is also less developed and more rural. Joblessness burdens Slovakia twice as much as it does the Czech Republic, running at 10 percent of the working population.

An Industrious Past

When the Communists took over in 1948, Czechoslovakia had a balanced economy and one of the higher levels of industrialization in Europe. Czechoslovakia's strong industrial tradition dates to the period when Bohemia and Moravia were the heart and lungs of the Austro-Hungarian Empire. Czechoslovakia has a tradition of democracy and a clear memory of stability arising from the period of its First Republic, from 1918 to 1938. People are skilled and educated; the transport system is well developed. But the country's factories are deficient in energy and lack an adequate supply of many raw materials, and their technology is 40 years old. The country's debt burden was only $3.7 billion in 1987, far less than in that of Poland or Hungary. Its principal industries are machine-building, iron and steel production, metal working, chemicals, electronics, transport equipment, textiles, glass, beer brewing, china, ceramics, and pharmaceuticals. Large-scale privatization of state-owned industry occurred in the second half of 1991. One in seven jobs in Czechoslovakia's state-run industry once depended on now-defunct trade with the U.S.S.R. The country has also lost its trade with former Comecon countries. The country's defense industry, which is located in Slovakia and employs 100,000 locals, was especially hard hit; from 1988 to 1990, sales by these plants fell from $8 billion to $1 billion.

To the end, Czech Finance Minister Vaclav Klaus, a free marketer, resisted giving the Slovaks the government credits, subsidies, and bailouts that they sought to lighten the burden of transition. Slovakian Prime Minister Vladimir Meciar called Klaus's bluff by mustering the votes to oust Havel and force the Czechs to divide the republics or remain mired in divisive political battle. The Czech and Slovak republics formally split on New Year's Day, 1993—ironically, the same day that Western Europe formally unified into a single market.

Country Capsule: The Newly Independent States of the Former Soviet Union (including the Baltic States)

Winston Churchill called Russia "a riddle wrapped in a mystery inside an enigma." Only the observer guided by this principle can hope to understand what once was the Union of Socialist Soviet Republics. On December 21, 1991, the Commonwealth of Independent States (C.I.S.) was formed, with the signing of a treaty in Alma-Ata; it included the Slavic Republic of Russia, Ukraine, and Belarus. Later, 11 of the 12 remaining former Soviet republics, out of the original 15, joined the commonwealth. Georgia remained aloof; the Baltic republics of Estonia, Latvia, and Lithuania had declared their independence from the Soviet Union earlier that year. Before looking at each "newly independent state" of the former Soviet Union, let's review what the Soviet Union looked like up until its dismemberment in 1991.

The U.S.S.R. spanned 11 time zones and was the largest country in the world. It was home to 290 million people, almost 40 million more than the United States, ranking third in world population, after China and India. Three out of four of these people live in one of seven former so-called European republics: the Russian Republic; the three Baltic states of Estonia, Latvia, and Lithuania; Ukraine; Belarus; and Moldova. The Ural Mountains divide traditional European Russia from Asiatic Russia. The republics of the Transcaucasus—Georgia, Armenia, and Azerbaijan—are home to only 6 percent of the total population. One percent of the total former Soviet population resides in the Central Asian republics—Kazakhstan, Kyrgyzstan, Tajikistan, Turkmenistan, and Uzbekistan.

Ethnically, linguistically, and in terms of religion, the former Soviet Union is a melting pot. More than 100 ethnic groups live in the former U.S.S.R.; 72 percent are Eastern Slavs. Seventy percent of these are Russians and the rest are Ukranians and Belorussians. The population is made up of the following ethnic groups: Russians 50.8 percent, Ukrainians 15.45 percent, Uzbeks 5.84 percent, and Belarusians 3.51 percent. Although each ethnic group (there are 170, all based on heredity rather than place of birth) has its own language (there are 200 languages and dialects), since Stalin the Russian language has been taught as a second language to all non-Russians. One of every five former Soviet citizens professes the Russian Orthodox religion; roughly 10 percent are Muslims. About 8 percent adhere to one of a panoply of other congregations including Protestant, Roman Catholic, and Jewish. All the remaining people (over 60 percent) had been assumed to be atheists under communism, but with the sudden disappearance of party policing of religious activities, many of these people have begun to practice religion (Fig. 3-9 and accompanying tables).

Locomotive for East-West Trade.   In the recent past, the U.S.S.R. purchased over $30 billion worth of goods from other countries per year. As of 1989, one third of that trade was with the Organization of Economic

Cooperation and Development (OECD) countries of the capitalist West; more than one half was with member nations of Comecon and other Socialist countries. In 1990–1991, the C.I.S. experienced a massive drop in ruble trade with former Comecon countries; all trade is now conducted in hard currency rather than rubles. The country was importing about $4 bil-

Figure 3-9. Map of the newly independent states of the former U.S.S.R. [*Business Information Service for the Newly Independent States (BISNIS), U.S. Department of Commerce, International Trade Administration.*]

The Former Soviet Union at a Glance

Total area:	22.4 million square kilometers
Population:	290.9 million (1990)
Labor force:	152.3 million (80% industry and other nonagricultural fields, 20% agriculture)
Ethnic groups:	Russian 50.78%, Ukrainian 15.45%, Uzbek 5.84%, Byelorussian 3.51% (approximately 170 nationalities)
Religions:	Russian Orthodox 20%; Muslim 10%; Protestant, Roman Catholic, Jewish, among others
Languages:	Russian (official); more than 200 languages and dialects are spoken

SOURCE: Central and Eastern European Trade and Technical Assistance Center, International Division, U.S. Chamber of Commerce.

Countries and Capitals of the Former Soviet Union

Former republic	Capital city	Population of capital city
Armenia	Yerevan	1.22 million
Azerbaijan	Baku	1.75 million
Byelarus	Minsk	1.6 million
Georgia	Tbilisi	1.2 million
Kazakhstan	Alma-Ata	1.13 million
Kyrgyzstan	Bishkek	627,000
Moldova	Kishnev	720,000
Russia	Moscow	9 million
Tajikistan	Dushanbe	584,000
Turkmenistan	Ashkabad	402,000
Ukraine	Kiev	2.6 million
Uzbekistan	Tashkent	2.1 million
Estonia	Tallinn	503,000
Latvia	Riga	900,000
Lithuania	Vilnius	700,000

SOURCE: U.S. Foreign Commercial Service, Central and Eastern European Trade and Technical Assistance Center, International Division, U.S. Chamber of Commerce.

lion from the United States per year, and selling to the United States about $700 million worth of goods annually. Principal American exports to the Soviet Union have traditionally been food-related—corn, wheat, dairy products, poultry meat, fertilizer, and soy beans—while the United States has bought mainly oil, chemicals, minerals, and tractors from the U.S.S.R.

Loaded with Resources. Energy resources are the commonwealth's most obvious asset—estimated at 25 percent of the world's total. Only South Africa produces more gold- and platinum-group metals. The commonwealth's timber and manganese resources are the largest in the world; the republics are endowed with ample supplies of lead, zinc, nickel, mercury, potash, and phosphate. The commonwealth lacks only two major minerals—tin and uranium. Forty-two percent of its exports are fuel and electricity; 9.5 percent consist of mineral ores and metals.

Yeltsin Schmoozes the Group of Seven. At present, all the Newly Independent States are seeking IMF assistance; and the Overseas Private Investment Corporation (OPIC) is pursuing agreements with each as well (see the table next page). The IMF and the Group of Seven have also promised $24 billion in aid to the former republics, much of which is earmarked to help stabilize the ruble and make it convertible. The IMF has backed down on its demands that Russia meet certain criteria in terms of its timetable for reforms. Not disingenuously, Yeltsin warned Michel

Status of Agreements between the United States and the Newly Independent States.

Republic	Trade agreement	MFN	GSP	OPIC	Eximbank
Armenia	Yes	Yes	No	Yes	No
Azerbaijan	Pending*	No	No	Pending†	No
Belarus	Yes	Yes	No	Yes	Yes
Georgia	Pending*	No	No	Yes	No
Kazakhstan	Yes	Yes	No	Yes	Yes
Kyrgyzstan	Yes	Yes	No*	Yes	No
Moldova	Yes	Yes	No*	Pending†	No
Russia	Yes	Yes	No	Yes	Yes
Tajikistan	Pending*	No	No	Yes	No
Turkmenistan	Pending*	No	No	Yes	Yes
Ukraine	Yes	Yes	No	Yes	Yes
Uzbekistan	Pending*	No	No	Yes	Yes

*Negotiations in progress (for OPIC, signing expected shortly; companies are encouraged to register projects with OPIC now).

†Awaiting ratification by country's parliament.

Note: MFN—Most-favored-nation status; GSP—Generalized System of Preferences; OPIC—Overseas Private Investment Corporation; Eximbank—Export-Import Bank of the United States.

SOURCE: U.S. Dept. of Commerce, International Trade Administration.

Camdessus, managing director of the IMF, that "There's a limit to what the people will endure, and after that, that's it. Patience will be gone, faith in the president will be finished, chaos will begin." While the risk of aid money being wasted may increase without the conditions, the risk that the conditions would upturn Russia's tenuous political stability may be reduced.

Wrenching Instability. Russia's teetering economy worries the West profoundly. Gross national product in the former republic was down 8 to 10 percent in 1990 while government debt increased almost 40 percent. Inflation soared to 140 percent per annum in 1990 after Yeltsin liberalized prices and has since shot up to 2,000 percent! The theory was that higher prices would create incentive for enterprises to produce more goods for the market; an additional incentive for producers will be that their production inputs will cost more to buy, and state subsidies for their purchase will no longer be available. But impasses have arisen. Because middlemen have a stranglehold on the distribution system (often former officials), many consumer products command prices up to eight times what they cost to produce and market. Ceilings set on wages have been removed so that managers can raise wages as the price of basic necessities soars (Yeltsin had already raised soldiers' pay by 90 percent), but the money to pay workers higher wages was simply not forthcoming from sales of enterprise products, since people and other producers were not able to pay the higher prices for them. When Yeltsin liberalized prices, neighboring republics raised their prices immediately also, fearing that the people in the Russian republic would stream over their borders to buy up bargain-priced goods. They had no choice but to follow Yeltsin's lead. The Ukraine began printing scrip to handle the demand for cash since the republic lacked printed rubles. There was a plan to print ration coupons that would bar nonresidents from buying goods in the Ukraine; but a consequence was that the coupons would become an alternative currency easily traded across borders. The government issued 8 billion new rubles in 1988, and 30 billion in 1990, further driving inflation and devaluing the ruble (the official rate has plummeted from two rubles per one dollar to 126 rubles per one dollar. Exports fell by 23 percent during the first half of 1991 compared to the same period the year before; imports dropped off 45 percent. Worst of all, oil and gas exports, from which the U.S.S.R. derived the lion's share of its foreign currency, dropped 54 percent, caused by shortages in the oil sector and, finally, by the dissolution of the Comecon trade bloc.

A "Grab-Now" Mentality Spreads.   With the selling off of billions of rubles in real estate and in company assets, the country, in the words of *Los Angeles Times* reporter Carey Goldberg, "resembles the beginning of a Monopoly game, when all kinds of choice property is about to go up for grabs—and the players, seeing the chance of a lifetime, are willing to cheat to win." In Russia's fast-forward gallop toward capitalism, the regulations—the checks and balances necessary to control capitalist transactions—have yet to catch up with the rush to make a fast buck. A mafia now controls virtually all of Russia's huge economy, and violent crime takes 60 lives a day in Moscow alone.

All of this brings back bad memories for older former Soviets, who remember that massive privatization has been tried before in the Soviet Union, with disastrous results. Between 1923 and 1930, Lenin initiated his so-called New Economic Policy (NEP), which allowed the privatization of a set proportion of industry and enterprise. Then as now, the experiment was aimed at fueling economic growth in response to stagnation. Also like today, the NEP created capitalists—rich peasants called *kulaks*, speculators, private entrepreneurs, and commercial traders—and was in the process of reestablishing a class of wage laborers. It also created gross inequalities of income and wealth. "At one end, the new Nepmen reaped an ungodly harvest from profitable opportunities; at the other, workers labored for little or, worse yet, were unemployed for long periods of time," John G. Gurley has written in his book *Soviets at the Edge*. By 1930, however, the program had failed, and those who had taken the initiative to privatize were either killed or carted off to Siberia. Soviet industry was renationalized.

A brief overview of each of the Newly Independent States follows.

The European Former Republics

Russia (or the Russian Federation). The newly independent Russian republic is now called the "Russian Federation" or "Russia." The nation occupies 77 percent of the land mass of the former Soviet Union and is home to half the former Soviet population (148.5 million). The population is 83 percent Russian, 3.6 percent Tatar, and 2.7 percent Ukrainian. The Russians adhere to the religion of the Russian Orthodox Church. Russia is endowed with most of the former Soviet resources, including oil, natural gas, iron ore, nonferrous metals, coal, and precious metals. Russia produces over 50 percent of the former Soviet Union's grain, potatoes, coal, and electricity output. It extracts 90.5 percent of the petroleum and 74.8 percent of the natural gas and generates 62.9 percent of the electricity. Every day the new nation produces 11 million barrels of petroleum and 544 billion cubic meters of natural gas. Siberia holds two thirds of the former Soviet Union's energy resources, half the world's coal reserves, and more than half the world's mineral oil and natural gas. The latest idea is to exploit enormous deposits in western Siberia (Urengoi, Yamburg, Tsapalyarnoye, and Medrestic). Natural gas processing occurs primarily in the Volga region.

Russia is divided administratively into provinces, metropolitan cities (Moscow and St. Petersburg), autonomous republics with their own independent goverments, 5 autonomous regions, and 10 national regions (Fig, 3-10). The country is a melting pot stretching from the Gulf of Finland to the Pacific Rim, where few ethnic groups have melted into one another at all; most regions and republics seek as much independence from the Russian-controlled center of Moscow as possible. Even Yeltsin's home region of Sverdlovsk has declared itself a "republic," and other regions have threatened to do the same, refusing to contribute their share of the federal budget.

Yeltsin's current economic reform package includes abolishing official exchange rates, releasing price controls, removing wage ceilings, and putting Russian enterprises up for sale in two phases. Small companies in trade, construction, food, and retail will be sold first; larger companies with over 10,000 workers involved in oil and gas refining, pharmaceuticals, and other strategic industries will be sold only with government permission. Enterprises directly involved in mineral extraction,

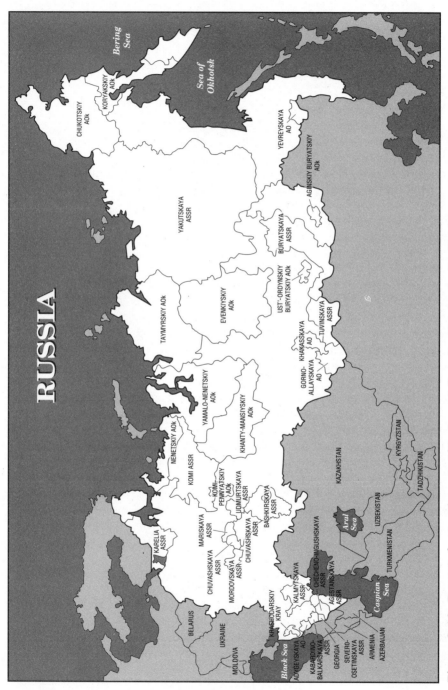

Figure 3-10. Russia's fractured empire. [Business Information Service for the Newly Independent States (BISNIS), U.S. Department of Commerce, International Trade Administration.]

banking, weapons manufacture, and key transport services will not be privatized. In the event that Yeltsin's reforms are given a chance to be fully implemented, prices should stabilize, but unemployment will sky-rocket as military plants make the shift to less labor-intensive production of consumer goods. If, that is, Yeltsin's reforms are enacted, are not vulgarized beyond recognition at the local level, and remain in place in the face of escalating social discontent. At the end of 1992, the reform package had come under siege by well-organized enterprise managers, and Yeltsin was forced to remove his economic reform czar, Yegor Gaidar. Reform, it was predicted, will proceed at a slower pace. In July 1993, however, Yeltsin won a key political victory with the ratification of a new constitution that significantly enhanced the power of the Russian presidency and will open the way for the abolition of the Congress of People's Deputies, a bastion of "go-slow" officials.

Ukraine. The Ukraine has the second-largest population (52 million people) of the former Soviet republics, and the second-largest population of Slavic people in the C.I.S. Known as Russia's breadbasket, as of 1988 Ukraine produced 22 percent of the Soviet Union's agriculture output and 16 percent of total GNP. It grows 22.4 percent of the former Soviet Union's grains and 17.7 percent of its potatoes; it produces 23.4 percent of the meat and 6.6 percent of the wool. Ukraine also produces 181.8 million tons of coal per year and 32.4 billion cubic meters of natural gas. It produced 46 percent of the U.S.S.R.'s iron ore, 20 percent of total chemical output, and 20 percent of mechanical engineering output.

In 1987, the republic exported 2.3 billion rubles worth of goods and purchased over 4.5 billion rubles worth of imports. Ukraine exports 8.7 percent of its total production output. Given its proximity to Central European markets, especially Hungary, the Ukraine may attract a sizable portion of future foreign direct investment headed for the former Soviet Union. Skeptics disagree as to whether Ukraine will be able to link itself to the EC as a nation independent of other C.I.S. economies. "[The Ukrainians] entertain the belief they are feeding other republics," writes Alexei Kiva in *We/MbI*, "and that their transition to an easier life and a place in the Common Europe House will be easier as a totally independent state. In reality, however, the situation is much more complicated. Ukraine will not be able to pull through without the oil, timber, and other materials provided by Russia. Furthermore, their coal mining, iron, textiles and other industries are in deplorable condition. Without cooperating with Russia, Ukraine will find it extremely difficult to pull itself out of its present mess. The Common European House? A pipe dream. From personal experience, I know that wealthy neighbors are in no haste to open their doors to beggars."

Belarus (formally Byelorussia).   Belarus, known before as the Byelorussian S.S.R., has a population of 10.3 million; 80 percent are Belarusians, 12 percent are Russians, and most of the rest are Poles. The nation's homogeneous population has afforded it a high degree of political stability, and its strategic position next to the Baltics, Poland, and Russia makes it an attractive investment site. Still operating as a command economy in which prices are fixed, Belarus has yet to confront the destabilizing impact of structural reform. Seventy percent of the population speak Belarusian; 28 percent speak Russian. The republic lacks natural resources other than peat fields and forests but produces a wide array of agricultural and industrial products. Agricultural products include potatoes, grain, and flax. As of 1988, Belarus produced about 10 percent of the former Soviet Union's potato crop, 3.27 percent of its grains, and 6.27 percent of its meat. There are major deposits of mineral salts, phosphorites and peat. Chief industries include machinery, tools, appliances, tractors, clocks, and cameras. Belarus is also a producer of motorcycles; it accounts for 20 percent of the total former Soviet Union's production and for 15 percent of total tractor production.

Heavily dependent on trade exchanges with other former republics, Belarus traditionally sold 70 percent of its output to other republics, while it exported only 6.5 percent. Belarus must import most of its energy, and the successful export of its farm products will likely be hindered by protectionist import policies in the EC.

Moldova (formally Moldavia).   Moldavia is tiny in population (4.3 million), land mass (33,700 square kilometers), and in resource endowment. Infrastructure is solid, however, compared to most other republics, and its strong agriculture sector produces sugar beets, vegetable oil, wines, and tobacco. The catch: Most Moldovians are ethnically Romanian (62 percent) and want to reunify with their Romanian neighbors across the Prut River. Moldova's Slavic minority (14.2 percent Ukrainian and 12.8 percent Russian), located mostly in the Dniestr region, has declared its own independence. The ostensibly impartial joint peacekeeping force sent by Yeltsin to enter Moldova numbers over 2,000 and include Ukrainians, Russians, Moldovans, Romanians, and Belarussians. The Moldovans, of course, object to Russian troops being included at all.

The Baltic States: Estonia, Latvia, and Lithuania.   Since their independence in September 1991, the Baltic States of Latvia, Lithuania, and Estonia have gained membership in the IMF, World Bank and the European Bank for Reconstruction and Development (EBRD), and have won associate status in the EC. The Baltic States can serve as a gateway from West to East, offering three warm-water ports and rail links with

Products Manufactured by the Baltic Countries

Latvia	Estonia	Lithuania
Telephone switches	Computers	Industrial robots
Electric railway cars	Electric motors	Computers
Buses	Measuring instruments	Auto fuel pumps
Motorcycles	Textiles	Televisions
Wool textiles	Shoes	Cassette recorders
Paper products	Fish products	Turbines
Biotech products	Skis	Chemicals
Synthetic fibers	Furniture	Furniture
Fertilizer	Veneers	Fish products
Radio sets	Cellulose paper	
Washing machines		
Dairy products		
Fish products		
Canned goods		

SOURCE: U.S. Foreign Commercial Service, Central and Eastern European Trade and Technical Assistance Center, International Division, U.S. Chamber of Commerce.

Russia. Lithuania has taken the lead in ratifying foreign investment legislation and privatization laws; but even here, it is uncertain whether former party senior officials will put the laws into action or just pay them lip service. Latvia has announced that it will soon pass new laws on private property, foreign investment, banking, and currency conversion. Estonia lags behind the other Baltic States in ratifying new laws, but the Estonians are further ahead in achieving a Western business mindset, perhaps because of their close linguistic ties to Finland and cultural link to Scandinavia. Despite jamming, Estonians have been exposed to Finnish television and radio programming for decades.

Prices have been liberalized in the Baltics, creating price increases between two- and fourfold. In Lithuania, the move has not been smooth, and the government has had to approve wage increases and provide additional social welfare services. The average citizen in Estonia, Latvia, and Lithuania continues to perceive economic reform, especially price liberalization, as serving only to line the pockets of officials and black marketers. Privatization programs have been initiated in Estonia, and foreign investment laws have been ratified in all three Baltic countries. However, Latvia's economy remains in a state of self-described "chaos" because of the devaluating ruble in Russia. Each Baltic State is in the process of issuing its own currency in order to strengthen and reorient its economy toward the West.

The Baltic States depend on imports of raw materials, especially oil and coal from the former Soviet republics. Sixty percent of Baltic GNP comes from trade: Raw materials in exchange for processed goods; oil for agricultural commodities. Barter agreements have been struck between the Baltics and the former Soviet Union. In 1992, the three Baltic States signed a cooperation agreement with the European Free Trade Association (EFTA), whose members include the Scandinavian countries, Austria, and Switzerland. The linking of their economies to the countries of EFTA will enable the Baltic States to reengage with Western capitalist economies. Scandinavian-Baltic commercial synergy should not be underestimated; of 250 Estonian joint ventures, 120 are with Finnish companies.

The Former Transcaucasian Republics

Of the three Transcaucasian republics—including Armenia, Azerbaijan, and Georgia—Georgia warrants a close look by investors and marketers.

Georgia. Georgia's 5.5 million population consists of 69 percent Georgians, 9 percent Armenians, 7.4 percent Russians, and 5.1 percent Azerbaijanis. Most people worship in the Christian Orthodox Church. After the ousting of President Zviad Gamsakhurdia in late 1991, by meance of a coup d'état, Georgians exhibited a collective will to pursue democratic reform and to put the country on a path toward a market economy, not just in word but in deed. The former Soviet foreign minister and Georgia native Eduard Shevardnadze was elected president in October 1992. Although most of the country has not been affected, separatist rebels began an offensive in Abkhazia, in the north, and in South Ossetia, in the east-central part of Georgia, in late 1991. This fighting and the imposition of martial law continued to the time of this writing.

The republic has a strong agricultural and industrial base that can be modernized and expanded. The republic's wineries, breweries, tea farms, and canneries can produce at close to world-competitive levels. The Georgians exploit their natural resources—coal, nonferrous metals, gold, and barite. As of 1988, Georgia produced over 6,000 tons of wool a year, accounting for 1.3 percent of the total output of the former Soviet Union. Tourism can be expected to grow since the republic borders the Black Sea and has many spas.

The Central Asian Former Republics

The five Central Asian nations of the Commonwealth of Independent States include Kazakhstan, Uzbekistan, Kyrgyzstan, Turkmenistan, and Tajikistan. The following table gives an overview of four of the Central

Asian republics. We will concentrate our attention on Kazakhstan, the most promising in terms of attracting foreign investment.

Four Central Asian Nations at a Glance

Uzbekistan

Population: 20.5 million

Area: 173,000 square miles

Main resources: Lead, zinc, copper, molybdenum, natural gas

Main commodities: Cotton, vegetable oil, fruits, vegetables

Manufactured goods: Cotton-farming machinery, chemical equipment, chemicals, excavators

- Uzbekistan has the largest population of all five Central Asian nations
- The former republic is one of the most economically backward former republics

Kyrgyzstan

Population: 4.3 million

Area: 79,000 square miles

Main resources: Antimony, mercury, coal, gold, marble, petroleum, natural gas

Main commodities: Cotton, wool, fruits, grains, tobacco, silk

Manufactured goods: Clothing, carpet, electronics

- The former republic possesses a productive agricultural sector, but is weak industrially
- Kyrgyzstan's Russian population (22% of total) is leaving the republic en masse

Turkmenistan

Population: 3.75 million

Area: 188,416 square miles

Main resources: Natural gas, oil, sulfur, sodium sulphate, iodine, bromine

Main commodities: Cotton, lamb pelts, wool

Manufactured goods: Refined oil, chemicals, textiles

A privatization program is well under way in the former republic

- The republic's cotton crop represents 18 percent of total cotton production in the former Soviet Union

- The former republic produces more natural gas than any former republic except West Siberia

Tajikistan

Population: 5.1 million

Area: 55,212 square miles

Main resources: Copper, zinc, lead

Main commodities: Cotton, fruits, vegetable oil

Manufactured goods: Hydroelectricity, electrolytic metal refining, aluminum reduction, electrochemical machine tools, refrigerators

Eastern European Investment Monthly calls this republic "perhaps the most economically crippled former republic"

- Tajikistan produced only 0.4 percent of Soviet industrial output and 1 percent of agricultural output

- The republic, however, produced 11 percent of the total cotton output of the former U.S.S.R.

Kazakhstan.   The former republic of Kazakhstan is the second-largest republic in the C.I.S. Although it occupies 12 percent of the total area of the former Soviet Union, it contains 20 percent of its arable land. Kazakhstan's population of 17 million is only 36 percent Kazakhs and nearly 50 percent Russians; however, where religion is concerned, most of the republic's citizens are Muslim. Kazakh is the official internal language, and Russian is the official international language in Kazakhstan. So far, ethnic strife has been subdued. The republic's reform-minded and politically deft president, Nursultan Nazarbayev, has implemented a privatization program that has already moved 40 percent of housing in the capital city of Alma-Ata into private hands. Primary industrial sectors include iron, steel, non-ferrous metallurgy, and a chemical industry. The Kazakhstanis need consumer goods, manufacturing capabilities, and food processing technology. Kazakhstan possesses oil, natural gas, metal ores, gold, and coal, which awaits extraction and more efficient exploitation. Kazakhstan also exports electricity to other former Soviet republics.

Kazakhstan produces a huge grain crop and 106,000 tons of wool per year, accounting for 23.4 percent of the total wool production in the former Soviet Union. It produces 18.7 percent of the coal and 13 percent of the grain. As of 1987, Kazahkstan produced 24.5 million tons of petroleum per day. Kazakhstan produces more meat than the other Asian republics and more than one fifth of the wool produced in the former Soviet Union. Loaded with natural resources, Kazakhstan holds about half of the zinc reserves in the former Soviet Union, and also has coal, petroleum, natural gas, iron ore, nickel, chromium, vanadium, titanium, molybdenum, thallium, bismuth, copper, lead, gold, silver, coal, bauxite, phosphorus, asbestos, and rare earth mineral deposits. Experts estimate that oil reserves lying beneath Kazakhstan equal those of Kuwait, about 97 billion barrels. The newly independent state has leased its Tengiz oil field to the Chevron Corporation, a megadeal that could become a hard-currency cash cow for the former republic for years to come. The French oil giant Elf Aquitaine lost only two days of negotiations during the August coup in pursuing an exploration deal in the republic worth $600 to $800 million.

Russia's Far East   The eastern coastline of Siberia in Russia—the Soviet Far East—commands growing attention because of its involvement in Pacific Rim trade. With unlimited resources, low-cost labor, port facilities in Vladivostok and Nakhodka, and emergent markets, the so-called Japan Sea Basin is a trade hub in the making, a potential vortex of economic dynamism where China, Korea, Japan, and Russia converge on the booming Pacific Rim. The Soviet Far East exports fish, minerals, coal, natural gas, and forest products. Japan's *keiretsu* (vast, interlocking corporate conglomerates), perhaps having the most to gain in this cold, bleak region, contemplate the use of Siberian resources as a cheap and politically correct alternative to exploiting natural resources in Southeast Asia. But there's a hitch. Japan will undertake massive investment in the region if, and only if, Russia returns to Japan the southern Kuril Islands occupied by the Soviet Red Army at the close of World War II. The standoff has been dubbed "the Northern Territories problem." Meanwhile, small, independent Japanese companies—literally, "briefcase companies"—venture into the Soviet Far East, where they rub shoulders with similarly underfinanced companies from the United States. Global independents are scrambling to nail down the best joint-venture partners in the region before the big boys of corporate Japan plow into the region if, and when, the Japanese government waves the checkered flag. Following their *nordpolitik* strategy, South Korea is also fostering ties with Moscow (behind North Korea's back), building up trade and investment relations in the Russian Far East.

4

Successful Selling

Researching the Market, Distributing a Product

Selling to Eastern Europe was once so easy. To sell to the region, you would travel to a capital city and talk to an industry-specific ministry. Each ministry was, in turn, linked to a foreign-trade organization, or FTO, where you would make your sales pitch. Once you penetrated the bureaucracy and inked a contract, you were an insider, and multiple deals could ensue for your firm over the years. It might have been a tedious process compared with cold-calling end-users in the West, but once you had signed a contract with the FTO, you could sleep at night knowing that you'd get paid. Foreign-trade organizations were accountable. "Once you were in, you were in," says David Kern Peteler, an attorney with Peat, Marwick in Los Angeles, whose clients do business in the former Soviet Union. "You knew you were going to get paid."

Now, when the Western marketer crosses the Danube or the Elbe, he or she confronts a business environment fraught with danger. No longer can you simply sell a product to a state-owned FTO under the auspices of a central ministry. Now you have to address the needs of end-users directly, while still maneuvering amid leftover state-controlled trading organizations. Now there's the fundamental problem of knowing who to sell to, of navigating broken bureaucracies and fledgling private sectors singlehandedly. And exporters have had to face not knowing whether they will be paid for their goods.

The Meaning of "Marketing" in Eastern Europe

The Eastern European marketing maven, setting out to research the potential of his or her product or service in the region, will discover a palpable dearth of available market information. Little real market research has been conducted in Eastern Europe and the former Soviet Union as of yet, and what has been done is rudimentary, often based on too few interviews in the field. Indeed, the "field" is changing rapidly; trends in consumer tastes and preference haven't yet settled down to a point at which a market snapshot can be taken. Most marketing in Eastern Europe, therefore, runs on the assumption that Eastern Europeans want what Western Europeans have. Certainly, this assumption contains a kernal of truth, but Eastern Europe is a new market, where having the essentials for mere *survival* often takes priority over obtaining luxury goods. A few Eastern Europeans have purchased stereos, compact disk (CD) players, and automobiles since the Wall came down, but for the great majority, needs are more dire, like the need for food and simple clothing. This is no reason, however, for Western marketers to ignore the Eastern European consumer market until incomes rise there, which could take years. Now is the time to serve *real* needs and to introduce product lines and brand names in hope of generating future sales.

Getting in Touch with Real Needs

Ruth Langhorst grew up in Germany, where she started a career in foreign trade working for the director of the foreign trade department of the Deutsche Bank. Later, she worked for a number of American manufacturers and eventually established her own export management company in La Jolla, California. There, I asked her what aspiring marketers can sell in Eastern Europe. She responded with a story. "After World War Two, we would get a care package from an uncle of mine in New York." Ruth's family had reached the point of starvation in war-ravaged occupied Germany. "He had a daughter my age, who would send me evening gowns. We didn't have anything to eat! We could have used some noodles, or a blouse, but not *evening gowns*."

She compared those evening gowns with what many American would-be exporters want to send to Eastern Europeans. "They don't understand Eastern European needs yet," she said. "You have to ask yourself: What would you send to a friend who has just lost everything in a flood?"

"In Eastern Europe, more than any place else, you need to know what these people *need*," Ruth continued. "I went to a conference at the University of Southern California recently, and I was sitting next to two very nice ladies. One of them thought she should export inexpensive jewelry to Eastern Europeans. The other wanted to buy Turkish sweaters and sell them to Eastern Europe." First of all, Ruth told me, the Eastern Europeans don't need *you* if they want a sweater from Turkey. And the idea of selling inexpensive jewelry to folks who are having trouble putting meat on the table is absurd. The same thing happened in the Soviet Union. In his book *Bear Hunting with the Politburo*, A. Craig Copetas chronicled the attempts by Americans to sell products to the Soviets during the first blush of glasnost. "There were New York entrepreneurs hustling collegiate football games, Georgia entrepreneurs trying to sell cosmetics and hair pomades manufactured for black people, even though there are no blacks in the Soviet Union, Virginia entrepreneurs vending lawn furniture (there are no lawns), and Arizona entrepreneurs flogging imitation hawk-feather dusters."

Two Marketing Successes in the East

Albert Jacmin has been selling the Romanians the right thing since the revolution. Albert met a Romanian fellow in Brussels, and they became friends. The Romanian told Albert that a lot of business could be done in Romania, selling goods in short supply. So Albert started a venture selling food and other basic items to Romanians. It worked like a charm. Here's how it operates.

First, he buys an old car, or an old truck, in Brussels. Then he fills it up with Western goods—basic necessities like baby food, meat, and cigarettes. He drives the car or truck to Hungary, where he loads up on other inexpensive goods like shoes and shirts. Then he drives on to Turkey, where he picks up more inexpensive items. With his truck full, he crosses the Romanian border. It takes three hours to get across the border, waiting for papers and goods to be checked. There are no duties or taxes on any of the essential goods needed for the people's survival. On cigarettes, perfume, and semiluxury goods there is a duty—upward of 40 percent, for example, on cigarettes. Once he crosses the border, he calls ahead to his partner in Bucharest, who starts setting up buyers of the goods. He parks the truck in the middle of the city, opens up the back, and starts selling the goods to Romanian consumers. Albert and his partner sell a truckload of goods in *one day.*

Albert then takes his "few thousand dollars in profit," which is in the currency of lei, to refill the truck with Romanian-produced goods, like T-shirts, sweatshirts, and shoes. He then drives the truck back to Brussels and sells those goods in Brussels. By this time he has made a significant profit, since he has spent lei buying Romanian goods produced by workers who earn only $30 to $40 a month. Also, his profit will be in foreign exchange. Who says there's no consumer market in Eastern Europe!

"What consumer goods will sell in Romania?" I asked Albert.

"Just about anything will sell in Romania," he snapped. He even sells French perfume there! It takes a few more days to sell, but it *does* sell. I couldn't understand how Romanians, who earn an average wage of $60 a month, could afford to buy goods out of the back of Albert's truck so voraciously. Albert enlightened me. "The rich class are the buyers," he said. For the most part, his customers are from the monied minority, who possess much disposable income in lei. (Romanians divide into a small upper crust, a small middle class, and a large lower class.)

Albert sells his wares in Bucharest and Constanta, Romania's port city on the Black Sea. He expanded quickly by buying a large retail shop in Bucharest, which he now supplies (through the system already described) with goods originating in Hungary, Turkey, and other inexpensive production areas. With his distribution network expanding rapidly, the sky seems the limit for this bold and enterprising entrepreneur. "Could an American sell to Romanians in the same way?" I asked naively. Albert told me, If you bring in a container load of essential goods in, you can sell the whole container in days—*if you have a sales network set up.* We'll get back to how Albert expanded his sales network in the next chapter.

Amway Corporation is an American marketing success story in the New East that is well known for its unique overseas sales network. Amway has cracked the Hungarian consumer market and plans to set up in Poland next. Selling mainly detergents and bathroom products, the company struck pay dirt with products of high quality, sold by individual sales representatives. Even with a huge rate of unemployment, thousands of Hungarians signed up to sell Amway products literally overnight. Hungarians possess little disposable income, but as consumers, they cannot do without detergent and shampoo. Amway's products easily outmatched the limited selection of products on supermarket shelves in Hungary. Pat Austin, a corporate interpreter and translator who has worked in Hungary for four years, first told me about the overwhelming presence of Amway products in Hungary. Pat and I tried to think of somebody we knew in the United States who used Amway products. Neither of us could think of anybody. "In Hungary," Pat said, "*everybody* had tried them." And many Hungarians use Amway products regularly. Amway responded to *real* needs with quality, selection, and an innovative marketing strategy. (The successful activities of Amway are covered in detail in Chapter 13.)

The Eastern European Consumer

Though the available marketing data remain weak and incomplete, we do know a few things about Eastern European consumers. Although they qualify as cash-poor, they *are* well exposed to Western consumer products. As an international marketer, you're not dealing with isolated countries on the order of Namibia, Laos, or Paraguay. There is tremendous unrealized demand among Eastern European countries for Western goods, which creates ample opportunity for large-scale exports as well as for sales by medium and small American producers. Kmart, America's second-largest retailer, was the first discount chain from the United States to set up in Eastern Europe. (It is rumored that Price Club is researching the market with the intention to enter soon.) Kmart bought up 13 of the best stores in a chain of state-owned stores in Czechoslovakia, before the country divided, investing $120 million in the purchase and renovaition of drab buildings. Guess what? The new Kmart store in Bratislava, the capital of Slovakia, outperformed all 2,400 Kmart stores in the United States in 1992, in terms of sales. Because of inefficiencies and costs, the store did not show a profit, but it is expected to do so within a couple of years.

Lack of cash and financing remains a major limiting factor, but there have already been surprising successes for U.S. exporters of big-ticket industrial items in the aircraft, medical equipment, food processing, telecommunications, and computer industries, among others. United States government-funded market reports cover opportunities for selling capital goods, but selling to Eastern European consumers entails hands-on research by the foreign supplier "in the trenches." Let's compare Eastern European consumers by starting with the basics.

The Size of the Markets

To put the size of the Eastern European market into perspective, one should realize that total U.S. exports to Eastern European countries in 1991, not including the C.I.S., came to less than the value of the amount that U.S. exports to France *increased* in that year (about $1.7 billion and $2.6 billion, respectively). United States trade with the former Soviet Union accounted for only 1 percent of total U.S. trade, less than the U.S. trade conducted with Indonesia or Colombia. Don't let these figures deceive you, however. With the region's total population of 400 million, many now-convertible currencies, and rising incomes, the market cannot be ignored now that it is open to Western suppliers.

Central Europe's largest population (in Poland) did not traditionally buy the largest amount of imports in dollar terms. In fact, Yugoslavia, before its dissolution in 1990, led the region in foreign purchases. Bulgaria entered first position after war broke out in Yugoslavia. Poland then ranked second (Fig. 4-1). Romania is virtually as big an importer of foreign goods as Hungary. I would venture to say that Romania, with its population of 23 million, qualifies as the most under-rated market in Eastern Europe. Romania's hard-currency exports plunged by 55 percent in the first eight months of 1990 compared to the same period in 1989, but total hard-currency *imports* were up over 150 percent, to $3.3 billion. The consumer-goods import sector was suddenly booming, as shortages of goods produced in Romania occurred.

Looking at the trade shares of the former Soviet republics, excluding Russia, one can easily pick out potential hotspots for exports (Fig. 4-2). Ukraine dominates by a wide margin over runners-up Belarus and Kazakhstan. Whether you're in search of barterable goods or markets, these Newly Independent States should be your first stops. Georgia ranks back in the pack, even though Georgians enjoy a higher standard of living than most former Soviets and the region borders the markets of Europe. Kazakhstan continues to import more goods than it exports, but this should change as oil extraction deals come on line. Ukraine has run similar deficits in the past.

Consumer Buying Power

Some of the positive predictions that I have made about Eastern Europe's markets may seem absurd when you look at the low level of wages most Eastern Europeans are paid (Fig. 4-3). While eastern Germans earn roughly 40 percent of what west Germans are paid, Bulgarians, former Soviets, and Romanians earn less per month than either Indonesians or the mainland Chinese, the two lowest-paid groups in all of the Asia-Pacific. Yugoslavians had been the second-highest wage earners in the region; now many workers there are being paid in IOUs because of the disruption of economies there.

Though consumer buying power will remain low as long as wages do, wages in Eastern Europe have climbed rapidly as workers begin to demand wages closer in line with those paid to workers in Western Europe doing similar work. For example, wages in Romania rose over

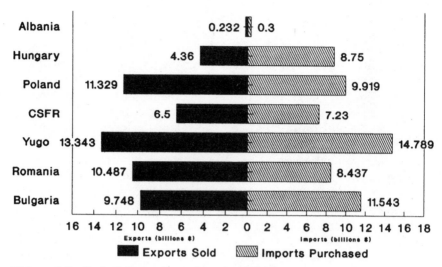

Figure 4-1. Central Europe's total trade (excluding Germany and the former U.S.S.R.); all figures 1991; hard-currency trade only. (*Department of Commerce.*)

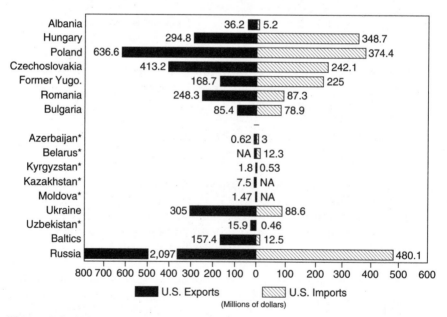

Figure 4-2. U.S. trade with Eastern Europe (including the former Soviet Union). All figures for 1992; for countries marked with asterisk (*) figures are for January to September 1992. (*U.S. Department of Commerce.*)

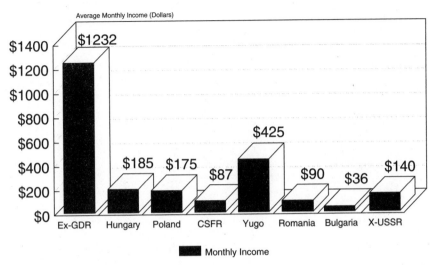

Average Monthly Income (Dollars)

Figure 4-3. Monthly wages across Eastern Europe.

300 percent between October 1990 and December 1991. One should also factor into any assessment of buying power the fact that "official wages" do not reflect the earnings of thousands of new private entrepreneurs in these countries. Albert Jacmin found a ready market in Romania selling to a growing population of new "privates" and made a killing. With higher numbers of workers being hired on to work in private sectors in these countries, buying power has grown but has not yet been statistically quantified. In 1991 one half of Poland's imports of $15.5 billion were purchased by private enterprises; private companies were responsible for 22 percent of the $14.6 billion in exports. Germany sold two thirds of these imports to Poland's private sector and 50 percent of the total imports. The trick for marketers in the United States is to target this growing segment of the population.

What Eastern Europeans Own. How "sophisticated" are Eastern European consumers? How like Western European consumers are they? To find out, let's look at what they owned when Western marketers streamed over the Wall (Fig. 4-4). Overall, the level of ownership of basic consumer appliances, automobiles, and electronic goods may surpass your expectations if you've been reading press reports about "economically devastated" Eastern Europe. Occupying the highest rung of consumer-goods ownership in the region, former East Germans owned 476 televisions, 409 washing machines, and 595 refrigerations per 1,000 people. They also owned more automobiles per capita than any other

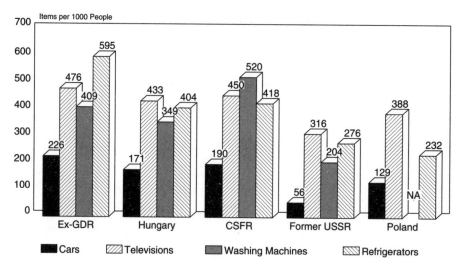

Figure 4-4. Consumer profiles for four Eastern European countries and the former Soviet Union. (*UN Statistical Yearbook, 1988; UN Human Developtment Report, 1991; Business International Ltd., October 1991.*)

Eastern European population. The consumer market in the Commonwealth of Independent States was surprisingly well endowed, with 304 televisions, 205 washing machines, and 276 refrigerators per 1,000 people. "Quality of life indicators" for Bulgaria, as measured by the U.S. Department of Commerce in 1987, were equally surprising; I will give them to you with the caveat that many U.S. government reports on Eastern bloc economic prowess were exaggerated in the past. The figures for Bulgaria: 94 percent of households had a refrigerator, 97 percent owned a television, and 39 percent of households owned an automobile.

Though figures on ownership patterns for other products are only now being collected, one can conclude from these figures that tastes and preferences for consumer goods in the East generally match those of the West in terms of desired goods and appetite for new and improved goods.

The Size of Consumer Markets. While Poland imports less than some of the other Eastern European countries in dollar terms, the country's 40 million citizens currently buy more *total* consumer goods than any other country in the region. When the Berlin Wall fell and barriers came down, foreign exchange purchases skyrocketed; now, with the money spent, imports have declined. Figure 4-5 indicates the share of retail sales of an assortment of consumer goods throughout the region in 1988–1989. The Czech showing is notable when one considers its small population, and so is Romania's purchases of footwear and watches.

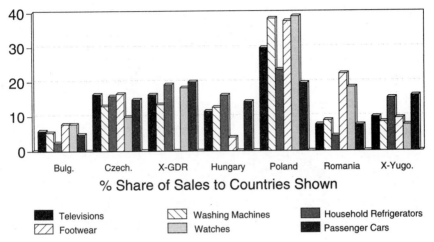

Figure 4-5. Comparing the size of the markets. (PlanEcon.)

Measuring Consumer Demand

We now understand something about the size of Eastern European markets, what consumer products Eastern Europeans own, and which countries buy the most consumer goods. But we haven't yet located where *demand* for imported products may be more intense than somewhere else. One way to measure import demand is to compare "retail sales" of a product with the amount of the product that the buying country produces domestically. If, for example, a country purchases 1 million shoes but produces only 500,000, the country has to be importing the difference. When retail sales of a commodity consistently outmatch production, shortages of needed goods will have to be imported. When one looks at retail sales versus production in Romania, one finds that Romania traditionally purchases about one half of all cotton and cotton fiber that sells in Eastern Europe every year, but it *produces* only 21 percent of that produced in the region each year. No wonder Albert Jacmin found a need for cotton apparel goods in Romania.

Now look at the relationship between retail sales and production in each country in Figs. 4-6 through 4-10. This will give us an indication of what the import needs are for a variety of consumer products (as well as an idea of goods that will be prime targets for import-substituting manufacturing projects). Notice that Poland buys 37.8 percent of the shoes that Eastern Europe buys yet produces only 24 percent of the shoes that Eastern Europe produces. Imports fill the gap, many of which come from Italy. Figure 4-7 shows that sales of televisions outmeasure production in Bulgaria, Czechoslovakia, and Poland. In Fig. 4-8, the purchase of refrigerators is shown to outmatch production in Bulgaria,

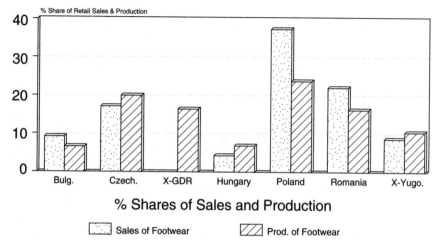

Figure 4-6. The demand for footwear: Comparing sales versus production. (*PlanEcon.*)

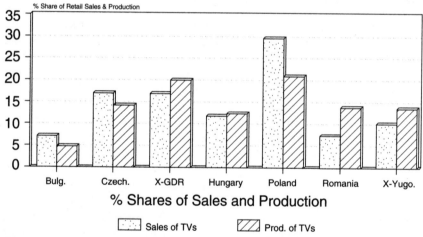

Figure 4-7. The demand for televisions: Comparing sales versus production. (*PlanEcon.*)

Czechoslovakia, Hungary, and especially Poland. A shortage of washing machines appears acute (Fig. 4-9) in Hungary and Poland, and shortages of domestically produced passenger cars appear significant in Bulgaria and Hungary (Fig. 4-10).

In Fig. 4-11, the huge share of retail sales and production held by the former Soviet Union relative to Central European countries is clear. The former Soviet Union *appears* remarkably self-sufficient in supplying its population with domestically produced consumer items. In

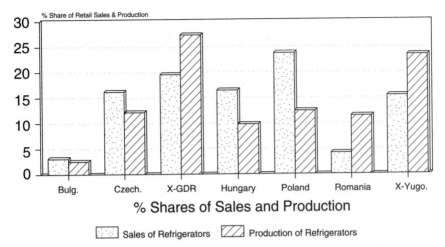

Figure 4-8. The demand for household refrigerators: Comparing sales versus production. (*PlanEcon.*)

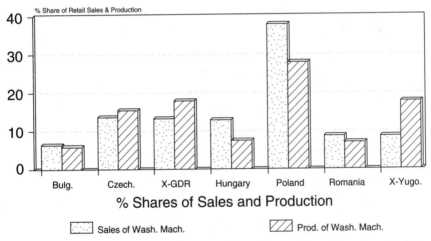

Figure 4-9. The demand for washing machines: Comparing sales versus production. (*PlanEcon.*)

reality, consumer goods were traditionally hard to find except on the black market, and imports of goods in short supply were tightly regulated. The black market in imported goods filled many gaps, but the size of this market will never be accurately known.

For the past 40 years, the majority of these consumer goods were produced domestically in these countries rather than imported. Now, however, the appetite for Western products of higher quality

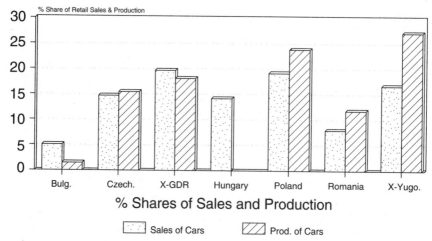

Figure 4-10. The demand for passenger cars: Comparing sales versus production. (*PlanEcon.*)

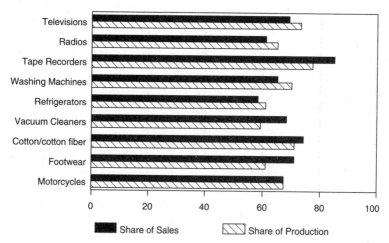

Figure 4-11. Consumer demand in the former U.S.S.R.: Share of retail sales versus production (percent shares of entire Eastern European region). (*PlanEcon.*)

and wider function has taken hold. Imports of consumer goods to replace domestic models are climbing, and so are manufacturing deals that substitute these imports. Either way, the trend bodes well for foreign suppliers of (1) finished goods, (2) the raw materials to make them, and (3) the licenses to manufacture them. Any of these three modes can be an entry pass into the market. Initially consumer-goods sales will be sluggish, but they will improve after infrastructure investments are made and the unemployment rate drops. In the beginning, niche products will have the greatest success in all sectors, and low-priced products will provide the best opportunities.

Here are some examples of initial marketing questions that you can ask to help gauge the situation.

Is There a Need for Your Product or Service? We've discussed *real* needs already. By utilizing the Department of Commerce and the mail, you can gauge the appropriateness of your product and service without spending more than the cost of stamps. Attending a trade show in Eastern Europe can confirm or refute your hopes in the most cost-effective way.

How Does Your Product Compare to the Competition? If German companies offer competitive products in the market already, you'll be hard pressed to outmatch their sales efforts and ability to get close to potential customers in Eastern Europe, especially the former G.D.R. and Poland, merely because of their close proximity.

Will You Have to Adapt Your Product? Most marketers move products into the East from Western Europe and keep adaptation for the East to a minimum. The small scale of the market doesn't warrant the expense of researching necessary adaptations. However, if you're moving a product from the United States into the East directly, adaptation of your product may be required. Can your company afford changes, and are its top decision makers going to be willing to deal with requests for customization?

What Type of Payment Will You Require? Will you be open either to helping the Eastern European buyer raise funds to purchase your product or to barter and countertrade arrangements, including straight barter, counterpurchase, offset, and buyback?

Does Your Product Meet Standards of Safety? Make it perfectly clear to the buyer or potential agent and/or distributor whether arrangements have or have not already been made for this testing. If European safety clearances are already in hand, demonstrate this without fail to potential buyers, agents, and distributors. If such testing has not been obtained, the expenses and risks involved will be items for negotiation with respect to an agency and/or distributor agreement or a potential sale. Your East European distributor will expect you to be willing to substantially share, if not shoulder, the costs of such testing, and perhaps also the cost of market testing and advertising.

Will You Be Offering After-Sales Service?   One-time sales of complex industrial equipment may result in disaster if your company is unwilling to service the machinery or to put a distributor in place who can. Creating a mess because you want to win a "quick-kill" deal hurts the reputation of all American suppliers trying to sell in the region.

Getting a Product Distributed

An enormous problem facing American firms trying to penetrate new markets in Eastern Europe is finding reputable and reliable agents and distributors of their goods, since the experienced dealers were snapped up in 1989 and 1990 by early comers. Commission rates have soared as well. A foreign firm now has to consider the reality of setting up an independent network of distributors in each country. A Western company typically sets up a network like this: First, a representative of the firm travels to an Eastern European country and advertises for sales reps; 10 to 20 competent salespeople are hired. Next, the firm rents a warehouse and hires the necessary transportation service to move products from their point of entry to the warehouse and then out to customers. Next, the firm brings in a local manager as a 20 to 40 percent partner who takes over the marketing operation; all the Western firm's expatriots are eventually brought home, leaving the show to the locals. That's it, in a nutshell. Following this strategy of setting up independent distribution networks, Woolworth has opened a 650-square-meter department store in Halle, in eastern Germany, the first of 10 that the company plans to open. Chrysler plans to establish a sales network in the former Soviet Union to sell its passenger cars, and Lotus has set up dealerships in 31 commonwealth cities. Sounds easy, but it takes a tremendous amount of time on the ground to round up the reps, find the right eventual manager-partner, obtain warehouse space, set up communications, and make the proper banking and legal arrangements along the way. What if you can't afford this level of commitment? A sound strategy might be to hire a distributor that has a selling network already set up in Eastern Europe. But how do you find or qualify one?

Finding an Agent or Distributor in Eastern Europe

Eastern European governments are eager to attract capital to rebuild and upgrade their production facilities rather than to just increase imports of foreign products. Importing of products will remain a necessity, but companies that concentrate on imports receive little assistance or support. Marketing, as a capital-creating service, is still not well understood. Thus, while new trading companies are springing up everywhere in Eastern Europe, they are often undercapitalized and short on experience. Good companies, however, can be found. Maxtor recently appointed an agent to market its computers and disks in Czechoslovakia. In Bulgaria, Motorola has appointed Systematix to distribute its computer systems.

Many startup companies prove to be excellent marketers, but most require strong financial assistance, extensive training, and a heap of patience. Don't expect to sign on an agent who will generate immediate large sales. Aggressive agents should be able to sell to the entire Eastern European market, so you should not limit the territory of an agent too severely. Few American companies will find that one market of Eastern Europe is large and profitable enough to justify sales efforts only in this area. The entire Eastern European market is a more profitable target, with the partner serving as the window. Plan on two to three years for market development before a break-even point is reached. Because of this situation, many American companies may choose to wait for conditions to become normal prior to attempting to enter the market. This strategy carries lower financial risk than immediate entry but may result in your company being blocked from the market by competitors who have taken the few qualified agents.

Because the agent and distributor network is underdeveloped, locating and qualifying a potential agent or distributor may require an extensive search. The Department of Commerce's Agent/Distributor Service (ADS) can help your firm locate and screen distributors and representatives. The ADS program can also help you prepare literature and brochures and get your product information reviewed by embassy employees in the country you have targeted. The ADS information may be ordered through your local U.S. Department of Commerce district office. To obtain the telephone number of your district office, contact the Eastern Europe Business Information Center (EEBIC). You can, and should, have background checks made on potential European agents, distributors, and buyers, either through your bank or an international credit agency or through the World Trader Data Reports (WTDR) available from your nearest district office of the U.S. Department of Commerce.

Attend a Trade Fair.   Exhibiting at a trade fair brings a good American product into contact with large numbers of Eastern European potential sales representatives (not to mention buyers). Trade fairs have traditionally been the primary mode by which Western Europeans have conducted direct sales of products and services, and Eastern Europe has joined the tradition. Czechoslovak importers, in fact, conduct 25 percent of their total trade turnover at trade fairs. The EEBIC offers a publication that highlights the trade fairs held throughout Eastern Europe. The National Technical Information Service (NTIS) makes videotape versions of trade conferences available that contain the names and addresses of participants.

If the above methods do not produce a suitable agent or distributor, consider conducting your own search in Eastern Europe. Signet-Armorlite sold to West Germany and now sells to eastern Germany through a western German distributor. The firm tried to find a local representative through advertisement and trade show exposure but was not able to find one. It finally canvassed *potential customers* and, through a customer, was referred to an individual employed by a marketing company who was the most appropriate person to distribute the product Signet-Armorlite offered. The firm then contacted this person, and the relationship has been very fruitful ever since.

Tracking the Market: Sources of Information

Gathering relevant market data on Eastern European countries is almost always a time-consuming proposition. Most information is not yet readily available, and much simply has not been published in any form. You can begin researching an Eastern European market by requesting marketing information from the following sources.

United States Government Sources

First, request a publication list from the EEBIC, a well-organized and well-staffed organization that can provide information on doing business in all the Central and Eastern European countries (except the former Soviet Union). EEBIC will also send you the informative newsletter *Business East Europe* free of charge. You may want to grab your phone right now and call EEBICFLASH, the organization's innovative recorded-information hotline, by means of which you can order information on markets, financing, and trade fairs. The information will be faxed to you free of charge. The phone number is (202) 482-5745.

Department of Commerce

The DOC has developed comprehensive studies of many sectors of Eastern European industry, which are organized both by country and by

region. *Romanian Bottling & Container Packaging Industry* and
Telecommunications in Poland are two titles.

National Technical Information Service

The NTIS provides access to current public legal texts of commercial
laws from all Central and Eastern European countries in the native
language or English. Prices for publications range from a few dollars to
over $100. If a large state library is nearby, you can save money by
copying needed publications from microfiche.

United States and Foreign Commercial Service

The U.S. and Foreign Commercial Service (US&FCS), represented by
commercial attachés stationed in Eastern Europe, offers a wide range of
programs to assist marketers, including Country Marketing Plans, Best
Prospects Lists, and Alert Reports.

National Trade Data Bank

This data bank contains basic export information, industry-country
information, and export and import statistics lists by commodity and
Standard Index of Traded Commodities (SITC) classification, and
includes a Foreign Traders Index. Call the Trade Information Center at
(800) USA-TRADE to find the NTDB location nearest you.

Chambers of Commerce and Business Councils

Your company does not have to become a paying member of the U.S.
Chamber of Commerce or a chapter of one of the numerous chambers to
acquire the marketing information that some of them publish. The U.S.
Chamber of Commerce operates the Central and Eastern European
Trade and Technical Assistance Center in Washington, D.C., which will
send you a publication list upon request. The U.S. Chamber of
Commerce has individual chapters, or councils, for each country of
Eastern Europe.

Eastern European Government Offices and Trade Organizations

Increasingly, the U.S. offices of Eastern European trade agencies and
commercial sections of their embassies supply top-grade market
information, often free of charge. I suggest visiting all relevant offices
and organizations that you can while in Eastern Europe. Other in-
country sources for marketers doing on-site research might include
customers, distributors, suppliers, manufacturers' associations, ad
agencies, and managers. "Local management is the only good source,"
writes Bill Liddell, managing consultant for Ernst & Young, in *World
Link.* Throughout Eastern Europe, Western-style managers have
grown in number, and many now operate in the private sector where

foreigners can easily solicit their assistance in formulating marketing strategies.

Newsletters

A veritable tide of business newsletters has washed up on my desk since I became involved with the Eastern Europe market. Many of these publications are useful, all are pricey, and some are of no use whatsoever. Newsletters may be country-specific or cover an entire region. Few, however, are industry-specific for the region, containing, for instance, detailed information on import composition, customer tastes and preferences, or recent purchases of capital goods. However, for general business climate information and updates, newsletters do prove useful, and some warrant their high cost. One suggestion: Call all the newsletter publishers listed in the appendix and request recent sample copies to make sure that your money will be well spent. (See Sources of Information for Marketers in the appendix for addresses and phone numbers.)

Secrets of Selling to Eastern Europe? There *Are* No Secrets

Successful selling to Eastern Europe can be boiled down to one Golden Rule: If you can sell to *Germany*, you'll be able to sell anywhere in Eastern Europe. Hence, we should seek comparative advantage in selling to Eastern Europeans by meeting the criteria necessery to sell successfully to Germany.

Forge Personal Contacts and Relationships.   The personal relationship drives the business relationship, assuming that quality, after-sales service, and long-term commitment exist. That is, if there are three or four competitors who all offer similar price, similar quality, similar after-sales service and similar commitment, the relationship that exists between the German buyer and the Western seller can tip the balance to produce a sale. The question is whether loyalty in a relationship will remain and keep business alive if price rises relative to that of one's competitors.

Eastern European firms, having once found a reliable business partner, *are* loath to break off the relationship (perhaps because they spend so much time and money choosing a partner). An American should not, therefore, enter lightly into either a supply contract or a principal and/or agent relationship with a firm. A carefully negotiated relationship can be a highly profitable, long-term arrangement.

Mind Your Company's Reputation.   Among Eastern Europeans there exist great respect and admiration for large American corporations like 3M, IBM, GM, and Ford—respect for their products, respect for the quality of their products, and respect for the way they treat their employees. The sometimes-unearned good reputation of an American company, just because it *is* American, is a clear advantage for you as a marketer. If your company is an unknown, you will meet with a bit more resistance than the well-known U.S. firm when attempting to crack the market, especially if you "make a lot of noise" in doing so. That is, if your firm enters the market with a lot of hoopla and cymbal-crashing, it will generate suspicion and possibly resentment. The Germans, for instance, remember well a smooth-talking American entrepreneur who arrived in Germany in the 1960s and set up a securities scheme that bilked German investors out of billions of marks.

Offer Low Price and Discounts.   Any marketer knows that certain industries are more price-sensitive than others. For example, lower-end consumer goods and foods that sell at high volume and lower price will be more price-sensitive rather than quality-sensitive or relationship-sensitive. But the countries of Eastern Europe vary in how they rank low price relative to, say, after-sales service and state-of-the-art technology. Cash-poor countries respond to low price more than promises of service or even top-notch quality. For example, in the former Soviet Union, quality takes a back seat to availability because of a long history of persistent shortages of virtually all essential consumer goods. However, you must...

Focus on Reliability and Specifications.   Often the buyer decision will boil down to a choice for top quality. Especially in Germany, an affluent society that wants the best, there is simply no room for cheap products. This tends to be true for most of Western Europe as well, and it is more and more the case in the East. When industrial goods are sold, it's important *not* to depend on Madison Avenue-style advertising, hype, or sizzle. Rather, it is vital to stress the mechanical and technical specifications of a product, instead of its associated image or emotional appeal. "Lifestyle" oriented consumer goods, of course, may be an exception.

In Germany most buying decisions are based on institutional surveys that scientifically compare products. The same style of buying decision marks the East, partly because of the heavy emphasis on academia and also because of the current strong influence of German business people and Germanic business style in the region. You're dealing with a *Consumer Reports* mentality—if it's the best, it's the best because it measures up in every tested category that can be verified. While marketers in the product-saturated West look not only to serve existing markets but also to *create* markets for new products, Eastern Europe is a region where needs are obvious and companies that can best serve them win contracts. "I don't think that you can *create* a market in Eastern Europe," echoes Ruth Langhorst. "If something similar to your product is on the market, and you have a better mousetrap, that's what does it." In short, look for underserved needs rather than addressing apparent needs with novelties.

Remember that German buyers (and, increasingly, Eastern European buyers) demand and expect *total reliability* from suppliers, American or otherwise. I cannot overemphasize this point. Promised delivery dates must be kept. If you are selling to a buyer for others, he or she will apply the same standards when quoting customers a delivery date. Many German firms would rather pay more for a product knowing that it will arrive when promised than pay less and gamble on delayed delivery time. As suppliers, Germans have a well-earned worldwide reputation for reliability and a willingness to install and service products which they manufacture and export, and as buyers, they expect as much of American manufacturers. Because Eastern Europians have been supplied by West German firms for decades, American companies are expected to meet the standards of reliability, support, and accountability set by the Germans.

Are American Firms Meeting the Challange?

I recently met Piotr Puchala, president of M.P.P. World Trade Company, at a reception given by a San Diego law firm. Piotr is a world trader who arrived in the United States three years ago to help set up an American subsidiary of his Polish company. His experience in trying to sell capital goods made in America reveals some of the generic weaknesses of U.S. firms trying to sell in Eastern Europe. To his chagrin, Piotr discovered that it was hard to convince Americans that the market in Poland holds promise, that it even *exists,* and that it will pay off. To Piotr, Americans seemed completely unwilling to back up their sales to the region with after-sales customer services, which is de rigueur in selling complex industrial production systems. "American companies do not want to go and set up two or three representative offices in Poland. They don't want to set up a service company in Poland to offer after-sales service to capital goods that they sell."

"The situation right now in Poland," says Piotr, "is that private companies are springing up either as green-field operations or as parts of state conglomerates that have been privatized. They have money to spend and the currency is convertible, and they want to buy machinery and they are willing to pay top dollar for it *if the after-sales service capability is included in the price.*" But he has found American suppliers generally unwilling to make this commitment to the market. Thus, Polish concerns opt to buy from the Germans and other European manufacturers. American firms remain unwilling to put the time, effort, and resources into capturing the Polish market. In fact, Americans *could* capture the market and make profits in Poland if they were willing to set up offices there and offer the services European suppliers can offer. He misjudged Americans in thinking that the capital-goods producers would be willing to make the commitment to the market in the short term—they have stayed on the fence.

The same lack of commitment can be said to be occurring throughout the Eastern European market. We need to engage with customers and partners more fully if we are to increase market share relative to the Germans and Japanese.

Committing to the Market: Pursuing the Partnership Principle

I asked Ed Mattix of USWest how the firm leverages to win its multimillion dollar bids in Eastern Europe. Is it price? Quality? After-sales service? Or relationships?

"It's all of that," Ed answered. "I think the key is that you build a strong partnership...it's building a strong partnership."

He elaborated on what partnership meant.

"It's knowing how to operate in that particular country. It's understanding their business and culture, how they do business and what the cultural differences are and how to manage those. It's not a question of outbidding someone. It's an all-around package. That's what [the Eastern Europeans] look for. They look for someone who wants to make a long-term commitment there, who's not there just to take money out in the short term and then disappear, but someone who wants to build a long-term relationship that's beneficial to both the venture and the country."

Werner Korel implements a "partnership principle" with buyers. Returning to his native Austria in 1975, he now directs Dow Corning's Eastern European business. Dow Corning's silicone products are required in a broad range of sectors from electronics to petrochemicals. "But I realized we couldn't just try to dump products on to the market," Korel says. "Don't bulldoze these people.

Don't think our way is the only way. Let them see how Western companies are organized and then allow them to draw their own conclusions." He has used the same concept in the former Soviet Union.

"Reinvent" the Export Culture of Your Firm. Before entering Eastern Europe as a marketer, you may have to reorient the culture of your company toward exporting to world markets. As an export manager, Ruth Langhorst deals constantly with a pervasive attitude problem endemic to U.S. manufacturers: They aren't interested in selling to foreigners. "When times are good," she says, "U.S. companies aren't interested in exporting; when times get tough, they get interested in exporting. *I see this all the time.*" Your company may not be ready to make a long-term commitment to Eastern Europe. It's better to know this before wasting your time and energy researching the market and locating an agent. Moreover, you cannot allow your company to fall into the trap of putting your new overseas market in second place whenever your traditional American home market begins to expand. This can have a nasty boomerang effect if domestic sales later drop and suddenly your overseas market becomes necessary to buttress these declining sales. Your neglected Eastern Europe buyer or agent-distributor is not going to welcome you back with outstretched arms after a period of neglect and half-hearted interest. Marketing in the East will involve *regular* visits abroad with major buyers, agents, and distributors. On these visits, you must be prepared to help and advise, free of charge. Your company will have to be available, interested, and quick to react to problems or complaints issued by Eastern customers.

Leverage for Market Access by Investing. Large contracts in the Eastern Europe market often go to Western companies that have made the commitment to invest in the market—bringing in higher technology, increasing export potential, substituting imports, training managers, and putting larger numbers on people to work. Investing in the market is the most powerful mode of leverage in the market. The next chapter will help you consider the potential promise, and the possible pitfalls, of making this longer-term commitment.

5
Why Invest in Eastern Europe?

Smart Strategies for Investors

The countries of Eastern Europe currently compete with one another for foreign investment and technical know-how. This contest for dollars, yen, and deutsche marks began the moment the Berlin Wall came down. In this chapter, we will examine the level and type of foreign investment moving into the region and define six investment strategies that investors in Eastern Europe follow. The aim is to help you decide whether, and how, your company should invest in Eastern Europe.

For Whom the Investment Tolls

During the first three years, the competition to attract investment to Eastern Europe generated large numbers of deals and a significant number of megadeals compared to the rate of investment in other "transitioning" countries. By the end of 1989, only one year after liberation from Communist control, over 5,000 foreign joint ventures had been signed in Eastern Europe. Eleven percent of these joint undertakings had been set up by U.S. companies, 26 percent by companies from Germany, and 25 percent by companies from Austria. Hungary attracted 29 percent of the joint ventures, Poland 26 percent, Czechoslovakia 3 percent, Bulgaria 1 percent, and the former Soviet Union 40 percent. By the end of 1990, nearly 10,000 foreign ventures had been established in Poland, Hungary, and Czechoslovakia.

Some huge deals got inked. ABB of Switzerland committed $50 million in Poland to make turbine engines with Zamech. Pilkington of the United Kingdom invested $140 million with HSO Sandomierz in Poland to produce glass products. In Czechoslovakia, Volkswagen committed *$6.6 billion* to manufacture automobiles with Skoda BAZ, and Linde of Germany invested $106 million there to produce gas products with Technoplyn. General Electric teamed up with Tungsram in Hungary in a deal capitalized at $120 million; General Motors made a series of large investments in car assembly and production plants throughout the region.

By 1991, it was apparent to observers that the Eastern Europe investment binge was not just the result of an initial flush of excitement about the opening of a 400-million-person consumer market. In the first quarter of 1991, Hungary pulled in $500 million in foreign investment, over half of its foreign investment in *all* of 1990. Poland successfully solicited $370 million in investments in the first quarter in 1991, nearly double what it did during the same period in 1990. The same trend occurred in Czechoslovakia: $100 million in investment entered the country in the first quarter of 1990, and $200 million was invested in the first quarter of 1991. The annual growth rate of direct investment was running between 100 and 400 percent. Even politically unstable Yugoslavia attracted a total of $1.2 billion in foreign investment by the time of its breakup. By 1992, U.S. investors led all comers, in terms of both the number of deals (219 from September 1991 to September 1992) and the amount of investment (almost $8 billion). Germany signed 80 deals in the same period in Eastern European countries, not including its massive number of deals in eastern Germany. Italy signed 60 deals worth $7.6 billion; Japan signed only 22, worth $8 million. "The U.S. investment surge is startling," Mark Dixon, editor of *East European Investment Monthly*, told *Business Week* recently, "in light of Eastern Europe's greater proximity to Western European countries and the economic and political ties it is forming with the European Community." The real surprise is the dilatory Japanese. "The Japanese will likely wait for Germany and America to pioneer a path," a Hungarian consultant told me, "and develop East Europe's investment infrastructure, and then come in to sell to the market. "The Japanese pursue a 'follower strategy,'" Karsten Finke, a consultant with Arthur D. Little in Berlin, told me. "They buy houses and land, but they let others develop the market. They'll serve it later. Right now, their cameras and CD players are too expensive for Eastern

Europeans, but they won't be later."

A Closer Look at the Numbers

The big winner in terms of numbers of foreign-invested ventures set up and dollar amount of total investment is Hungary. Part of Hungary's success is certainly due to the dynamic created by Europe becoming a single integrated market in 1992. The country has privatized over 130 enterprises thus far, with an investment flow of $1.3 billion *since* March 1990—an outstanding performance compared with the investment raised in Poland and Czechoslovakia. Western companies with joint ventures in Hungary have already repatriated over $20 million of profits. *Doing Business in Eastern Europe* reports that "7,000 joint ventures, around 60 percent of which are estimated to be operational, were registered in Hungary by mid-1991." Sixteen percent of these deals were struck with American companies, representing 41 percent of the total investment. German companies set up 37 percent of the ventures, and Austrians set up 24 percent. However, American investors have invested the lion's share of foreign capital in Hungary—about $650 million. German investors have brought in about $350 million; Austrians have invested $400 million. In addition to joint ventures, some 70 wholly owned foreign firms had been set up in Hungary by mid-1991.

The jury is still out on investment in Poland. The numbers seem to indicate that investment is moving into Poland slowly; Poland had attracted a total of $400 million in investment by the end of 1989, U.S. investment accounting for $15 million of the total. The following year, Poland attracted only $200 million. One must remember, however, that Poland's investment law was ratified only in July 1991. By mid-1991, Poland had signed 2,800 joint ventures; 214 set up by American companies, and 981 by German companies. Yet, only 954 of the joint ventures had actually started operations, and roughly 70 percent of them were companies run by Polish individuals rather than corporations. Poland's Industrial & Commercial Chamber of Foreign Investors has reported that "the majority of joint ventures are operating in the clothing industry (19%), followed by the cosmetics and plastics sector (11%). The remaining ones are primarily in household products, construction, food processing, electronics and medical equipment production." Poland's joint ventures are concentrated in the Warsaw area, where they number 182 and employ 22,000 people. Poznan, Katowice, and Lodz are other focal points for joint ventures.

In Czechoslovakia, 2,894 joint ventures had been set up by mid-1991, 861 by Germans—a whopping 85 percent of total foreign investment. American companies had set up only 132. German companies have found in Czechoslovakia a next-door source of highly skilled, low-cost labor where industrial capabilities are sufficient for the production of low- and medium-technology capital goods.

The passage of Romania's foreign investment law in March 1991 has provided an unexpected boost to the number of joint ventures and investment in Romania. In 1990, before the law was passed, only 1,589 joint ventures, worth a total of $112.4 million, had been signed. Over 1,500 joint ventures were penned in Romania between January 1990 and April 1991, worth a total of $150 million. However, 1,443 of them conduct foreign trade or offer services; only a small minority are involved in manufacturing, construction, food processing, and electronics. There *now* exist 8,022 joint ventures in Romania. Germany leads in the number of joint ventures, and France leads in total capital invested. France has invested $58.8 million in 369 ventures. (You may recall that France and Romania share a common Latin-based language and common cultural tradition.) The United States ranks second in investment, with $32.2 million in 470 joint ventures. Germany has invested $30.0 million in 1,181 joint ventures. Sixty percent of Romania's joint ventures are based in Bucharest, 8 percent are in Timisoara, and 5 percent are in the port city of Constanta.

In the former Soviet Union, 3,400 joint ventures had been set up by mid-1991. However, only 948 of those were active at the time. Forty-two percent claim to be involved in industry and services, and 27 percent in advertising and/or publishing. These joint ventures employ 117,000 people, 115,000 who are former Soviets. Roughly one out of four joint ventures set up in the former Soviet Union provides "business services." Many of these ventures were simply phantom companies established to import foreign computer goods for resale in Russia or to move foreign exchange out of Russia and into outside bank accounts. Figure 5-1 shows the situation as of 1992. Where the former Soviet Union is concerned, American companies had pledged about $3 billion of investment but had committed only $400 million by 1992.

Remember that most joint ventures in Eastern Europe are small. Seventy percent of the joint ventures set up in Poland, for example, are valued under $100,000. The average value of joint ventures in Romania is only $25,000 total investment. Over 1,300 joint ventures in Hungary have equity of less than $1 million; 82 were between $1

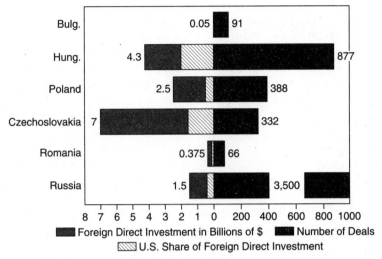

Figure 5-1. For whom the investment tolls: Total foreing investment and deals. (Note: The number of deals for Russia covers only joint ventures.)

and $5 million; 15 ventures were between $5 and $10 million. Only 10 foreign joint ventures in Hungary represent investments of over $10 million.

Foreign Investors, Not Traders!

Let's go back a few years. When Eastern European countries first liberalized their laws to allow foreign investments in, they were attempting to attract Western investors rather than Western merchants. They wanted to use foreign investment to enhance the manufacturing base of their countries, and thus their export potential. Since as early as 1987, the region has been trying to attract *investors* and has been neutral to, or even negative to, traders. "If investors had the opportunity to just sell their products [in Eastern Europe], they would," says Gerry Rohan, coordinator for Ernst & Young's consulting services in Eastern Europe and the former Soviet Union. "But it seems that they need to take a long-term outlook and earn money in the currency of the country in order to pay workers and hopefully develop an operation that will fuel the latent demand for consumer products."

The era of barter in Eastern Europe declined quickly after 1990. Retailing then ran its course, and distribution came of age. Manufacturing in Eastern Europe is the wave of the future. "People in the

West think that Poland is an empty country where you can sell every-thing and make a lot of money." says Dariusz Linert, president of Daro Trade Company in Poland. As is the case elsewhere in Eastern Europe, this formula doesn't work any more because Poland has been decapitalized of disposable cash after a binge of import buying. Now, foreign companies are asked to set up a production facility and make a product to be sold in Poland for zlotys. "Now is the time to invest in production and services," says Dariusz. "The time of trade is finished. It's too late to simply send products to Poland to be sold there." Investment officials in the former Soviet republics seek ventures that generate hard currency, such as oil and gas projects, or that overhaul existing factories and increase their efficiency, and that increase the numbers of workers employed in the free-market sector of the econo-my. They have tired of Western investors coming in and not produc-ing something; of the 3,000 joint ventures that have been signed, only 20 percent are operational: Many were set up merely to be fronts for trading organizations. In short, Eastern Europe wants and needs for-eign investment, not foreign traders.

Many different strategies have emerged and been pursued by American companies in Eastern Europe. Some have looked to Eastern Europe thinking that they could find attractive deals on business acquisitions. Although investors perceive the European Community (EC) as a more mature market than Eastern Europe, the required investment there is high and the regulatory environment is not always amenable to foreign investors. Meanwhile, Eastern European countries were going out of their way to attract investors. "There was a much more obvious welcome mat at the Eastern European and Soviet Union doors," says Ernst & Young's Gerry Rohan. Also, investors had a vast number of opportunities from which to choose that weren't available in the EC. "There wasn't *one* television plant; there were twenty, or a hundred, manufacturers of television sets," says Rohan. Investors were concerned, of course, with the low quality, real cost, and mar-ketability of what Eastern European businesses produced, not to men-tion the undeveloped distribution systems in Eastern Europe for get-ting their products to market.

Six Investment Strategies to Consider

In formulating your business plans for Eastern Europe, first decide on one of two basic approach strategies: One based on a fast return on investment, the other based on long-haul presence in the region. In the first, you need to devise an extremely clever and innovative business idea and find a perfect partner to help implement it. In the second, you need to project success over a 10- to 15-year period, build a visible presence in the region at low cost, and establish a permanent positive business reputation that will result in affording you special status and privilege in regional business communities. Generally, U.S. companies considering manufacturing in Eastern Europe have one of the following objectives in mind: Penetrating regional domestic markets; exporting to neighboring hard-currency markets, usually a Western European one; or exporting to the former Soviet republics or other Eastern European countries. To date, probably the most common investment strategy used by Western companies, especially large ones, in Eastern Europe is a combination of strategies. In the short term, companies often try to penetrate domestic markets as an effective way to support an investment project for the first year or so. In this case, companies typically repatriate only small amounts of profits earned through domestic sales, preferring instead to reinvest the bulk of earnings in the venture. As a medium-term strategy, companies aim to refine their product enough so that it is marketable in Western Europe. Once this is accomplished, the company can begin generating earnings that are substantial enough to be repatriated. A company enjoying success in this manner can afford to wait several years or more until economic changes in Eastern Europe and the former Soviet Union proceed to the point at which the company can begin to exercise its long-term strategy—namely, penetrating these large and untapped markets.

All of the following strategies should be considered before committing time and resources to investing in the region; let's look at them in detail and at some of the companies that have pursued them in Eastern Europe.

Strategy 1: Penetrating a New Market

Almost all companies considering investment in Eastern Europe want to penetrate the domestic industrial or consumer markets—if not immediately, then at some future point. The most popular investment strategy pursued in Eastern Europe aims to capture new markets by setting up operations in-country, behind tariff and non-tariff barriers, via any number of different business forms, including joint ventures, cooperative agreements, and wholly owned subsidiaries. To gain access to the market, the foreign firm must offer concessions. These often include transferring advanced technology, sourcing supplies from domestic sources, exporting a certain per-

centage of production, and offsetting a percentage of production to
indigenous producers.

The automobile industry finds this strategy essential in building
sales in new markets. General Motors' European business has generated more profits in recent years than its U.S. operations. GM's investment in Eastern Europe has risen to $800 million. GM's largest invest-
ment in the region is its $650 million assembly plant in Eisenach, in
eastern Germany, which plans to sell cars in unified Germany. GM's
venture with Fabryka Samochodow Osobowych (in English: Passenger
Car Factory) in Poland will assemble 35,000 Opel Astra cars per year,
most to be sold in Poland. GM's $295 million automobile manufactur-
ing plant in Hungary, the largest single foreign deal in the country,
builds Opel Astras that sell for $13,310 each in Hungary, about seven
years' salary for the average Hungarian. GM plans to sell the cars
mainly to Hungarian businesses. "GM's strategy in Hungary is characterized by investments in local production facilities to secure a permanent presence, supported by a wide distribution and service network,"
Christopher Mattingly, GM's coordinator of public affairs for Eastern
Europe, told *Business Eastern Europe*. "GM's network will be composed
of sales agents and ASOs [authorized service outlets], all organized
under a subsidiary."

Selected deals aimed at penetrating Eastern European markets:
Philip Morris has cooked a joint-venture deal in Hungary to produce
and market its coffee and chocolate products; Coca-Cola has signed a
joint-venture agreement to produce Coke, a 50:50 deal worth $14.7
million. In the former U.S.S.R., General Electric has entered a joint
venture with a consortium of French companies and Aeroflot, to produce jet engines, worth $1 billion. The engines will be installed on
Soviet-made IL-86 jets. Gillette has signed a joint venture to manufacture razor blades, shaving systems, and disposable blades in a venture
of which it owns 65 percent and in which it maintains manufacturing
control. And Otis Elevator has signed a joint venture to build, market,
install, and upgrade elevators, of which it has a 55 percent stake.
Franchising in Eastern Europe, which has gained many adherents
among Western companies, fits into this strategy to penetrate new
markets. Shell International (U.K./Netherlands), Coca-Cola, PepsiCo,
McDonald's, and Burger King (all American) have all signed franchising agreements in Hungary, for example.

Several caveats about this strategy should be made, however. First,
some countries have populations that are small even by Eastern
European standards, and certainly in comparison to the former Soviet
Union (286 million). Second, the existence of investment screening in
Eastern Europe may act as an impediment to penetrating the market

via an investment project. In Hungary, for example, for all foreign investments in which the share of the foreign partner(s) will exceed 50 percent, a license must be obtained from the Ministry of Trade. Since the Hungarian government generally prefers investments that will be at least partly export-oriented, and earn hard currency, the requirement gives the government the chance to screen out projects intended to produce only for domestic sales. In this case, the foreign partner may want to forgo majority ownership of the venture in order to get around the licensing barrier and remove the need to emphasize exports.

Strategy 2: Explore for and Extract Natural Resources

The natural-resource sector in Eastern Europe—and especially the former republics of the Soviet Union—will be absolutely key to overall regional modernization. In the former U.S.S.R., natural resources will be *the* primary source of hard currency with which to finance overhauling state-owned industries, cleaning up the environment, and raising the population's standard of living; sales of oil and gas provide 80 percent of Russia's hard currency. Mineral and fuel resources found in great quantity in the former Soviet Union include gold, zinc, silver, phosphate, salt, tin, lead, aluminum, bauxite, coal, natural gas, petroleum, and magnesium. In 1988, the former U.S.S.R. produced 2.4 metric tons of aluminum and 4.6 million metric tons of bauxite. The republics also produced 11 million karats of diamonds, 273 metric tons of gold, and 248 million metric tons of iron ore. The U.S.S.R. produced 15.5 million metric tons of salt, 40 million metric tons of phosphate, and 95.2 thousand metric tons of magnesium in 1988. Most important, the former U.S.S.R. produced 4.55 million barrels of crude petroleum in 1988 and 770 billion cubic meters of natural gas in the same year. In fact, commonwealth oil fields hold more black gold than the Middle East.

The world's earth-resource development companies have flocked to the former Soviet republics, and throughout Eastern Europe, to make investments as part of their quest for new sources of raw production inputs such as coal, oil, lumber, copper, and uranium. Often, resource-exploitation projects in Eastern Europe find their funding through government loans and aid packages made available by the European Bank of Reconstruction of Development (EBRD), the World Bank, and other international banking institutions. The added costs of pursuing this strategy have involved infrastructural development to facilitate the transportation of raw materials from the interior of the source country to the receiving country.

American companies lead the pack in supplying oil- and gas-indus-

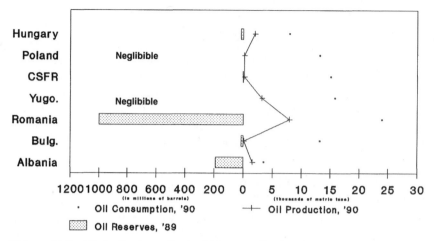

Figure 5-2. Oil in Eastern-Central Europe: Production, consumption, and reserves. (*PlanEcon Report, vol. 7, March 8, 1991, and CIA Handbook of Economic Statistics, 1990.*)

try field machinery and services in Eastern Europe. In the former Soviet Union, Mobil Oil is planning to prospect for oil and gas on Sakhalin Island. In Bulgaria, Maxus Oil has signed an agreement to drill for oil in Central-Northern Bulgaria. Texaco Oil is prospecting in the Black Sea as a result of an agreement with Bulgaria (Figs. 5-2 and 5-3).

Strategy 3: Manufacturing for Export

Three recent deals epitomize a third corporate strategy pursued in Eastern Europe. In Hungary, General Electric has invested $100 million in Tungsram to produce light bulbs; the factory will be GE's main manufacturing plant, supplying GE products to all of Europe. In the former Soviet Union, Allied Plywood has signed a joint venture to market timber, plywood, fiber, chipboards, pulp, paper, and furniture in the United States in hopes that the C.I.S. obtains most-favored-nation status, so that finished products can be sold to the United States. In Bulgaria, Barry Stevenson, a private investor, has signed a cooperative agreement with Tonet Enterprise to manufacture and market furniture. The investor is providing the fabrics and the designs; the output is to be exported to the EC and Japan.

An export-platform strategy aims to increase the price competitiveness of a product line by cutting the cost of production. This end is attained by employing cheaper labor, renting cheaper land to place a

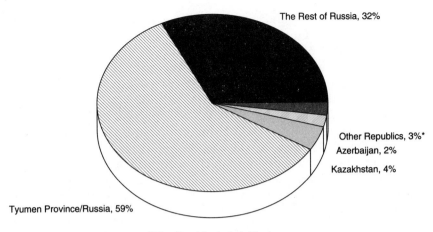

The Rest of Russia, 32%

Other Republics, 3%*
Azerbaijan, 2%
Kazakhstan, 4%

Tyumen Province/Russia, 59%

*Other Republics include Ukraine,
Turkmenistan, Uzbekistan, and Belarus.

Figure 5-3. Oil-rich republics: Russia holds a monopoly. (*Petroleum Industry Research Associates and the Los Angeles Times, February 11, 1992.*)

factory, locating where taxes are low, etc. Companies can also acquire cheaper, locally sourced raw materials. Using this strategy, as taxation has outstripped wage in importance as a percentage of production, companies have been locating throughout Eastern Europe on the basis of preferential regulations concerning taxes, fees, and rental rates as well.

Many companies consider Eastern Europe a prime manufacturing location from which to export to neighboring hard-currency markets—usually Western Europe. The Getz Corporation and Schwinn Bicycle have chosen Hungary as a site to manufacture for European customers; United Technologies Automotive/UTA, the subsidiary of the U.S. conglomerate, purchased a plant in Hungary as part of the firm's overall European strategy, in which market penetration in Eastern Europe was secondary. In order to meet "just-in-time" delivery demands from its customers, UTA ranked "proximity to market" as an important criterion in selecting Hungary, rather than a country in Western Europe, as its strategic "European" location.

There are a number of positive aspects to such a strategy. First, the Eastern European governments are very eager to attract investment projects that will expand their industries capacity to produce high-quality value-added products that can be exported for foreign exchange. Eastern European governments and firms are often willing to go to great lengths to accommodate export-oriented investment projects, including offering significant tax breaks and allowing low minimum capitalization. Second, companies have found that manufacturing costs in Eastern Europe (especially labor) are still low, which can give products manufactured in Eastern Europe the price advantage necessary to win a share of competitive Western European markets. Third, several key market barriers between Western and Eastern Europe have fallen; as of January 1990, the EC began phasing out quantitative restrictions on most Eastern European exports and, for example, made about 4,000 Hungarian products eligible for a duty-free import program. It has become both easier and cheaper to export from Eastern Europe into the EC, and this will remain the case even after the EC market is integrated in 1992. (Poland, Hungary, Czechoslovakia, and Romania have been granted associate status and now enjoy much more favorable tariff rates.)

General Electric looked at its deal with Hungary's Tungsram as an entryway into the European market as a whole. In fact, 70 percent of Tungsram sales were to Western Europe at the time of acquisition, while sales to the Eastern bloc amounted to less than 30 percent of sales. I spoke to company spokesperson John Betchkal at GE about GE's objectives. "Our objective was to be number one, or number two, in the world lighting market. We were a strong number two [in the world] and a strong number one in the United States market. In order to become number one [in the world], we developed a strategy to strengthen our position by becoming stronger in the European market. We had two percent of the European market; we picked up an additional seven percent with the acquisition of Tungsram. Since then, we have gone further with the later acquisition of GE Thorn in England. We paid one hundred and fifty million dollars for fifty percent of Tungsram and since then we have increased our ownership share to seventy-five percent."

The main disadvantage to a European export strategy is that many U.S. companies already have manufacturing operations in Western Europe and do not want their Western and Eastern European operations competing for the same markets. In this case, companies may want to explore the production in Eastern Europe of one or more midstream manufacturing inputs, which can then be used to supply (at a reduced cost) downstream manufacturing operations in Western Europe. Or, they may want to explore other hard-currency export markets reachable from Eastern Europe, such as the Middle East or North Africa. Many former Yugoslavian companies, for instance, have sold to these regions for decades. Also, setting up behind tariff barriers in Europe may not remove the problem of protectionist tariffs completely. "I know a company that is involved in an agricultural project in Poland," says Gerry Rohan. "The EC's restrictive tariffs on exports from Poland to the EC make it not very economic." Agricultural protectionism between EC countries is intense; between the EC and non-EC members, it is even worse.

Although classic "offshore export manufacturing" along the lines of the *maquiladora* model cannot be said to be flourishing in Eastern Europe yet, the strategy should generate increasing interest as investors realize that the tactic represents a double cost savings. If you set up in Poland, for example, you gain a cost advantage at the outset. Later, when Poland becomes part of a single unified EC, you will already be producing *within the EC*. Thus, this strategy offers both short- and long-term benefits. Companies currently pursuing Poland as a site for low-cost manufacturing include laser printer manufacturers, component manufacturers, and consumer electronics manufacturers. This strategy can be best applied in Albania, Bulgaria, and Romania, where wages are the lowest in Europe, and in Poland, Czechoslovakia, and Hungary, where companies can set up labor-intensive manufacturing operations that can harness abundant intellectual capital.

Although the stereotype might indicate otherwise, you can find value-added manufactured goods being produced in Eastern-Central Europe that match similar goods produced in the West in quality, and that can be purchased at a fraction of the cost. Take, for example, cuvettes, which are small glass laboratory containers. A company in the West bought thousands of them from a Western supplier until it found a Hungarian firm that produced a similar product of exactly the same quality, and at half the price. Other goods that may match Western quality, or that can be upgraded easily to do so: furniture, wood flooring, crystal goods, jewelry, carpet, household goods, clothing, and shoes. Poland wants to increase exports of raw resources like coal (which is cheaper than in England), copper, and silver. Poland also produces good vodka, great ham, and machinery that it traditionally sold to the Soviet Union but now sells to the EC at a fraction of Western prices. Germany has found a fantastic source of low-cost machinery in Czechoslovakia. More products will hit this list every month; Westerners who keep a sharp eye out for them, and attend trade shows, will find the bargains first.

A variation on this strategy entails manufacturing in Eastern Europe with the intention of exporting to other Eastern European countries or to the former Soviet Union. However, trading with former Comecon countries cannot be said to be easier from Budapest or Warsaw than it is from Brussels or Paris. I spoke to Arthur Anderson's Karsten Finke about whether eastern German companies could provide a U.S. firm with the connection and clout to sell to former Comecon countries. "East Germany is no longer a window on Eastern Europe," he said.

"The old relationships are gone." However, eastern Germany *did* retain connections with Soviet buyers and western German companies were able to utilize these old relationships to penetrate the Soviet market. The U.S.S.R. lacked funds, of course, but loan guarantees were one thing that western German firms could bring to the bargaining table. The Germans also consider Poland a stepping stone to the commonwealth market.

Strategy 4: Acquiring Ground in a New Market

In Hungary, Colgate-Palmolive is selected by privatization authorities to purchase Caola, a household cosmetics manufacturer. In Poland, Pepsi-Cola purchases 40 percent of the widely known confectionery factory, Wedel, now listed on the Warsaw Stock Exchange. In Czechoslovakia, Procter & Gamble enters an accord to acquire Rakona, a detergents enterprise, for $20 million, with future investments to equal $24 million. These acquisitions of Eastern European firms put on the auction block by their governments represent a strategy of grabbing market share by purchasing a key supplier on the market. Although the most competitive companies with the best reputations and largest market shares have been snapped up, hundreds remain to be sold into private hands. More broadly, with the development of new technology and the acquisition of older technology by Eastern European firms, some once-noncompetitive companies are quickly entering the fold of the world economy as producers of manufactured products. To maintain market share in the face of potentially growing economies-of-scale in Eastern Europe, many U.S. firms have entered venture agreements simply to hold ground in emerging markets where, before long, indigenous producers could acquire state-of-the-art technology in order to produce marketable products on their own.

Often, corporate rivalry—for instance, that between Pepsi and Coke, or Xerox and Fujitsu—gets superimposed on a new playing field, and both players try to nail down deals with the partner with the biggest market share. Guided by this strategy, Procter & Gamble and Unilever bought up detergent companies in Czechoslovakia and Poland almost simultaneously in June 1991. Two weeks after R. J. Reynolds Tobacco International set up a joint venture in Russia to produce 20 billion cigarettes a year (in response to the nation's 100 billion yearly shortage of cigarettes), Philip Morris Products cranked up production of Marlboros in Russia in tandem with Samara Tobacco Factory and an automobile giant, Autovaz. PepsiCo signed its first deal in Russia in

1973 and was able to freeze out its competitor Coca-Cola until 1985. For some time, Pepsi had remained furlongs ahead of Coke in the C.I.S. "cola derby." Its lead began in 1959, when Donald M. Kendall, former chairman of PepsiCo, handed Nikita Khrushchev a Pepsi just before a historical picture taking. That was long before Coca-Cola responded to the Pepsi challenge with Operation Jumpstart in 1992, investing heavily in Eastern bottlers, public relations, and "presence." In Hungary, it set up direct-delivery systems, expanded sales forces, and teamed up with a privatized bottler that provided Coca-Cola direct control over marketing and distribution. Meanwhile, Pepsi remained bound to a lethargic state-owned bottler in Hungary that cannot deliver directly to stores. Market shares in Eastern Europe tell Coca-Cola's comeback story. In Hungary, the company now holds 43.9 percent of the soft-drink market to Pepsi's 30.0 percent. In most other countries, the contest is closer: The cola war appears to have only just begun.

Strategy 5: Sharing in Research and Development

Under this investment strategy, a firm usually forms a joint-venture partnership with a counterpart that possesses the in-house resources and/or government backing to share the expense of developing a new product that it cannot afford to develop on its own because of high cost and high risk. In Eastern Europe, this strategy will grow in popularity as the cost of developing technologically sophisticated products skyrockets worldwide. (There will be no comparable lessening of the inherent risk that the new product may fail in the marketplace, even with a concerted research and development effort behind it.) Also, the increasingly modular nature of global industrial systems (in which separate parts of a complex product are developed by different countries) demands that firms share and coordinate their technological endeavors with widely dispersed business partners. Since most scientists and gifted engineers tend to want to remain citizens of their countries, rather than take jobs in the West, Eastern European firms will increasingly be entering partnerships of this sort with Western companies.

Many times, technical partnerships will merely involve technology transfer via licensing. For a firm that has no presence in a burgeoning Euro-market, licensing may be a way to lessen the negative effects of not participating directly in the market, especially if its competition has a secure presence already. The selling of state-of-the-art, and older, Western technologies to Eastern Europe has only just begun, and I believe that it will grow enormously. The problem becomes one of finding the customer. You need to search out the companies that want to upgrade or expand their product lines without purchasing an entire set of new equipment. Import substitution will involve building low- and medium-technology goods after purchasing the technology and (possibly) used equipment from foreign suppliers. The United States is too far away for shipping used equipment to be feasible, but an international company should think of shifting old equipment out of its EC plants directly into Eastern Europe. Licensing deals will often depend on putting the financing together; if, however, you can obtain the funding, a deal could be put together that would supply the Eastern company with a new technology that it could use to produce goods that it could, in turn, market to the West, paying you (and the lender) a royalty on all sales. While Ashton-Tate complains about software pirating in the former Soviet Union, Sun Microsystems has hired local talent to conduct software development, and an ethnic-Pole vice president at Cray Computers has enlisted Polish programmers to write software. Digital Electronic Corporation will study electric properties of silicon in a cooperation agreement with Budapest Technical University. In the former Soviet Union, Apple Computer has reached a cooperative accord with ParaGraph International, a Soviet-U.S. venture, to obtain its handwriting-recognition technology and other recognition technologies to be developed in the future.

Eastern Europe is also a place to conduct basic research science at a fraction of normal cost. Because the Soviet Union imposed its high priority on science and technology on them, Eastern European countries have developed a truly massive scientific research apparatus far larger than the size of their economies would warrant. Currently, 50,000 thousand Ph.D.s in Poland alone are at risk of losing their jobs, and they can be hired at low salaries. Scientific people in the East have moved quickly into the modernizing corps in governments and institutions, set up research consultancies, and formed numerous joint ventures with foreigners.

Product development and testing can be done inexpensively in the region as well. Any company that intends to develop a process to create a new product must carry out laborious and expensive testing. In Eastern Europe firms can hire an underutilized laboratory to conduct this testing for a fraction of the usual cost. Regulatory barriers may be lower in the East than in the West, allowing for faster progress in experimentation. Environmental impact statements and multilevel approvals may be less stringent and less time-consuming in the East than in the West. I'm not implying that Western companies should endanger the East with environmentally hazardous scientific experimentation. Any development work that is done must be totally safe; the point is that conducting the work will entail less hassle and be much less expensive.

One last possibility worth considering: Eastern European Socialism supported and groomed specialists in a spectrum of endeavors who you may be able to commercialize in the West. In the East there is a rather odd assortment of highly skilled and trained people who are now in surplus. Translators, singers, musicians, circus performers, and sports people are among the sort in oversupply. Using a fax machine, a company could, for example, set up a translation service specializing in the languages of the entire region that would cost a pittance compared to hiring translators in the West.

Strategy 6: Acquiring New Technology

When a parent firm cannot afford to develop new technology, it can opt to form a joint venture with an overseas firm that has already developed it, in an effort to acquire that technology. This pursuit may be urgent if the newly developed technology represents a radical breakthrough that threatens the competitiveness of the firm's present product lines. As technological innovation becomes more globalized, many firms will enter Europe simply for technological survival: If they don't, their products will soon become obsolete.

Matching Business Structure with Business Endeavor

Should an investor link up with a joint-venture partner, set up a wholly owned company, or purchase a company that is being privatized? It depends on what your strategy is and where the greatest potential exists to pursue that strategy. Take, for example, the case of an American agricultural products company that set up in Poland. Its executives knew of a *particular firm* in Poland that they wanted to acquire. Originally, they wanted to pursue this objective by forging a joint venture, because at the time there was no other vehicle with which they could link up with this company. In the middle of their negotiations, Poland's privatization law was introduced and the Polish company was offered for sale. The American company decided to acquire the company outright and discard the idea of forming a joint venture. If this same U.S. company moved into Russia, it would set up a "green-field" project because there is no company in Russia that has the type of plant or production capabilities that its executives are looking for. There is simply no partner in Russia that would be attractive to them. Similarly, when the joint-venture law was ratified in the Soviet Union in 1987, there was no other option other than to set up a joint venture if one wished to get into the market as an investor. When the law was changed to include 100 percent foreign ownership, many companies considered outright acquisition as an option.

Some companies will look at privatized companies and see them as a good investment, possibly as a smart way to obtain a toehold in a market. Others will decide that such a purchase will cost too much money to turn around and gear up for competing in the world market and will decide that simply starting from scratch and building a new plant is the best way to go. Some companies follow clearly defined global strategies that sometimes condition their approach in Eastern Europe, too. Hewlett-Packard, for instance, opened a 100 percent-owned subsidiary in Warsaw in 1991, and a 100 percent-owned subsidiary in Prague in 1991—the same strategy it has pursued in China.

Even though it is legal to go in and acquire or set up your own business in most countries of Central Europe, you have to make certain that the purchase price is fully discounted to reflect the portion of company debt to be assumed, the quality of the assets, and the responsibility for environmental problems.

A Joint Venture May Not Be Best

A joint venture with a foreign entity is the business form of choice in Eastern Europe because such a venture increases production through foreign investment and equity rather than through debt. Take note, however, that most joint ventures are relatively weak production agreements that do not give the Western partner any degree of control or influence if the Eastern European state-owned partner company is privatized. In other words, a joint-venture partner may not be allowed to buy the enterprise. After the sale of the enterprise, it may lose its position in the market if a competing firm purchases its partner! Charles Jonscher recently gave an example, concerning Fiat. "[Fiat] has had a major joint-venture relationship with the Polish car manufacturers FSO and FSM for nearly 20 years and is now competing fiercely with newcomer General Motors for the acquisition of FSO." Soon after that comment was made, GM successfully forged a deal with FSO worth $75 million to produce 35,000 Opel Astras per year. Let this be a warning—joint venture doesn't always equal permanent market share.

Cooperative Strategies

In lieu of entering a joint-venture deal or making direct cash investments, a foreign firm may decide that a better first step toward penetrating the Eastern European market would be to participate in a "cooperative agreement" with an Eastern European company. Cooperative agreements can take many forms and can also be considered building-block agreements on the way to extensive technology-transfer engagements. Some cooperative strategies include:

1. The Western firm provides an Eastern European company with advanced production equipment, technical documentation, and training. The Eastern European company begins production and sells products domestically or to foreign countries stipulated in the contract, and pays the Western vendor with products produced or with other goods that it obtains locally.

2. In other agreements, the Western company may provide know-how and documentation in exchange for products produced; yet the value of such "software" can be hard to justify among Eastern European managers.

3. Coproduction of a product by a Western company and one in Eastern Europe means that each company produces components or subassemblies which go into a final product that will be marketed by both sides. This form of agreement will become more common as Eastern European companies become more adept at marketing internationally.

4. Production and assembly agreements utilize inexpensive labor in Eastern Europe; the Western firm simply provides the specifications and/or parts to be assembled and pays the Eastern company a production fee. Deals of this nature do not interest Eastern European companies at present unless the component to be manufactured or assembled represents a high level of technical sophistication. Romania, Ukraine, and Belarus could emerge as assembly sites in the future, however, and become exceptions to this rule. A new "South China" in Eastern Europe does not appear to be emerging, as of yet.

5. Two partners may also jointly finance the engineering and prototyping of an entirely new product, as well as its eventual manufacture. A Western firm might fund research by an Eastern European company in exchange for the right to use the research results.

6. In other coproduction agreements, two firms may simply swap technical licenses, documentation, and training programs.

6
Deciding Where to Invest

Weighing the Potential and the Pitfalls

To decide where to place investments overseas, investors analyze prospective countries and consider the investment-climate variables. Some look at a handful of key variables, including a country's gross domestic product (GDP—as an indication of productivity), infrastructure (to gauge the cost of transportation and energy needs), tax incentives, and the buying power of local consumers. Others look at a broader number of variables (including the exhaustive list of criteria in Table 6-2). We want to compare countries with these criteria in mind, but the *first step* that you, as a would-be investor in Eastern Europe must take, in considering Eastern European investment sites, is a review of the state of your *industry* in each country. After you have done this—and this will certainly involve on-site visits to the region—you can move on to conduct a "country comparison," which we will do in a moment.

Industry First, Then Country

The U.S.S.R.'s "satellites" in Central Europe were forced to focus their industrial efforts to meet the objectives of Moscow's economic plans. Each country specialized in whatever Stalin's whim demanded. East

Germany, for example, became an efficient producer of grinder units, presses, cultivators, and household electrical appliances including vacuum cleaners, refrigerators, washing machines, televisions, and radios. Czechoslovakia became known for its cutting lathes, bearings, tractor seeders, spinning machines, and weaving machines, not to mention vacuum cleaners, refrigerators, and washing machines, and Hungary turned out high numbers of televisions, refrigerators, tape recorders, and canned meat and vegetables. (Country and city specialties are listed in the Appendix on pages 338 and 339.) In many cases, foreign companies have chosen to participate in an Eastern European *industry*, like the electronics industry in Bulgaria, without much concern about the *country* in which that industry is located. Both criteria—country and industry—have a bearing on whether an investment will be a good one.

In your search for an investment site, a first stop should be at an industrial almanac to research industrial priorities in each country. No doubt, the majority of enterprises in the industrial sectors that are technologically modern enough to interest Western companies exist on a scale that far exceeds the needs of their national markets. Hence, they are geared more to employing people and serving the Soviet market than to serving the needs of their domestic markets. Many Eastern European enterprises now simply sit in entirely nonstrategic locations. Figure 6-1 provides an indication of where manufacturing was emphasized most, as a percentage of total gross domestic product (GDP) in each country of the region. Though one would guess that Czechoslovakia would possess a large manufacturing sector, the surprise here is how much of total output in Romania and Bulgaria is due to their manufacturing sectors. The data in Table 6-1 show the structure of former Soviet industry. You can see the emphasis on machine building, light industry, and food processing in all the former republics. It may surprise you that Georgia leans heavily toward light industry and food production and is weak in machine building and metallurgy compared to all of the other republics. Belarus looks surprisingly strong as a producer of chemicals and as a site for machine building and metallurgy.

Figure 6-2 shows the heavy emphasis on engineering and machine building throughout the region, ranging from 26 percent to 31 percent of total industry in each country of the region. Radio and television production was disproportionately emphasized in East Germany. Radio production was high in Poland, as shown in Fig. 6-3. Eastern Germany and Hungary produced high quantities of chemical goods: 20 and 19 percent of the total industrial output was chemical products, respectively (Fig. 6-4).

Figure 6-5 gauges the industrial productivity of each of the former Soviet republics by showing both per capita output of citizens in each republic and each republic's share of the total net material product.

Table 6-1. Structure of Industry in the Former Soviet Union

	Former U.S.S.R.	Russia	Ukraine	Baltics	Kazakhstan	Belarus	Georgia
Heavy industry	8.7	9.5	8.6	6.0	12.8	2.3	4.0
Electric power	3.7	3.8	3.2	3.1	4.6	2.9	2.0
Fuels	7.7	8.6	7.3	3.3	8.5	5.6	2.0
Ferrous metallurgy	6.2	5.8	12.9	0.9	6.0	4.1	0.6
Nonferrous metallurgy	4.0	5.1	1.2	0.1	11.5	0.1	—
Chemicals and Petrochemicals	7.0	7.6	6.2	4.9	6.0	9.3	3.0
Machine building and metal working	27.0	29.9	24.4	22.9	17.3	32.0	13
Wood and paper	4.5	5.5	2.5	6.5	2.8	4.5	3.0
Construction materials	3.7	3.6	3.3	3.9	6.0	3.4	5.0
Glass	0.4	0.4	0.5	0.4	0.1	0.4	—
Lighting products	15.3	13.2	11.8	21.0	16.3	20.1	20
Food	17.4	14.5	20.3	27.7	18.6	17.7	39
Other	0.7	0.8	0.7	0.7	0.6	0.9	—

SOURCE: PlanEcon; all figures, 1985.

Notice that, in terms of productivity, Russia is equaled by Belarus, Estonia, and Latvia, and Ukraine lags behind.

Once you have reviewed the scant literature that covers Eastern European industrial capabilities, which are in a state of complete flux, the next step is to broaden the analysis on your own by interviewing factory managers in the region or hiring a consulting company to undertake a formal industry review.

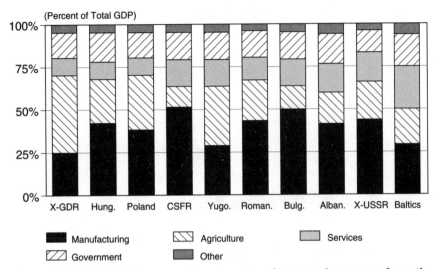

Figure 6-1. Total GDP by economic sector: Manufacturing the engine of growth. (*Economic Intelligence Unit Ltd., Country Reports, 1992.*)

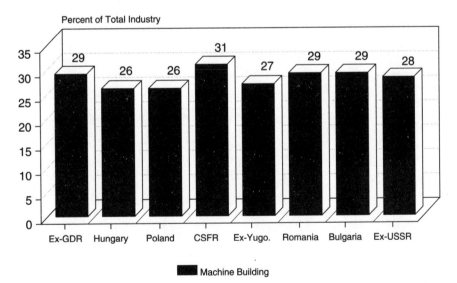

Figure 6-2. Machine building in Eastern Europe: A mature industry poised to modernize. (*PlanEcon.*)

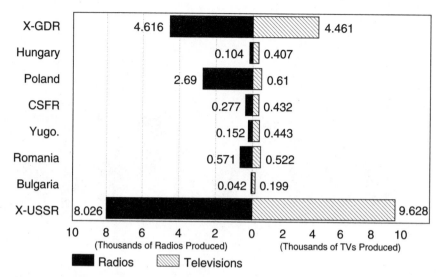

Figure 6-3. Radio and television production, 1986: Former East Germany and former Soviet Union as key players. (*PCGlobe 4.0, 1990, PCGlobe, Inc.*)

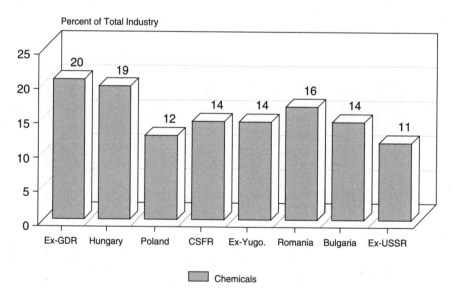

Figure 6-4. Eastern Europe's laboratory: A glance at the chemical industry. (*PlanEcon.*)

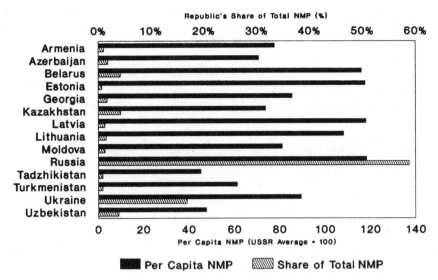

Figure 6-5. How productive are the former Soviet republics? Per capita output and share of total national material product (NMP). (*PlanEcon; all figures 1988.*)

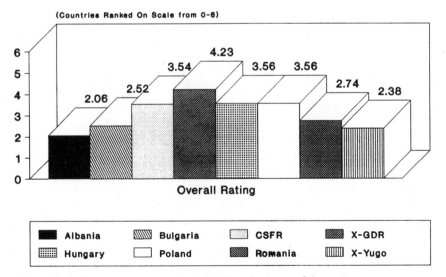

Figure 6-6. Comparing investment climates: A survey of the region.

Ranking Eastern European Investment Climates

After rating each country in terms of the 35 criteria listed in Table 6-2, we arrive at an overall rating for each country. Figure 6-6 compares the overall investment-climate rating for each country. Obviously, the investment ratings will change from month to month. Use this matrix of criteria to update the overall ratings that are presented here. Now let's look more carefully at a few of the ingredients that go into an "investment climate." Again, you should remember that all these aspects of the commercial atmosphere are, as of this writing, in a state of violent transition. Now let's look at how Eastern European countries compare with regard to the most salient investment climate variables.

Forms of Investment Allowed

All countries of the region accept investment in cash or kind. They differ, however, as to whether foreigners can own real estate. Joint ventures and wholly owned enterprises are acceptable everywhere except in areas vital to national security. Options for business structures in the region include joint stock, limited liability, association, private companies limited by shares, limited partnership, partnership limited by shares, and general commercial partnership. In all countries of the region, including the Commonwealth of Independent States, 100 percent ownership of enterprises is permitted.

Minimum Capitalization

Eastern European policies do differ, however, as to minimum venture capitalization. As of this writing, Hungary requires 1 million forints to set up a limited liability company and 10 million forints to start a joint stock company. In Poland, $1,000 is required to start a limited liability company, and $26,000 is needed to start a joint stock company. Setting up a joint stock company in Czechoslovakia will require a minimum capitalization of 100,000 korunas, but there is no capitalization requirement to start a joint venture. In the former Yugoslavia, the requirement was 2,000 dinars to start a limited liability company, and 15,000 dinars to start a joint stock company; these figures may differ in the new nations of former Yugoslavia. No capitalization requirements exist in Romania or the Commonwealth of Independent States. Bulgaria requires 50,000 lev to start a joint venture.

Tax Rates

Corporate tax rates on venture profits vary from country to country and have changed rapidly over the past two years. As of this writing, the tax rates on profit for joint ventures are as follows. In Hungary, you will pay 35 percent tax on a base profit of $60,000 and 40 percent on more. A 20 percent tax reduction is possible through negotiation with government authorities. In Poland, there is a 30 percent tax on dividends. In Czechoslovakia, the rate is 25 percent on dividends and 50 percent on total wages. The West German tax system has been fully implemented in eastern Germany. Currently the highest marginal tax rate for corporations in Germany is 53 percent. Some special tax incentives for the five new eastern states are currently under discussion. Tax rates in the former Yugoslavia differ depending on the republic in which you are doing business; the corporate tax in Slovenia is currently 40 percent. Two- to five-year tax holidays are negotiable in Romania; corporate tax runs between 30 and 40 percent there. In Bulgaria, the tax rate is 40 percent and 10 percent on dividends. In the Commonwealth of Independent States, the tax rate for enterprises with a foreign share of 30 percent or less is 45 percent; for firms with more than 30 percent foreign ownership, the tax rate is 30 percent. In Russia's Far East, you may be able to negotiate a tax rate of 10 percent.

Local-Content Requirements

Local-content requirements, whereby ventures are forced to source a certain percentage of inputs in-country, are not being imposed on joint ventures anywhere in the region.

Profit Repatriation

Repatriating profit can be accomplished anywhere in the region, with some notable differences in restrictions. In Poland, 100 percent of hard-currency profit may be repatriated. In Czechoslovakia, hard-currency profits may be repatriated provided that the joint venture meets its hard-currency requirements. In Romania, profits may be taken out with an additional 10 percent tax. In Bulgaria and the Commonwealth of Independent States, hard-currency share of profits may be repatriated.

Table 6-2. Rating Eastern Europe's Investment Climates (Countries Ranked on a Scale of 1 to 6)

Criteria for comparing investment climates	Albania	Bulgaria	Czech and Slovak Republic	Former East Germany	Hungary	Poland	Romania	Former Yugoslavia
Regulations on foreign ownership of property and enterprises	4.5	4.2	6	6	6	6	6	6
Attitude and policy concerning foreign investment	3	1.6	4	5.5	2	3.6	4	3.5
Regulations on repatriation of profits out of the country	6	4.2	6	6	6	6	4	6
Size of the economy in the form of GNP	0.5	1.4	2.1	6	1.2	4	2.8	2.9
Convertibility of the local currency into foreign exchange, and the stability in the rate of exchange	4	3.5	4	6	4	3.8	2	3
Inflation rate, especially in light of the potential for demands for wage hikes to match inflation	4	0	1.1	5	2.1	4.3	1.7	0.5

Indebtedness of the country, and how it affects economic policy	5.5	1.5	4.5	2.6	1.1	1.1	5.7	1.9
Corporate tax rates and breaks	4	3.3	3.3	1	2	3.1	3	4.2
Per capita GNP, as an indication of worker efficiency	0.5	2.9	4.8	5.1	1.2	4.1	2	2
Existing business services, like law offices, banks, communication centers, and accountancies	0.5	1.5	4.5	5	5	4	1.5	4.6
State of transportation networks, including roads, ports, and airport facilities handling cargo shipments	0.5	3.8	3.7	5.1	2.5	3.3	1.5	3.8
Exposure and adoption of Western-style business practices, ethics, and protocol	0.2	1.3	2.8	5.2	5	4.6	2.3	2.8

Table 6-2. (*Continued*) Rating Eastern Europe's Investment Climates (Countries Ranked on a Scale of 1 to 6)

Criteria for comparing investment climates	Albania	Bulgaria	Czech and Slovak Republic	Former East Germany	Hungary	Poland	Romania	Former Yugoslavia
Rental rates for expatriate apartments and office space	3.1	5.2	4.2	1.5	3.8	2.3	5.2	0.7
Crime rate and health risks, including sophistication of hospitals and availability of doctors	1.1	3.8	3.4	1.5	4.9	3.2	3	1.1
Economic growth as an indicator of expansion or contraction of industry	3	4	5	5.3	2	1.8	2	1.8
Wage level, and trends in wage increases, if any	6	6	4.9	0.5	3.6	3.9	5.1	0.9
Education and skill level of workers and managers	3.4	4.1	5	5.1	5.2	4.6	3.2	3.3

Tax incentives for ventures fulfilling certain nationally defined objectives	1.5	2.5	3	3	4.5	3	4	4.5
Environmental damage and scale of cleanup in the country, and the region where the venture is to be located	4.5	2.5	1.5	2.5	3.5	2	3	5
Foreign commercial presence in the country in the forms of joint ventures, subsidiaries, banks, lawyers, hotels, and expatriate community	0.2	1.2	2.3	5.7	6	5	2	0.7
Flexibility of labor laws, and the power of workers and labor unions vis-à-vis foreign and domestic managers			4	3			1.1	1

Table 6-2. (*Continued*) Rating Eastern Europe's Investment Climates (Countries Ranked on a Scale of 1 to 6)

Criteria for comparing investment climates	Albania	Bulgaria	Czech and Slovak Republic	Former East Germany	Hungary	Poland	Romania	Former Yugoslavia
Distribution network, including availability of trucking services, freight forwarding, and Customs efficiency	0.5	1.7	1.9	5.3	5.1	4.9	2.8	2.3
Speed of investment decision-making apparatus and the necessity to "lubricate" the system in an unorthodox manner	2.2	2.1	6	3	0	0	3	3
Industrial strength and diversity of manufacturing endeavor—what "pockets of excellence" exist?	0.2	0.5	2.5	4	1.9	4	3.1	2.3

Pace of large-scale privatization; i.e., how many large state-owned firms have been sold?	1.8	1.5	4.6	4	3.5	2	0.7	1.5
Pace of small-scale privatization, including the growth in number of private enterprises and size of private sector	0.5	6	3.2	6	5.3	5.8	6	1.2
Number of public-sector firms that have been put up for sale to foreign interests	1.5	1.3	2	3.1	3	3	4.1	3.5
Availability of financing for foreign ventures, both in the country and globally	0	0.5	3.7	6	4.2	1.1	0.5	0
Depth of foreign relations, including most-favored-nation status, trade pacts, and political treaties	0.5	1.5	3.8	6	4.5	3.9	1.7	0

Table 6-2. (*Continued*) Rating Eastern Europe's Investment Climates (Countries Ranked on a Scale of 1 to 6)

Criteria for comparing investment climates	Albania	Bulgaria	Czech and Slovak Republic	Former East Germany	Hungary	Poland	Romania	Former Yugoslavia
Political stability, including ethnic relations, potential for coup, and overall social discontent	1.3	3	4.2	6	4	6	4.2	0
Financial support of the IMF, World Bank, and EBRD	3	3	4	6	4.5	5	2	3.5
Level of production technology in place, and intensity of application	0.5	2.5	3.5	4.5	3.8	3	1	3.5
Managerial skills, as well as "manager mentality"	0.5	1.1	3.5	3.7	3.1	3.1	2.1	2.9
Production material supply, potential for disruption of supply	0.5	1.5	4.1	5.5	5.1	4	1.9	2
Overall rating	2.06	2.52	3.54	4.23	3.56	3.56	2.74	2.38

Special Enterprise Funds

Be aware that in some countries of Eastern Europe a joint venture may be required to put aside a certain percentage of profits for social welfare purposes. For example, as of this writing, in Poland an 8 percent after-tax profit must be deposited in a reserve fund. In Czechoslovakia, a joint venture may be required to deposit revenue in a reserve fund, a remuneration fund, and a fund for social needs. And in the Commonwealth of Independent States (C.I.S.) a joint venture may be required to put aside certain funds for social needs as well.

Joint ventures are not integrated into state purchase plans in Eastern Europe. One rule in Bulgaria, however, limits state purchases from a joint venture to two thirds of the venture's total output.

Hiring Requirements

Throughout the region, there are no formal restrictions placed on joint-venture managers to hire people, whether workers or managers, of a certain ethnic background or nationality.

Real Estate Ownership by Foreigners

Nearly every former Eastern bloc country and republic has liberalized its investment laws to allow foreign investors to either buy land or lease it virtually in perpetuity. However, a great deal of confusion over who owns specific pieces of property that investors want to purchase continues to vex business partners on both sides. In fact, David Roche, managing director of Morgan Stanley International, has written that the ownership dilemma "provides the most frequent explanation (or excuse) for big companies and multinationals doing nothing in East-central Europe." (We'll return to the problems of assessing ownership in Chapter 9.) A foreign-owned company or a foreign person can buy or lease land in Poland, but most companies lease land to avoid the hassle of obtaining a permit from the Ministry of Interior to buy land. Investors in Czechoslovakia can own real estate, provided the deal meets certain requirements. Land can only be leased in Romania. More information on this topic, pertaining to the former Soviet republics, is given later in this chapter.

Inflation

As of this writing, inflation runs highest in Bulgaria (316 percent per annum) and lowest in Poland (peaked in 1990 at nearly 350 percent and had fallen to 32 percent per annum by the beginning of 1991). Inflation is spinning out of control in the former Yugoslavia and most of the former Soviet republics. (See Fig. 7-1 in Chapter 7.)

National Debt

In terms of foreign hard-currency debt left over from the Communist years, the C.I.S., taken singly, is the worst-off country of Eastern Europe, with over $58 billion owed in convertible currency. As of 1989, Poland (which owes $47 billion to foreign lenders) and the U.S.S.R. owed 60 percent of the region's total debt. Hungary carries a heavy debt load as well, relative to the country's population and industrial exports. Romania and Czechoslovakia carry light debt loads.

Joblessness

Unemployment in Eastern Europe is careening out of control. Accurate statistics are hard to come by, in part because so many people may have lost their jobs and yet continue to "moonlight"—working one, two, or three part-time jobs. Joblessness is, however, very real in Eastern Europe, and one can expect it to get worse before it gets better. Two forces driving unemployment and underemployment are at work in the region: First, hundreds of state-run factories have been forced to cut work forces or close completely; and second, inflation has forced workers to augment their income by finding second and third jobs. Grim estimates for eastern Germany predict that as much as 50 percent of the working population could find itself out of work. By mid-1991, 10 percent of working-age Romanians had lost their jobs; over 1.3 million Poles, representing 4 percent of the working population, had also lost theirs. (See Fig. 7-2 in Chapter 7.)

Infrastructure

The Big Three—Poland, Hungary, and Czechoslovakia—enjoy well-developed business infrastructures. Supplies of power and water present few problems; a private service can be hired to ensure proper water and power access in these countries. In the Balkans and former Soviet republics, however, it can become extremely difficult to communicate, especially in West Siberia and the Far East, purely because of insufficient telecommunication links. "The mail system doesn't work worth a darn," says David Kern Peteler. "The transportation system doesn't work very well outside of the major cities, and even within the major cities it's not as good as it could be." I asked a desk officer at the Department of Commerce whether the infrastructure in the former Soviet republics varied much. She recounted a story: "We did a trade mission to West Siberia. The communication to put the mission together took months. We had to talk to these people, and you can't dial direct. You have to go through an operator, which takes a tremendous amount of time, if it's even possible. Telexes aren't widely available there yet, so we had to locate someone in a city nearby that had a telex machine. It was complicated. But that's Russia."

Wages

Throughout Eastern Europe, wages are on average 90 percent lower than in the West. Monthly average income ranges from $36 per month in Bulgaria to $425 per month in Yugoslavia. Hourly labor cost in eastern Germany runs about $7; in Hungary the figure is about $1.88; and in Poland one can expect to pay $1.58 per hour for unskilled labor. In comparison, hourly labor costs $16.29 in Italy and $11.60 in Spain.

Legal Guidelines

All the Central European countries have issued new, clear investment laws and regulations concerning business interaction with foreign companies. These are available from the embassies of each country in the United States. Romania, Bulgaria, and Albania have lagged behind the other countries in ratifying new investment laws. The former republics of the Soviet Union are in the process of writing their own investment, taxation, and export laws. "The problem with some of them is that they simply adopted the old Soviet laws," says Gerry Rohan. "These laws often contradicted new laws that are being written in the republics." Will investors have to abide by republic, as well as central, laws? "There may be, at some point, when they get organized, some sort of federal tax to worry about," says David Peteler, "but I think foreign investment is something the various republics are going to want to control as much as possible by themselves. They aren't going to give up much authority to the new center if there is a center."

National Wealth

Per capita gross national product (GNP) can give us some idea of a country's national wealth and worker productivity. In Fig. 6-7, you can see that former East Germany was the most efficient economy in the region. Czechoslovakia is a strong second; Hungary and Yugoslavia rank third and fourth, respectively. With Yugoslavia's economy now in

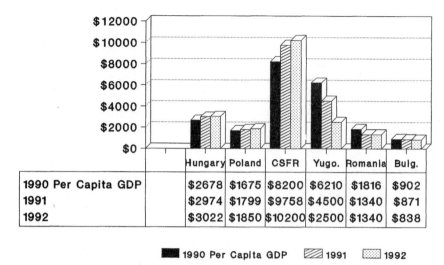

	Hungary	Poland	CSFR	Yugo.	Romania	Bulg.
1990 Per Capita GDP	$2678	$1675	$8200	$6210	$1816	$902
1991	$2974	$1799	$9758	$4500	$1340	$871
1992	$3022	$1850	$10200	$2500	$1340	$838

■ 1990 Per Capita GDP ▨ 1991 ▒ 1992

Figure 6-7. Per capita GNP, 1990: East Germans stand alone.

turmoil, Poland has moved into the fourth-ranked position. Also of note, Bulgaria ranked in front of Yugoslavia in 1989. In terms of total GNP, all the countries of the region took a beating during 1989 and 1990, as Soviet customers became insolvent, oil prices skyrocketed as the result of the Gulf War, and Eastern European firms were put up for sale. During this time, GNP declined 9.1 percent in former East Germany, 12.9 percent in Poland, and 15 percent in Bulgaria. In 1990, industrial production in these countries plummeted by 23 percent in Poland, 5 percent in Hungary, 3.7 percent in Czechoslovakia, 20 percent in Romania, and 10.7 percent in Bulgaria. Remember that GNP figures can be deceptive since they do not reflect the fact that thousands of private enterprises have mushroomed during the past two years to eventually replace faltering state-owned enterprises.

Cost of Conducting Business

Office rents vary widely throughout the region. Per square meter, office space in Hungary will run between $15 and $50; in Poland, $4 to $200; in Czechoslovakia, $15 to $25; in Yugoslavia, $40; in Romania, $7; in Bulgaria, $3 to 20; and in the C.I.S., as high as $50. To rent a four-room unfurnished apartment in a capital city, expect to pay $280 a month in Hungary, $361 a month in Poland, and $373 a month in Czechoslovakia. With regard to customs duties on imports of assets to a joint venture, few restrictions exist anywhere in the region.

Comparing Countries Close Up

Referring to our ranking of investment climates in Table 6-2, one can gauge the advantages and disadvantages of investing in each country of Eastern Europe, starting with eastern Germany.

Eastern Germany. Eastern Germany came out on top with high ratings in "freedom to repatriate profits," "convertibility of currency," "size of its (now unified) economy," and "political stability." Upon unification, the former German Democratic Republic (G.D.R.—one of communism's more ironic titles) inherited a body of well-documented, complete, and sophisticated business law. Investors would not have to wait 5 to 10 years for an accountable and stable legal atmosphere to take form in eastern Germany, the way they would in Poland, Hungary, and the former Soviet Union. The equivalent of over $100 billion has flowed into eastern Germany from western Germany, guaranteeing eastern Germany's eventual transition to a market economy. Top German investors include Volkswagen, which has acquired Automobilwerke Sachsenring, Zwickau GmbH, Barkas GmbH, and Automobilwerk Eisenach, for a total investment of $2.3 billion. Daimler Benz has acquired Ifa Automobilwerk Ludwigsfelde, Siemens has purchased 16 former G.D.R. enterprises, and Telekom plans to modernize and expand a telephone network in the former G.D.R., with total investments of 55 billion deutsche marks through 1997. Foreign investors have purchased just 81 companies in eastern Germany, mainly through their subsidiaries in west Germany. They include Coca-Cola (United States) and Danisco De Dankse Sukkerfabrikken (Denmark). Coca-Cola will spend $450 million over the next couple of years, one of its largest overseas investments yet. Very few deals with American companies have been penned with the Treuhand thus far, and now it's probably too late for Americans to find bargains. "You Americans come late," I was told by Ewald Hiltenkamp, a representative of the Treuhandanstalt in Koln. "Investors from Germany, Japan, Belgium, Netherlands, England, and France have taken the best firms already." Many American firms have been frustrated in dealing with the Treuhand, which they have criticized as being overbureaucratized and exclusionary.

Virtually all U.S. business marketing is done via west German subsidiaries. For example, General Motors has entered eastern Germany through its subsidiary Opel. Procter & Gamble and Coca-Cola have entered east Germany through west German subsidiaries as well.

Your desire to invest in eastern Germany may diminish as you consider following five points. First, the infrastructure stinks. Second, eastern German managers suffer the same deficiencies as other managers in the region: They lack management skills and knowledge of marketing standards. Third, the issue of property rights has yet to be resolved; foreigners still cannot purchase real estate in eastern Germany. Fourth, the public-sector bureaucracy suffers from slow decision making; its officials are accustomed to directives of great detail being issued from above and lack initiative to move unilaterally to improve the system or assist foreigners. And fifth, eastern Germany has suffered massive environmental damage, and to some degree, foreign investors are expected to finance the cleanup.

Some bright spots include: No restrictions on joint ventures; foreign companies can buy all or part of the assets of a local corporation; and all rules against holding a majority position in a company, as was the case in the former East Germany, have been rescinded. Every form of European business incorporation is allowed. You may form a limited-liability company (GmbH), a publicly held corporation (AG), a limited partnership (KG), or a sole proprietorship. A firm is also permitted to operate as a branch office of an American company without formal local incorporation. Moreover, the five new states will also be included in the 1992 unification of the European Common Market, making an investment in eastern Germany a cost-effective avenue of getting around EC trade barriers.

Czechoslovakia. Czechoslovakia rates high in "speed of investment approval," "freedom to repatriate," and in willingness to allow foreign ownership of enterprises. With the division of the Czech and Slovak Federal Republic concluded, many investors that have been poised to enter Czechoslovakia as investors will now move forward. Czechoslovakia has received endorsement from European CEOs as being the most promising investment site in Eastern Europe because of its well-developed industry. The country's devastated environment aside, the comments of Dr. Carl Hahn, chairman and CEO of Volkswagen AG, speak volumes about Czechoslovakia's potential as a destination point for foreign capital moving into the New East: "In the 1930's, [Czechoslovakia] was one of the strongest industrial nations in the world....I would have to rate Czechoslovakia as offering one of the best opportunities for manufacturing investment in the world today....The country has managers, engineers, skilled workers, and highly literate people in abundance. For a small country, it has amazing capacities in steel, machine tools, aircraft, and just about anything else."

Foreigners investing in Czechoslovakia can own 100 percent of their enterprises as well as real estate, provided certain requirements are met. Almost all industrial sectors have been opened wide to foreign participation, and 100 percent profit repatriation is permitted. Especially beneficial to foreign managers, the country's labor laws covering hiring and firing of workers seem to be more flexible than elsewhere in Eastern Europe; a worker can be fired with two-month's notice. Privatization has moved quickly. You won't have to sit on your hands waiting for investment approvals, and with concern over the division of the country into two halves now a self-fulfilled prophecy, political stability should become a magnet for fresh foreign investment.

Hungary. Hungary rates high in allowing easy repatriation of profits, a strong "foreign corporate presence," and an open attitude toward foreign ownership of enterprises. American companies have been more active in Hungary than in other countries of the region, attracted by the country's central location and proximity to Vienna, its relatively well-developed business infrastructure in major cities, and the presence of foreign financial services in-country. But Hungary is a small country of only 10 million souls, and it's small geographically, too. Only 10 million people live in Hungary, and 2.5 million of them live in Budapest.

Hungary enjoys a tradition of private commerce, especially in the service sector, which has produced thousands of well-educated entrepreneurs that now seek partnerships with foreigners. Since the mid-1960s, Hungarian individuals have been permitted to own and operate their own businesses and to employ up to four workers. Production services that were allowed to be privatized also included small manufacturing companies.

Poland. Poland excels in allowing foreign ownership of enterprises, easy repatriation, a strong corporate presence, and political stability. Many reasons exist for setting up shop in Poland. First, in five to seven years, Poland will become a member of the EC, which means free trade without tariffs. Second, 300 million people of the former Soviet Union live next door to Poland, and they "need everything." Poland's joint-venture law is probably the most liberal and investment-oriented in the region. It allows for 100 percent participation without any special permit and for 100 percent convertibility of company profits into hard currency. You can convert your zloty profits at the end of the month at the official rate into hard currency and take it out of the country, after taxes. Although social security payments may seem high (you have to pay benefits totaling roughly 60 percent of total wages), when you consider that a worker's total monthly wage is around $300, the total labor bill will be small relative to elsewhere in the developed world. The government is trying to keep a lid on wages in order to hold down inflation, so investors can expect Poland to remain a site for inexpensive labor. Poland has a significant pool of talented people, especially Ph.D.'s in biotechnology and electronic engineering, a formidable natural resource for foreign high-technology businesses to tap into in order to promote and pursue their R&D effort in Eastern Europe at a significant cost savings. The average postdoctoral fellow earns between $500 and $700 a month in Poland.

Moreover, it's easy to set up a wholly owned foreign subsidiary; there are no special permits required unless your venture is in a specialized industry such as law, banking, or insurance. For a manufacturing plant, real estate operation, or hotel, no permit is needed. You simply set up a Polish company with a minimum capitalization of $1,000 and file the paperwork with the local court, all of which takes a total of four to six weeks. The basic corporate tax rate is 40 percent. Special tax credits are available if your total investment is in excess of $2.4 million and the investment increases employment, enhances environmental protection, and brings new technology in to the country. If these four criteria are met, you can apply for a dollar-for-dollar credit; that is, for $2.4 million invested, you would receive a $2.4 million tax credit.

Poland is more industrialized than Hungary but less so than Czechoslovakia. However, Poland possesses more raw resources than Czechoslovakia. Poland will probably become both (1) a site for assembly and processing that uses cheap labor and (2) a center for manufacturing and designing technologically sophisticated products. With Poland's highly skilled and educated scientists and managers, both goals are obtainable. A recent treaty between the EC and Poland, lowering tariffs on products shipped from Poland to Western Europe relative to tariffs on products shipped from the United States directly to Western Europe, adds to the benefit of producing in Poland for sale in Western Europe.

Romania.   After Poland, Romania occupies the next rung on the ladder of overall investment climate rank, with high ratings in number of private enterprises and a light debt burden. Investors in Romania enjoy overall political stability, a welcoming attitude toward foreign investment in most industrial sectors, freedom to repatriate 100 percent of their profits, and the right to own property outright, with the exception that land can only be leased. On the downside, conversion of currency can occur only if the profits equal 8 to 15 percent of the capital invested, workers must be hired locally, and worker negotiation power is significant. Investment approval takes over a month unless you have the right connections. Large-scale privatization of public firms proceeds at a slow pace. Romania has well-developed maritime and river navigation facilities as well as a good railway network. Free trade zones have been set up in Constanta Sud and Sulina port.

Bulgaria.   Bulgaria rates well because it offers low wages, a thriving private sector, and a low cost of doing business. However, its tenuous political climate has delayed massive privatization of state-owned industry. This hurts the country's overall investment climate by limiting the number of public sectors that accept foreign investment. Moreover, investment approval requires the patience of Job. On the bright side, foreigners can own 100 percent of their enterprise and land, if they build on it. Convertibility of current account profits and capital remains limited.

Albania. Investors in Albania can lease but not own land, and they can own 100 percent of an enterprise. Most sectors have been opened to foreign participation, and investors can freely repatriate profits. Albania's overall investment climate is hindered by the country's slow pace of privatization, lack of tax breaks for investors, and most of all, political instability, which, though improved since the victory by the Democrats in 1992, will continue to be shaky, as predicted infighting within the new government takes hold and the potential for Serbian aggression in neighboring Kosovo builds.

Former Soviet Republics. The former Soviet republics have only recently begun to compete for investment dollars. It remains to be seen how actively the newly independent states will seek foreign investors, what their attitude will be toward providing foreigners a role in their economies, and how rapidly they will ratify investment laws. Also unknown is how C.I.S. laws being written (and rewritten) will affect and/or contradict laws enacted in the former republics. One thing is certain: All the former republics pursue their own agendas; thus general statements about investing in the former Soviet Union are utterly meaningless. Some highlights, however, at this early stage of market development in these new countries, can be offered.

- Although *Armenia* has been slow to enact a body of investment law, its electronics and computer industries should attract investor attention, especially members of the Armenian diaspora. Key export industries include trucks, tires, electronics, and instruments, but a number of plants were destroyed in the devastating 1988 earthquake and must be rebuilt. Armenia is currently trying to expand markets for its products in Iran and Turkey and seeking trade pacts with other former republics. The republic is home to the highest of specialists, possessing the highest educational level, of all the former republics. A program to privatize both land and major industries has moved very quickly.

- *Azerbaijan* has recently adopted a body of investment law designed to attract investors mainly in the oil and natural gas industries. If not for war, pogroms, coups, corruption, and both Islamic and communist revivals, the tiny republic might be able to lure Western companies to tap its estimated 4 billion barrels of oil lying offshore in the Caspian Sea. Amid the chaos, Turkish and Iranian business people have forged joint ventures with Azeris, deals often struck between Azeris living in Turkey and Iran and those living in Azerbaijan.

- *Belarus* has moved quickly to ratify investment laws aimed at moving the country's economy into a market-oriented mode of commercial exchange. Foreigners can buy property (but may only lease land) as well as Belarussian companies up for privatization. Tax incentives have been offered, and the country's stable economy and political scene bode well for future investment. However, Belarus has not yet weaned itself of its command economy, in which prices are still fixed. In the near term, change may be forced upon Belarus from outside rather than initiated from within; problems of inflation and joblessness are already spilling over Belarus's borders from adjacent former republics.

- *Estonia* is participating in the investment contest by offering tax incentives and exemptions and permitting investors to own property, including real estate. A handful of firms have been put on the auction block, and large-scale privatization is imminent. One destabilizing factor could be the issue of Estonian citizenry; only 60 percent of the population is Estonian and friction between Russians and Estonians may become intense.

- Georgia is now open to foreign investment and allows foreign purchase and ownership of Georgian companies. Foreign ventures thus far have focused on the oil sector and import-export trading services, many of which involve Georgians now living in the United States. Observers predict that the country's recently elected parliament will move quickly to begin work on a body of investment legislation which will replace preexisting all-union laws currently used to regulate foreign investment and the business activities of foreigners in the country.

- Most locals agree that President Nursultan Nazarbayev is not just a former Communist who has donned a reformist hat. He truly desires to put oil-rich *Kazakhstan* on a road to economic reform in pursuit of a market economy. The Export-Import Bank is there. OPIC is there. Kazakhstan is a member of the IMF and eligible for EBRD loans. Investors should keep a keen eye on oil deals; each megadeal represents regional development projects on a massive scale for which services of all types will be needed.

- Although *Kyrgyzstan* has cast out its past Communist taskmasters, economic stagnation may only worsen as the country's Russian population (22 percent) returns to Russia. This migration will probably encourage Russia to curtail assistance to the newly independent state. Foreign investors will be sought to help, but few will do so.

- *Latvia* has enacted incentive-creating investment legislation that guarantees 100 percent foreign ownership of property, tax incentives, the leasing of land, and 100 percent repatriation. Privatization has also been started, with some initial success, though the number of firms open for acquisition remains low. Also, no one knows how long the animosity that exists between Latvians and Russians (who make up nearly half the country's population) will remain nonviolent.

- *Lithuania* has started an ambitious, if uncomplicated, system of privatization and has taken steps to actively attract foreign investment. However, convertibility of currency remains elusive, there are few tax breaks, and foreign ownership of property and land is limited.

- As a member of the IMF and the World Bank, *Moldova* is attempting to carry forward financial reform and industrial restructuring, as well as encourage foreign investment. Key opportunities will be in infrastructure development (financed by international loans), food processing, and agriculture.

- Investment laws in *Russia* have been liberalized overnight, and this has generated significant new investment from abroad including an estimated 360 joint ventures with U.S. firms by the end of 1992. Approval of investment still comes slow, many sectors exclude foreign investors, and ownership of property and land is limited. However, 100 percent repatriation of earned rubles can be accomplished through exchange and 100 percent ownership of enterprises is allowed under the Russian law on foreign investment of July 1991. Industrial production in Russia fell 8 percent in 1991, and another 13 percent in the first two months of 1992, says the International Monetary Fund (IMF). Retail prices in Russia jumped twofold in 1991, and threefold in January 1992. In February 1992, retail prices rose 40 percent and scarce goods were less scarce—reason for optimism, says the IMF. Political risk continues to loom as the greatest deterrent for investors. The Russian agency for International Cooperation and Development has created a billion dollar program to provide political risk insurance for investors in Russia and also is setting up investment banks in conjunction with major international financial institutions.

- Little investment action has occurred in *Tajikistan*, the most backward of all the former Soviet republics. *Eastern European Investment Monthly* reports, however, that the newly independent state seeks Western investors and has opened the Tadjik Development Agency in London to link foreign investors with Tadjik partners, for a fee.

- *Turkmenistan* will soon launch a program to privatize 75 percent of its industries during the next three years, though the state will maintain ownership of oil, gas, minerals, and agriculture, which- make up 80 percent of the economy. Some favorable laws for investors have been enacted, but little action has ensued as yet; there is currently no direct U.S. investment in the former republic.

- *Ukraine* is being advised by various Western economists to launch its own version of economic "shock therapy," including price liberaliza- tion, budget balancing, and privatization. But the Ukrainian govern- ment has balked, fearing economic chaos. Reforms are moving ahead, but at Ukraine's own pace. A new currency may become convertible, because it will be backed up by a reserve of precious gems and metals.

- Political instability and an absence of new investment law (and the apparatus to enforce them) will keep *Uzbekistan* off the investment road map for some time to come. Economic reform ranks low in pri- ority among the country's often-corrupt and authoritarian former Communist leaders. The trained and educated Russian population (8 percent) is leaving in droves, and economic relations with Russia have become highly charged; at this juncture, trading between the two former republics has virtually ceased. A rising Islamic funda- mentalist-separatist movement in Uzbekistan may be the spark that sets this tinderbox alight.

Pioneering in a Land of Political Perils

The pioneering American companies that have set up inside Fortress Europe can only hope that their competitors will find it difficult to pen- etrate Eastern Europe markets as latecomers. Many American compa- nies will, like most Japanese firms, choose to wait for Eastern Europe's economic crisis to pass and for political stability to return to the region before making financial commitments in the region. Political uncertain- ty is felt more by Fortune 500 companies because they tend to be more sensitive to instability than small companies; their efforts in foreign countries cost more, and their projects generally involve large cash investments. Middle-sized companies with fewer layers of manage- ment to answer to are quicker to react to opening markets and are more aggressive. The smaller the company, the more quickly it can move into countries like those in Eastern Europe; such companies can adjust to the business risk inherent in markets that are politically unstable. Moreover, smaller companies have not necessarily moved into Eastern Europe as part of a wider penetration into Europe's single market; they have gone to Eastern Europe in much the way American firms originally stormed into China in the mid-1980s: to pioneer new markets before the competition catches on. As Eastern Europe opens, they want to be there first; for them, penetrating Western Europe is probably just as hard, if not harder, than penetrating Eastern Europe. Their move into Eastern Europe cannot be said to be a natural evolution from the West to Eastern Europe. These are speculative pioneering ventures. "None of my six clients have been doing business in Western Europe," Andrew L. Kozlowski, an international business attorney with Jennings, Engstrand, & Henrikson in San Diego told me. "They've gone straight into Eastern Europe." This helps to explain why per-venture capital investment is relatively low. The *number* of ventures, however, is far more important than the per-venture dollar investment. A vast array of market-driven joint ventures that happen to be very small in terms of initial investment is far more important to Eastern Europe than three or four big deals. Eastern Europe need microenterprises upon which to base their new capitalist economies. For companies remaining on the fence, the economic and political instability present in Eastern Europe equals palpable business risk. And they are correct. But business risk can be managed. The first step is understanding that the risk of doing business in the New East is inextricably linked to the challenge that each country in Eastern Europe faces in making the changeover from state socialism to capitalism. This "transition," as it's called, should be viewed as the stage upon which any business interaction with the East takes place. We now must set that stage.

Best Prospects for Investment

Hungary

Food processing and packaging
Telecommunications equipment
Tourism
Computers and peripherals
Construction equipment
Medical equipment
Pollution control equipment
Household consumer goods

Czech and Slovak Republics

Computers and peripherals
Pollution control equipment
Computer software and services

Telecommunications equipment
Telecommunications services
Electrical power systems
Information services
Education and manpower training services
Management consulting services
Financial services
Travel and tourism services
Aircraft and parts
Avionics
Medical equipment
Franchising
Accounting services
Drugs and pharmaceuticals
Food processing and packaging equipment
Hotel and restaurant equipment
Renewable energy equipment

Bulgaria

Industrial electronics
Digital machinery
Robotics
Computers
Laser and optics technologies
Biotechnology
Agriculture
Tourism
Chemicals
Household consumer goods
Energy conservation
Pollution control equipment
Food and soft drink processing and packaging
Fast food restaurants
Financial services

Poland

Telecommunications equipment

Food processing and packaging equipment
Management and consulting services
Printing and graphic arts equipment
Pollution control equipment
Air conditioning and refrigerations equipment
Household consumer goods
Computers and peripherals
Electrical power systems.
Hotel and restaurant equipment
Furniture
Sporting goods
Medical equipment
Industrial process controls
Consumer electronics
Travel and tourism services
Automobile parts
Construction equipment
Textile products
Automobiles and light trucks

Romania

Telecommunications equipment
Agricultural machinery and equipment
Agricultural chemicals
Medical equipment
Mining industry equipment
Computers and peripherals
Food processing and packaging equipment
Electrical power equipment
Printing and graphic arts equipment
Pulp and paper machinery
Textile machinery and equipment
Computer software and services
Automotive parts and service equipment
Hotel and restaurant equipment
Security and safety equipment

7

Riding the Waves of "Transition"

Managing Business Risk

As was the case in the People's Republic of China in the mid-1980s, American business has rushed into Eastern Europe and found opportunities somewhat offset by business risks inherent in an environment where much is changing, yet much from the Communist era remains the same. Remnants might include tight ministerial oversight over the economy, vertically oriented bureaucracies, payment of subsidies to nonproductive enterprises to the detriment of productive ones, coddled workers, and managers who must answer to officials outside their factories. Unquestionably, business risk in the New East is inexorably linked to the region's ability to escape its Socialist legacy and enter into the world's capitalist economy. The $64,000 question is: Will Eastern Europe make the transition? The answer is a resounding Yes! But each country will encounter unique challenges along its chosen path.

The Magnitude of the Transition

Glance for a moment at the sheer magnitude of what is under way in former Communist Europe and the former Soviet Union—at what is really meant by what we casually call "privatization": First off, it means creating a suitable institutional framework for a market economy to exist, with all the checks and balances that a Westerner takes for granted, like legal systems, regulatory institutions, and representative organizations. It means removing rigid administrative barriers embedded in ministerial structures left over from Soviet-style state socialism. It means creating an attractive investment climate to bring in the capital needed to rebuild defunct and outmoded industries, whether from venture capitalists or international aid organizations. It means encouraging entrepreneurial thinking and behavior through the intensive retraining of managers, workers, and especially those forming private enterprises, starting with the business ABCs and ending with the most advanced management institutions. It means modernizing the structure and the technical level of production while transforming state enterprises into new private company forms like joint ventures, limited liability companies, and joint stock companies in hopes of improving their productivity and profitability.

We're talking about the sale into private hands of a vast number of state-owned enterprises that together produce the overwhelming majority of productive output in every country of Eastern Europe. In the mid-1980s, the state-owned sector in these economies was almost totally responsible for value-added output, which is a primary indicator of a country's creation of wealth. Ninety-seven percent of value-added productivity was in state hands in East Germany before 1989, for example. Eighty-two percent was in state hands in Poland, and 96 percent in the Soviet Union. Even in Socialist France, the figure is only 17 percent; in capitalist West Germany, it's 11 percent, and in the United States, the figure is 1 percent.

Eastern European countries intend to sell not part, but virtually *all*, of their economies. The number of firms to be privatized dwarfs any privatization attempt that has occurred before. Poland, for instance, has 7,500 state-owned enterprises that account for 75 to 90 percent of the country's industrial output! Czechoslovakia plans to sell 4,800 state-owned enterprises; Hungary has 2,300. In England under Margaret Thatcher, 25 firms were privatized, representing a mere 5 percent of the country's value-added productivity, and that program was an enormous project. In Chile between the years of 1973 and 1989, the biggest privatization undertaking in history entailed the sell-off of only 470 enterprises, which accounted for only 24 percent of value-added productivity in the economy. And many of Chile's privatized firms were only being *returned* to their previous owners after having been nationalized under Salvador Allende, 20 years earlier.

Moreover, an estimated 20 to 30 percent of these enterprises in each country actually require more money to operate than they earn, year in and year out. They *subtract value* from their economies rather than add value. How do you sell a so-called value subtractor enterprise to a private party? In most cases, you can't. These often-monstrous factories will simply have to be dismantled—their debts written off, and their workers relocated. Further, Eastern European citizens lack the disposable cash to buy back state industries from their governments. "The problem," says Vasily Kiselyov, regional deputy of Novosibirsk in Russia, "is how to sell property that belongs to nobody, and has no value, to people who have no money." That's where foreign investors come in. Many of the productive firms have already been sold, however, while the remaining hundreds of large firms sell at a rate of only 10 to 30 firms a year.

That's *10 to 30 firms a year*. Officials in Poland, Hungary, and Czechoslovakia, where 75 to 90 percent of industrial output remains in state portfolios, plan to privatize half of their state-owned enterprises by 1994; at the current pace, that would take *30 to 40 years*. The question is whether the new thousands of small, privately owned service and retail firms can offset the crumbling weight of the literally thousands of manufacturing complexes that will remain in state portfolios for decades to come. The quandary faced by all Eastern European countries is whether to sell enterprises to workers and managers in the form of stock sell-offs and share giveaways or to sell enterprises and their assets to foreign companies for much-needed hard cash with stipulations that foreign technology be brought in, environmental improvements be made, and Western managerial techniques be implemented. In the absence of cash from private citizens and the slowness of foreign investors in acquiring state-owned enterprises, most countries have been impelled to permit so-called spontaneous privatization of enterprises, whereby a company's management oligarchy commandeers the breaking up or selling off of all, or part, of an enterprise placed under its control, often "selling" the enterprise into its own hands. At first privatizations by managers or officials, or any other individuals who stand up and pronounce themselves in charge, took place in large numbers. Then the governments responded by setting up state privatization agencies to keep manager-barons from selling their enterprises to the highest bidder and instead encourage them to sell to new owners who would retool the business, train workers, find new markets for products, and bring in advanced technology.

Spontaneous privatization can best be characterized as one part theft (whereby managers obtain de facto control of an enterprise theoretically owned by the people) and one part reform (whereby they enter a position in which they can make the assets placed at their disposal more productive). In one deal, writes John Thor Dahlburg in *The Los*

Angeles Times, "Takeover artists crafted a mega-deal, worth a billion rubles or more, that would have won them control of a big chunk of the former Soviet military-industrial complex, including a Moscow air base. The resulting conglomerate, called Kolo, would reportedly have been able to make everything from samovars for brewing tea to satellites and rockets capable of orbiting the Earth." Those behind the deal to siphon off state assets were party functionaries-turned-capitalists— high-ranking officials of the now-defunct and banned Communist party Central Committee. Valery A. Makharadze, chief state inspector in the Commonwealth of Independent States (C.I.S.), is in charge of preventing surreptitious management buyouts of enterprises in the C.I.S. Unfortunately, this agency has only 90 staff members for its operations in *all* of Russia.

What Each Country Is Trying to Do

Each country in Eastern Europe has pursued its own transition strategy; they all, however, pursue similar objectives. First, they try to control inflation with austere budgetary and monetary policy by curtailing the issuance of credit, reducing state subsidies, restructuring the banking system, and reforming taxation policy. Second, they try to reduce state ownership of assets and property and put in place legal guarantees so that all types of ownership will be treated equally. Private enterprises, joint stock companies, and foreign-invested enterprises must be legalized and properly regulated with new and enforceable law. Existing state-owned enterprises, which maintain the dominant position in the economy, must be largely denationalized via privatization by allowing domestic and foreign equity participation. Third, state-set prices must be liberalized, especially prices of foodstuffs, fuel, and rents—the traditional areas where state subsidies were used to maintain artificially low prices. Fourth, government command over the economy, including enterprise inputs and outputs, must be abolished, and ministries must be trimmed down and made to focus on phasing-out Socialist-style programs while creating incentives for entrepreneurship. Fifth, state monopolies on foreign trade must be broken and foreign-trade corporations must be made to produce a profit or fold. Foreign investment must be allowed to flow freely, and import barriers must be brought down. Internal convertibility of the currency has to be achieved in order to translate all trade into the language of world prices. The sixth, and probably the most difficult task, is to set up the necessary functioning institutions of a market-based economy, including banks, regulatory agencies, employment agencies, commercial courts, stock exchanges, and trade promotion offices. All these changes must be carried out without overtaxing citizens or newly formed businesses, which would only flatten growth. Russian private enterprises, for example, already pay out a monstrous 60 to 70 percent of their income for taxes, fees (e.g., telephone "registration"), and protection against criminal elements.

"Shock Therapy"—the Approach of Choice. Policymakers grappled with three basic options in designing their transition tactics. One option envisioned an American-style free-market capitalism. Another was a social democracy à la Sweden. Last, policymakers considered a managed mercantalism like Japan, Inc. Everyone agreed on the objective of transition from socialism to market capitalism; they differed, however, on the question of modus operandi. The so-called shock therapy approach, rather than one in which reforms would be initiated in sequence, gradually, won the day. Industry would be privatized quickly through the auction of enterprises to the highest bidder. Prices would be liberated and currencies devalued. Private business would be given every advantage and incentive to generate new wealth. Citizens suffering the impact of inflation and job loss would be asked to endure a few years of hardship, and later enjoy the fruits of capitalism. Government policymakers hoped that they could end-run predicted political opposition by carrying out reforms as fast as possible, by actively promoting a private class of job-creating entrepreneurs in hopes that their new incomes would "trickle down" to those being disenfranchised by privatization.

The hoped-for economic upturn came more slowly than anyone expected, however. The past egalitarianism of Socialism was suddenly and savagely transformed into a nasty strain of social Darwinism; those who couldn't take advantage of privatization opportunities began to starve. Recipients of disability payments slipped through gashes in social safety nets. In came the international banking community to the rescue, including the International Monetary Fund (IMF), the World Bank, and the newly formed Bank of European Reconstruction and Development. The 1989 Support Eastern Europe Democracy (SEED) Act in the United States initiated the setting up of enterprise funds to support democracy in Eastern Europe through the funding of private ventures there.

One crucial event, I believe, exemplifies the new relationship between the democracy-promoting capitalist West and the emergent New East. Fred Zeder and Howard Hills, representing the Overseas Private Investment Corporation (OPIC), went to Gdansk to meet with Lech Walesa at Solidarity's world headquarters in 1990. Walesa was very animated and enthusiastic in his presentation to Ambassador Zeder about the fact that, in his view, Great Britain, the United States, France, Italy, the Group of Seven (G-7) countries—were like a group of bicycle racers in a race. They were in a pack, and they wouldn't open up and let Poland come into the pack. He went on in this vein, talking about the need for Poland to have an opportunity to enter the competition, and of the need for the developed countries to help Poland. Howard Hills was impressed by Walesa, but his boss, Fred Zeder (says Hills), "felt that he owed it to Lech Walesa to do more than just sit and listen."

Zeder interrupted the translator, says Hills, and said to Lech Walesa: "Listen, it may be true that the developed countries are like bicycle racers who are in a pack and won't let Poland in, but Poland won't have a chance to break into the pack as long as it's riding a rusty old bicycle built by the Communists. You need to get a *new* bicycle if you're going to compete with the developed countries. You've got to get a banking system in here. You've got to get some financial infrastructure in here. Some accounting. Some valuation. You've got to move into the modern world of business and market economics." Lech Walesa agreed that financial and business infrastructure needed to be put into the country and went on to talk about the importance of having OPIC come in. In response to that, Ambassador Zeder said, "In telling me you want OPIC in your country, you are preaching to the choir." The translator thought about that one for a minute and then explained it to Lech Walesa, who threw his head back in a roar of laughter and clutched Zeder in a bear hug.

East and West were coming to terms.

However, before lending desperately needed capital, the lending institutions of the West set conditions on Eastern Europe's economic policymakers. For example, they demanded that a certain percentage of these economies be privatized at a specific rate, that prices be decontrolled, and that government loans and subsidies to enterprises and to underprivileged citizens be significantly cut back. Interest rates of 50 to 60 percent were set to tighten money supplies and curtail inflation, and yet these same rates starved enterprises of capital. Never mind the masses, who had depended on state subsidies for decades. Never mind the swelling legions of jobless. Or the public outcry. In each country, "transition" became a gladitorial game of Beat the Political Clock. Consolidate reforms, obtain loans from Western lending institutions—all before the populace bled too much. Beat political fragmentation due to discontent. Beat a possible Communist backlash. Beat worker strikes. Even humanist Vaclav Havel gave in to his shock therapist finance minister, Vaclav Klaus, to initiate privatization reforms rapidly in order to obtain international assistance.

The "transition" took the form mainly of mushrooming new private enterprises. Over 1 million private businesses formed in Eastern Europe during the 15 months after the Berlin Wall crumbled. "Before, you couldn't shop on Sunday because no place would be open," said university professor Tadeusz Slawek, who lives in Cyzszyn, Silesia, as we strolled by the storefronts on the medieval town square. "Now you can, and there are no shortages." We walked through the small town with his 16-year-old son and talked about "ground-floor capitalism," a term referring to the way Poles whitewash the first floor of their apartments and open storefront businesses. Small retail businesses, filled with televisions from Korea, VCRs from Japan, furniture from Finland, and condiments from France, now fight for attention along Cyzszyn's narrow lanes. Though private enterprises in trade and retail sectors have formed quickly and have generated growth, the question remains, What is to be done with the large state-owned enterprises that foreigners won't buy? How do you distribute the assets of a country in which there is no capital? And how do you do so fairly and to the benefit of all? This issue has generated some extraordinarily creative schemes throughout the region. The basic approach has been to give large enterprises to the people by issuing funny money (vouchers) so that they can purchase shares in these companies.

For many leaders in Eastern Europe, however, the bear hug with the West became, in reality, a choke hold. As the negative social impacts of shock therapy took hold, it became clear that the Swedish model (where most industry is in private hands, but the government maintains strong social and economic regulation of the economy) could become the alternative of choice for Eastern European governments, which must face either the IMF or an angry and politically well-organized population that votes its stomach.

Privatization Scorecard

Czech and Slovak Republics

The Czechs freed 85 percent of their country's prices in 1991 and made the kroner convertible for business. Most, if not all, trade barriers have been lifted and tariffs on competing goods are few. However, the country's private sector still accounts for only 2 percent of gross domestic product (GDP) and only 6,000 state shops have been auctioned off. The pace of sales of large state-owned behemoths has proceeded painfully slowly and plans to open a stock market are on hold. Many Czechoslovakians sought to reclaim land and property nationalized in 1948. This has slowed down privatization since real ownership cannot be granted until past owners have had a chance to make their claims. Small companies were auctioned, and large ones were sold via a voucher system; yet small shops and restaurants were auctioned with only a two-year lease to the property.

The Czech and Slovak republics' voucher system for privatization of state-owned industry is the most innovative privatization scheme in the region. Each citizen can purchase a booklet of coupons worth the equivalent of $35 (one week's salary), or 1,000 points, to be converted into shares in companies. The person can "invest" the coupons during two huge auctions in state-owned companies of his or her choice; 1,492 firms are on the auction block. Each share will "cost" three points at the start. When all the shares are distributed, a stock market will be set up and citizens will be permitted to trade shares as stockholders in firms and to turn their shares into cash. Ultimately, the companies that nobody invests in will wither and sell off their assets to budding entrepreneurs. The ones that receive investment will prosper. The wealth of the republic will thus be transferred to individual shareholders.

The question remains, however, Where will *real* money come from to buy new equipment? Foreign investors? It's possible, but the flow of investment to Czechoslovakia has been glacial in relation to the country's immediate needs. Moreover, foreigners are locked out of the first round of company auctions, though many Germans have gotten around this by investing through their family members living in the Sudetenland. If the plan works, the Czech Republic will look like the American model, in which investment is raised through markets, rather than the Japan-German model, in which funds are raised by banking institutions that also guide and direct their credit firms.

Poland Leads the Way

Poland's economic Big Bang was detonated in January 1990. With inflation and a black market in zloty fueling public discontent about the transition to capitalism, Poland's minister of finance, Balcerowicz, cut the money supply by curtailing loans and wage hikes. The black market disappeared, and the zloty stabilized. Inflation plummeted. The Poles set up the Warsaw Stock Exchange, sold off or leased over 60,000 state shops, and started privatizing state-owned factories through liquidation, management buyouts, joint ventures with foreign companies, and foreign acquisition. About 20 enterprises per week moved into private hands, mostly via management buyout or spontaneous privatization. Over 1.2 million registered private businesses now employ over 2.7 million people. Private interests now hold over 70 percent of the retail sector. Roughly 15 percent of Poland's economy is now in private hands; the figure was 5 percent only three years ago.

The Poles are poised to launch a voucher system, too, but not as fast as the Czechs have. Poland has set up mutual funds to buy up shares in privatized companies and maintain oversight of their performance; later, shares will be sold to individual shareholders. The Poles want to distribute shares in actual funds run by banks; the masses won't be entering ownership positions, as in Czechoslovakia. The Polish system emphasizes management of firms, rather than fast distribution of their assets to individual stockholders. Worker councils, however, are so powerful in Poland that one half reject placing their enterprises in the privatization program at all, since they realize that such a move bodes layoffs of workers. All adult Poles receive equal shares, and trading of shares is set to begin in 1993.

Hungary

The privatization achievements of Hungary rival those of Poland. Hungary has sold off about 10 percent of its state-owned sector. The private sector now accounts for 20 to 25 percent of GDP. Foreign investment has rushed in, nearly $1 billion of it involved in the privatization of over 50,000 Hungarian companies. Trade barriers and tariffs on competing products have all but been removed. Prices have been liberalized across the board.

Hungary has pursued none of the above-mentioned voucher systems to redistribute wealth and assets; it has followed a decentralized reorganization of property whereby ownership of firms has been transferred to limited-liability companies. These companies are, in turn, owned by other companies or banks, both private and state-owned.

Hungary currently has plans to privatize 2,180 companies; the government has approved the sale of 380 of them, worth $400 million. Only a handful of companies, however, have actually been sold as of this writing; the others have been corporatized but are still owned by the government. Roughly 90 percent of the enterprises in Hungary remain state-owned. The government wants to reduce this figure by another 20

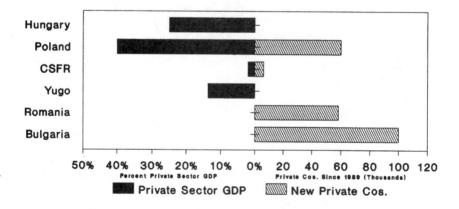

Astounding growth in new private companies and in number of economies led by private enterprise (late 1992).

percent, but this may be a pipe dream since foreigners want to buy only factories that operate. A stumbling block to selling state shops has been the question of who owns the real estate and who has the authority, therefore, to sell it.

Romania

Sweeping reform has been slow to take hold in Romania, but there is no doubt about the initiative of Romania's entrepreneurs, who have formed 58,375 private enterprises in a country where virtually none existed before. However, of these private companies, the lion's share (31,931) employ fewer than 5 wage earners and operate primarily in the service sector. Those employing 5 to 20 workers number 16,573, and those employing 21 to 50 workers number 9,281; only 60 private enterprises in Romania employ more than 100 workers.

The prices of goods and services necessary for subsistence, such as rents, energy, and basic foods, remain fixed in Romania. However, little government debt burdens the country because Nicolae Ceausescu's government sapped the country's economy dry in order to repay nearly all of it before liberation.

Bulgaria

Bulgarian reformers have liberalized most prices, excluding 13 basic foods and the cost of transportation, while reeling in inflation to 1.8 percent annually. Although the lev has been allowed to float, Bulgaria's currency remains only partly convertible. State-owned commercial banks have begun operation, exports are climbing as interest rates come down, and over 100,000 private businesses have sprouted since 1990, mostly small companies involved in trade and services. Import tariffs remain high, but restrictions on imports and foreign investment are gone. Unfortunately, Bulgaria shoulders an enormous annual government deficit, amounting to 13 percent of its gross domestic product (GDP). A populace which fears the hardship that shock therapy entails has stymied sweeping reform; the recent reelection of the country's "go-slow" leadership expressed this trepidation.

Russia

Boris Yeltsin clearly desires to follow the "cold shower" route trailblazed by Poland, eschewing transitional policy in favor of an immediate, mandated transfer to market-oriented economics. The attempts of economic reformer Yegor T. Gaidar to liberalize prices, convert the ruble, curtail inflation, and auction off state property mirror Poland's policy exactly. Shops and stores are set to be auctioned off first, to be purchased by consortiums of workers or entrepreneurs. The plan, which *The Los Angeles Times* has termed a "forced march to a market economy" that could push down living standards in Russia by 30 percent—calls for the elimination of government subsidies for consumer goods and the consequent freeing of prices, the privatization of thousands of state-owned enterprises, and the breakup of most of Russia's 24,000 state and collective farms. Russia has already created 128,000 private firms.

Moreover, Russia has implemented its own voucher system, based on the laissez-faire system of the Czechs. Each citizen receives 10,000 rubles worth of coupons to use to bid on shares of enterprises sold at public auction. Most people hardly understand the system and prefer to play the lottery or gamble at a casino, but at the public sales of state-owned enterprises, some "investors" do plunk down hundreds of vouchers on a single company, vouchers they have obviously obtained through healthy speculation. However, with inflation rising 1 percent per day, it's presumed that most Russians will want to part with their 10,000 ruble vouchers sooner rather than later, before they become worthless. Dividends will be paid at the end of 1993 to investors of profitable companies. Land does *not* come with shares, but it *may* in the future, predict hardcore speculators. To prevent takeovers, initial bidders are limited to 5 percent of a company's shares. A voucher system has also been started in Lithuania, where officials hope to privatize 20 to 30 percent of state-owned industrial assets in the near term.

In January 1992 six republics of the commonwealth were admitted to full membership in the IMF and the World Bank, which furthered Yeltsin's drive toward free-market reform by giving the former republics access to billions of dollars in development loans. Yeltsin has shown that he is willing to forgo central control over the old command economy, share financial data about the commonwealth economy, and accept institutional oversight—all requirements for membership in the funds.

Ominous Outcomes of Shock Therapy

Shock therapy's negatives directly affect the risk of doing business in the region. It's not hard to see why. Eastern European governments were forced to adopt the Western notion that private capitalist entrepreneurial endeavor must be the prime mover of an economy. In so doing, they upheld an ideology that victimized their countries more than it helped them, at least in the short term. Incipient governments faced a boomerang effect as public dissatisfaction grew and elections were held.

First, while the masses demanded equality and fairness, the gap widened between rich and poor. Overnight, thousands became paupers. For example, Poles lost one third of their purchasing power in the 12 months after liberation from communism as inflation rose throughout the region (Fig. 7-1). Average GDP for Bulgaria, Czechoslovakia, Hungary, Poland, and Romania fell 8 percent in 1990 and another 8 percent in 1991; industrial production in these countries fell 17 percent in 1990 and 11 percent in 1991. Although former East Germany has probably hit bottom in terms of output, production is

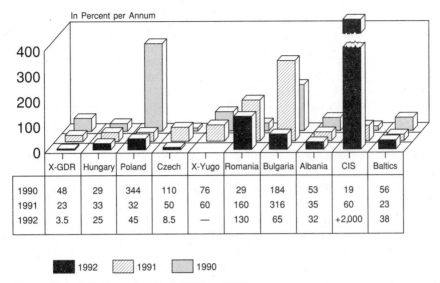

	X-GDR	Hungary	Poland	Czech	X-Yugo	Romania	Bulgaria	Albania	CIS	Baltics
1990	48	29	344	110	76	29	184	53	19	56
1991	23	33	32	50	60	160	316	35	60	23
1992	3.5	25	45	8.5	—	130	65	32	+2,000	38

■ 1992 ▨ 1991 ☐ 1990

Figure 7-1. Inflation rates from 1990 to 1992.

still declining in the other countries while unemployment soars. Two thirds of the working population in East Germany is underemployed or unemployed. Over a million Poles have lost their jobs, and in Hungary, one out of ten people is now jobless (Fig. 7-2). It didn't take long for Eastern Europeans to see that in capitalist countries a signifi-

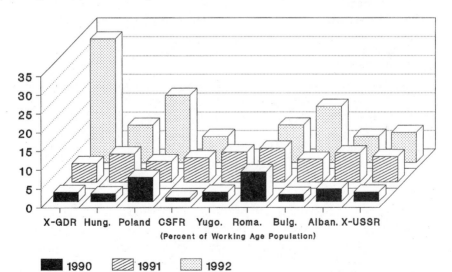

■ 1990 ▨ 1991 ☐ 1992

Figure 7-2. Eastern Europe's joblessness grows: Percent unemployed from 1990 to 1992.

cant percentage of the population doesn't "make it" without safety nets, regulations, and controls—for example, the old, the handicapped, and the very young. Market forces have split Eastern European societies into two camps: Those who must watch out for their jobs because they're employed by state industries, and those who can't make it because they've been fired and have fallen through the cracks. These people never intended to be entrepreneurs: Often they're pensioners. The few rich people drive Porsches and Mercedes, and growing numbers of people live in the streets. While one third of all Russians suddenly found themselves living below the poverty line, the Moscow business weekly *Commersant* estimates that 3 million Russians now earn monthly incomes between $500 and $1,000, while 90,000 Russians earn over $2,000 a month.

"There are two parallel Moscows now," writes David Brooks in *The Wall Street Journal,* "the red ruble Moscow of shortages and queues and the green dollar Moscow of high octane gasoline and cellular phones." Only dollars will buy high-quality imported goods or goods in scarce supply. Those who have green *bakks*—mostly *biznessmeni* and mafiosi—hang out at the new casinos and discos taking in the floor shows, while those earning in rubles pawn what they own on street corners to survive the reforms.

During the first flush of liberation, those who spoke about inequalities were labeled proto-Communists. To mention the gashed safety net implied that you wanted to impede market forces and the implementation of a market economy. "Suddenly," says Ray Shoenholtz, "you had Lech Walesa to the right of Ronald Reagan. Walesa's whole attitude is, `Let's strip the whole edifice of regulatory [measures] and let market forces go.'" The result was predictable. People can't pay their rent or buy food.

The old and infirm are discriminated against in the hiring practices of new private enterprises as well. Many help-wanted ads in Prague newspapers, for instance, state bluntly that you need not apply if not "under 30, good-looking, and speak a foreign language." The result: the total disenfranchisement of the older generation. The legions of homeless now roaming the streets of Prague are 50 percent elderly people.

Strikes and Insolvency.   Other results of subjecting enterprises to market forces have been, and will continue to be, bankruptcy and strikes. All the countries of the region are putting in place bankruptcy law, since many enterprises will not survive. Thus far, Russia has not allowed enterprises to fold—because of the political price tag—but if reform proceeds, eventually it will. Already, workers are intolerant of taking on additional hardship. Labor unions in Moscow say that 90 percent of the city's massive defense plants, most already virtually bankrupt, now face imminent strikes. Meanwhile, state enterprises in the C.I.S. chug along on state subsidies, running up debts, between January 1992 and July 1992, of 2 trillion rubles, close to $20 billion. They buy and sell from each other using IOUs instead of cash in the hope that Yeltsin will give in and bale them out. To survive politically, he may have to.

Political Fragmentation. In reaction to the impacts of shock therapy, political parties emerged throughout the region which addressed the widening social maladjustments, all supported by few but fervent supporters. Over 100 political parties sprouted in Poland; 60 arose in Czechoslovakia. By mid-1993, Lech Walesa himself was *publicly* denouncing the party he formed—Solidarity trade union—because it refused to support his alliance of independent groups in elections held in September 1993. Coalitions fell apart as readily as they were formed, and voters grew disgruntled and cynical, expressing their cynicism by avoiding the voting booth. Typically, only 35 percent of the people vote in Eastern European countries, and when they do vote, their vote is widely splintered.

The final outcome of shock therapy has been the pressures it has brought to bear on the region's fledgling democracies, which are extremely fragile. Eastern Europe's newly erected democratic institutions have no experience with the kind of enormous social fragmentation taking place there; market forces have put huge pressure on these institutions, and they could simply cave in and stop functioning—representing not only risk to the business person in the region but also political risk for Europe in general. Already, Russians are losing faith in Yeltsin, and in government generally. *Nesarisi Maya Gazet,* a Moscow newspaper, conducted a survey in late 1992 and found that 68 percent of the Russians it questioned don't trust the government. William G. Hyland writes in *Foreign Affairs:* "One can hope that Russia will break with its history and firmly implant the roots of democracy. But more likely is the eventual revival of an autocratic state, probably well armed and potentially hostile toward its neighbors....It is also foolish to believe that out of chaos and crisis will come a well-ordered market." Ominously, Kazakhstan voted recently to transform itself into a free-market economy, but the players, from Nursultan Nazarbayev on down, are former Communists, rather than emerging democrats. Ukraine became independent, but who's ruling it now? A former Communist party member. In Lithuania's first election since independence, in October 1992, a parliament controlled by "reform-minded" former Communists was elected. In public opinion polls commissioned by the U.S. Information Agency in Poland in the early 1990s, one could see the waning public support for economic shock therapy in hard numbers.

Although 56 percent of Poles supported fast reform in early 1990, only 30 percent did in late 1990, and only 17 percent by mid-1991. By that time, 72 percent preferred gradual reform. Sixty percent of now-cynical Poles no longer take the time to express their opinion in public elections.

The situation is most precarious in Russia, where opposition to privatization, in the form of 400 mostly women protesters, appeared during Russia's first company privatization auction in late 1992: They shouted, "Shame, shame" at then-economic minister Gaidar and other officials. "The government is forcing us into classes again, and it will be the owners versus the employees, the merchants versus the consumers, the haves versus the have-nots. Prices will be raised to increase profits....Simply and clearly, the people as a whole will suffer," said Irina Krasnikova, a schoolteacher in Gorky, to a *New York Times* reporter. A poll conducted by the newpaper *We/MbI* of 1,012 Russians in 12 cities in August 1992 showed that only 37 percent of Russian citizens wanted the reforms to be continued. About one third wanted to return to a planned economy, and the last third "didn't know." Public contempt for market-oriented reform is in essence a business risk, since it could slow or stop the process of market opening and the welcoming of foreign investment.

Why Has Large-Scale Privatization Failed?

"Every Eastern European country has failed, and failed significantly, to find new owners for state-owned enterprises," concluded Harvard economist Jeffrey Sachs recently. Why has the process of large enterprise conversion been so slow, painful, and piecemeal, one enterprise at a time? Why are Latin American countries generally succeeding with privatization while the transition in the East moves so slowly, even with price liberalization, more stable currencies, and more open trade? The answer, in part, is that foreign investment has failed to materialize in the East. Chile, Mexico, and Argentina lured $7.8 billion in foreign investment in 1991 alone, while Czechoslovakia, Hungary, and Poland together netted only $2.2 billion. Also, Eastern European enterprises lost 60 percent of their trade after the collapse of Comecon (the Warsaw Pact trade organization), and European Community (EC) countries have refused to accept their most competitive products—namely, steel, textiles, and agricultural products. Five underlying factors should be considered in trying to place blame for Eastern Europe's slow transformation.

1. *The quality of existing enterprises to be sold.*   First and foremost, the

hitch in carrying out massive overnight privatization in Eastern Europe comes from the fact that most of the large state-owned plants for sale are, in reality, hollow behemoths. The problem with these companies isn't the workers, or even the products they produce, which could be improved and sold on the open market. The problem, investors have found, is the factory, and its surrounding industrial structure. Typically the factory area suffers heavy pollution. Its production lines don't use robotics. There's no computer system. Internal telephone lines don't function. Electrical systems are shot. Moreover, enterprises carry more debt than the value of their assets; to purchase these companies is akin to buying the right to lose money. Quite succinctly, often there's *nothing there to buy.*

Only a small percentage of Eastern Europe's factories can be said to "operate," in Western terms. So foreign investors have sought to "buy the raisins and leave the cake," as the Hungarians complain. Here's an example: A factory complex in Hungary produces trucks, gear shifts for buses, machine tools, and bicycles. Of all the company's divisions, only the bicycle division is profitable. Schwinn comes in and buys the bicycle unit, but only the bicycle unit. Schwinn doesn't care about the rest of the company's divisions. It just wants the bicycle unit, and the Hungarian managers agree to sell it. The outcome is reflected all across the region: the Hungarian company soon finds itself with only its nonproductive divisions, while continuing to need and receive state subsidies to pay its remaining workers, who for the most part now sit around waiting for orders that will never materialize. (The trucks and gearshifts that the company produced had been shipped to the Soviet Union before the Wall came down.) Layoffs and plant closings are the result.

2. *Bureaucratic inertia.* A completely new group of high government officials have taken over from Communists in all the countries of Eastern Europe. But in the next level of the bureaucracy, many of the players are the same as they were before 1989. The progression toward becoming a market economy is often halted by the self-preservation needs of these elites. Are these people stalling the privatization process simply because they are former party people? No. They occupy important positions, but so do nonparty people who might be just as much a force of inertia. Everybody behaves in a self-preserving manner, regardless of party affiliation. It's not *political* resistance in any respect; it's simply that they want to hold on to what they've got.

3. *The need to look out for workers.* One problem in most, but not all, countries of Eastern Europe is that privatization authorities have worked to prevent workers and managers from receiving shares in newly private companies, creating few incentives for workers and man-

agers to increase the value of their companies. This has created a grand canyon of political disagreement between the people in official positions of power and the workers and managers—people who are needed by political people as allies in order to implement economic reforms. The cleavage between labor and new owners (that is, the ministries of privatization) is most conspicuous in Poland presently, but the dynamic has taken hold throughout the region. Poland's liberation was initiated by its industrial working class in the form of Solidarity. Workers in Poland's state-run industries are represented by councils that have the right to hire and fire managers and snuff out privatization deals affecting their companies. Solidarity fears mass privatization of large enterprises will lead to *Nomenklatura* privatization. Privatization officials have found, however, that looking out for workers' interests has a high price tag because foreign investors shun deals that involve stipulations that they will maintain a large, unproductive work force.

4. *An intransigent "Socialist mindset."* "We have no problems with our economy or our politics," says Polish entrepreneur Dariusz Linert, "but we have a problem with the mentality of our people." The Communist party no longer exists, but Eastern Europeans were trained to believe in whoever speaks up. Leaders have been trained to usurp authority and tell people what to do. The masses have been trained to accept that authority and not ask questions. The typical Eastern European tends to look *up* for solutions, not *within.* Eastern Europeans are typically not ambitious or entrepreneurial, and this is understandable. What they had they were given by the state. They were given jobs, their possessions, their apartments for free. At the same time, they're envious of a neighbor who has more than they do. People once took pride in not allowing others to slip through the social net. The reverse side of the coin, however, was that possessing ambition and initiative was cause for ostracism, was to flirt with becoming an outcast. To excel, if not done strictly to benefit everyone, was considered immoral, even criminal. With the opening of these societies, however, Eastern Europeans now want what they have been denied, but few acknowledge that they will have to work for it. The Russians, says Barbara Chronowski, a professor of marketing who lectures in the former Soviet Union, have a profound sense of *entitlement.* They believe, like most Eastern Europeans, that Westerners have had a high standard of living for a long time, and now it's time for them to have it, too. Moreover, many Russians feel that the West should hand over its high standard of living, free of charge. East Germans saw on television that the West Germans were wealthy, but they didn't believe it. Now that they have seen that the wealth and modernization are real, they want the accoutrements of the West German lifestyle given to them on a platter; they're

resentful that these trappings are not being made available to them quickly. Meanwhile, their expectations have created a deep current of resentment among West Germans, who view the *Osis* as ungrateful, spoiled, and lazy. What people in the East tend to forget, they say, is that the West Germans did not build their country into an economic powerhouse in a year, or a decade, or a generation. It took 40 years.

Most Eastern Europeans remain innately risk-averse and unwilling to break out on their own, in great measure because they fear disengaging from the gift horse of the state. For decades, the typical Czech has supplemented his or her $200 to $300 monthly salary by moonlighting at other jobs. For instance, a worker at a state-owned dairy might earn an additional $600 a month as a part-time veterinarian. However, the worker would not consider this activity a "business," per se. The worker offers a value-added service and charges more than the state would charge but doesn't keep books, doesn't have a license…is not a *business person.* Few people really wanted to "go into business for themselves," as a full-time endeavor. "What if I fail," they might think. Says Duane Best, who has worked in Prague and studied Czechs at the first stage of capitalism, this "mindset will take five to ten years to change."

5. *Lack of financial support for private enterprise.*   Even if mass-privatization schemes result in the sale of Eastern European enterprises, they alone won't create genuine market economies. An efficient financial industry, the armature of capitalism, will still be absent. Decentralized market-oriented economies work well only when supported by financial institutions, including commercial banks, savings banks, investment banks, stock and bond markets, and foreign exchanges. Healthy companies need capital to modernize, and new private enterprises need capital to start up. Where will the capital come from, when state-owned banks are under tremendous debt burdens and stock markets are only embryonic? One approach has been to form commercial banks, separate from state-owned central banks, that can loan money to private enterprises. Ironically, these private banks are skittish about lending money to any enterprise that is *not* state-owned, and interest rates on commercial loans are surreal, 186 percent in Russia, for example.

Western observers have suggested privatizing state-owned banks throughout the region, but there are problems. These banks carry huge numbers of bad loans to state enterprises, many now near total collapse. Their portfolios must be cleaned before they can be sold to private interests. Their past loans were made according to state plans, not based on the ability of the enterprise to repay. Many loans made were not secured, and many were low interest and long term. New loans would have to be made at high interest rates to remedy past losses.

Controlling the Risks of Doing Business in Eastern Europe

Considering all that I've said about "transition" in the East, the Western investor has to realize that although the pendulum of change has been swinging in the direction of market reform since 1989, it could reverse direction at any time unexpectedly. Eastern Europeans have found that foreign investment is no magic bullet for solving their economic problems. By 1995, the region should be attracting $7 billion a year in direct investment and should have received a total of over $20 billion in loans from aid agencies and private banks. But all of this, Eastern Europeans now realize, will have little impact on what are embedded structural problems. The promise of foreign joint venturing may leave the masses with a bad taste in the mouth about dealing with foreign companies at all.

One has to anticipate that in any Eastern European area in which one has invested, the political environment is such that the local population could suddenly begin to *blame* foreign investors for somehow causing their country's problems. At any moment, anywhere in this economically ravaged area, citizens could begin to balk at welcoming foreign investors as potential saviors of their economies and begin to view them as perpetrators of their problems. One can certainly expect a psychological letdown in regard to foreign investment since it has flowed into the region at a vexingly slow rate. It remains possible that the region's complaints to the West about the slow rate of investment could turn to caustic words blaming the West for the failure of reform in the region, with the finger pointing at investment already in the region as being exploitative rather than helpful to the region's modernization. This scenario presents a palpable business risk to the foreign investor in the region.

Forms of Business Risk

In Eastern Europe, one must come to grips with three distinct forms of business risk.

Sociopolitical Risk.   Austere economic reforms may lower standards of living and end social welfare programs; jobs and subsidies and employment benefits may end and cause political strife: All this, collectively seen as a consequence of the end of communism and the transition to capitalism, spells sociopolitical risk to foreign businesses. Economies may become monopolized by private interests instead of public ones. This may create a public outcry against any faster move toward a market economy. If the number of people falling through the "social safety net" continues to grow, the number of underprivileged Eastern Europeans who turn against foreign enterprise altogether may grow, too.

Regulatory Risk. A cellular phone company offered phone cards to foreign business people in Moscow so that they could make 3- to 5-minute international calls from a special booth without having to wait the typical 48 hours. Although the Ministry of Telecommunications approved the service, when it saw how much foreign exchange the foreign company was raking in ($70 per phone card sold), it annulled the agreement. Call it "regulatory risk"—the changing of investment, tax, import, currency rates, and labor laws that can spell disaster for a fledgling venture.

Geopolitical Risk. The secession of the Slovak Republic from the Czech Republic; civil war in the former Yugoslavia and the tenuous independence of its republics; Romania's tensions with Hungary over disputed territory in Transylvania; and violence in the separatist Abkhazian region of Georgia are all tremors in the geopolitical landscape of Eastern Europe that can negatively affect foreign enterprise. HNC's venture in Belgrade is a case in point. Since war broke out in former Yugoslavia, its computer distribution joint venture, says HNC Chairman Robert Hetch-Nielsen, "has apparently gone dormant. The orders have stopped coming in, though they still want to be distributors." The company's chief sales consultant in charge of helping customers make final purchase decisions decided, "for personal reasons," to return to the United States for a while, says Hetch-Nielsen, "to avoid being bombed." At this writing, Hetch-Nielsen was predicting that his company's activities would survive intact, but for the time being, interrepublic trade for the distributor had ceased.

Managing Business Risk

To gauge long-term business risk in a formal risk analysis of a specific country, look at five impacts of transition:

1. The direction and momentum of reform policies

2. The intransigence of obstacles, both economic and managerial

3. The impact of reforms on social welfare, i.e., standard of living, employment, and cost of living

4. The attitude of the populace toward foreign-invested enterprises and investment in general

5. The strength of emerging democratic institutions, e.g., chambers of commerce and trade unions

The prudent investor should also investigate political risk insurance in the interest of protecting investments.

Insuring Your Investments.   The Overseas Private Investment Corporation (OPIC) works with the private political-risk industry and with the U.S. private sector to develop strategies for managing cross-border risk. The particular forms of coverage that OPIC offers generally are not the same as the insurance that can be procured from the private political-risk insurance companies, which provide three types of coverage. The first is a 20-year policy covering the risk of war, insurrection, political violence, expropriation or nationalization, and inconvertibility of currency. If your company is earning profits in a local currency and finds that it cannot obtain or repatriate hard currency by going to the country's central bank, OPIC will exchange your local currency for dollars. Many businesses have found this coverage to be critical to their success in Eastern European markets. In Hungary alone OPIC-insured projects amount to over $188 million, with $141 million of coverage for General Electric investment in Tungsram. For more information, contact:

Overseas Private Investment Corporation
1615 M Street, NW
Washington, DC 20527
Tel: (202) 336-8400
Fax: (202) 872-9306

The Multilateral Investment Guarantee Agency (MIGA) of the World Bank provides insurance against risks similar to that offered by OPIC. For more information, contact:

Multilateral Investment Guarantee Agency (MIGA)
1818 H Street, NW
Washington, DC 20433
Phone: (202) 473-5419

Finding a Safe Niche: Linking Up with a "Perfect" Partner.   The

best way to protect your investment is by finding the right venture partner in Eastern Europe, one with the clout to allow your partnership to
prosper in the face of all three forms of business risk. At the outset, you
should avoid spending all your time circumventing convertibility problems or fretting over changing joint-venture laws. Spend your energy
finding the "perfect" business partner; this is your best protection. The
next chapter will help you to find, and qualify, an Eastern European
business partner and enterprise.

8

Finding the Perfect Partner

Qualifying People and Enterprises

Many American business people expect to waltz into Eastern Europe, network at a conference reception, and find the "perfect" business partner. In reality, what they encounter are vultures. At the typical trade conference Eastern European business people wait like land piranha, with literally hundreds of business proposals to pitch to their deep-pocketed American friends. The Americans enter wide-eyed, ready to do business. Here's what happens.

"*What business are you in?*" the American asks the Eastern European.

Answer: "*We make bathroom fixtures, and we're in the tourist business. What is your business?*"

The American answers: "*Nuclear reactor shielding.*"

Answer: "*Oh, we do that too!*"

The scammers are merciless. One Russian real estate agent recently requested 25 years worth of rent up front from a Western company, and with a straight face. Then there were "castle deals"; for some time in Hungary after the Wall fell, Westerners were constantly approached with deals to renovate castles into first-class hotels. Of course, rarely did the Hungarian actually own or control the real estate on which the castle stood.

Where Networking and Cold Calling Don't Work

The problem is that many Americans go to Eastern Europe thinking that business people there are going to do business in a Western manner, that they are going to work with them *ethically*. But few of them realize—before they get burned—that there is no tangible body of working business law in many of these countries as of yet and that, if you sign a contract there, it's basically meaningless. Americans often just arrive in Bucharest or Moscow or Sofia and start prospecting. They are approached by business people pitching "perfect" deals 24 hours a day, most of which are worthless.

The phrase "Potemkin village"—an imposing or showy facade concealing a shabby or embarrassing condition—derives from the pristine Soviet villages, made of cardboard, that Gregor Potemkin built to impress Catherine II during her visit to the Ukraine and Crimea in 1787. Russians (and Central Europeans, too) have a special knack for presenting eager foreign business suitors with spellbinding Potemkin villages, whether in the form of an all-too-perfect deal or a cache of suddenly available hard currency or anything else that may trick the foreigner into making a tangible commitment. So you've got to be on guard, and savvy. You've got to do your homework *before* you travel to the East, and you should have something very specific in mind in terms of the type of business that you want to start. Otherwise you will quickly get lost in the "opportunities" and taken for a ride.

First, you must find people who are trustworthy as well as business-minded—no easy task—and qualify people in places where few carry résumés and reputation is relative. (If they *do* carry a résumé, don't take its reliability for granted.) You must actively share information about Eastern European people and their companies with other Western representatives. Visiting Moscow is enough to convince the observer that U.S. Company X doesn't know what U.S. Company Y is doing in the same city, even though executives from the two companies are both posted there and both are members of the same business associations.

Getting Introduced to "Real" Partners

With a partner you can trust, train, confide in, communicate with, and respect, your chances of success in Eastern Europe will be significantly enhanced. How do you find the perfect partner and the perfect factory in your industry? Before venturing off to Eastern Europe and snooping around promising-looking factories (which is a good idea), start with any one (or more) of the following sources of introductions, all of which can help:

- Government privatization ministries
- Published joint-venture partner lists
- Trade associations
- Consultants
- Chambers of commerce
- U.S. Department of Commerce
- Accounting firms
- Lending institutions
- Business newsletters

Perhaps the best place to start in a partner search won't cost you a dime, a dinar, or a ruble. As part of a program called *American Business Initiative,* the Eastern Europe Business Information Center (EEBIC) has created an information service entitled "Eastern Europe Looks for Partners" designed to help U.S. businesses locate partnership opportunities in Europe. For copies, contact the EEBIC at (202) 377-2645. Also, many Eastern European enterprises and former trading ministries operate offices in the United States where you can meet counterparts and start networking. (See the appendix for a complete listing of Eastern European business contacts.)

A proven method for finding a partner is to send a representative to Eastern Europe who speaks the language and who knows the local business scene. This person can't just "find somebody" for you to do business with, stopping blokes on Gorky Street and asking them whether they do business. Your representative has to find the person who will become your sponsor in Eastern Europe, who is introduced to you through your person, whom you have sent as emissary. This person becomes your mentor. Through this person, you will be introduced to others as somebody who knows business and has money to do it. This person puts you together with the right counterpart under the right circumstances. Remember, however, that the introduced counterpart must still prove to you that he or she has the wherewithal to do a deal and is accountable.

Lawyers and Consultants as Introducers

Too few companies take advantage of cross-cultural experts and consultants who can offer introductions to appropriate counterparts, not to mention identify markets and opportunities, introduce appropriate officials or private interests to deal with, help negotiate letters of intent or protocols, participate in long-term negotiations, and help structure financing. In some of its business activities in the region, USWest at the outset depended on services of a consulting firm to supply introductions. In fact, says company representative Ed Mattix, "one of our primary consultants in the Soviet Union was former senator Gary Hart. Senator Hart has a lot of experience in the Soviet Union. It was one of his primary interests when he was in Congress, and he has an excellent understanding of their culture, their business, and the people in government whom you need to contact to begin negotiating projects." I asked Mattix whether a company needs someone like Gary Hart more, or less, now than in the past. "I think probably less," he said, "because of the way the governments are opening up for competition to serve....It's important to have someone who knows the right people, but the people are changing so quickly that you can be talking to someone today and they might not be there tomorrow." He went on to say that, "while it's good to have someone who has those kind of contacts, I wouldn't say it's a key to winning it any longer. It really comes down to your capabilities and what you offer in your bid." USWest now has people in-house who have been hired because they have either specific backgrounds in telecommunications or specific backgrounds in Eastern Europe; the company now has a "mix of both."

A consultant can be especially important at the outset, during the search for a suitable partner. But you need to do your homework before hiring a consultant. First, a consultant should have the verifiable potential to introduce a company to the highest echelon of potential customers and appropriate government officials. A consultant's value should not be measured by estimated *costs*, but by the estimated *savings* of money, time, and resources spent on gaining fast entry into a desired Eastern European market. American businesswoman Anne Devero, who has set up a jewelry manufacturing venture in Poland, employs a consulting firm to update her when legislation or trade-law changes affect her venture, and she has the information given in writing. "The charges [for this service] aren't high if you're very explicit in your request," she says. But you need to be very specific in what you want the consultant to do, and put it in writing. You need to ask for an estimate of the fees up-front. You need to understand who's working on your work, and understand exactly what their billing rates are. If you think they're too high, negotiate. Consulting firms *are* negotiable. Always get an estimate before you authorize any work to be done.

Beware the Local "Consultant" Liaison. With layoffs of thousands of government officials and technocrats from the Socialist era, formal commercial consulting groups have sprouted like mushrooms all across the region. Most technical institutes have spun off consulting groups mandated to earn hard currency from foreigners; some are good, others are worthless. Well-written performance contracts are the order of the day in consultant shopping; and this goes for U.S. consultants as well as the indigenous variety. The consulting company must have genuine Eastern Europe expertise; don't hire a briefcase company that has no in-house Eastern Europe expertise. You don't have to hire somebody specializing in say, computer-related products; rather, hire the company that specializes in the country that you want to deal. Beware, also, of large consulting firms. "They're just too broad and cannot specialize in anything," says Russia expert Olga Ringo. Of course, some do specialize, but you have to check and obtain references.

Hire the consultant located closest to where your product is to be built, distributed, or developed. The consultant must be able to send someone from his or her office, wherever it is, to the desired area to conduct research on potential partners, the industrial setting, and so on. The consultant should research a number of different locations and present you with options as to where to go to set up. After you decide where to go first, the consultant should set up the meeting with the factory owner. Do not allow the meeting to be held in a capital city when the factory is located somewhere else. You want the meeting to take place at the factory itself, and you must attend. Do not allow the consultant to become a permanent barrier between you and the producer, "protecting" you from the realities of the factory. Go and deal with the producer directly and see your product being made. (Who knows where it might get made if you aren't there to see for yourself?) The objective is, of course, to cut the consultant out as soon as you acquire the expertise that he or she offers. Pay the consultant an up-front fee or, when the deal is done, a percentage of any resultant business.

Business "Types" in Eastern Europe: Whom Can You Trust?

The foreigner in Eastern Europe deals with one or more of a limited number of business personalities, all differing in background and priorities: Government administrators, factory managers, former Communist party bureaucrats-turned-dealmakers, scientists and engineers, and private entrepreneurs. With so many business "types" besieging you with deals, how do you find out about a person's background? Start by interviewing business people who know the person and have had dealings with him or her. Be prepared, however, for the fact that business people in Eastern Europe are not generally accustomed to being interviewed by Westerners. You may want to carry out this task through a local representative, though you can't hire just anybody to do your checking, as that person might simply fabricate the credentials of the potential partner in exchange for a favor or kickback. Perhaps the best method is to work with a foreign-owned consultancy that has extensive contacts and an office presence in the area of Eastern Europe where you plan to do business. Ernst & Young, for example, has a subsidiary that will check on a potential business partner. Other companies that will carry out the same activities have sprung up throughout the region.

You will run into many business types in the New East, but there are few "typical characters" to look out for; depending on your needs, you will want to involve yourself with some of them, and you will want to avoid others.

The Former Comecon Trade Official

Within the old foreign trade organizations and their local affiliates were people who, in principle, were salespeople. And some of them were good salespeople. Unfortunately for them, their sales experience doesn't amount to much if the factories they deal with won't respond to the needs of new customers. A former Comecon salesperson may be able to cook a deal for the sale of autobuses to be delivered in two months, but if the factory misses the delivery date, which inevitably occurs, the deal falls through. After this happens two or three times, no customer wants to see the salesperson again. In response, many of these talented people have set up private marketing companies; others have kept their positions at state-owned foreign trade companies, many of which still exist.

Former Comecon people were all party people, and they don't hide this fact. They were good administrators and often possess contacts with enterprises that are still run by the state. In principle, they are attempting to motivate production enterprises to produce products of high quality while meeting contractual delivery dates. In practice, they are trying to find a safe niche for themselves in a swiftly changing system because they realize that they are not going to be able to motivate the producers. For most of these people, life is a question of surviving until a new opportunity comes along. Moreover, they may prove to be effective in structuring a barter deal since many of them dealt directly with supplies and buyers in numerous Eastern bloc countries under the old regimes.

The Party-Member-Turned-"Entrapparatchik"

Many talented and creative Eastern European people discovered relatively early in life that if they wanted to get ahead, and if they wanted to get done what they wanted to get done, the smartest thing to do was to join the Communist party. Many politically minded individuals felt that the only way their country could be reformed—the only way that sober-mindedness could win out—was if they joined the party and worked within the party toward that end. There were two basic types of party people. The first was the "careerist"; the other might be called an "honest and sincere Communist." The disillusionment of the latter is now much greater than that of the former. The sincere Communists had tried to reform the party for a decade only to see it suddenly collapse; they were *believers*, and are now bitter. As far as business is concerned, neither type should be avoided. Many of these people are articulate, politically shrewd survivors who are quite capable of functioning in a market economy. Some of them probably still possess useful contacts, though you have to check because their contacts may no longer be current.

The Former Socialist Manager

Long-time factory managers who are trying to survive the company's transition to capitalism will rarely be practitioners of deceitful tactics, especially with foreign parties. Four decades of culturally enforced corporate honesty has ingrained in Soviet-style managers a profound fear of the penalties associated with lying and corruption by the manager of an enterprise. You can usually trust an enterprise manager from the Communist era, as well as a scientist at the Academy of Sciences, but CEOs, private entrepreneurs, former ministry officials, former party hacks, and former Comecon people require a background check.

The Fixer

Every venture in Eastern Europe needs a "fixer," the person who can work wonders, procure anything, and get what's needed overnight. Pat Austin has a fixer in the family: "I've got a cousin. He's a Hungarian. He's the manager of a hospital and also does scientific research. Recently, he was elected by the hospital to manage the expansion of the hospital." Why would they need a research physician to handle this? Pat asked him: "He said he knows exactly who he has to bludgeon to get across something that he wants to get across. He's been the manager of the hospital for a year and a half. The hospital has undergone a complete reconstruction, which the regular administrators hadn't been able to complete in twenty years. He had to literally pound the people on the head who had to do the design. He had to pound the people at the ministry who had to approve the funds. And he had to hound the people who did the bricklaying." In short, the fixer is a person who can *do*. Fixers have a political sense; they know who to promise what to (it doesn't have to be money, but must be some sort of a favor). Fixers have a sense of whom to threaten and what they can use as a threat. And they know how to use threats and favors from the inception to the completion of a major project. If you find a fixer, put this person on your payroll, and never let him or her go.

The Westernized Young Person or Graduate Student

Students tend to have more open minds and a more Western conception of business ethics because they haven't been spoiled by the privileges of party membership. They speak English and want to work for Western corporations while maintaining deep-rooted ties to their home countries. You might also meet scientific and R&D types associated with either a large institute like the Academy of Science or a newly formed lab spun off from such an institute who want to become your business partners. On the one hand, Westernized young people can make fine employees in a foreign venture because they are free of the symptoms of the "Socialist mentality" I spoke about in the last chapter. On the down side, they are Young Turks despised by many working-class people who can no longer make ends meet and prone not only to idealize capitalism but also to emulate its worst qualities. "Keep the youthful Eastern European entrepreneur on a short leash," recommends one business executive I spoke to.

The National Hero Turned Dealmaker

Each country has its sports- or national-hero turned entrepreneur: Like the guy who wins the gold medal in downhill skiing or lacrosse, moves to the United States, works hard, and amasses a small fortune— which he invests in his home country—where his clout and influence are still great—when the Wall comes down in 1989. One such "sportsman" invested $200,000 in a one-hour photo lab in Budapest; it soon multiplied into a chain. He took the profits and bought a Hungarian crystal factory. Finally, he took the profits from that venture and bought a department chain. The companies are purchased as "joint ventures," but he runs the companies himself. And he's grown rich. As potential partners, the former cosmonaut, Olympic medalist, or film actor may lend your venture clout in getting high-level meetings. If they have had experience as business people in the West since their heyday, they may be excellent venture partners, in part because they have the stomach to go back to their home countries and deal tirelessly with all the frustrating exigencies of doing business there. But remember that often they are merely trying to cash in on their past notoriety among foreigners who seek an open door. Use them for this only if they don't possess personal hands-on commercial experience.

The Private Entrepreneur

A number of people in Eastern Europe conducted private "speculative" business under the Communist regime, often in the shadows, often illegally. Now, they are the first group of people in the New East who know how to undertake the pursuit of profit. Even in the former Soviet Union, there were small groups of business people in the U.S.S.R. who speculated, invested, and accrued profits through the years. Many of these clandestine entrepreneurs got trained in the import-export business through their black market experience. These people now operate in the legal private sector. As partners, they can make you money because they understand where the emerging opportunities are and how to get through bureaucracy fast. They can procure anything a venture may need. As a Westerner, don't try to pull the wool over the eyes of these people. They learned the not-so-gentle art of capitalism in an environment in which speculation was a crime worse than rape. Deal with somebody who has been involved with private business for a long period of time (prior to 1989), rather than a newcomer. Can you trust these people? Yes, but you *must* spend time with them in order to build up personal trust before doing business. It's up to you to weed out the bad potatoes, and in these "wild West" business posts there are many bad potatoes that live by the creed that a sucker (foreigner) is born every minute. "Nobody but the big crooks have the money," complains Sepp Leimgruber, the area director of Hungary and Czechoslovakia for Rank Xerox, Ltd. "And the question is whether you, as a respectable company, want to do business with the crooks." The sort of private entrepreneur you should look for in a potential partner might be Dariusz Linert, a young and successful Polish entrepreneur who is no crook.

The Making of an
Eastern European Private Entrepreneur

Dariusz Linert is one of Poland's a Young Turks, increasingly sybaritic with exposure to the West, swift-thinking, and ready to cash in on transition. Dariusz's father was an adviser to Solidarity in Silesia, in South Poland; when he was 13 and Solidarity became outlawed by Jareszelski in 1982, Dariusz took to the streets to fight the police. He was thrown in a detention center for two weeks. He decided to emigrate.

"There was no place for me. It was still a Communist country. There was no opportunity to do something for yourself," he recalls. In 1983, Pope John Paul went to Poland and admonished the Polish people to stay in their country; he said that freedom was on the near horizon. And sure enough, in 1986, it became possible for Poles to talk about democracy openly. In 1989, Poland's first freely elected government came to power; this changed the world for Dariusz. "At that moment, I found in Mister Balcerowicz's financial program many possibilities to start to do business just for my own. Everything was clearer." How did Dariusz know that he wanted to be his own boss and an entrepreneur? "The idea was born out of the background of my family, and I always wanted to be independent. I couldn't imagine working for somebody else. I could work *with* somebody, but not *for* somebody." Dariusz's mother, a trained economist, had been the director of Fiat in Milan, later becoming a dealer for Honda in Silesia. She was international in perspective, and her attitude rubbed off. Before 1986, travel wasn't easy; Dariusz could not carry a passport at all. Since, 1986, however, he has been able to travel freely. He visited friends in West Germany, Denmark, and other European countries.

How did he come to find what would make him wealthy and independent? "During the last three or four years, many companies in Poland imported products from Western countries. Cars, clothing, furniture...everything. Everything you can imagine. Even food. They established warehouses, retail shops, and large distribution networks," says Dariusz. The influx of Western products started in 1983; but as of 1987, it gained steam...But the prices they charged for Western products were high compared with Polish products, because of duties, tax, and transportation costs. Dariusz could see that there was a big difference between the price of foreign-made products and those made in Poland. Most of the imported Western products were not made in Poland at the time, but some, such as simple kitchen utensils and plastic containers, were. Not televisions or VCRs or automobiles, but essential household products. "Everything that the housekeeper needs everyday, like dishes, spoons, plastic boxes..." remembers Dariusz.

Dariusz, then 21 years old, packed his suitcase and traveled to Poznan to attend the largest trade fair in Poland. "I tried to find Polish products I could distribute to the Polish market, with good quality and good price." He wanted to find a product he could move in quantity, with a narrow profit margin. He wanted to sell quality, in great quantity, and create economy of scale. He found what he was looking for in a producer of plastic goods located in North Poland, seventy miles from Gdansk. He

discovered that the company was not marketing its product in South
Poland, only in the North and to international markets. In short, the
company lacked a distribution network outside its local area, a problem
most Polish producers suffered from at that time, and which many still
have not addressed. Under communism, production and sales had been
localized; Dariusz recognized that this company could benefit from a
motivated marketer like himself.

The owner of the plastics company told Dariusz that he had no idea
how to put together a distribution network or how to compete with the
foreign products that were becoming available in Poland. The owner
was a manufacturer, he said, not a marketer. (Remember, this was the
first year of legal private enterprise in Poland.) The owner gladly
accepted the idea of having Dariusz represent his line of products in
South Poland. Product samples in hand, Dariusz visited retailers and
wholesalers in the South. Two weeks later, playing hooky from school,
he sent the owner of the company an order for $100,000 worth of
household plastic ware. Were the buyers surprised that the products
were made in Poland? "They were very surprised," says Dariusz,
"because they had been buying only foreign products, until this twenty-
one-year-old guy comes in to sell them Polish stuff." Since 1983,
wholesalers and retailers had been able to buy foreign products out of
catalogs at high prices, but they hadn't ever seen Polish products
because they were not being distributed or advertised outside the areas
in which they were produced. "The price of a spoon from the West was
two dollars," recalls Dariusz. "Our price was only twenty-five cents.
Some of the people I talked to actually started crying because they had
paid so much for a similar product from a foreign company only one
week before. `Why didn't you come before?' they said."

Dariusz's network grew quickly to include over 2,000 wholesalers and
retailers in South Poland. He diversified his list of products by signing
up 25 new producers, for whom he now distributes products through
his distribution network. He has diversified his list of products. He
bought trucks. Hired drivers. Rented a warehouse. Now, his private
enterprise sells $1 million worth of household goods a year. Dariusz has
put his mother in charge of the company while he continues his
education in import-export trade in Long Beach, California. The future
looks bright. He's 24.

Appraising the Eastern European Enterprise

The three types of businesses you may get involved with in Eastern
Europe include (1) state-owned enterprises, (2) cooperatives, and (3)
private businesses. Because there isn't a Dun and Bradstreet with
which to qualify Eastern European enterprises, you have to conduct
your own investigation or what lawyers call "due diligence." Start by
locating the prominent companies in your industry; contact them one

after the other until you have appraised them all as possible partners. Companies that have been designated by the government as "ready to privatize" will probably be in sad shape, but a company whose management is in the earliest stages of considering whether to privatize itself may be in relatively good shape financially; it may intend to bring in a foreign partner to expand or upgrade production. You will have to locate a company of this sort by visiting the country and conducting interviews and seeking introductions, as such companies may not be listed by any privatization organization.

Remember also that there have traditionally existed two industrial worlds in Eastern Europe: The military-industrial complex, and all the rest. Defense-related firms possess the best and brightest scientists and managers, have had access to the highest technology, and could obtain foreign exchange for purchases of necessary imports of capital goods. In fact, your first stop in seeking a manufacturing partner in Central Europe and the C.I.S. should be a defense-related company, or a consortium of companies, that is in the process of converting to commercial production. Managers in these companies maintain contacts among elite decision makers, and their employees will be more skilled and more highly educated, and will have been exposed to Western-style management practice.

State-Owned Enterprises

State enterprises—inefficient, enormous, and victims of lost markets in the Soviet Union and rising energy costs—are typically run by managers woefully ill-equipped to deal with competitive world markets. Richard A. Jenner and Joseph Gappa studied eight businesses in Poland in 1990, including two large state-owned manufacturers, four trading companies, one privately owned firm, and a cooperative bank. The results of the study revealed managerial deficiencies that you can expect to find in virtually all state-owned Eastern European enterprises as they face new pressures brought on by exposure to a competitive free-market. They included (1) passivity on the part of managers, (2) a tendency on the part of managers to wait "for foreign agents and suppliers to tell them which new products to produce or market, (3) weak marketing skills combined with a general disinterest in learning about ways "to implement systems for product development, design, and marketing," and (4) an almost total lack of strategic planning, which appeared "limited to assigning productive quotas or targets to various products or outputs throughout the business's system." The enterprises were also little concerned with enhancing their level of technology or the technical skill level of their employees. Communication systems suffered, as did other aspects of surrounding production infrastructure on which the enterprise depended.

In a large state-run firm, production processes, quality control, and data collection will all be geared to satisfying the production quotas set by the old system of central planning. In the past, manufacturing decisions were not made after analysis of complete and quality data; managers simply followed production directives issued from entities outside the enterprise. Hence, while the workers might be technically capable, the factory's purchasing ability, accounting systems, and commercial design will not be developed. You may find Western equipment in a factory in the East, but because of lack of spare parts or financial restrictions, the equipment may not have been maintained. Moreover, often you will find that equipment purchased from the West 10 to 15 years ago looks nothing like it originally did; again, because of a lack of spare parts, the machinery has been patched up, modified, or reworked just to keep it in operation, to the credit of the line workers.

Although most state corporations are in abysmal shape, there are notable exceptions. Some are perfectly successful despite their imperfect management and are attractive to foreign buyers. An excellent example is Orbis, the state-run travel agency in Poland. Orbis operates a nationwide chain of hotels and other tourist-related services and earns a significant profit. The company's problem is a shortage of hotels in Poland. Orbis hardly loses money, and yet its assets are not being utilized as efficiently as they could be.

The problem with most state companies that have been placed on the auction block is that they lack a ready market for their products since their Soviet customers have become insolvent. Moreover, managers of state companies tend to have little grasp of how to find, create, or serve foreign markets. Recently, a Hungarian entrepreneur wanted to purchase a state-owned factory that produces strain gauges, a precision instrument not produced in many Western countries. The company possesses the most advanced equipment in the world for producing strain gauges, and it had been put up for sale. The Hungarian entrepreneur decided to buy it; he contacted a group of American investors and invited them to come and see it, in the hope that they would provide the capital for the purchase. Of course, the first question the Americans had was why hadn't the state company begun selling to international markets on its own, given that demand existed for its products around the world. What they learned was instructive. They found that the company was, indeed, aware that companies throughout the world needed high-quality strain gauges; yet it had made absolutely no effort to contact these companies after it

lost its ruble-paying Soviet customers. It hadn't even informed potential customers about what it offered. Worse, the company's managers
couldn't even understand the *concept* of contacting potential customers
in markets outside the former Soviet Union. The experience was a
vivid reminder of how foreign trade in Eastern Europe was a government monopoly. State-owned companies were traditionally not permitted to operate their own foreign-trade departments; separate state-
controlled foreign-trade companies handled all trade transactions with
the outside world. Only gradually were rules about foreign trading by
state enterprises relaxed. Some large state-run companies were permitted to handle their own offers and submit their own quotations.

Many state-owned enterprises have, however, been nimble in
responding to the clarion call of capitalism. "If we had continued
doing business the old way," says Kazimierz Brezeszczynski, director
of manufacturing at Dresso's hundred-year-old sportswear factory in
Poland's textile capital of Lodz, "we probably would have gone bankrupt by now. We have recognized how vital it is to improve quality
and productivity." The company quickly moved into fancier, more colorful designs and created incentives for workers to raise productivity
because it could no longer depend on automatic distribution of its
products by the state. "Now we have to win over customers," says
General Manager Wlodzimierz Weglarczyk. "That wasn't the case
before." The company sensitized itself to customer needs and preferences and watched its exports climb 43 percent in one year. Dresso's
sales and marketing director says: "When people have less money,
they become more selective, so we have to work hard to make sure we
are offering them what they want."

Cooperatives

Americans may be acquainted with a "co-op" in the sense of an enterprise set up to sell products at prices below what the market will bear,
for the benefit of the community, while profits are shared by the
employees of the enterprise. The altruistic, semi-Socialist "co-op" of
the West is not what Eastern European entrepreneurs have in mind
when they set up a cooperative. A cooperative is a free-market capitalist enterprise whose managers set their own prices for the factory's
production and sell for what the market will bear. A cooperative often
enters into leasing agreements with a large state firm to occupy a
given premises, rent certain equipment, and utilize given inputs which
it obtains through a purchasing contract paid for in cash or kind
(sometimes in the form of a kickback to an official in the parent firm).
The output of the cooperative will usually be marketed by the parent

firm; its directors will normally come from the parent firm, as do its raw inputs. An appendage of the main firm, the cooperative operates independently from, but in symbiosis with, a state enterprise.

In the former Soviet Union, a state enterprise may dissolve itself into a number of cooperatives and an assortment of small enterprises. The small enterprises might act as repair centers or assembly units, while the cooperatives will employ a large number of workers and take on the responsibility for product development and/or R&D. For example, a firm in the Ukraine that makes consumer goods recently set up a cooperative to (more quickly) design new products while the parent state-owned factory produces the prototypes. In this case, the state enterprise continues to enjoy guaranteed access to raw inputs, while the cooperative is more flexible and fluid in developing innovative consumer products on a Western-style fast schedule, a typical objective in organizing a cooperative enterprise.

Cooperatives in Eastern Europe generally suffer from both government interference and a lack of government financial support. Recently, in the independent state of Russia, the state failed to enforce its laws against extortion and outright vandalism against cooperatives. Cooperative managers couldn't trust the state militia, so they met their demands for kickbacks and protection money. Many co-ops then hired the armed services of security firms, which, fittingly, were typically co-ops themselves. Successful Russian co-ops were then blamed for gobbling up basic goods in short supply, and state-owned suppliers of these goods withheld them from the co-ops, after which the state levied price controls on products produced by cooperatives. To add insult to injury, many managers and owners of cooperatives were detained as hooligans, speculators, and exploiters of the people.

Like a state enterprise, a cooperative may leave a lot to be desired in terms of entrepreneurial know-how. A U.S. textile company recently sought to set up a business presence in Hungary. It couldn't find a private partner who was strong enough, so it met with a cooperative. The co-op had an elected management, an all-female working staff, and a decrepit office in a nice part of town overstaffed by six secretaries whose salaries, as well as the high rent, were swallowing up the co-op's profits. "They were totally and one-hundred-percent incompetent," said a consultant who worked on the project. "They couldn't price an object that they were, in principle, supposed to sell." The Americans mentioned the issue of competition from China, but the Hungarians shrugged off the issue and said, "No, we're not going to lower our price because of Chinese competition." Next, the Americans wondered why they imported their fabrics from France when they could get the same quality of fabric from Pakistan for one third the price. They were told that the Pakistanis wanted to sell in quantities that were twice what they normally purchased. The Americans asked why that was such a problem since the co-op would certainly use the fabric. "It takes too long," was the answer.

Private Enterprises

A privately owned company that has already achieved success and has proved to be efficient and well managed is perhaps the most attractive potential partner. In short, *deal with enterprises in the private sector, if you can.* One characteristic virtually all private enterprises have in common is a lack of capital. Many of these companies have been in existence for only two or three years, and they're generally small. They would be larger, even more vigorous companies if they possessed working capital to expand and managerial expertise, both of which U.S. investors can provide. These companies have not lost their markets, as is the case with most state-owned companies. They simply can't expand to serve their existing markets adequately. They typically enjoy a high growth curve in terms of both revenues and productivity. In many cases, with the addition of a few state-of-the-art machines and a dose of Western managerial and marketing know-how, these companies can become megagrowth companies that can serve international customers in Russia, Western Europe, and elsewhere.

Some of the most innovative and entrepreneurial new private firms in Eastern Europe are spontaneously generated out of a state-owned conglomerate. Crosna, a new private company in Russia, was started with 2,800 rubles which its owner earned by selling VCRs. He took over an operating factory, privatized it, fired its director, and started building satellite dishes. He outlawed boozing during working hours, docked workers for faulty workmanship, and offered bonuses for good performance. Soon, the company commanded a monopoly of the satellite dish market in Russia and began raking in profits. Its high-profile customers include the Japanese embassy in Moscow.

Small enterprises have difficulty starting up independently, partly because of extremely tight monetary policy and high interest rates on business loans. Most are in no position to plunge into a market economy without the benefit of state-subsidized supplies, research and development, transportation, political protection, and so on. In the former Soviet Union, a new enterprise typically takes root in the fertile ground of a state conglomerate, taking advantage of cheap state-obtained inputs that it acquires for its own uses by exchanging its output in "noncash" barter agreements. Characteristically, the state-run parent firm nurtures the new enterprise in exchange for a piece of the action—that is, a share in future profits.

Let's look briefly at the plastics company that Dariusz Linert works for, since it represents the type of firm that you will want to look for as a potential partner in Eastern Europe. The company had been a privately functioning company for 20 years. The owner sold 60 percent of his production to West Germany and Denmark *before* the Wall fell, and he reinvested all of his profits in new machinery and warehouses. Other producers possessed machinery and markets, "but they did not develop their companies by reinvesting in them," says Dariusz. "This guy, he invested always. He didn't buy a nice car, nice clothes," and other luxuries. Other companies ate their profits; they purchased the accoutrements of Western lifestyle and squandered the investment that they should have put into their companies to ensure their survival.

Qualifying an Enterprise: Initial Questions to Ask

Who owns the enterprise?

Find out who holds what percentage of its shares and how the ownership breaks down between various banks, the parent firm, workers, and the managers. Ascertain which entity appears to be monopolizing shares in order to attain complete control of the enterprise. Ideally, the managers are becoming the owners with some worker-ownership, and the state-owned parent firm is losing shares.

What is the external relationship between the enterprise, the surrounding bureaucracy, and the economy?

Especially in the former Soviet republics, one must learn which entity, if any, currently has control over the enterprise: a ministry in Moscow, a ministry in the newly independent republic, a concern, a parent firm, a cooperative, or one or more private owners. You may find that the enterprise managers don't know which entity controls their firm, since the transition from control by Moscow to control by a ministry in a republic may not be complete. The foreigner may become frustrated with managers who do not know what agency or government entity they must answer to; rest assured, however, that your irritation is more than matched by that of the managers who remain in the dark while bureaucrats debate the fate of their enterprise.

Where do the funds come from to upgrade the enterprise and/or spin off cooperatives?

Do they come from the state, investors, or from profits generated by the enterprise? Remember that state inputs may have been redirected to purchase new equipment for a newly private or cooperative enterprise.

The state may come back to haunt the small enterprise, however. For example, often the parent enterprise loans state money to a newly forming small enterprise at low, or no, interest. The small enterprise will, however, have to pay back the loan to the parent enterprise.

Who is the manager, and what is the internal position of management?

Decision making may be centralized among a few managers or may be decentralized among subdivisions of the enterprise that may already have been privatized. Most managers respond slowly to the call to reorganize, delegate, and manage for a market economy. The foreigner must appraise the manager of the Eastern enterprise with this variable in mind. The key manager will likely be a "go-slow" entrepreneur in approach and attitude; you are looking for the rarer manager who wants to move quickly to take full advantage of privatization reforms. As business relationships become vital to fledgling enterprises, the goodwill and accountability of managers who sign contracts with each other have grown in importance. A manager can't be just a cog in the system anymore. He or she must foster respect, accountability, and integrity, among peers and colleagues; otherwise, managers of other enterprises will be unwilling to enter into deals with his or her enterprise that are based on personal trust as much as on binding contract. You must ascertain whether the manager has accomplished this.

What kind of resources can your enterprise partner marshal, in cash and kind?

Perhaps the toughest challenge for an Eastern European manager is the timely procurement of inputs and services, whether the need is for a computer system or writing paper. Your partner *must* have clout and informal connections if your venture is to get anything accomplished efficiently. The partner with connections can obtain a phone line in two weeks rather than six months. "No problem" will be the reply to your request for a phone line to be secured so that he or she can call you directly in the States. Supplies and logistical support will materialize on schedule. Ask around to find out how much clout the partner wields in his or her industry, and to what extent geographically.

> *If the enterprise has been released from ministerial control, you need to find out where it is getting its production supplies, and whether it is guaranteed access to those supplies.*

Independent enterprises often rely now on contracts with suppliers which may not have provided reliable delivery thus far. Find out whether deliveries have been disrupted. Most important, when an enterprise has been cut off from its supply line, you need to judge the efficiency of the response by the managers in ameliorating the problem.

What level of technology is the factory using, and what level of technological upgrading can it readily assimilate?

"A good technology may exist in one plant, but it is not diffused throughout the industry," says John W. Kiser, president of KRI, Inc., in

Washington, D.C. "Or, a factory may be in the Dark Ages by Western standards, but have one or two pieces of production equipment that are highly advanced." Make a detailed assessment rather than basing your analysis on an initial overview.

How much does the enterprise pay in taxes, and to what agency or ministry?

Find out whether taxes on the enterprise's output have been increased or decreased with reforms. The managers may have responded to avoid state taxes, for instance, by restructuring the ownership of the enterprise to put it in a different tax bracket.

What is the enterprise's relationship to domestic and international banks?

At the outset, find out how indebted the enterprise is, relative to earnings. Many enterprises own shares in a privatized bank, which makes it easier for them to obtain funding. You might also ask whether any of the enterprise's managers have banking experience or hold a seat on the board of a banking institution.

How strongly represented are the interests of workers?

When a company is undergoing privatization and foreign parties are invited in, foreigners will find that they must deal with well-represented workers' interests, which will influence the context of negotiations. Worker power varies dramatically from country to country in Eastern Europe, even from plant to plant, depending on whether you're dealing with a single plant or a strategic industry like steel or coal.

Why does the enterprise want to enter into a partnership with your company?

Ask yourself this question periodically throughout negotiations with an enterprise in Eastern Europe. Hidden agendas and ulterior motives abound in East-West commercial courtships. For example, an Eastern European enterprise may want to form a joint venture with your company merely to set up a subsidiary of the venture outside the country. The subsidiary can open a legal bank account in a foreign country where hard-currency earnings (from your venture or others) can be deposited out of reach of tax collectors in the home country. Roughly one fifth of the first 2,000 joint ventures in the Soviet Union were given permission to set up subsidiaries, many for this unstated purpose. A reasonable objective in forming a partnership, but maybe not your company's objectives.

9
Negotiating and Financing a Deal

You've found a business partner and selected an enterprise in Eastern Europe to acquire or in which to invest jointly. You're ready to open negotiations on a contract to acquire company assets, modernize the factory's production line, streamline its work force, restructure management, upgrade technology...all to the end of comanufacturing for profit with an Eastern European enterprise. Hope and bonhomie run high on both sides of the negotiating table. The bright future envisioned for the venture by all present, however, belies many negotiating and management storms that loom ahead.

Four Challenges Faced by the Foreign Negotiator

When you want to acquire an interest in an Eastern European enterprise, your first challenge will be to cajole a privatization agency or ministry into selling to you a specific enterprise that you want to buy. This means deciding how you want to participate in the privatization of an existing company and understanding how the various players in a factory privatization—that is, workers, managers, and officials—conduct the decision making on a foreign project. Second, in tandem with these parties, agreement must be reached as to what the enterprise you are purchasing is worth and, indeed, who owns it and can lawfully sell it to you (no small feat in Eastern Europe).

Your third challenge is to submit a winning bid in order to acquire an interest in an Eastern European enterprise by addressing the priorities of a specific privatization authority, of the factory's workers

and managers, as well as the interests of the surrounding community. Fourth, your company must obtain the necessary financing to
acquire the enterprise, possibly turning to international lending institutions, which are specially geared to evaluating and funding foreign-invested ventures in the region, rather than dealing only with
American entities.

Plugging into the Privatization Process

We looked at the different methods of privatizing state-owned companies in the preceding two chapters—company auctions, voucher systems, and "spontaneous" privatization by managers. Where does the
foreign investor want to enter this complex morass of options? How
are decisions about the sale of a state-owned enterprise made? To
answer these questions, let's take a closer look at the priorities held
by the Treuhandanstalt, the privatization coordinator for eastern
Germany and the most successful privatization agency in Eastern
Europe.

The Treuhandanstalt offers a wide range of 8,000 companies for sale
to foreigners in the fields of mechanical engineering, electrical engineering, and textile industries as well as ones in tourism, construction,
and services, and the Treuhand offers investors use of its user-friend-
ly, computer-aided database of companies held in its trust.

Three Modes of Enterprise Conversion

Three types of privatization schemes are possible through the
Treuhand. The first is the takeover of an entire enterprise (stock purchase), which is sold in existing form. The enterprise is simply transferred in its original size and structure to the buyer. The second
scheme involves the takeover of individual parts, or groups, of companies. Partial sales of this sort are possible when no prospective buyer is
interested in purchasing the entire enterprise. The Treuhand will consider such piecemeal purchases if the remaining parts of the enterprise
will still have a chance of selling. In the third scheme, a foreign entity
may take over a number of fixed assets owned and operated by an
enterprise. "Asset sales" by the company to a buyer are allowed only
when schemes 1 and 2 are not possible.*

---

*This description of Treuhandanstalt practice is adapted from an investor brochure pub-
lished by the Treuhandanstalt.

As in eastern Germany, Poland's Ministry of Ownership Transformation pursues three major schemes of privatization of Polish state firms. The first is *pure liquidation* of companies, in which a previously state-owned company is purchased for its assets, the buyer perceiving a ready market for those assets. Outright liquidation is taking place most often in heavy industries where plants and equipment are most outmoded and would require total retooling to become competitive. The workers in such a company would have already been relocated. The second mode of privatization is *acquisition*. The purchaser buys a going concern in Poland, in part or in total, and makes it into a subsidiary or division. Acquisitions are not limited to large firms; the ministry lists small acquisitions such as retail outlets, small restaurants, and small hotels as well. The third scheme of privatization in Poland involves the *transfer of shares,* held by the treasury, to individual stock holders. This scheme will help large Polish companies become privately held firms with their stock eventually held by individual citizens via mutual funds.

So You Want to Buy an Eastern European Company?

Assuming that the foreign party wants to *acquire* a state-owned firm in Eastern Europe, the following scheme, which is specific to Poland, is typical. Other countries follow similar decision-making routines, though all are in a state of constant flux. The following detailed case is provided to give the Western dealmaker a sense of how many interest groups must be addressed in a large acquisition and of how many decision-making steps will be required. (To make initial contacts, see Privatization Organizations in Eastern Europe in the appendix.)

Most Eastern European firms exist in a form that is legally unacceptable in international investment circles, and they must be converted into a corporate entity first. In Poland, the conversion of a major state firm is called "privatization through restructuring," a process that allows company managers to participate actively with foreign parties in the privatization of their enterprise.

Step 1: Preparation of a Business Profile

First, either the board of directors or the Worker's Council of the Polish company solicits an independent consulting firm to prepare a brief investor's prospectus, or business profile, summarizing the company's financial situation, technical facilities, and future commercial plans, and to provide a credit rating for the firm. Consulting firms are asked to complete the business profile and to wait for payment until the enterprise is purchased.

Step 2: Announcement of the Competition

The Board of Directors or the Worker's Council announces the opening of bidding competition for the restructuring plans for the privatization of the company, which is announced in national newspapers.

Step 3: Preparation of the Restructuring (Business) Plan

The "Management Groups" taking part in the competition purchase a business profile about the company from independent consulting firms and, on the basis of information they have gathered by themselves or through hired consultants, prepare their own Restructuring (Business) Plan for the corporation. The Restructuring Plan is submitted to the company's Board of Directors along with an estimated value of the company. The plan contains information pertaining to the company's strategy for developing the enterprise, its operational goals in restructuring—proposed price of goods and commission for distributors, etc., a preliminary valuation of the company, and a detailed time schedule for the plan's fulfillment. Plans are then evaluated by the Ministry of Ownership Privatization.

Step 4: Preliminary Selection of Restructuring Plans

When the deadline for submission of plans expires, the Ministry of Ownership Privatization sends the plans to the Board of Directors or the Worker's Council for initial selection.

Step 5: The Competition

The competition-auction is conducted by the Ministry of Privatization and includes representatives of the ministry as well as representatives of the Board of Directors, the Worker's Council, banks, suppliers, and other organizations outside the company. There are four phases in the competition-auction: individual meetings with Management Groups to discuss the restructuring plans and the initial value of the company, negotiations with the Management Groups in order to set the highest initial value proposed, general meetings with all the Management Groups in order to announce the highest negotiated initial value of the company (with an open auction a possibility), and the selection of a Management Group. At this juncture, the management group that won the competition-auction must propose the structure of the management of the enterprise.

Step 6: Entering into the Business Contract

The Ministry of Ownership Privatization enters into the contract with the Management Group that won the competition-auction. Once a

Management Group is chosen, state-owned enterprises will be transformed into state treasury stock companies and a Board of Directors will be formed. The Executive Board, proposed by the Management Group and appointed by the ministry, will be paid salaries negotiated by the Executive Board and Board of Directors.

Step 7: Supervision of the Restructuring Process

The Board of Directors supervises the restructuring process implemented by the new Executive Board and has the right to terminate the business contract if it concludes that the Management Group is not implementing the restructuring plan and/or is operating to the detriment of the company.

Step 8: Preparation for the Sale

The Management Group is responsible for the restructuring activities and thus for the preparation for sale. The group conducts all the initial activities specified by law—i.e., provides the definition of ownership rights, prepares the economic and financial analyses (verified by the independent auditors), executes the preliminary appraisal of the company's value, constructs the company's prospectus, and specifies the means of the company's sale. The failure to sell a minimum of 51 percent of shares obligates the group to continue restructuring activities.

Step 9: The Sale

The sale is made by an independent brokerage house. In the case of an open auction, the company directs the negotiation process, with a closed auction, the company invites potential investors, and with a public offering helps in preparation. The Management Group suggests the appropriate time for the sale of shares. A state-owned company is considered to be sold (privatized) when at least 51 percent of its shares are in the hands of private investors, including the shares awarded to employees. The Ministry of Ownership Privatization gives up its active role in managing the portion of the company remaining as a property of the state treasury. The Management Group receives a commission in the form of shares.*

The Well-Represented Interests of Workers

Before an offer is accepted, the investor must obtain the approval of the enterprise's Worker's Council, which can be a sticking point in the purchase of a Polish company, *and of any company throughout Eastern*

---

*This section adapted from Polish Ministry of Privatization, "Poland's Privatization Program," *The Insider*, Warsaw, Dec. 9, 1991 (special information supplement).

Europe. The Worker's Council represents the interests of the work force of the factory you intend to buy. It is not a worker's union; it is a council of representatives of the workers in the factory. Its mandate is to look out for the benefits of the workers. The Worker's Council wields great power in any kind of acquisition because, in almost every Polish company, there are 30 to 40 percent more workers than needed. This means that, in nearly all cases, an acquisition by a foreign company will entail massive layoffs. Tension almost always grows between the acquirer and the Worker's Council over what specific adjustments are to be made in the new company. In short, you have to negotiate an acquisition with both the Management Group of the factory and the Worker's Council.

The problem is that two opposing sides often exist across the table: Management and workers. They both have different, often contradictory, demands, and a compromise must be achieved between them before a transaction can be signed. In most cases, the management's sole objective is to see the transaction approved, whereas the Worker's Council will probably fight for contract clauses stipulating that a large number of workers will be retained in the factory after purchase. This is often a snag in transactions with foreign buyers. In Germany, the Treuhand actually *requires* that investors stipulate in the contract the number of jobs to be retained and created in the future. If you later abandon employment and/or investment plans without compelling reason, you may have to make compensation payments. As of this writing, in Poland only a dozen or so outright enterprise acquisitions by foreign parties have been signed; another dozen or so are in the pipeline. Time will tell whether the interests of the workers remain influential in acquisitions or give way to managerial prerogatives in the future as the need to speed up the privatization process intensifies.

The Challenge of Valuating an Enterprise

"Valuation has been, and will continue to be, the biggest challenge" to the foreign investor in Eastern Europe, says Ernst & Young's Jerry Rohan. In the Eastern Europe economic system, more value was placed on the *assets that were utilized* in an enterprise than on the ability of the enterprise to create cash flow and profits using those assets. International consulting firms working in the region use a complicated technique to arrive at a fair valuation of an enterprise. Nevertheless, it's never an easy process. "We've done privatization work in all of Eastern Europe and the Soviet Union, and it's never easy to demonstrate to people that the value of a business is its ability to generate profit," says Rohan. "If you built a plant for one hundred million dollars and it produces one pack of cigarettes a year, is it really worth a hundred million dollars?" The countries of the region have invested millions of dollars in plant and equipment. Officials and managers in these countries are naturally concerned that foreign investors—and their accounting firms—may take unfair advantage of them by placing a low value on the firms that are for sale. Eastern European managers typically measure the value of their companies' assets—the equipment in the factory—by their physical value. You may find it impossible to convince them that, if their company has no *market* for its product, the value of its equipment does not amount to anything. With no real asset valuations or cash-flow analysis, valuations of Eastern European enterprises, even when conducted by an international accounting firm, are rarely more than guesswork.

Management groups and the government privatization authority often don't agree on the valuation of a firm because, from the outset they have different agendas. "The government generally wishes to maximize proceeds, while the enterprise management, which may be seeking to participate in the privatization, will wish to see valuations held at the lower end of the calculated range of values," explains Bill Liddell, managing consultant with Ernst & Young, in *World Link.* "This discrepancy highlights the biggest fear management and employees have, which is to not be able to participate actively in the future, privatized company. Employees usually know their company's shortcomings and see privatization as a panacea for all of them. And of course they want to keep their jobs. Directors often see privatization as a vehicle for a majority management buyout. A high valuation, though pleasing to the seller, puts the company or even shares of the company out of the range of interested local participants." Moreover, most firms have not compiled reliable accounting records that are compatible with Western accounting practices. "In the United States and Western Europe," says Lawrence Danzig, director of valuation services in Eastern Europe for Ernst & Young, told *Tracking Eastern Europe,* "we value a company in terms of past, current and future performance. However, in Eastern Europe, we must value operations based on the future, because past performance is not really relevant."

Thus, you may have to hire the services of a consulting company to "translate" the data into Western terms. To valuate an enterprise, the analyst must consider the following:

- The overall characteristics of the enterprise being privatized
- The enterprise's competition

- The financial condition of the company
- The historical performance of the enterprise
- The future outlook for the privatized company
- Comparable known values of other in-country firms
- The macro outlook for the local industry and economy
- The firm's potential for profit making

Valuation conflicts may pivot on the percentage split in a joint venture between multiple partners; that is, one party on the Eastern European side may fight for a higher asset evaluation purely for the purpose of increasing its equity share from, say, 49 percent to 51 percent. When conflicts arise, bring in a third party. The third party needs to base its judgments on *recently* placed orders won by the enterprise (to determine the marketability of the products) and on whether the customers who placed them can really pay for the goods. Valuation of the preexisting Eastern enterprise should be followed by a valuation of the proposed joint venture, taking into account all the value added that the foreign side will be bringing to the venture. The percentage difference in value between the Eastern enterprise alone, and the joint-venture enterprise, should roughly correspond to your company's equity share in the venture.

Who Owns the Factory? The Land?

Foreign investors also find that, in dealing with a privatizing company, they encounter "the ownership dilemma." Property-rights laws remain one of the biggest obstacles to foreign investment in Eastern Europe. The problem with acquiring a formerly state-owned company is one of ownership rights. If private owners ran the company before the Second World War, they often come out of the woodwork to reclaim their property, which was confiscated long ago by a Soviet-installed government. You buy a factory, and two months later the "owner" calls up and wants his or her factory back. *This happens!* Eastern Europe's governments have had to strike deals with the original owners of some of these enterprises in which the owner takes a chunk of cash and agrees to walk away. In other cases, an investor is asked to offer the original owner a seat on the board! You may also be asked to pay off people who claim they once owned the enterprise, simply to get them out of the way. Worse, you may be asked to share profits with them. Foreign parties should initiate a deal like this only when they are 100 percent certain about the factory's history of ownership. Start by finding out whether the company was owned by the central government, local government, or by the town's city hall. Talk to people living near the factory as a starting point for research on a firm's hidden pedigree.

Real Estate Ownership.   The question of ownership of real estate creates the worst nightmares. (The ownership of the plant, buildings, and equipment assets is usually clearer.) Often, past owners surface to claim different combinations of parcels of land. Often, survey maps differ from deed maps, and deed maps are often different from those registered with the official registry of land. One map might indicate that a 10,000-square-feet piece of real estate consists of 10 parcels, each 1,000 square feet. Another map might have different 1,000-square-foot parcels, the total equaling 10,000 square feet. In other words, each map has different configurations of the parcels. One version of a parcel looks like a square, another like a rectangle, and a third like a pentagon!

Even renting shop space, for example, may be a travail. Your first step: Go to the place you want to rent and ring the doorbell. Ask the person who answers the door (possibly the concierge) who owns the building. Generally, it will turn out to be the local council, which is similar to a county or borough. In other words, the property is probably state-owned, which means that it might be owned by any one of a number of entities. The city of Budapest, for example, is divided into 22 districts, each with a local council that controls land. Once you've traced the owner, hire a lawyer, since it may turn out that whoever is responsible for renting the place is the kind of bureaucrat with whom you could spend hours, days, weeks, or months and still not have a lease. If you get a lawyer who has done this before and who knows how to pin down bureaucrats, you will probably be able to rent the place. Find the lawyer locally, for he or she must know the local laws, speak the language, and have worked in the system. Local laws in Eastern Europe are changing fast. You don't need a generalist!

Investors should also note that because there is a shortage of usable land in Eastern Europe, arising from lingering questions of titles and zoning, the purchase of an outmoded factory may be a faster way to set up a new factory. After the original assets are disposed of on the used-equipment market, the building and land are yours to use as you please.

Winning the Bid: Making Your Offer Attractive

Before a privatization agency such as the Treuhand will approve the sale of a state enterprise to a foreign investor, the investor must submit a written offer containing a careful and detailed plan for the ongoing operation of the Eastern European company in addition to a purchase bid price. Normally, a purchasing plan comprises investment and financial projections; a plan for hiring, firing, and training employees; and an overview of the company's proposed commercial relations with customers and suppliers.

Purchase Price May Not Be Paramount

I cannot overemphasize that Eastern European privatization officials evaluate submitted plans from investors with an eye for (1) a solid financial package and (2) a clear agenda for future investment and betterment of the indigenous firm as well as the surrounding community and industry. German authorities look for a "promising business concept, which will ensure or create jobs and guarantee investments." In other words, your purchase price will, by no means, be the primary criterion in gaining approval to buy formerly state-owned firms in Eastern Europe. If you base your bid only on the bottom-line purchase price, you may not win in a competition for the purchase of an extremely attractive company. In fact, the French chemical company Elf Aquitaine may beat out Dow Chemical in a bidding war for the acquisition of one of Czechoslovakia's largest companies, Chemicke Zavody Sokolov As. Dow offered $53 million (plus $96 million for upgrading production later) in exchange for a 51 percent interest in the firm. A preliminary agreement was signed—to great fanfare in the press. Then Elf Aquitaine submitted a privatization plan whereby the company would agree to buy and sell some of the Czech company's products toward the end of increasing production and ensuring years of growth. Elf also agreed to pay for later production upgrading. The Ministry of Privatization seems to be leaning toward the Elf proposal as of this writing.

The topics considered important to Eastern European privatization evaluators, which you will want to underscore in your proposal, include:

1. Plans that keep current workers and staff employed and expand the number of high-paying skilled jobs in the future.

2. Innovative and competent managerial leadership which augurs well for the company's future.

3. Large amount of total investment injected over time.

4. Marketing scheme that will generate export earnings in hard currency.

5. Willingness to train workers and managers.

6. Amount of debt relief to be given on behalf of the enterprise by the purchasing party. In Germany, the Treuhand acts to determine the amount of debt relief to be made by the investor. Naturally, the amount of debt relieved will affect the total purchase price bid.

7. Environmental cleanup commitment. Privatization agencies are often willing to share the burden of cleanup, as well as the cost of future environmental damage for a specific period beyond the time of purchase.

Committing to Environmental Cleanup. Throughout Eastern Europe, numerous bills are pending regarding the liability of foreign investors for environmental cleanup and impact. For instance, the Treuhand asks foreign purchasers of state firms to "accept responsibility for ecological damage caused by the purchased enterprise"; this would terrify even the most gutsy investor. I recommend that would-be investors observe the following guidelines for existing, accumulated, and future environmental damage. Before investing, carry out a thorough appraisal of the land, buildings, and other assets in order to detect any environmental damage. Deduct the cost of the existing damage from the purchase price of the acquisition. If cleanup of the existing assessed damage cannot be performed before or at the time of purchase, an assessment should be made to cover the accumulated cost, fines, and other fees covering the period until complete cleanup can be performed. Often, these initial costs borne by the new owner will be reimbursed by the national privatization agency, provided that an agreement was reached between the new owner and the agency at the time of purchase. In all cases, you must forge an agreement such that the cost of environmental cleanup detected *after* the time of purchase will be covered by the national privatization authority.

Decision Making on Foreign Projects

The primary issue in getting a project approved is finding out who needs to approve the deal. Few enterprises can unilaterally approve anything, and finding out who needs to sign off can be trying. There are three levels of government in Eastern European countries: The central or national government, the provincial government, and the local government. The trend is for the local government to get a significantly increased amount of control over foreign-invested projects. Hence, for projects that are not extremely large, you will be dealing almost exclusively with the local government, which is called the *gmina* in Poland. The gmina consists of a mayor and city council, and it runs somewhat like a municipality. Often the land which you might be interested in buying or leasing will be owned by a gmina rather than the national government. Thus, you will probably be dealing with a gmina over the issue of leasing or selling land, as well as on the issue of getting your project approved. This proves to be a great advantage for foreign investors in Poland and elsewhere; they must pitch the deal to the gmina, generating enthusiasm for it at the local level, and need not concern themselves with generating enthusiasm for the project higher up. Also, in cases in which a gmina strongly desires a certain project to be undertaken in its area of jurisdiction, you may be able to negotiate added concessions, or at least push harder than you would if multiple layers of decision makers were involved. You can effectively play one gmina off against others to get the best possible set of investment incentives. This basic approach applies throughout the region.

Influencing a Deal: Creating "Push" and "Pull" for Approval.
As a project moves through the later stages of negotiation, both sides of the venture must join forces to get the project approved—that is, to convince high officials in the central government to pull for the project and to convince local officials to push the project through the bureaucratic steps necessary for final approval.

Any acquisition deal requires a patient negotiator on both sides of the table. Eastern Europeans realize that the longer the negotiation process, the greater the possibility that foreign investors will withdraw from the deal. Markets change. Or worse, personnel changes can occur in the top echelon of management in the Eastern European enterprise; these changes can derail the deal. In other cases, laws must be changed in order for a deal to proceed; the Eastern European negotiator is then at the mercy of government policymakers. "The bureaucrat and the red tape serve a valid purpose," wrote Jacob Byers in *Business in the U.S.S.R.*, general director of Management Partnerships International, the American partner of a computer-oriented joint venture in Russia, before the fall of the Soviet Union. "Preventing the Westerner from getting something for nothing." His advice is still valid throughout the region: "If you try to exploit the Soviet labor subsidy, for example, you will come back with horror stories about how the negotiations took months and the JV [joint venture] took years to put together. However, if you approach the Soviets as true business partners with legitimate needs, risks, and rewards, and approach the deal with a sense of how you can solve a problem for the common good, you will be greeted with open arms and the overwhelming bureaucratic process will work in your favor. But if the Soviets feel you are trying to exploit a vulnerable market, the administrative hurdles will never end."

Bribes, Kickbacks, and Commissions. Are there palms to be greased at every turn? "It's not that desperate," says Pat Austin, who then offers a big sigh as she tries to find a way to describe how bad the corruption is in Hungary. "First, you have a government that knows it's not going to hold on to power for very much longer. At the same time, many in government feel it will be in power forever. On the other hand, since the government may not be in power forever, it's a good idea to get one's hands on all the privileges and prerogatives that officials had amassed in the past over the course of forty years in office."

Petty corruption permeates Eastern European societies, and indeed, has been part of all Socialist societies throughout history—not that it is limited to those societies. In the past, the Eastern European citizen would walk into a store and hand the person behind the counter an envelope of money, and the sweater that he or she might otherwise have waited three weeks for would materialize out of thin air. Informal barter and favor-giving were the modes of commerce. Indeed, this system was perhaps most insidious in the medical profession, where medical professionals were historically grossly underpaid. You would simply not get what you needed done unless you slipped something to the doctor or the nurse. That is not to say that the medical practitioners would respond only if you gave them money. The point is that the patient *would not think* of asking for medical help without offering something under the table. The system was ingrained. The fear was that if you did not tip the surgeon, he or she might forget to sew up an artery. Now, especially in the former Soviet Union, "You can't get anything without bribes," as a private store director in Russia told a "bribery hotline" run by the newspaper *Komsomolskaya Pravada*. He said: "I get a delivery of cigarettes—10 percent goes to the…distributor. Looking for space for your store? That'll be 10 grand on top."

Eastern European officials may be part of the educated elite, but they usually pull down a lower salary than their counterparts in the private sector. For this reason, they sometimes drag their feet unless properly motivated with a small cash incentive. The "grease" may be as innocuous as a small appliance or as unabashed as a handbag full of cash. Price kickbacks are a now-ubiquitous method. You should, however, *never* involve yourself directly in the paying of commissions. Let your Eastern European joint-venture partner, or distributor, handle the actual payment. Often a local manager receives an inflated salary which enables him or her to "tip" all the people who help prevent a business from being strangled by delays in delivery, approvals, and so on. And do not give gifts and favors indiscriminately. If a favor-inducing gift is to have a beneficial effect, it must be given to the right person—namely, the person in the loop of decisions that affects your venture. Spend the time to find out exactly who this is before making your move. Again, your Eastern European go-between will know best. Once you have a personal tie with him or her, your go-between can make most of your commission decisions for you.

Go-betweens can be hired as business facilitators in any country. They help get the goods off the dock, lobby a key person in government for special consideration of a proposal, and use their personal connections to help make the foreigner's business run smoothly. Always pay a go-between "on spec"—when the job is done, they get paid. Advice to the foreigner: If the "fee" is huge or if permits get approved quickly, you can assume that a bribe has been paid. Many U.S. firms accommodate extorters, budgeting in "bribes" as a part of doing business in the former Soviet Union. Overt corruption in the rest of Eastern Europe is certainly prevalent but less of an obstacle to the foreign business person wanting to set up shop.

Other Modes of Influence: Public Relations.   Any benefit you can bring to a company will play a part in the decision-making process regarding your product and the attention your business receives. You might offer to upgrade a local factory by bringing in needed office equipment, setting up a welfare fund for workers, or sponsoring star workers with scholarships for overseas training. All these perks can nudge a decision maker without money changing hands. Back-room politics should not be underestimated as key to the survival and prosperity of investments. Consequently, learning the power games common in local politics should be at the top of the "must-do" list for foreign business people. Start by reading the Eastern European press and committing time and money to efforts that Western businesses broadly define as "public relations." Scan the business scene, conducting intelligence gathering on what is occurring month to month in local and central politics, especially regarding specifics of reform implementation. Public relations by a foreign company should not be limited to contacting people in the bureau in which the enterprise exists. If you operate in the Balaton Lake region of Hungary, you must make the requisite trips to Budapest to find out how far and how fast the government is pushing implementation of reform programs that may either benefit your venture or threaten it.

Other activities could include grass-roots endeavors which will further the image of the firm at the local level. As the "new kid on the block," your firm could be the target of antagonism from local enterprises if it produces products similar to theirs but of higher quality. As a foreigner, one must always be careful to not appear threatening to local workers and managers who have significantly more clout with local suppliers than a new foreign venture. Work to get the venture accepted into the social and economic landscape. Keep your company profile low but do not be secretive: Such an approach will only engender suspicion and animosity. In short, invest in grass-roots philanthropy rather than Madison Avenue corporate image-making. Utilize *local* trade organizations and professional services. The local business environment will respond to a time-honored business relationship based on trust and responsibility to the community. For instance, R. J. Reynolds Tobacco International president Dale Sisel handed over a $100,000 check to its new joint-venture partner in St. Petersburg to "show our new neighbors in this city that we will try to make life for our workers here, and in the whole city overall, better." The money will be used by a school to train managers. Up against decades of anticapitalist, anti-West propaganda in Eastern Europe, companies from the West have had to conduct serious work in public relations and to put their money where their mouth is. Pizza Hut delivered pizzas to defenders of the Russian Parliament during the August coup; IBM has donated computers to a Russian Orthodox Church; and after winning a multibillion-dollar oil-exploration contract, McDermott shipped in humanitarian aid by air and sea to Sakhalin Island.

The Power of the Press. Keep in mind that the press is *extremely* influential in Eastern Europe. You must deal with it constantly and use it to your advantage. In extraordinary instances, public-relations cases taken to the world press can serve as a de facto appellate court to bring about resolution of problems unsolved through the normal channels. Do *not* avoid the press; doing so will be more damaging to your corporate image than speaking publicly about your venture's problems.

During the decision making on a large privatization project, public opinion plays a critical role in whether your firm will be permited to purchase all, or part, of a privatizing firm. For this reason, you should consider teaming up with managers, workers, and local officials to develop and implement a public relations program designed to lobby for your interests in the comunity at large. A last point of advice: Get bilingual staff—preferably local nationals—into the region as early as possible to monitor and manage your business relationships. This will ensure you a good "ear to the ground" and will lessen the chance for miscommunication and misrepresentation by your company.

Financing Your Venture in Eastern Europe

Count on one thing when you try to finance a venture in Eastern Europe. Low-interest financing will not be readily available to your company, or its venture partner, from a commercial lending institution in Eastern Europe or the former Soviet Union. "Banks do not have any financial or legal instruments at their disposal which would encourage investment," complains Piotr Matysiak, director of Polmicon, an investment liaison service in Warsaw, in an interview with the *Warsaw Voice*. The problem in Poland and elsewhere in the region: Interest rates on credit are astronomically high. "Nowhere in the civilized world," complains Matysiak, "do people demand a guarantee of 200 percent of the amount of credit to be granted. I get the impression that Polish banks would like to see guarantees in the form of chests of gold or sacks full of precious stones." The result: Only the shrewdest wheeler-dealer Eastern European business person involved in pure "speculation" can afford the risk of taking out a loan or procure the required guarantees to obtain credit.

Don't Be Discouraged

Although current international banking attitudes portend very limited commercial bank lending to projects in Eastern Europe and the former Soviet Union in the near future, the U.S. government and multilateral institutions do offer a variety of programs to assist investors and traders in financing transactions, investments, and development projects (Table 9.1). The number and types of programs vary from country to country and naturally are in a state of flux. The list of financing sources that follows is not all-inclusive and covers only sources available to companies operating from the United States. This information is adapted, in large part, from U.S. government publications; some specifics are likely to change. Contact the Eastern European Business Information Center (EEBIC) for updates on these and other financial institutions involved in Eastern Europe. I have divided funding sources into (1) financing sources for trade transactions and (2) financing sources for investments. The contact information for each institution is current as of this writing but may change.

Financing Sources for Trade Transactions

Export-Import Bank of the United States. The Export-Import Bank of the United States (Eximbank), an independent U.S. government agency, supports the export of U.S. goods and services through a variety of loan, guarantee, and insurance programs. For more information, contact:

Export-Import Bank of the United States
811 Vermont Avenue, NW
Washington, DC 20571
Tel: (202) 622-9823

Table 9.1. Samples of Funds Made Available to Finance Export Trade and Projects with the C.I.S., Baltics, Poland, Hungary, and Czechoslovakia

Group	Amount	Destination	Type of program
		1992	
The World Bank (International Finance Corp.)	$300–$350 million	Central and Eastern Europe	Financing development of capital markets and financial institutions
	$30 million	Russian Republic	Financing technical assistance programs for fiscal reform, taxation, and privatization
U.S. Department of Agriculture	$1.25 billion	All former Soviet Republics	Credit guarantees for agricultural products, including rice and grains
U.S. Agency for International Development	$26 million (U.S. funds)	Hungary	Financing investment and export increases
The Export-Import Bank	$52 million	Russian Republic	Available, but not disbursed yet
Consortia of American Business in Eastern Europe	$500,000 grants for each of five businesses	Poland	Construction, food processing, agriculture, telecommunications, and waste management
U.S.-Hungary Enterprise Fund	$41 million	Hungary	Financing investments and technical assistance programs
		1991	
The World Bank	$29 billion (total)	Poland	
	$200 million		For growth of private banks and development of capital markets
	$280 million		For privatization efforts
	$100 million		For reorientation of rural cooperatives
	$17 million	Bulgaria	Financing technical assistance
	$450 million	Czechoslovakia	Financing structural adjustments
	$250 million	Hungary	Financing structural adjustments

Table 9.1. (*Continued*) Samples of Funds Made Available to Finance Export Trade and Projects with the C.I.S., Baltics, Poland, Hungary, and Czechoslovakia

Group	Amount	Destination	Type of program
		1991	
The World Bank	$300 million	Yugoslavia	Financing development of thermal capacity
Polish-American Enterprise fund	$69 million	Poland	Financing privatization of banking and financial institutions
Trade and Development Program	$4 million	Poland	Feasibility studies for major development projects with large U.S. export potential
Small Business Administration	$123 million	C.I.S./Russia/ Eastern Europe	Financing of export promotion programs
U.S.-Hungary Enterprise Fund	$19 million	Hungary	Financing investments and technical assistance programs
		1990	
Export-Import	$3 million	Hungary	Varied
Bank	$1 billion	Poland	Varied
	$25 million	Czechoslovakia	Varied

SOURCE: *East/West Executive Guide*, April 1992.

Foreign Credit Insurance Association. The FCIA, an agent of the Eximbank, is a private association that provides export credit insurance to cover commercial and political losses. The FCIA facilitates exports by (1) protecting against the failure of foreign buyers to pay for commercial or political reasons, (2) encouraging exporters to offer competitive terms of payment, (3) supporting an exporter's prudent penetration of higher-risk foreign markets, and (4) providing exporters and their banks with greater financial flexibility in handling overseas receivables. For more information, contact:

Foreign Credit Insurance Association
40 Rector Street, Suite 1622
New York, NY 10006
Tel: (212) 466-2950

U.S. Department of Agriculture. The U.S. Department of Agriculture supports the sales of American agricultural products (including freshwater fish and forestry products) through the Commodity Credit Corporation (CCC) and the Export Enhancement Program (EEP). The CCC guarantees repayment of short-term loans (six months to three years) made to eligible countries purchasing American farm products. For more information, contact:

Export Credit Program Development Division
U.S. Department of Agriculture
Room 4524, South Building
Washington, DC 20250
Tel: (202) 720-5319

Financing Sources for Investment Projects

Overseas Private Investment Corporation. The OPIC offers a finance program in which it makes direct loans of up to $6 million to small businesses from its cash reserves of $1.6 billion, and investment guarantees of up to $50 million. The OPIC does not loan to the American investor, per se. It loans to the project, requiring that the equity position of the U.S. investors be upward of 20 to 25 percent, in hopes of encouraging them to "play for keeps and do their utmost to make the project a success," says OPIC representative Howard Hills. Roughly a third of all companies that seek OPIC assistance are small firms with no international experience. For more information contact:

Overseas Private Investment Corporation
1615 M Street, NW
Washington, DC 20527
Tel: (202) 336-8400

The Eastern Europe Enterprise Funds

Set up by President Bush as part of the Support Eastern Europe Democracy Act of 1989, these funds are designed to promote private-sector development in member Eastern European countries through equity investment insurance grants, loan guarantees, and training. All the enterprise funds follow similar general investment guidelines. Small and medium-sized companies are given preference; large companies and those involved in major infrastructure programs are of little interest. Target areas for investment are wide; even trading companies that will help develop distribution networks and thus promote manufacturing operations will be evaluated. Projects that will employ locals, utilize domestic resources, and improve Eastern European living conditions in the short term are most sought after. For more information contact:

Polish-American Enterprise
  Fund
535 Madison Avenue, 33rd Floor
New York, NY 10022
Tel: (212) 339-8330

Czech and Slovak-American
  Enterprise Fund
1620 Eye Street NW, Suite 703
Washington, DC 20006
Tel: (202) 467-5480

Hungarian-American Enterprise
  Fund
1620 Eye Street, NW, Suite 703
Washington, DC 20006
Tel: (202) 467-5444

Bulgarian-American Enterprise
  Fund
33 W. Monroe Street, Suite 1213
Chicago, IL 60603
Tel: (312) 629-2500

Other Assistance Funds

Environmental Enterprises Assistance Fund.   The Environmental Enterprises Assistance Fund invests in promising energy-related projects which, if they result in profitable business, will return funds for further development. The fund provides technical and management assistance, loans, and equity, and acts as a catalyst to overcome nonmarket barriers. The fund manages a $20 million portfolio. For more information, contact:

Environmental Enterprises Assistance Fund
1611 North Kent Street, Suite 600
Arlington, VA 22209
Tel: (703) 522-5928

International Finance Corporation.   The International Finance Corporation (IFC), an affiliate of the World Bank, is the world's largest source of debt and equity assistance to private sectors in developing countries. The IFC invests in most types of enterprises, usually limiting its debt and equity participation to 25 percent of project costs. The IFC arranges financial packages by coordinating funding from commercial banks, export credit agencies, and other institutions and can facilitate syndicated large loans and arrange debt for equity swaps. For more information, contact:

Department of Investments
Director/Europe
International Finance Corporation
1818 H Street, NW
Washington, DC 20433
Tel: (202) 473-1234

U.S. Agency for International Development.   Under the American Business Initiative, designed to increase the participation of small and medium-size American companies in Eastern Europe, USAID will implement projects covering agribusiness, energy, environment, housing, and telecommunications that will facilitate the transfer of U.S. commercial expertise and the flow of U.S. capital to Eastern Europe. The USAID may provide funds to recipient governments, which will in turn issue tenders according to USAID's procedures. The USAID may also request proposals and issue tenders directly. For more information, contact:

Office of Development Resources
Bureau for Europe
U.S. Agency for International Development
Washington, DC 20523-0053
Tel: (202) 647-9734

U.S. Trade and Development Program. As an independent agency of the U.S. government, the TDP promotes economic development by funding feasibility studies, training programs, consultancies, and seminars in developing countries. Host government agencies must request financing, either directly of the TDP or through the local U.S. embassy, but U.S. companies may bring these projects to the attention of the TDP. Developmental agencies such as the USAID and TDP announce projects in the *Commerce Business Daily*, P.O. Box 5990, Chicago, IL 60680; phone (312) 353-2950. Also, the publication *USAID Procurement Information Bulletin* is a valuable source for potential contacts. For more information, contact:

U.S. Trade and Development Program
SA-16, Room 309
Washington, DC 20523
Tel: (703) 875-4357

U.S. Small Business Administration. The SBA offers loan guarantees to help qualifying companies start up international business or expand their existing activities. For more information, contact:

Office of Business Loans
Small Business Administration
409 Third Street NW, Sixth Floor
Washington, DC 20024
Tel: (202) 205-6570

The International Bank for Reconstruction and Development, or the *World Bank.* European countries have been the target of increasing World Bank funding. If your company wants to bid on an IBRD project, you must maintain a close liaison with the responsible ministry or agency in the borrowing country. Relatedly, the procurement procedures for consulting services are described in the World Bank's *Consultant*

Guidelines. The International Business Opportunities Service (IBOS), a subscription service, announces World Bank projects. For more information, contact:

The World Bank
1818 H Street NW
Washington, DC 20433
Tel: (202) 477-1234

European Bank for Reconstruction and Development. The EBRD commenced operations in April 1991 at its headquarters in London, capitalized at approximately 10 billion European Currency Units (ECUs), approximately $12 billion, with a mandate to (1) provide advice, loans, equity investment, and debt guarantees designed to foster the transition to market-oriented democracies and to (2) promote private and entrepreneurial initiative. Albania, Bulgaria, Czechoslovakia, Estonia, Hungary, the Commonwealth of Independent States, Latvia, Lithuania, Poland, Romania, and Yugoslavia are all eligible for EBRD project funding. For more information, contact:

European Bank for Reconstruction and Development
122 Leaden Hall
London EC3V 4QL
UNITED KINGDOM
Tel: 71-338-6424 or 6126

10
Managing the Venture

Promoting Change, Communication, and Conflict Resolution

There are basically four types of foreign joint ventures in Eastern Europe. First, there are those that have been signed and are functioning, authentic ventures. However, there are three categories of joint ventures that are *not* functioning. The first type has failed because something happened and it never got off the ground. The second type got off the ground; planning work was done, but disagreements arose, and no energy went into bridging them. The third type got under way, but a whole series of issues arose—like supply, quality control, efficiency, chain of command, decision making—that were not addressed early, and the Western partner withdrew believing that the venture was too hard and too complicated.

With regard to the last two types of joint-venture enterprise, where the partners went forward and then withdrew because it became too difficult, one can argue that the foreign partners misperceived the nature of the challenge of managing a joint venture in Eastern Europe and that false assumptions and misperceptions became the seeds of ultimate failure.

Remaking the Enterprise in Your Image: Controlling Hopes and Projections

In short, the foreign partners perceived the challenge of a joint venture in Eastern Europe *in Western terms*. They never tested their assumptions about Eastern Europeans. Assumptions such as "The Eastern Europeans are not market-oriented people," or, "They are not incentive-oriented," or, "They're not capitalist-oriented." Operating on the basis of these perceptions, the North American often feels himself or herself to be a white knight striding into Eastern Europe to introduce a market economy, to bring capitalism to the East. In short, the Westerner thinks he or she is re-creating the East in the image of the West, and to a great extent this is true. And, in most cases, the Westerners who venture to the East get treated like messiahs of modernity—in fact, treated much better than they might be treated in the West: Picked up at the airport by the mayor and taken to dinner and out for entertainment, for example. The North American never stops to question his or her basic assumption that Eastern Europeans don't understand how to manage a business (incidentally, this is *not* really the case). In fact, sharpening the manufacturing *support services* in an enterprise—especially data collection and application—will be a much larger task for the joint-venture manager than upgrading the management of manufacturing methods of the Eastern enterprise. The data *can* be collected and *are* available; it's just that the typical Eastern manager has never seen the need to obtain the data.

Getting To Know Eastern European Managers

In fact, the Eastern European manager *does* know how to manage a business—he or she has just never been given the opportunity to manage one *autonomously*. Managers have never been given the opportunity to do their work in a way that North American managers would do their work. Eastern European managers traditionally had no control whatever over the revenue generated by their productive efforts. Company profits were distributed by an appropriate ministry so that companies that suffered a loss would share in the profits that a productive enterprise had earned. Thus managers had no reason to work to increase profits because they would not benefit directly from increasing them. They would receive bonuses for high company performance, but they had no authority over the reinvestment of profits in their enterprises. At the middle and lower levels of management in an enterprise, the bonuses would not be enough to change a manager's lifestyle significantly. Therefore, middle managers and workers cared little about the profitability of their organization. Since no personal benefit would come from extra effort, few workers were willing to go the extra mile to improve the performance of their company.

Eastern European managers realize that they must decentralize and delegate responsibility in their enterprises, but precious few have done so. Most factories (70 to 80 percent) in Eastern Europe still exist on the state dole, and their managers are often satisfied merely to show some forward progress toward privatization or profit-oriented behavior—evidence that they are responding to the market rather than pursuing privatization. It's possible that a manager might ask you to formulate a letter of intent when you want to get started on a final contract. But many managers may lack the motivation to move quickly. The state may not yet have given managers an ultimatum to produce a profit or watch their company go bankrupt.

In most enterprises, the manager will be preoccupied with mundane details that a factory manager in the West would not be responsible for, such as the volume level of the background music in the workers' canteen, pension plans, and other nonproduction-related issues. In most firms, the manager remains a sort of czar overseeing the factory's every activity, unwilling to share the slightest degree of responsibility for operations. Organizational restructuring at such enterprises will take place only as a last resort—for example, when the demands of workers for better pay become so intense that management is forced to begin market-oriented reforms. Large state-run enterprises often must adhere to strict wage controls, and thus, restructuring occurs when management realizes that, to meet the wage demands of workers, it must reorganize the enterprise, often breaking it up into smaller enterprises.

Feelings of Powerlessness. Typically the Eastern European manager suffered from an overwhelming feeling of impotence with regard to improving the enterprise and the lives of the workers. "Hungarian managers worked in a hierarchical structure in organizations, occupying a niche," says consultant Sue Gould. "They might be a vice president, or a first deputy director, but they would have a boss above them who made the decisions that they followed." They, in turn, made decisions that their subordinates would follow and not question. "They felt sandwiched in, as does everyone else in that structure," says Sue. "They couldn't stretch their elbows." During Sue's training in Hungary, managers expressed feelings of being constricted, immobile, straitjacketed. Mind you, these were managers working in the state sector and collectives. They were mainly people in their forties, very successful, who wielded great power

within their organizations. Yet they felt totally powerless to change anything that did not fall within their specific domain of authority. For example, one manager of a kitchen at a large hotel had control over equipment
purchases, and that was all. None of the managers had control over workers' salaries or authority (or input) in the decision making concerning
wages, raises, firing, hiring, or any other aspect of creating worker incentive. "They had no way to motivate anybody because they didn't have the
power over the cash revenues of their departments," says Sue, "and they
feel money is the only thing that motivates anybody."

Manager Authoritarianism.   While complaining about a constrictive
hierarchy, managers themselves were reinforcing that hierarchy in their
authoritarian and exclusionary behavior. They tended to embody an
"extremely Prussian" philosophy about authority which was reflected in
the way they dealt with their bosses and subordinates. Everybody subordinate to them had to be subordinate to them *at all times.* They would not
tolerate disobedience in thought or deed. Further, status differences were
clearly defined and enforced by social customs. In Hungary, for example,
people ranking below a manager were called by their first name, whereas managers would expect lower-ranking people to address them formally using their last name. They did not allow their subordinates to
participate in their decision making.

The Eastern European Manager's Response to the Westerner.   In
an East-West joint venture, a climate is suddenly created in which the
lower-level Eastern European worker and manager can exercise his skills.
What happens? First, the Eastern experiences an enormous amount of
uncertainty about the trust level that's being given, since he or she has no
experience with the sort of incentives and freedoms that have been given.
The North American entrepreneur operates with an enormous amount of
trust and presumes that, given the incentives he or she offers, the
Easterner will respond the way a Westerner would. No time is spent,
however, on dealing with the fears and anxieties of workers and managers and how *they* work through problems and deal with conflict.
Remember, most Eastern managers lack the extensive managerial skills
necessary to effect significant organizational changes in a joint venture.
For years, managers spent their time finding ways of satisfying politically
motivated party officials and the local welfare interests of their enterprises instead of concentrating their energies on implementing modern management techniques in their factories to upgrade production performance.
   What happens in this Eastern European-Western enterprise when
things aren't going right? The rational response for the Eastern
European manager is to hang low and not say much. When Eastern

workers respond in this way to problems, the North American concludes that it's hopeless and withdraws. The North American doesn't understand the Eastern European's anxiety and uncertainty, The uncertainty comes from the fact that they're being asked to manage and work in a Western style, using Western methods, but they don't know how their own system can accommodate those methods. As a foreign manager, you must respect and remember the fact, as you carry out training, that the Eastern European manager has the ability to become the kind of manager you want him or her to become—and that you must make extraordinary changes in the Eastern European enterprise in the face of culturally ingrained attitudes and thinking processes that work against the acceptance of new ways of doing things.

Promoting the Three C's: Change, Communication, and Conflict Resolution

All people fear change to some degree, but when changes enacted by foreign parties in one's place of work are felt as a direct threat to one's ability to put food on the table, the resistance to change can be adamantine. Children in Eastern Europe don't get weaned on Cinderella stories or Horatio Alger stories. People *expect* life to be tragic, for things *not* to work out, for life to be hard. The idea of work is resolutely anchored to the notion of sitting around, drinking tea, and complaining to each other. Eastern Europe's masses are only now making the connection that if they are more productive personally, they will better their lives and their national economies. Many, however, still lack the incentive to transform themselves.

Ruby Maxham deals with low self-esteem and defeatism when trying to motivate newly enlisted Amway distributors in Hungary. Most Hungarians don't believe that they can make themselves a success, she says. "You have to *inspire* them. You have to make them realize that they can make something of themselves by working hard and changing their negative attitude." This is part of the psychology of capitalism that must be imparted to people in the East—along with its economic fundamentals. Some people have been exposed to the culture of capitalism; others have not.

Gauging Attitudes Toward Change

In any given state-owned enterprise in Eastern Europe, the attitudes toward change divide workers and managers into three distinct groups: (1) those who want change—the *change agents*, (2) those who are waiting to see before they change, and (3) those who have no intention of changing. To deal with this situation, you have to create empathy in each group for the imperatives of the others and encourage compromise among them. As a manager, you must *validate* change and *reward* people for speaking up, while creating ways for them to do so. This is the first step in bringing new values into the Eastern European workplace. As a salesperson, trainer, or manager in Eastern Europe, you need to realize that the perception of and response to new systems of management will vary across the spectrum of workers and managers in an enterprise. That is, your work force will probably be out of sync in its attitude concerning how far and how fast your ideas should be implemented.

Most Easterners don't yet *believe* that they can achieve success through creativity and personal enterprise. Getting them to *try* is the first step; your worst mistake is to throw up your hands when they don't try and leave the region in frustration, thinking "These people will never learn." Many have learned, and have learned very fast. Others will astound you as entrepreneurs because they have operated as shadow capitalists under Socialism all along. "We are sure we will do better since we will be working for ourselves," Elvira Nikolayeva told *The New York Times* recently. She's the elected commercial director of a newly privatized "worker's collective" called the Radio-Technika Store in Nizhny Novgorod, Russia. "We know our market, we know our products, and, most important, we realize the rubles we earn go into our own pockets, not the state's."

Creating an Atmosphere for Open Communication

Management depends on the effective flow of applied information. The problem is that inside the Eastern European enterprise, constructive communication between factory managers and workers and between workers themselves in the presence of managers is virtually nil. Eastern managers may be able to define a problem, but the reasons for failure are neither accepted nor explored. They eschew organized meetings in which open discussion concerning management difficulties or operating failures occurs, fearing ostracism from superiors if they are perceived as culpable if a problem becomes known. Easterners may not want to get into a meeting in which they have to talk about problems. No one seems willing to commit to anything until the problem has been solved. For 45 years under Soviet communism, workers and managers operated in a system in which they had to be careful about how they spoke about a problem, about conflict, or about any aspect of the production unit that was not working right. Speaking out on a topic that had implications beyond the factory might result in a person being considered a troublemaker, a sociopath, or subversive—someone trying to undermine the integrity of the state process. Self-sufficiency is an important value in American business. If a problem develops on the job, Westerners are trained to come up with a solution and go to their boss with a plan. Eastern Europeans, however, were conditioned to respond to a problem by throwing up their hands and saying, "What can I do?" If a worker *did* voice a solution to a problem, he or she could get into trouble with management. The result was that most people suppressed their opinions out of fear and avoided openly expressing problems they saw.

But an effort can, and should, be made to get workers and managers talking to each other and to their foreign counterparts. If you are involved in a venture employing a fair number of employees, it is extremely important to quickly develop communication-skills and management-skill training programs that legitimate the expression of concerns and the revelation of production problems. In most foreign ventures, there's not enough communication about *how to communicate.* There's a lot of communication about what the contract is, and what the product is to look like, and when it is to be delivered, and at what price. To win a contract, the manager on the Eastern European side may be reluctant to raise objections or point out potential problems. If the Westerner probes for problems, the Easterner may think that the Westerner is looking for ways to leverage or test them as to whether they know their job.

The American manager might mistake the make-no-waves behavior of an Eastern European for merely acquiescing, or being polite, and not recognize the psychological dimension that has to be overcome. It is necessary to give people *permission* to speak about ways of improving things, about doing things better, and communicating these things through new channels. Otherwise, Eastern European managers will not talk about problems and mishaps, even though they realize that by not addressing them, or correcting the conditions under which problems have arisen, they may not be able to meet the standards to which they are held under contract with the foreigner.

Democratizing Communication Channels. In the face of traditionally hierarchical Eastern European management organization, you must democratize the workplace. If you are buying or entering into a joint venture with a large factory, you must educate yourself so that you will understand how the nondemocratic psychology operated under the old regime. The problem is not a lack of understanding or a lack of education (these are very well-trained and educated people for the most part) but rather a psychological dilemma about what is permissible and about what are the channels through which one can raise issues without being penalized.

Let your workers know how their opinions will be acknowledged (through what channels), who will acknowledge their opinions, how their opinions will be used, and whether there will be some reward for expressing opinions. Explain the philosophy of the company regarding the discussion of problems, how problems get flagged, and what the vehicle is for responding to them.

You need to explain the culture of your company. You need to be thorough in explaining not only what you want Eastern European workers and managers to do but *why* you want them to do it. Help them visualize what the end result of your requested action or change will be. Understand that Eastern Europeans do not possess the experience necessary to quickly grasp the philosophy behind your actions or requests.

When communicating, assume that the local manager does not possess a working knowledge of Western-style managerial technique. Persuade your partner to accept a change—such as adopting your strategy for ordering, documenting, and shipping by showing *why* your system is necessary. Do not simply present it as "this is the way it's always done in the West." Illustrate the benefits that your method will bring to the enterprise. Also, highlight the mistakes you made in the past that have led you to believe that your method works. Without being patronizing, explain why you want to change something and why the manager should do it your way.

Make a concerted effort to build trust and rapport. It is vital that the American manager encourage the Eastern European manager to feel safe in asking for help. You've got half the battle won if the manager can feel perfectly at ease in coming to you with questions, comments, his or her mistakes, and suggestions. If the manager feels uncomfortable revealing his or her weaknesses and mistakes, you're in trouble. The Eastern European does not conceal his or her mistakes and ignorance of Western management practice for some other cultural or political reason. The issues are human pride and uneasiness. Be willing to teach without acting like a tutor. Ideally, communication training ought to be part of an original joint-venture agreement so that the effort is made jointly. Ray Shonholtz, founder of Partners for Democratic Change in San Francisco, advises foreign partners to sponsor *residential* training programs in their venture to get to the process of converting the culture of the enterprise as early as possible. "If you don't go in with the investment in the people, to develop the business culture as understood by the North American, and draw out Central and Eastern Europeans as to their limitations in their own work experience in embracing the North American business culture, and work through that, you are destined to see your venture fail," says Shonholtz. "The North American companies that go in cheap are the joint ventures that fail."

The Gentle Art of Conflict Resolution

Inside any Eastern European enterprise undergoing the transition to becoming a private company, will be both residual and fresh conflict—between managers and workers, between managers and bureaucrats attached to the firm, and—when the foreigner arrives—between the joint-venture parties. All parties want their interests protected. When the foreign manager enters the scene, he or she must acknowledge the vital importance of understanding the tensions and animosities that have built up in the enterprise over years and must understand how to reduce new friction as it arises.

The Inevitable Financial Conflict. Financial conflicts, especially over the issue of how profits should be reinvested, seem to go with the territory, since most Eastern European enterprises are under extreme financial pressure. The prudent foreign partner enters into a joint venture only after thorough review of the fiscal well-being of the prospective venture partner; this review may entail conducting a financial appraisal at the partner's expense. Take a look at what happened to Freissler-Otis (Austria), a subsidiary of Otis (United States), in Hungary. Otis signed a joint-venture agreement with Gep es Felvonoszerelo Vallalat (GFV) in Budapest worth $1.6 million in start-up capital. Otis has a 51 percent stake. The joint venture had sales of $3.5 million in its first year of operation. At the end of 1990, a conflict arose between the partners over the allocation profits. "Freissler-Otis wanted to reinvest all profits during the first three years of operations," reported *Business Eastern Europe*. "On the other hand, GFV—which has had serious liquidity problems—wanted to use its share of JV profits to bail itself out....The problem has been compounded by having two differing sets of accounts, one for local needs and the other to meet U.S. shareholder requirements. The books based on U.S. accounting rules show much higher profits, which Otis wished to fully reinvest. But the Hungarian side wanted to use their net profit share—as per local accounting rules—to improve on the financial plight of GFV." As of this writing the conflict was yet to be resolved, though sales were climbing 100 percent a year.

Conflict over the use of profits scuttled another, smaller joint venture. Cary Harrell, a veteran marketing director in the United States, found an opportunity in selling out-of-season American goods in Estonia that her former employer, the Michigan Trade Exchange, could help her buy at low prices at so-called distressed sales. As profiled in *The Los Angeles Times*, she had hired some Russian émigrés to travel to Russia in search of lucrative business opportunities. They returned with a plan to link her to an Estonian couple, Andres and Kuellike Neeme, who wanted to form a joint venture. They owned a café and had been bitten by the American dream; in fact, more than anything, they wanted to own a Buick. Harrell and the Neemes opened a hard-currency store that sold American goods—"American style," that is—in Tallinn, the capital of Estonia. Harrell was backed by Paul Rosenberg, a Los Angeles investor. The Neemes would locate the real estate, pay the necessary bribes, and finesse the red tape. Harrell's side provided the capital, store fixtures, and merchandise. The partners would split the profits 40:60, with the larger share going to Harrell. Sounds charming. "We buy at close-out prices, twenty cents on the dollar, and mark it up 100 percent. We're able to bring it in duty-free," Harrell told *Los Angeles Times* reporter Tamara Jones in April 1992. But then things got strange. The Neemes were, as Harrell said, "stealing us blind." She attempted to sever the partnership. "The perception is that every American is a millionaire," Harrell says. "[Andres Neeme would] come in, take things out of the store and sell them for hard currency in his café. He'd demand the keys to the warehouse from the kids working here and go load up his truck. He demanded $1,000 for coffee machines for his café."

The next step on the machinations of the Neemes was to close the store, saying that the venture hadn't paid its taxes. Things probably got even uglier, but in their out-of-court agreement to "divorce," each partner vowed to maintain confidentiality. Harrell does claim that the Neemes stole over $21,000 worth of merchandise. The Neemes feel, however, that they are the victims. "We are totally innocent people!" says Mrs. Neeme. "Cary shamed us before all Estonia. We haven't done anything wrong." Mr. Neeme says: "We were supposed to get 40 percent of all profits. After we had been working half a year, the American side announced that there was no profit at all; [the venture was] in debt and therefore due nothing. The shop was making huge profits, though. Nobody believed this." Although Harrell says the store now clears $21,000 a month, the bills associated with paying customs bribes and start-up costs had to be paid before the venture could be said to be making a profit. The Neemes could not understand this and apparently started taking what they perceived to be "profit" directly out of the warehouse and selling it at their café.

Harrell got nasty when she found out and read them the riot act: "You walk away. Take what you've stolen from me. Or, we go to Sweden and I file criminal charges and use every resource I have to ruin your family name." The Neemes settled and did walk away from the deal, which Harrell now operates as a wholly foreign owned venture. A store in Minsk and an outlet in Moscow are on the drawing board. "I want American-style stores all over the former U.S.S.R," she says. Meanwhile, the Neemes linked up with some Finns and Germans and plan to open a department store, another shop, and a restaurant. "My feeling is that the American side took advantage of my husband's work," says Mrs. Neeme. "They will profit from it for the next 10 years. The Americans fly here and fly back. They come and go, but we live here; we're trying to build ourselves a life. The big misfortune for Estonians is we don't know how to do business. We just don't know the rules. They have won. We have lost."

Joint-Venture Management Guidelines

- If Eastern managers are bogged down making decisions on minutiae, it follows that the incoming foreign manager may be drowned in requests to decide on trivial matters also. "You have to work on decentralizing your decision making process," says Andrew Wnuk, a manager working for a joint venture in Krakow, Poland, between Continental White Cap and Opakomet that was formed in 1990. "You want to push those decisions down, but you can't push them down too quickly." This is because workers in Eastern Europe still expect a manager to rule over every aspect of the enterprise. "If you ask other people to make those decisions, you're [viewed as] incompetent," says Wnuk. First prepare workers for the fact that you will be delegating decision making, and when they are ready to handle a new responsibility, give it to them.

- You may find that few managers in the enterprise want to wield real authority and take responsibility. Keep an eye trained on the work force for those individuals who will. Resourceful people rise to the fore in Eastern European enterprises as they respond to market forces. For example, a line-assembly person might possess leadership ability; put this person in charge of one of those "trivial" decisions that you don't want. Delegate to those willing to lead. Put your work force under a microscope until you find these people, because they may not feel empowered to come to you.

- The Eastern European tends to view a new venture as an opportunity for workers and managers from the production unit associated with the Eastern partner company to gain employment. Almost all joint ventures suffer from overstaffing. Many workers are holdovers from the previous enterprise. These redundant workers create a problem because the foreign partner often brings to the venture substantial amounts of new technology that require a smaller, more skilled work force. The foreign manager should not react by slashing the size of the work force. Firing people goes against the moral imperative rooted in Socialist Eastern Europe: the promotion of egalitarianism. Managers do not want to be guilty of causing their neighbors to starve. Though you may be forced to agree to keep an original work force intact for a specific number of years, you can reduce the number of workers through early retirements, maternity leaves, and, most important, by enforcing new disciplinary rules which will result in some firing. Most countries have made it simpler to carry out work force reductions. But don't fire employees abruptly or mercilessly, as the public relations cost will be high. Many U.S. firms gain some control over hiring and firing in the initial phase of start-up through an examination process that includes intelligence, psychological, and manual dexterity testing.

- In the past, Eastern European workers enjoyed little or no role in the management of the enterprise beyond the chance to resist changes if wages were not raised. How do you motivate Eastern European workers to take responsibility? "The first way is with money," says Polish private entrepreneur Dariusz Linert, who pays his workers the normal salary of $200 per month plus a monthly bonus linked to performance. Among other incentive-creating techniques are offering upward mobility to workers by training them as versatile managers, teaching them skills that will further their career outside the joint venture; ensuring worker satisfaction by helping with housing and welfare; and giving the factory interior and exterior a new look and cleaning up working environments, adding lighting, renovating workshops, etc.

- Work groups should be encouraged to share responsibility and divide labor among themselves. Work groups should be rewarded for innovation and efficient productivity. Group tasks should be rotated so that each group begins to acquire a more general knowledge of the workings of the joint venture. Concentrate on creating an organization that is highly respected by both employees and the community at large—in short, an organization capable of inspiring *loyalty*....an organization which helps its employees to better their lives and the lives of those they love and which promises to do so on a continuing basis. Set up a lounge in the joint-venture factory, construct a recreation room, provide entertainment, sponsor classes, provide a library, install shower and bath facilities on the premises. Safety, cleanliness, and good food should also be part of the joint-venture regimen.

- Real-time data collection was never part of Eastern European enterprise management. You have to make it clear that timely data about the enterprise's activities must be collected and used appropriately to enhance its productivity. Your first request for production data will likely be ready for your review a month after the request. Request that it be done faster, again and again, until everyone in the enterprise understands that data can be collected, and used, in real time.

- Possibly the shortest route to conversion of the working culture of a former state-owned enterprise is through retraining, especially in the States. United Technology (UT) pursues a plan to become what it terms a "multidomestic company," with administrators and managers being local nationals. (Its venture in Hungary is operated by Hungarians.) As reported in *Doing Business in Eastern Europe*, "UTA employees [in Hungary] from all levels will be trained in the West at other UTA facilities. Since many of the employees have never been in the West before, the firm plans to send interpreters along and train two weeks in the West, two weeks back in Hungary, and then back to the Western facility for another stint. The training will not only be an introduction to new technology and Western financial accounting methods, but an induction into the U.S. firm's work habits."

Send the Right Manager to Eastern Europe

It goes without saying that managing in Eastern Europe requires a special type of person to represent the interests of the foreign joint-venture partner and implement all the advice outlined in this chapter. Western companies have asked executive search organizations to find local nationals, rather than Westerners, to operate their businesses in Eastern Europe. "To our surprise," says Michael A. Pappan, vice chairman-international at Ward Howell, an executive search organization, "that's been more than half of our business." An executive with the personnel search firm Paul Ray & Carre Orban International told me: "There aren't a heck of a lot of people that have the level of contact and familiarity that a company needs to deal with what is a very unstructured situation in virtually all of the countries of Eastern Europe."

A primary motive on the part of companies in looking for a local national is, of course, the cost break in terms of salary. But there are other motives. A manager who has been running a factory outside of Budapest or Bucharest or Warsaw someplace where it's hard to get parts, the machinery is old and has to be fixed all the time, and the power supply goes out daily, is a manager who has been struggling in extremely difficult circumstances, and he or she will likely make a very resourceful manager. There need to be, in fact, both presences in a joint venture: Staff people who understand the locals because they are local people and staff from the West who can be the change agents, who can change the culture of the company.

I spoke with Michael A. Pappan about his company's move into Eastern Europe. "We started out our [Eastern European business expansion] thinking that the bulk of our business would be the recruitment of Western businessmen to that part of the world, who may have an ethnic background in Eastern Europe, language ability, and some cultural affinity, but who primarily had Western business experience. It turned out that was not the case. More than half of our search assignments in Eastern Europe are looking for local nationals, although there are certain positions that the local national can't fill, like being the general manager of an operation in Hungary [because] it's very unlikely that we're going to find somebody in Hungary, unless he has spent a lot of time in the West." Pappan predicts that eventually even production and administrative functions and, as time goes on, finance and marketing positions will be filled by local nationals. "Local nationals have the one thing that people from the U.S. don't have: Knowledge of the language and a cultural understanding of the people that are working for them," says Pappan.

How do you find talented local professionals? "That's where our local offices come in," says Pappan. "It's a different process than here. They don't have databases or industry reference manuals. It has to be done much like it was in the old days in the United States, through word of mouth and the old-boy network. Because of the lack of databases [Eastern Europeans], have a much better developed old-boy network than we do anymore here."

If you are from the West and are looking for a job in the New East, here's what search organizations are looking for. First, language ability is vital. Cultural knowledge, too, based on years lived in Eastern Europe during the Communist era. Plus, you need to be an experienced manager. "What we're looking for," says Pappan, "once you get beyond the technological training and hopefully some language and cultural affinity, is *management ability*—success as a manager in a Western organization. Someone who has proved that he can run something. An effective motivator who is organized and can build a business."

Hiring a Western Representative

The first rule in filling an Eastern Europe management post: Don't send a middle manager with a background as an accountant or lawyer to manage a plant, just because he or she speaks the local language. Send the person who has worked the whole assembly line from top to bottom, who gets under the machines, who gets his or her hands dirty. Send the practitioner, not the theorist. A solid, hands-on knowledge of the production line earns the foreign manager the acceptance and respect he or she will need in order to make changes in an enterprise. Moreover, the Western expatriate may be more effective in an administrative capacity like human resource management, finance, or marketing, where his or her Western-style expertise will have an immediate impact. Local nationals or émigrés will typically be more adept in finessing the local bureaucracy and procuring needed resources for the venture.

One key consideration must be acknowledged before hiring someone to work in Eurasia: Does he or she possess an extraordinarily *patient and tolerant* disposition? Eastern Europe is defined by paradoxes. To work in the region, an expatriate needs to be able to deal with irreconcilable contradictions and exhibit an almost inhuman tolerance for inconsistencies. "One can sit in a Moscow office," says Jonathan J. Halperin, president and founder of FYI Information Resources in Moscow, "with the capacity to send a television image around the world at the flick of a switch but without sufficient paper to produce a press release." Some people have infinite patience; nothing surprises them. Other expatriates lose composure easily and, in worst-case scenarios, bad-mouth the locals. Nothing can do the image of your firm more harm in Eastern Europe.

Get the CEO into the Action

Don't allow the home office to become a distant player in your company's business in Eastern Europe. Keep company heads updated on your activities, hardships, and successes in order to prevent sudden changes in corporate direction initiated by uninformed executives.

Michael Mears, former head of the U.S. Commercial Office in Moscow, has said: "There's a big crack between the poor fool who is here trying to do business in this labyrinthine mess and the Board and Directors and politicians back in the States who are reading perestroika stories." A CEO not totally on board and committed to your endeavors in the New East is an impediment far worse that any of the potential pitfalls in the market we have discussed thus far.

Joint-Venture Management Success: GE and Tungsram

When General Electric formed a joint venture with Tungsram in Hungary, it took over not just one factory but in fact 12 Tungsram factories, 11 in Hungary and 1 in Austria. The factories were what you'd expect to find in an Eastern European country. In terms of hardware, the factories had the equipment to manufacture a broad range of light bulbs, including incandescent, fluorescent, and specialty bulbs like automotive light bulbs and Christmas holiday bulbs. The quality of Tungsram's products was not the issue; Tungsram enjoyed a reputation for high-quality products in Eastern and Western Europe. In fact, there were jokes in Budapest that GE had to teach Tungsram how to build *lower-quality* light bulbs in order to sell more light bulbs to consumers and thus generate a profit. "There's no technological reason that you can't make a light bulb that will last 25 or 30 years," GE spokesman John Betchkal told me, and Tungsram was making them. "But the bottom line is that people don't want to pay, say, fifteen dollars for a fourteen-watt fluorescent light bulb that will last ten thousand hours if they can pay seventy-five cents for an incandescent light bulb that will last seven hundred fifty or one thousand hours."

The monumental task for GE managers was human engineering needed to make Tungsram competitive in the world market. General Electric inherited 18,000 people who worked in a variety of jobs at Tungsram factories spread all over the company. General Electric didn't know what most of the workers really did or if they were any good at what they did; there were simply too many workers. However, it soon become clear that most were good workers. George Varga, GE's head manager of the venture, described the typical Hungarian worker at Tungsram to *World Link:* "We didn't find a lot of the 'lazy Communist workers' one hears so much about. These guys work. They are diligent and get upset when the raw materials are wrong or managers give stupid orders."

While Varga applauded the workers, he found that Tungsram's managers left a lot to be desired. "Our biggest problem came at the management level," says Varga. "Many of the managers had to get over their past experience and the autocratic mind-set it had engendered." Levels of middle management that ascended stepwise from the assembly floor to the top executive had to be reduced in number from nine to three. "The most difficult part is the human software," remembers Varga. "New ideas were discouraged, there was very little initiative and zero sense of ownership." No longer could Tungsram directors focus all their energy on generating hard currency for the state. With their new partner, they now had to focus on generating sales, lowering costs, increasing productivity, and earning a profit. Moreover, with GE managers, they had to somehow streamline Tungsram's costly internal network of social services including schools, holiday homes, and three professional sports teams!

General Electric hired International Management & Development Group Ltd. (IM&D), a New York-based consulting firm, to draw up plans for the Tungsram transformation. The GE/Tungsram transition "model" pursued clearly defined objectives that other joint-venture partners should include in their restructuring plans. General Electric had to find the right combination of American, Hungarian, and European management style. First, GE set up a system to identify new employment opportunities for workers who would have to be terminated. Although massive layoffs in Hungary had not been seen or tolerated previously, GE reduced Tungsram's labor force from 17,600 to 14,297 (the reductions fall short of Varga's target of 10,000). Varga felt that if GE came in like the American bully and put 4,000 people out on the street, trust between GE and Hungary's working population would be destroyed. (Five hundred new employees were hired who had skills needed to raise productivity. Wages have gone up because of inflation and because GE has wanted to attract and keep talented professionals.)

Second, the company made it a priority to train laid-off workers and enhance their skills so they could find new jobs. As part of this effort, Tungsram and GE assisted local business start-ups so that new jobs would be created for laid-off workers. IM&D helped GE relocate 84 former Tungsram employees. With a loan from Tungsram and a facility donated by the local government, a local business person established a factory in Kisvarda that makes overalls and packaging materials, among other products. Tungsram's Employee Venture Fund was set up to provide grants and loans of up to $3,000 to employees who have promising business ideas.

With these radical social policies under way, GE set about upgrading the skills of workers through retraining. This effort went hand in hand with the modernization of Tungsram's production technology. "We introduced such things as pay-for-performance," says Betchkal, "and while that was alien, people discovered that if they were smarter, more effective, or more clever, they would make more money." The joint-venture also articulated a clear corporate mission that emphasized teamwork between the two sides, attention to customers, and responsibility to the company's work force. *Industry Week* summarized GE's statement of shared visions and values: "[Our] vision is to make Tungsram a world-class, customer-oriented company by uniting the best attributes of Tungsram and GE. At the same time, it is our goal to have highly productive, well-paid people and provide them with excellent working conditions and a work atmosphere which allows for freedom of initiative, self-determination, and job satisfaction."

When I asked how the "two sides" have gotten along since, John Betchkal replied: "I kind of cringe at the 'two sides' term. We've been there a fairly long time now. We've got Hungarians going back and forth from Budapest, and the other plant cities, to Cleveland. Our people go back and forth and talk on the phone. I stood in a guy's corridor for about fifteen minutes this morning. He's a research scientist manager and he was talking to a guy in Budapest; they were working something out together. We're at the point now where people are beyond the initial reaction [to the venture] and are now into running the business, and making it competitive." But did it work? "The biggest criticism that we heard from the Hungarian employees was that we weren't moving fast enough," says Betchkal. "We are, by nature and practice, the kind of company that takes a [long] look at a situation. The Hungarians had been looking at Tungsram for twenty years, so they were saying, 'Let's put in new machinery, change this, change that,' but we wanted to make sure it was the right decision." I sense that the "two sides" have, indeed, merged into one in this venture, but George Varga's words will remain true for some time to come: "Attitudes will be the most difficult thing to change," he said of his challenge. "It's not a problem you can just throw money at."

11
Mastering the Technology-Transfer Game

It is a widely held notion, as far as science and technology are concerned, that communism causes brain death.

JOHN KISER III, PRESIDENT OF KRI, INC.,
WASHINGTON, D.C.

Remember Rubik's Cube?

"Rubik's cube was a mechanical miracle," says Robert Hecht-Nielsen, chairman of the board of HNC, Inc., a neural network hardware manufacturer in San Diego. "Devilishly clever."

You might be surprised to learn that Rubik's cube, which came on the international market in 1980 with great success, was invented by a Hungarian teacher named E. Rubik. Hecht-Nielsen's eyes light up: "And there are *many more* Rubik's cubes in Eastern Central Europe and the Soviet Union....Whoever finds them, stands to win—and win big." It's true. From the time Peter the Great made technology acquisition from the West a national priority in Russia in the nineteenth century, the sophistication of Russia's scientific community has far surpassed the country's economic position relative to other countries. That legacy was passed on to all of the Warsaw Pact nations.

Technological Excellence in the East

Working with bare necessities in the way of laboratory equipment, Soviet and Eastern bloc scientists in ministry-affiliated institutes or the Academy of Sciences pioneered more than their share of breakthrough technologies. "There is nothing like shortages, obsolete equipment and poor-quality raw materials," writes John Kiser, president of KRI, Inc., a technology transfer company in Washington, "to stimulate the mind." Savvy Western companies have not ignored the basic research and product development that has taken place in Eastern-Central Europe and the U.S.S.R. since World War II. For example, the soft contact lens was developed from technology founded on the inventions of the Czech chemist Otto Wichterle—technology which Bausch & Lomb licensed, to great benefit, in the 1960s. U.S. Surgical Corporation was going nowhere in the 1970s until it licensed Soviet technology for surgical stapling; now, it's a leader in medical suturing with annual sales of $250 million. The list of acquired technologies from the East is long. General Electric has purchased a license from Hungary for a compact flywheel energy-storage system for use in X-ray machines. DuPont has purchased a license for a cardiovascular drug from the Soviet Union.

Over the past three decades, the Soviet Union sold over 300 processes, inventions and innovations, to companies in Western countries, the lion's share of Eastern European sales of technologies. Numerous German, Belgian, Swedish, Italian, British, Spanish, Austrian, and U.S. firms have purchased technology from the Soviets in sectors such as ferrous and nonferrous metallurgy, process engineering, the food industry, agriculture, machine building, chemicals, industrial construction, microbiology, and medical equipment production. Foreign buyers have included Nippon Kokan (Japan), Italimpianti (Italy), Newton Chambers (U.K.), and Altos Hornos (Spain), the last buying a license for production of dry coke quenching equipment. The Japanese purify industrial waste using U.S.S.R.-developed treatment plants. McDermott (U.K.) bought a technology license for welding large-diameter pipes.

With the former Soviet military industrial complex selling its secrets, the opportunity to pick up proprietary technologies at extremely reasonable prices achieved critical mass in the early 1990s. American purchases of sensitive Russian high-tech products include a space-station nuclear reactor generator called the Topaz, to be set up for experimental use at the University of New Mexico. The Topaz is a space-vehicle propulsion unit used to propel satellites in space. The United States has also purchased plutonium-238 from Russia, which is used to fuel satellites on deep-space missions.

Combining the talents and technologies of the United States and the former Soviet Union could take human beings to Mars. In fact, the Russians are urging that such a mission be undertaken; it would be especially symbolic, given that the space programs of both Russia and America were offspring of the Cold War. The Russians sent cosmonauts up with their space station for long-term space flight; that experience could be useful in planning a mission to Mars. NASA put a man on the moon. "There's a reservoir of skills, facilities, and capabilities in the former Soviet Union that ought to be used for common objectives," says John M. Logsdon, a space-policy expert at George Washington University. "It makes no sense to throw it away." Both sides see the mission as a way to keep former Soviet scientists tied to their desks, rather than accepting job offers in Libya, Syria, and Iraq. "The manned exploration of Mars is something we can't pass up," says Bill Spencer, president of Sematech, a government-industry consortium in the United States. "But [this is something] we ought to do as a planet. We don't have to be macho and do it ourselves any more."

Scientists for Hire!

Central-Eastern Europe and the former Soviet Union are home to a community of creative and well-educated technical specialists, who have labored in a repressive scientific environment in which they had little opportunity to see their innovations come to fruition in the form of product prototypes. "Yet hidden in this failed system," says Eastern Europe technology expert John W. Kiser, "is a 'use what you have' approach that can yield tremendous competitive benefits, when put into the right hands. 'What they have' is a collection of very well-trained, mathematically oriented engineers and experimentalists. Solutions with high ratios of brainware to hardware mean sophisticated results using simple, cheap equipment—an investor's dream."

These people possess "hands-on" technical competency that remains a largely untapped source of advanced product ideas. Moreover, their discoveries, processes, and prototypes are ready for licensing or joint manufacture and marketing by Western technology hunters. In Eastern Europe the inquisitive Westerner can find state-of-the-art technologies as well as alternative sources of high-tech expertise and manufacturing capabilities. For example, Corning, Inc., has hired more than 100 Russian scientists to undertake research in fiber optics. In another arrangement, AT&T Bell Laboratories will hire 27 Russian scientists from St. Petersburg's A.F. Ioffe Physico-Technical Institute to research semiconductor physics and semiconductor lasers. Salaries, travel expenses, and equipment will cost AT&T under $100,000 for an entire year of research work. United Technologies has joined forces with the Institute of Structural Macrokinetics in Russia to develop novel high-strength ceramics.

To begin hunting for the future Rubik's Cubes of the East, you should be acquainted with both the indigenous technological capabilities and the nature of the R&D environment in the East.

Eastern Europe's R&D Landscape

Like industrial production, scientific research in the Eastern bloc was forced to conform to Stalin's vision of "Soviet reality." Each country in the Soviet sphere was directed to specialize in a particular technological niche created to serve the needs of Russia's defense-oriented industrial establishment. "Our computer industry was deliberately created for the Soviet market," says Venko Karov, head of a Sofia research institute, in Bulgaria, the country selected by Moscow to build computers. Poland's scientists concentrated on electronics and electrical engineering (51 percent of science and technology staff) and chemicals (18 percent of science and technology staff). Insulated by the Iron Curtain, the Eastern bloc pursued science and technology endeavors without considering of the needs and preferences of non-Communist end-users. "Inside Comecon, we were a great power," recalls Venko Karov. "For fifteen years, the Cold War was good for us." But after the Cold War, and the end of Comecon, Karov visited the computer industry in California, and his tune changed. "I've been to Silicon Valley. There is no basis for comparison. It's hopeless....The only way out [for us] is to work under the guidance of a Western company."

Pockets of Eastern Technological Excellence

C.I.S. (Commonwealth of Independent States): Defense-related technology, pulsed power, microwave, advanced materials, heavy industry, electronics, sensor capabilities, space technologies

Eastern Germany: Flexible manufacturing systems, software for industrial applications, optics, machine tool technology, advanced welding technologies

Poland: Shipbuilding, coal mining, chemicals

Hungary: Pharmaceuticals, agriculture, computer software, electronics

Czechoslovakia: Machine building, machine tools, textile machinery design, weapons manufacturing, process chemistry

Bulgaria: Computer technologies, electronics

The Structure of Eastern Bloc Science and Technology

The organization of scientific research was similar throughout Eastern Europe, and thus science and technology suffered the same basic problems in each country. Science-related institutions introduced in Central-Eastern Europe after World War II mirrored those in the Soviet Union, so we can speak about the subject in general terms for the entire region. To varying degrees the "system" still exists in Eastern European countries.

Government-run scientific institutions were divided into three groups: research institutes under the control of academies of science, R&D institutes and laboratories controlled by branches of industrial ministries, and universities and various schools of higher education. In each country, the three groups performed different tasks and were not linked "horizontally."

1. The academies of science played a dual role as high-level government-controlled science institutions and as matrixes of research institutes conducting research at the highest level. Their scientists enjoyed access to the best equipment, free travel, and few teaching responsibilities.

2. Various ministries involved in agriculture, trade, forestry, health, and so on, governed and financed the R&D. These institutes contracted to *develop* scientific research into usable technologies, and thus they became influential and rich, though they were home to relatively few Ph.D. holders. In Poland, they consumed 80 percent of total science and technology funds. These institutes conducted research and development with the aim of resolving technical problems encountered in state-owned enterprises under each ministry. Since no market existed, virtually none of the R&D performed in these institutes was implemented in a final product.

3. The universities and other educational institutions, recently stripped of much of their status and research resources, were the second bastion of scientific research, though they were considered stifling to creative experimentation and highly paternalistic. The extreme compartmentalization of research endeavor tended to exclude interdisciplinary research and to keep constructive criticism of a scientist's work to a minimum. Rather than rise in the scientific community through the merit of one's work, one got ahead by climbing a ladder of degrees, titles, and positions while locked into permanent job positions based on tenure. Young graduates leaving universities, of course, found few opportunities

awaiting them in educational and research institutions (Figs. 11-1 and 11-2).

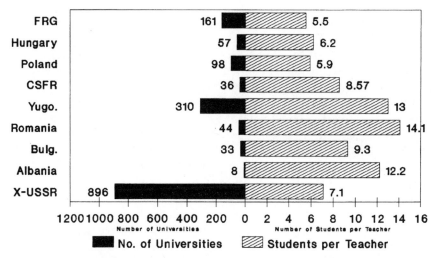

Figure 11-1. Finding a college and a teacher: Number of universities and teachers. (*Statisticki Godiahjak Jugoslavije 1990, for Yugoslavia; and EUROSTAT Central Eastern Europe, 1991–1992.*)

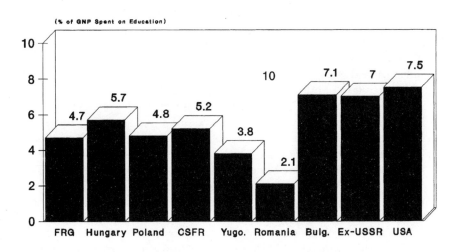

Figure 11-2. Varying priority on education: Percent of GNP spent on education. (*UNESCO, Statistical Yearbook, 1989.*)

Moreover, a gulf existed between the research institutes and universities which removed the possibility for synergy between education and research. Money spent on applied research was often wasted because end-users of the research either did not exist or were little interested in a scientist's results; R&D was centralized geographically in the capital city of each country. Of all R&D institutes in Poland, for example, including those affiliated with the Polish Academy of Sciences, almost half were set up in Warsaw. Krakow, Poznan, Lodz, Katowice, and Wroclaw—the country's five largest cities—accounted for another 41 percent.

Czechoslovakia's science and technology landscape was typical of Eastern Europe. Czechoslovakia developed an extensive network of scientific research organizations under a centrally planned Socialist economic regime, including (1) numerous institutes under the academies of science, (2) multifunctional applied research and technology development institutes, each under the auspices of specific economic ministries, and (3) universities and colleges of higher education.

Basic research was conducted at the academies of science. About 140 research institutes, each run by its own administrative staff and supported by independent services, conducted research activities outside the purview of the academy. Unlike the situation in the West, universities played only a minor part in scientific research, and research institutions generally did not exchange information and ideas with each other. Within the Czech and Slovak republics, a high degree of duplication of specific research facilities existed, in no small measure because each republic built independent institutions without much analysis of the plans of the other. The same duplication of scientific endeavor occurred in other Eastern countries.

During the decades of Socialism, Czech and Slovak specialists found little incentive to conduct applied scientific endeavor in an efficient or profit-oriented manner. In fact, their job mobility depended more on political activity than on the significance of their scientific research. Research tended to be "basic," not geared to solving practical problems by developing new technologies. In 1991, however, everything changed in Czechoslovakia's science and technology sector, and indeed in science and technology sectors throughout the region. First, and most important, the system of financing scientific research from state budgets was radically reformed. Although Eastern European governments continued to provide temporary financing from state budgets to research centers (since to do otherwise would force the closure of virtually all of them), science and technology policymakers began to require industry, including state-owned industry, to pay for its own R&D efforts with revenue earned through exports to world markets.

In short, funding for innovation has been drastically cut, which is unfortunate, since scientific innovation is exactly what Eastern Europe needs to develop the products to sell in order to survive in a competitive world economy. Rather than the state paying for science for science's sake, without a profit objective in mind, *grant systems* were set up in both the academies of science and universities throughout the entire region in most areas of scientific research. Funding for scientific endeavor at research institutes and universities could now come out of the state budget in the form of research grants for *specific* projects, with independent councils of scientific scholars deciding what projects would see the light of day. In Poland, one third of science funding is now allocated in the form of research grants awarded after open competition between scientific groups proposing projects. (The figure is not expected to top 50 percent.) Similar systems have been implemented all across Eastern Europe.

The hope is that grants will remove personal ties as a factor in winning financing and put long-overdue emphasis on scientific merit and profit potential. Also, as Polish scientist Andrzej Ziabicki said in a lecture, "Grants give real opportunities to able and young people who, especially in Poland, might have to wait many years for advancement within the hierarchical structure of academia." Indeed, Poland's scientists responded to the new grant system enthusiastically. The proposals came in lorries, filling three rooms to the ceiling: 9,600 projects were submitted in the first round, totally overwhelming the filing system of the new committee in charge of evaluating them. The following three months were dedicated solely to creating a computer registration system for grant applications.

Who do scientists have to convince that their project proposals are viable? Ironically, the same people who ran the academies of science and the military industrial complex in the past—the same drone managers who were there under the Communist regimes. Although the only change in R&D personnel so far has been that some older R&D Communist managers have been retired, and a number of younger people in the apparatus have been promoted to higher decision-making positions, decision makers do have a new list of criteria to use in deciding which scientists get funded. To get funded, scientists must address real market issues and innovate for profit.

The R&D game right now consists of scientific people demonstrating how energetically they can address the world technology market and earn foreign exchange. The more convincing that demonstration is, the more regularly they eat, literally. If an R&D endeavor has the potential to earn foreign exchange on the world market, government support for that activity most likely continues unabated. Some scientists and researchers have been nimble and have found ways of involving themselves in activities that seem to have a future. Others have faltered, or their labs have faltered, in making the transition to a market orientation, and they face unemployment. Almost all labs are now under tremendous financial pressure, and most have fragmented into groups led by competing managers, each vying for government support in the form of grants, in competition against the others. Most have no access to the necessary funding to move their innovations to market. "We could make a big profit if we just had a little money for production," Russian scientist Viliam L. Sanderov told *The Los Angeles Times* recently. He says he has developed a smaller, more reliable, and cheaper microchip than now available, utilizing aluminum film instead of gold wire. "But we have no investor," he says, "so we cannot get started. We don't even have enough money to pay for having a patent processed [abroad]. So someone could steal our idea." Like many others, Sanderov has no support from the government to start up production or seek partners overseas, not even to pay for the translation of a letter to companies in the States which he believes would be interested in his invention. "We're not used to this," he admits. "We're used to defense funds paying for all our projects and assuring us a comfortable life. Now we have to get adjusted to a whole new world."

Faced with unemployment and complete uncertainty about their futures, hundreds of Eastern European scientists have emigrated and/or taken jobs offered by Western companies. Unfortunately, the people who emigrate are often the most outstanding. The number of scientists who are leaving should not be exaggerated, however. The number of former Soviet scientists who will eventually leave their homeland will probably remain around 10 percent of the total former Soviet science community. About half of these people have left the country as part of government programs, without specific jobs lined up in the West. Not to paint too grim a picture, I should emphasize that a number of labs in Eastern Europe have come under extremely competent and market-sensitive leadership by top-notch technology managers. In these organizations, technologies are being developed for market by instinct, without any need for directives from above. Labs like these are rare, but they do exist in Eastern Europe.

Technology Licensing Opportunities

Eastern Europe is ripe for technological modernization, and American firms can supply that technology either directly through sales of high-tech equipment or indirectly through technology licensing and training. Indeed, Eastern European governments offer concessions to foreign firms that exhibit a willingness to transfer their advanced technology. It follows that for North American corporations to compete effectively in the region, they must offer technological upgrading as part of a deal and must implement that technology smoothly. A perfect first step to take in doing this is to license the use of your technology or process to an Eastern European enterprise.

Selling Licenses

Most Western firms that have entered into coproduction or licensing agreements in Eastern Europe report that the experience has been positive. You will find high-level technical expertise in Eastern European enterprises. Their managers exhibit genuine respect for patent and trademark rights; this keeps theft to a minimum. Also, they have performed well in upgrading quality control standards at the foreign partner's request. A Western manager who has worked in the Czechoslovakia market for seven years told *Business Eastern Europe:* "Our [licensing] agreement was an unqualified success by any measurement one chooses to use. We encountered no major headaches uncommon to licensing in other parts of the world."

Literally thousands of Eastern European enterprises are technology hungry; some are surprisingly experienced technology purchasers already. For example, Videoton is Hungary's largest manufacturer of electronics and a major purchaser of Western technology licenses. Employing 20,000 people, Videoton first specialized in radio and TV receivers, but during the 1970s, it moved into the manufacture of data processing equipment, purchasing licenses from France's CII for minicomputers, U.S. Data Products for line printers, and Siemens for computer memory and various computer components. In the area of computer banking, Videoton paid more than $300,000 in 1980 to SEMS of France to update its minicomputer, and $700,000 to Data Products for a license to manufacture computer printers. Through a joint venture that started in 1984 with Walters Microsystems of the U.K., Videoton bought a license from a U.S. company for a head-printer assembly. Videoton has also been building video recording equipment, after purchasing a license along with know-how in 1984 from Akai Electric of Japan. By 1988, Videoton had started efforts to produce CD players after buying a license from Philips.

Licensing technology can lead smoothly to a joint-venture manufacturing arrangement. Companies that sold licenses during the 1970s and 1980s have found that their Eastern European customers are contacting them about joint-venture possibilities. Many companies have been pleasantly surprised at how easy it is to initiate a joint-venture with a past customer since the company will already know the American's manufacturing methods, processes, and the specifics of its line technologies.

Eastern Europe technology acquisitions are motivated by a desire to both earn hard currency through exports and to avoid incurring new debt through the purchase of imports. The range of criteria that will be used in considering the purchase of a Western license will include:

- Cost

- The technology's hard-currency export earning potential

- The import substitution potential of the technology license

- Type of equipment needed to produce a licensed product

- Needed raw materials

- Energy needs to manufacture the product

- Start-up date

- Competitiveness of domestic R&D organizations to supply a similar license

- Unique strengths of a foreign license relative to competing ones

Tips for Licensers

- Long delays between the purchase of foreign licenses and putting them to use in production have caused criticism from Eastern European government authorities. As a negotiator, you should emphasize that the purchase of associated equipment will shorten the time to get the license producing. You can point to official complaints about delays in trying to convince your business partner to buy essential Western equipment to initiate production of the licensed product as soon as possible.

- Experienced technology negotiators demand contract clauses that protect their image in case products of inferior quality are manufactured under license. Also, they limit their liability if a licensed product does not meet specified standards, since quality problems are often the result of faulty materials being used by subsuppliers rather than a consequence of negligent behavior on the part of the foreign partner.

- Negotiate a licensing deal with probable delays in production start-up in mind. After the license is purchased, it will take most Eastern European enterprises years to produce the product efficiently, let alone sell it internationally. For this reason, you may want to concede marketing restriction clauses in a contract in exchange for some other sweetener.

- Given that delays will occur in getting a licensed technology up and running, it follows that licensees often want to extend the license's guarantee period. Be reluctant to extend unless you are sure that purchased machinery has been properly stored in an area protected from damage. Use a local attorney or consultant to negotiate the technical provisions in a licensing contract, such as the exact type of technical property rights being purchased, protection of your technological secrets, and market territory restrictions. Local counsel will often be effective in handling the patent, copyright, and trademark applications.

Acquiring Technology in Eastern Europe

Technology acquisition deals can be truly "win-win" deals. You may be able to swap manufactured goods and production equipment for patents or for the extended services of a group of scientists and their technologies. Or you may merely provide a set of production equipment to an enterprise in Eastern Europe in exchange for a quantity of high-tech products it happens to produce. Consider also the cost benefit of conducting contract research in Eastern Europe, where $30,000 to $50,000 will retain a Ph.D. and a laboratory technician and also cover laboratory overhead for a full year. General Atomics of San Diego, a contractor for the Energy Department, has hired the Kurchator Institute in Russia to undertake one year's worth of hot-fusion experiments using its Tokamac reactor at the lilliputian cost of $90,000. You not only get more for your money, you get access to extremely well-trained scientific minds which may bring a revolutionary perspective to your R&D activities

Funding Patents in Exchange for Technology Rights

One problem for the Eastern European scientist in selling his or her technology to a Western interest is lack of patent protection. A potential deal bogs down because the Easterner cannot normally afford the cost of properly conducting a patent search in the West and then filing a binding patent in the States. The cost in hard currency prohibits these scientists from licensing technology to a foreign party. The solution: A Western company links the originators of a proprietary technology in the East with an appropriate patent attorney in the West. The attorney conducts a patent search and files the researcher's new patent in the United States and is paid by the Western company. The originator signs over ownership of the technology to the Western company, but the patent for the technology is filed under his or her name. The Western firm then develops the technology and brings a product to market, paying the originator a royalty on all sales. The Easterner will consider such technology-sharing deals akin to attaining nirvana; they bring instant status to the former-Eastern bloc or Soviet scientist while validating his or her work in the eyes of the organization where the work was performed. Few deals like this have been done; the potential remains untapped.

Potential for Software
Development Deals

Negotiating a software development deal with the East can be just as simple. The first contact you should make is with the software development department at the academy of science in the country where you are doing business. Resident software developers will bring their own products to your attention in hopes, no doubt, of soliciting your assistance in marketing them in the West. Some of these packages will hardly impress you; others will knock your socks off for their ingeniousness and practicality. Inventive Machine Corporation of New Jersey, for example, is marketing an artificial intelligence technology, known as the Invention Machine System, owned and developed by 27 scientists and engineers in Belarus. The software allows one to solve technical problems on-line while obtaining input and suggestions generated by 300,000 existing patented inventions.

Two-way deals can be readily arranged that allow you to market a piece of indigenous software in exchange for research, development, and documentation performed in Eastern Europe on a software program of your own. In one ground-breaking deal, Philips of the Netherlands traded a quantity of its lower-end electronic products in exchange for the full-time use of a group of expert Russian software programmers over a period of several years. Sun Microsystems of Silicon Valley has hired Russian scientist Boris A. Babayan (pronounced *bob-ee-YON*) to set up a laboratory in Moscow. Babayan will employ 50 software and hardware designers, each paid a few hundred dollars a year in dollars. Software developers in Eastern Europe and the C.I.S. are known to be *five times* better educated that their counterparts in the West. As Hecht-Nielsen says, "The United States has hackers; Eastern Europe and Russia have computer scientists who are better educated than ours—and they're cheap and hard-working."

A truly unique opportunity in Eastern Europe exists for Western companies that can put to good use underutilized scientific talent in the region. Eastern European scientists and postgraduate students are well informed and efficiently organized. However, they are not adept at harnessing their abilities to create new products for Western markets. That's where Western companies can play a mutually beneficial role.

How to Bring Eastern Technologies to Market in the West

Dr. James Baur, owner of Science Solutions in La Jolla, California, is a technology hunter who has scoured the former Soviet Union in quest of undiscovered and—it is hoped—revolutionary, new technological inventions. Science Solutions deals with a number of scientific groups in the former Soviet Union which have been told to make their own way and do their own business. "They are willing to accept and adapt to our business and financial practices, with no reservations," says Jim. Within a few months, Scientific Solutions was overwhelmed in its efforts to handle all the ideas and prototypes offered by the Soviets. Science Solutions has agreements with a number of Soviet groups that have prototype products that it will market for the Soviets.

Qualifying Science-Oriented Businesses in Eastern Europe. When you shop for technological businesses to get involved with, what criteria do you apply? Briefly, look at the *product* the enterprise is producing. There will always be an operation that can take over the marketing of any product that you find. For instance, let's say that Jim Baur goes to a large institute in Russia that produces optical equipment and talks directly to the director, the vice director, and the scientist who invented the equipment. The first thing the directors say is that if Jim finds a market for the optical equipment, the institute will set up a production facility to produce it. When the meeting is over, however, the vice director hands Jim a manila envelope containing descriptions of other products that have been developed by the institute and are being manufactured at an enterprise down the road. Then, at dinner that night with the inventor-scientist, Jim is told that if he can find buyers for the optical equipment, the inventor and three of his buddies have an enterprise a few miles away that could produce the product as well. In one day, Jim has been offered three different production facilities to produce a device for the Western market. In other words, production and R&D

are still entirely separate endeavors in Russia, and one must, therefore, *focus on the product* rather than the enterprise when shopping for high-tech products to sell in the West. Eastern Europeans have plenty of workers to take care of orders; let them worry about production.

Also, beware the miraculous "breakthrough technology" designed to transfer your currency from your pocket to the Eastern European scam artist: Like Elate Intelligent Technologies, Inc., in Moscow, whose commercial director claims that, by using electrical energy, the firm's technology can change the weather over a 200-mile-wide area to a customer's liking. Cost to you for desired weather: $200 a day.

Qualifying Scientists: Whom Should You Deal With? At your company in the West, you might qualify scientific specialists and inventors by looking at their résumés, contacting their references, and making some judgments about them based on their personality. This isn't difficult since you all speak the same language. But how do you size up a Russian specialist, or a Hungarian inventor, or a Bulgarian software developer? What criteria can you apply, given that they probably will not possess a standard résumé that would be acceptable in the West?

Jim Baur doesn't waste any time deciding whether the Soviet or Eastern European scientist he is talking to is a bona fide "developer" or an "assembly-line person." He's dealt with both. Whenever possible, he tries to weed out the latter and deal with the former.

"As you move into the business area [and out of the scientific area], it's tougher to weed out the bad apples," says Jim, "because they haven't been doing business in the way they are now trying to for very long. They can't come to you with a résumé that shows good *business* [as opposed to scientific] experience."

Jim's approach is simple: He sets up a desk at business conferences and meets face to face with potential scientist-partners. They come to him and pitch their ideas and their expertise. Then the weeding-out process, which is based on Jim's own personnel selection criteria, begins.

"One person might be relatively uneducated, but is opportunistic, forthright, and doesn't try to overly impress me." These are good signs.

"Another person may not be very aggressive, but is persistent and patient. For example, I was seeing people fifteen minutes at a time and getting first impressions. This guy kept coming back and making another appointment to see me." That was a good sign, too.

What about negative signals on the part of Eastern scientists? Who does Jim try to avoid? He steers clear of "technical people who have discussed their technical idea with me and cannot respond to friendly criticism. If they can't respond to friendly criticism, I tend *not* to want to work with them. If you've got a system for doing science and business there, and we've got a system of doing science and business here, both sides have to adjust their methods, or you're not going to mesh. If they cannot let me look at the workings of their product and let me ask questions, like: 'Why does it work like this?' or, 'Would it be better to use a different wavelength?' without getting defensive and saying, 'Nope, I can't do that,' that is a sign that the person is not going to work well in our system."

Let's call it scientific arrogance. Avoid it at all costs. Sometimes, a *closed business attitude* on the part of a potential innovation partner will put off an American partner. Though you may run into scientific people who are naive about business, you must realize that this is to be expected considering the system that Eastern scientists have toiled under. Most Westerners entering Eastern markets are naive in some sense, too. Being an ingenue is perfectly acceptable, especially if the inventor possesses an idea, on paper or in the form of a prototype, for a "better mousetrap" or revolutionary product. However, if the inventor you meet feels fundamentally committed to entering into a *particular form of business arrangement* and will not budge on the issue to discuss other arrangements, or fails to exhibit a reasonable degree of flexibility in forging a business agreement, you may want to avoid engaging that person in further discussions. When a potential innovation partner pursues a predetermined notion of the type of venture he or she wants the foreign party to enter, perceive it as a red light—an ominous sign of inflexibility, hidden agendas, or a scam.

Jim concludes: "If the Soviet person sits down with me and is unwilling to listen to give and take on what kind of deal we might be able to structure, then they're not much use to me." He offers an example of the sort of flexibility he's after. The people who approached Jim and put the project together receive only 2 percent of the resulting profits. At least this was the situation until mid-1991. After the union took its 40 percent tax, the republic took its share, and the institute extracted its share to pay salaries and production costs, the scientist and the lab were left with approximately 2 percent of the profits. "If you're a Soviet businessman and you're talking about your idea that you want me to market, if you're not willing to listen to a way that I can get you more money than your two or three percent—if you've got it all figured within the old system—it's not going to work with us." How would Jim increase their income?

Let's say the Russian built a device that Jim sold for $2,000 in the States. The profit for the Russian was $500. Jim would suggest that the money be put in an account in the United States and used to fly the Russian over to the States to give a presentation to potential customers. During his or her stay, the profits that had accrued to the Russian would be used to buy Western products for resale in Russia, at a tremendous profit to the scientist and to his or her institution. Ultimately, Jim would set up agreements to include the purchase of his company's products by the Russian scientist for resale in Russia, using the profits from the original sale of the Russian's device. (Suddenly in November 1991, the union law changed to allow such profits to be used to purchase foreign products rather than requiring them to go directly to the union treasury. Jim's idea had been legitimized. But then the union fell apart, and the commonwealth was formed.) This sort of arrangement has become easier to put together, and Science Solutions recently penned the deal "it had hoped for" since entering the market.

Don't Push Scientists Too Hard.   Western technology hunters have to recognize that most Eastern European scientists are not interested in jumping immediately into a market economy. They want to *embark* on the transition. Their institutes will support them for two or three years if they develop an avenue along which an international market can be pursued. Indeed, such action will elicit marked support from the organization. The task of developing an actual business plan and signing a contract, however, is an enormous undertaking for them.

The impetus for engaging a foreigner in business discussions may simply be part of the scientist's agenda to keep the gravy train chugging, so to speak. They may be using the time spent with a delegation from the West to create an influx of capital from their overseeing organization that will keep their endeavors afloat.

Thus, keep this warning in mind: You may participate in time-consuming and costly preliminaries only to find that your innovation partner fails to follow through simply because, by talking with your company, he or she will have achieved enough. With a nebulous deal in the pipe, they can coast a while. You will be warmly received; no doubt about that. But Eastern scientists will not (normally) be motivated to move on to the next stage of business courtship quickly. A finalized contractual agreement and commitment remain scary for the majority of them. Don't expect to deal with "go-getters." Scientists will not (yet) be working from a "bottom-line" mentality. In fact, 70 percent of them are still on the state dole. Their organizations are in the *process* of becoming private; they are not there yet, however.

Priority Is Placed on *Effort* Rather than *Results*.   For members of this fast-changing science community, scientific effort has traditionally been valued more than actual practical results. Real personal and business risk suddenly looms when they begin to consider linking their inventions to the competitive world market. "Why expose oneself to such risks?" "What happens if the product fails to sell?" "What then?"

Hecht-Nielsen was introduced to a scientific success story at the Academy of Sciences in Russia—a young man who had written a piece of software that he had successfully licensed to a company in the West which pays him a foreign exchange royalty on all sales. The developer splits the royalty with his partner and has to turn over 50 percent to the academy. But he is considered a true hero of scientific entrepreneurship whose achievements seem outside the realm of the possible for virtually every scientist in the former Soviet Union.

Unfortunately, says Hecht-Nielsen, the man is not yet widely emulated. He's respected, that's for sure. But because of a false sense that the odds for success are heavily stacked against them, most scientists perceive the young man's success as otherworldly. "It's as if the guy had won the lottery," Hecht-Nielsen says. Overwhelmed and disheartened by the transition to market-oriented scientific endeavor, most Eastern scientists just give up. If they spend time in the West, they adjust and become more enterprising, but currently in the former Soviet Union, few scientists have the confidence and ambition to try. In Central Europe, however, initiative is greater: Possibly two thirds of the scientists there are ready to try; the remaining one third *will* try, and perhaps succeed. The percentages will not change much in the years to come; the fact is that the process of matching personalities with entrepreneurial challenges is under way. Those who have responded well are the people to link up with as research and development partners; the unaggressive and unresponsive will soon find themselves operating the centrifuge in a lab or carrying out other mundane lab tasks as part of research teams under the leadership of the self-starters.

Plugging Into Eastern European R&D

How do you get plugged in to Russian R&D? A number of trade organizations affiliated with the markets of the commonwealth have cropped up. This may be a good first step. Contact the U.S. Commerce Department, the U.S. Chamber of Commerce, or the embassy of the country you are interested in, for an introduction. Some of the countries now have technology specialists in their embassies in the United States. Trade shows are important. If these avenues are unsuccessful, consider hiring a consulting company that specializes in technology transfer and offers select introductions in your industry.

Forging a technology link may be the best way to begin researching Eastern technological opportunities. P&G has linked up with Leningrad State University, from which it gains access to talented, knowledgeable people who understand the former Soviet system, as well as the university's significant physical resources and infrastructure. "This is a small, exploratory first step for us," said P&G president John E. Pepper to *Eastern Business Report*. "Our objective is to begin to learn how to market, sell, and distribute consumer products in the Soviet Union, and Leningrad State University is an excellent partner for us as we begin this learning process."

The Ethics of Technology Sales

The liberalization of COCOM rules regarding Eastern European nations has made it easier for U.S. business to export goods to the region. (COCOM is the Coordinating Committee for Multilateral Export Controls.) Exporters of dual-use technologies, which have military and civilian applications, once faced stringent export licensing requirements, since most of the diversion of sensitive technologies into the U.S.S.R. went through Central Europe. Since June 1990, however, COCOM has reduced the so-called core list of civilian technologies with potential military applications for sales to the Soviet Union and its Eastern European allies by 83 percent.

COCOM agreed to relax export restrictions to countries that agreed to implement safeguards and allow on-site inspections. Poland and Hungary met these requirements in October 1990, and Czechoslovakia instituted a comprehensive safeguards regime not long after. As a result, exports of high technology to these three countries will be treated favorably by COCOM members. Albania, Romania, and Bulgaria have not yet established the safeguards necessary for such favorable consideration. For information about COCOM's Core List contact: the Bureau of Export Administration's office of Public Affairs at (202) 377- 2721.

Dealing with COCOM: A Conversation with USWest

Telecommunications giant USWest entered Central Europe in 1986 and has since become one of the few successful American telecommunication companies in the region. The company's experience in dealing with changes in the former Soviet Union, and with COCOM, which delayed a major deal in Russia, will be of interest to anybody pursuing a technology transfer arrangement in the region. I spoke with Ed Mattix at USWest about the company's progress in the region so far.

How does USWest go about trying to lobby or persuade COCOM to relax rules on fiber technology?

About the only thing you can do is do a lot of talking with them, and that's what we've done since the very beginning of the project back in 1988, just continuing discussion with the government. You explain to them what you're doing, try to tell them why you want to do it, how it will benefit them. And they have to make the evaluation. It just comes down to the U.S. government having to make a decision based on what they see as the facts, and until just recently, they haven't been willing to change the restrictions on fiber. And they've generally cited national security reasons, and I think it's pretty obvious to anyone who knows anything about fiber that it's a technology that's very difficult to tap. You can't listen in on fiber conversations as well as you can something that's transmitted by microwave. Of course, anything by microwave you can pull out of the air and listen to. Coaxial cable is easy to tap and those types of things so they've generally cited national security reasons for their unwillingness to change their restrictions on fiber.

What level of restriction is in place on sales and technology to the Eastern European C.I.S.?

There are still a lot of restrictions, and what level they should be at is really for the U.S. government to decide. We can only propose, and then they have to make the decision. They're the only ones who know what is going to be a threat to national security, and we've said all along that if they say we can't do it, we won't do it. And we certainly do not dispute the fact that if they have some issues, they have every right to make those decisions and we'll go along with them. So, we can't tell them what we think are the right levels. What we can tell them is what we think is happening in the industry: What's happening to the availability of fiber. Who could provide it. How it can be manufactured. And you know, it's one of those things that's ultimately going to happen. It's just how long can you hold off the inevitable.

Are there other countries that have it that could offer it?

Certainly. I think one of the reasons you're seeing some changes now is that there is a German company that was formerly in East Germany that had signed an agreement with someone (we don't know who, but some company or some organization in the commonwealth) to provide them some fiber-optic cable. I think that's one of the things that has led to some of the changes you're seeing right now. Other people are going to provide this if we don't at some point. Certainly reliable, quick communications are important in a democracy, and the ability for people to communicate helps keep people free because they can talk among themselves, tell one another what's happening, and be better informed about the state of their country than if they didn't have communications. That's certainly one of the reasons why they restricted communications to a very few people in the Soviet Union, and why you didn't have a lot of access to calling into and out of the Soviet Union.

What advice would you offer other U.S. firms who may confront restrictions like those USWest has?

The best advice, I would say, is just be open with the Commerce Department and the U.S. government about what you want to do. Provide them as much information as you possibly can and talk with them and answer their questions. That's all they really ask. They just don't want to be left in the dark. They don't want you to catch them off guard with anything. Certainly that's not too much to ask of anybody. You just make sure that our government is fully informed of what your intentions are, and how things will work, and that you are fully open to answering those questions as quickly and as thoroughly as possible. That's the best thing you can do and that's what we've done all along.

Adopt High-Technology Export Principles

Nonetheless, national security issues remain a serious concern in U.S. trade relations with Eastern Europe. Some of the Central Asian nations of the former U.S.S.R. possess nuclear weapons, and their possible manipulation by Middle Eastern countries such as Libya, Iran, and Iraq is something that makes many people in the West lose sleep. From Russia, Iran has purchased MiG-29's (advanced fighter jets comparable to U.S. F-18 Hornets), Su-24 fighter bombers, and nuclear-powered submarines. The illegal sale of nuclear warheads and the dispersion of former Soviet atomic scientists have become a distinct eventuality. Former Soviet officials were told all their lives that capitalism means "the devil take the hindmost"—cut your own deal, look out for yourself. So that's what they're doing. It's possible to buy just about any military item on Eastern Europe's immense black market. Everything is for sale. Everyone is cutting deals and being encouraged to do so. In this climate, global security should not take second place to the pursuit of the almighty buck. "The business community must take the lead," writes Stanley A. Weiss, chairman of American Premier Corporation, in *World Link*, "to halt the spread of weapons of mass destruction by asking not only if it is legal, but if it is right."

Business Executives for National Security (BENS), a private nonpartisan organization of business leaders based in the United States, has addressed the problem of unlawful and/or unethical export of sensitive technologies overseas by creating a set of principles for high-tech exporters to follow voluntarily. The organization believes that such a code of conduct will help stop the spread of nuclear, biological, and chemical weapons. The author hopes that high-tech exporters to Eastern Europe will adopt these five maxims as part of their corporate mission.*

1. Our company is committed to halting the further spread of nuclear, biological, or chemical weapons, or missile systems designed to deliver them.

2. Our company will support the letter and spirit of current and future laws against the proliferation of such weapons.

3. Our company will not knowingly export products, technologies, or services likely to be used in the unlawful or unconscionable development of such weapons.

4. Our company will make every effort to discover and document the ultimate destination and use of such products.

5. Our company will urge domestic and foreign businesses to abide by these principles.

*Adapted from Stanley A. Weiss, "The BENS Principles: Guidelines for Exports," *World Link,* vol. 5, 1991.

12
The Etiquette Edge for Eastern Europe

You might think that Western business people would make fewer mistakes in Eastern Europe than they do in Asia or Latin America because of cultural similarities between Westerners and Eastern Europeans. But such is not the case. Western business people make the same culturally based mistakes in Eastern Europe that they make elsewhere in overseas markets. A Hollywood production company that had been shooting period films in the streets of Moscow brought in a planeload of pasta to feed to a Russian film crew. But it turned out that Russians don't eat pasta, and the crew refused the food. What happened? Food had to be bought in Moscow, with foreign exchange, cutting into the planned budget for the project. Another example: An American was asked by his eastern German host whether he had seen Berlin before. The American replied: "Only from the air, when we bombed it during the war."

A last, more complex, example underscores how delicate it is to deal with a region of multiple nationalities. It happened at the San Diego Soviet Arts Festival held in 1991. The visiting performers were both Georgian and Russian. The organizers, however, were insensitive to the fact that these are two nationalities. In fact, when the festival was first conceived, it had been named the *Russian* Art Festival. The Georgians were deeply offended because the word *Russian* implied the Russian nationality, to the exclusion of Georgians. To make matters worse, the Americans on the mayor's committee in charge of organizing the festival continued to refer to the visiting members of the delegations from the Soviet Union as "Russians," regardless of whether the people they were speaking to were Ukrainian, Georgian, or Russian. When Georgian folk dancers arrived and saw that the festival was being billed as a "Russian" festival, they asked to be put on their plane and taken back to Georgia. They would not even sit with the Russians at banquets, much less talk to them. "San Diego would like to say that the festival was a success," says Barbara Chronowski, a Russia expert who coordinated the translators and interpreters on the project, "but in terms of interaction between the Americans and the different Soviet nationalities, it was not so good."

Protocol Basics: Authenticity, Efficiency, and Formality

In Eastern Europe strict rules of business protocol do not exist to the degree that they do in countries like Japan and China. You don't need to modify your behavior to smuggle yourself into some traditional mode of doing business in Eastern Europe. Communism rooted out any ancient, traditional mannerisms of commercial intercourse that might have existed, and any residual differences have been done away with by television. (The first TV show I saw in the Palast Hotel in East Berlin was the American program "Dynasty.") Most Easterners want to do business like Westerners do. Thus, rule 1 is: *Be yourself.*

Rule 2: Don't waste their time. Eastern Europeans are generally very efficient. After initial pleasantries, get down to business. Build a deeper, trusting, personal relationship once business discussions are under way. At the first meeting, be businesslike. Set the agenda. Define time limitations.

Rule 3: Remember that *Eastern European society is formal*—in communication behavior, negotiating, and attire. Fred Martin, president of the Bancroft Group, an international business consulting firm in Washington, took his client to meet with a real estate agency in Budapest in a search for space in which to locate a copy shop. The meeting didn't go well. Afterward, Martin's translator intimated "that the people at the real estate agency had thought Paul [the client] was a con man. He didn't wear a suit and tie, for one thing, and his manner was suspicious: He rejected outright the idea of buying a store or building, and he kept repeating what the partnership was after and what it was prepared to pay. All this struck the real estate agent as a little pushy, undiplomatic, even tasteless."

Fred Martin elaborates on the experience of dealing with the formality of Hungary: "The Hungarian way is to observe the formalities—to respect one's opposite, to negotiate rather than say No, to respond politely, formally, even ornately. Hungarians are very careful to preserve the dignity of a situation. They will not telephone someone for you unless they know that person's full name. "Mister X" will not do, and using the first name alone is unthinkable....They offer refreshments at every business meeting, to show respect for their guest. When a business discussion has concluded, it is common to adjourn to a large dinner accompanied by wine and toasts, even if the prospects of making a deal are obviously remote. I was amused by an American guy in a buffet line, whose Polish business partner asked him to enter the line ahead of him, out of politeness. "You always do that to me!" the American said, and made the Polish guy go first for once." Indeed, Hungarians might insist on walking to the left of a woman or honored guest. "Our Polish technology director kisses hands!" says an incredulous Richard Fischer of General Electric Aircraft Engines in Warsaw. In Eastern Europe, you will not witness male bonding in the American sense of back-slapping and rib-poking and the like. Your Eastern counterpart may accept such behavior, but you won't see him participate in it with his colleagues. Rules of formality only increase if you are dealing with a female business person in Eastern Europe.

The drawback is that as long as this sort of formality persists, the people you are dealing with will have no idea of where you are coming from. The Eastern European will accept a person who behaves informally; such a person may even allow them to relax. A group of Hungarians, for example, would never think to remove their jackets in a hot meeting room. However, the moment an informal American stands up and says: "Whew! I can't stand this. Let's take off our jackets," the Hungarians will jump up and take off their jackets. A thick layer of formality will exist until you break it down. You must be careful in doing so, however, because the warm, friendly, open, and informal business style of the West may irritate and alarm your Eastern business associate.

Western German business people are the most formal in their behavior. The western German style is stiff and impersonal; the eastern German style is warm, physical, and open. A friend of mine spoke at a conference in Berlin recently. Afterward, the western German came up and shook his hand and spoke to him coolly and formally. Suddenly, a man approached and cried, "Thank-you!" and clutched him in a bear hug. He was from East Berlin...an eastern German. You will find, doing business with western Germans, that their formal behavior will not vary much over time; they aren't likely to suddenly "loosen up." You will not find yourself on a first-name basis quickly, if ever.

Making a Stellar First Impression

First impressions in the East start with punctuality. Eastern Europeans are generally very punctual. Arrive two to five minutes early for all arranged meetings. Next comes your clothing. A noticeable difference between American and European business representatives is their clothing. Middle-class Europeans are at once much more conservative and more class-conscious than Americans. Custom requires people in certain kinds of vocations to dress in certain predictable ways that indicate social and professional status. The relaxed and frequently colorful dress preferred by some Americans is uncommon in upper levels of European business circles. It will quickly identify you as an American, but it can also incorrectly signal a certain inexperience, an unprofessional attitude, and a lack of seriousness in your effort. Conservative colors and fashions are the predominant features of the Eastern European business dress code. At a trade fair, for example, almost no one will be casual and wear an open-neck shirt—except perhaps at sporting goods or recreational trade fairs.

For your first meeting with an Eastern European, wear a suit and tie. But for ensuing meetings you may dress more casually; a blazer and oxford shirt without a tie is fine for men, and a conservative work skirt and blouse is appropriate for women. Although you should wear a suit and tie for all business meetings, you may find that your counterparts don casual clothing. (Before his ouster, President Havel of Czechoslovakia decreed that one day per week his cabinet could wear casual clothes, calling it "sweater day.") Remember that while men in business wear a suit and tie, professors and scientists can get away with wearing a jazzy shirt without a tie. Managers, consultants, and officials may wear the denim and polyester made in government factories, or, if they have the money, designer clothes imported from the West—"new chic." Wear a dark suit to an official event or wedding. A "formal occasion" means that men should wear a tuxedo and women should wear a long dress. If invited to a home for dinner, dress up a little; men should wear a tie. When visiting a mosque anywhere in Eastern Europe, remember to leave your shoes outside.

No Ostentation. Display of wealth is bad form. Successful indigenous entrepreneurs, especially the flashy "overnight success" type, may go in for conspicuous display of wealth, but for most, an ingrained egalitarian ethic keeps the peacock feathers hidden. In fact, until recently, most Eastern Horatio Algers lived like paupers, seemingly motivated less by cash than by idealism and upbringing. Chic is making an alarming comeback, especially among the nouveaux riches in Russia.

Greeting Rituals

The Western-style handshake is used throughout Eastern Europe, with a few notable variations. When close friends or relatives meet in Poland, they touch cheeks—one side, then the other, then the first side again. Titles may replace your last name, as in "Mister Manager" or "Misses Director." Foreign men should shake the hand of a Polish woman only when greeting. However, an old-school Polish man may kiss the hand of a foreign woman when greeting, so women should be prepared to offer their hand. Tomasz Gruszecki, privatization minister in Poland, "kisses the hands of women when he greets them, and graciously pours tea into porcelain cups," reports Jacqueline Gold in *Financial World*. Eastern Germans shake hands at the beginning and again at the end of each encounter whether meeting friend or stranger. The handshake is always appropriate. Greeting etiquette is identical to that in Western Germany. In eastern Germany shake hands and wait to be introduced before striking up a conversation. In Bulgaria, shake hands to greet people and wait to be introduced. When greeting people in any of the five independent states of Yugoslavia, shake hands and don't be surprised if you receive a peck on the cheek. Return it. Wait to be introduced before shaking hands. When greeting people in Romania, shake hands. Men rise when introduced. Romanian men, like Polish men, may rise and kiss the hand of a visiting woman. As a male or female foreigner, shake hands with Romanian women when greeting. Close Romanian friends traditionally peck each other on the cheek when greeting, and some kiss each other on the mouth. Wait to be formally introduced to a Romanian person before thrusting out your hand. When greeting a Hungarian, shake hands. Good friends in Hungary might embrace and touch cheeks, first the left and then the right. Close women friends might embrace without a handshake first. Wait to be introduced before shaking hands or embracing anyone. Shake hands when greeting someone in the Czech and Slovak republics. Be introduced before starting up a conversation. Czech men may give flowers to female business people whom they are meeting for the first time.

Names and Titles

The fairly elaborate courtesies in addressing business contacts may surprise you in Eastern Europe. Eastern European professionals won't address a new acquaintance by his or her first name. Indeed, they may not address someone they have known for several years by first name unless they have become close personal friends. The average Eastern European would be visibly taken aback if you were to address him or her by first name following the exchange of business cards. Although such familiarity by an American won't scare a visitor away, it will make the person feel uncomfortable.

Most important, use only the person's family name, preceded by the title—such as "Doctor" or "Professor"—if this information appears on his or her card. Introduce people by their title. Carry your translated business cards always, as they are required when introducing yourself at a company or government office.

Regional Differences.   In Germany, use "Herr" and "Fraulein" before a person's title or last name, even if the person speaks fluent English. A German executive will not call his female secretary by her first name, but rather by the title "Fraulein" only. If you socialize with a German over time, you will eventually be prompted to link right arms, with drinks in hand, and toast "Bruderschaft," or brotherhood. After this, you can consider yourself on first-name basis with that person. In Poland, allow yourself to be introduced, and use "Mr." or "Mrs." or the person's title with the last name. You may be asked to switch to a first-name basis over drinks, ceremoniously. When a Polish woman marries, her name changes; she takes her husband's surname, but changes the last letter of it to "a." For example, Mr. Koslowski's wife would be called "Mrs. Koslowska." In Bulgaria, use the person's title with the last name if the person is a doctor, architect, priest, engineer, manager, or professor. In the Czech and Slovak republics, use a person's title with his or her last name. The same goes for the former Yugoslavia and Romania. In Hungary, use the person's title or, if the person has no title, say "Sir (Smith Úr)" or "Mrs. (Smith ne)" or "Madam (Smith asszony)". Hungarian names are in reverse order from Western names, with the family name first and the given name second. The word for "Mister" is úr, or "lord." Talking to Mr. Gould, a Hungarian would say, "Gould Úr." If they were talking to Sue Gould, they would say, "Gould Ne," which translates to "Mrs. Gould." (Sue Gould could also be called "Gould Thomas Mrs.," if she is married to Thomas Gould.) If they do not want to use this formal address, they might address Mr. Gould by saying, "Úr Am," which is possessive, with "úr" meaning "lord" and "am" meaning "my." Thus, this is a polite and deferential form of address that has the tone of ingratiating oneself to another. This formal address serves to show the other party that there is positive rapport.

Dos and Taboos for Negotiators

First of all, be punctual to meetings in every country of Eastern Europe; many enterprises may use the same meeting room, and scheduling is tight. Remember that between noon and 2 p.m., many companies take a long lunch break. Second, do not send a low-status representative of your company to an initial meeting with a Russian company. The Russians, especially, are extremely status conscious and might take offense at this gesture and/or consider it an indication of only casual interest on your part in investigating the possibility of collaboration. A high-level representative should be sent to a first meeting, but there is little need to send a large number of staff members to accompany this person. Make sure that the person's title is specific and have business cards for the person translated into Russian. Because hard currency is limited in every Eastern European country, deals involving the spending of foreign exchange are considered with great care. Negotiators on the Eastern European side will, therefore, usually include top people in their field. Hence, they will expect your company to send executives with the personal authority to sign a deal. Don't send an underling, or you will only antagonize your partner.

A special note on Russian negotiators: Expect Russian business people to be more aggressive in negotiations than the typical Westerner. Many long-time shadow capitalists have waited for years to conduct business in the open. They're raring to go, and patience may go by the wayside. (On the part of the Russian bureaucrat, however, the desire for quick profit will likely be outmatched by a need to adhere to bureaucratic formalities, ad nauseam.) Russian negotiators are typically more pugilistic than Americans, less flexible, and more educated. They can be *antagonistic.* In response, be forthright with your proposals and constantly on the lookout for the hothead.

Meeting Setting

Rarely do Eastern Europeans conduct meetings with foreigners in offices; you will likely be seated at a rectangular conference table in a conference room, with Eastern Europeans on one side and foreigners on the other. One exception is that some CEOs have conference rooms in their offices, along with their desks. Senior-ranking people are introduced first. You don't have to bring a gift to a first meeting, but do bring a souvenir from the States to give to each of your counterparts and start the conversation. The possible absence of smiles and warmth while negotiating, especially with Russians, should not be taken as a show of hostility toward the visiting delegation. At the meeting table in the former Soviet Union, you will find soda water, Pepsi, and kvass, a yeasty nonalcoholic beer. At higher levels, you may also find a bottle of vodka and/or wine. Don't open one of these. They are for celebration only. If a deal is signed, they'll break out the vodka. Be persistent in bringing down the interpersonal barriers by establishing rapport and making positive comments about your counterparts' home country. Eastern European entrepreneurs may move quickly from small talk to business talk; however, many will not. Be sure that *you* devote ample time to developing the necessary interpersonal relationships to make business interaction smooth.

Don't Assume Anything

Enter negotiations with a totally open, "uneducated," frame of mind. Don't reject a partner, an enterprise, or a business concept based on what you've heard or read or assume. For example, don't enter Russia thinking that you won't be able to sell products for hard currency; with the right connections and the right arrangements you may be able to. Don't avoid talking to representatives of a "high-security" Ukrainian defense plant because you assume that they won't be permitted to sign with a foreign partner; they may desperately want to sign with one. Don't assume that you will be able to arrive in Warsaw, pick up the *Yellow Pages,*and make cold calls.

Be Flexible

"Anything the law does not prohibit is allowed," says a pamphlet published by Novosti Press Agency in 1988 and distributed in the Soviet Union at airports and train stations. The same goes for business conducted with foreigners. Business in the region is not a simple matter of adapting a Western model for a business and transplanting it to Minsk or Moravia. Innovative deal structuring—that may *not* yet be formally legal—is one key to success.

Show Respect

Expect your partners to strongly desire (1) to be taken seriously, (2) to be treated with respect, and (3) to convince you that they are nobody's fool as business people. There is a palpable feeling of mistrust, even fear, in the way Central European negotiators interact with Westerners, in part because they learned under the Communist regime that they can't trust *anybody*, but also because there have been raw deals for them in their experiences with Westerners since the Wall came down (though not many with Americans). You *must always* negotiate in good faith, while working on building a trusting business relationship in order to dispel apprehensions.

Actively Engage in Q&A

Be prepared to answer questions specifically and in detail. You may be given a prepared list of questions; do not feel that you have to answer them immediately. Inform the team that you will study the questions and prepare answers for the next meeting. If you prepare a written document of answers to such questions, it should be translated. In fact, present all your documents in the local language, if possible. Bring multiple copies of all documents to be handed over to the Eastern European side; a copier may not be available except at the top hotels.

Don't Be Rushed into a Deal

Eastern European negotiators are typically under enormous pressure to sell an enterprise and may suddenly become impatient and threaten to sell it to another interested party. They might "lay all their cards on the table" at the outset and then become indignant when you "need time to consider" a deal. Simply explain that no foreign company wants to jump into a deal without considering all angles. A related problem: Often, competitive tenders in Eastern European privatizations are obligatory, even when only one foreign company is interested in purchasing the enterprise. The deadline for bids is typically set for one month hence. Most potential investors can't put a proposal together in one month and thus avoid the deal in the belief that an investor must already have been found. The original investor drops out, the Eastern European enterprise is left unsold and, the negotiators become embittered.

Using a Lawyer

The role of the lawyer in Eastern European business negotiations is crucial. A foreigner who does not understand Eastern European business law should utilize two lawyers—one from the United States, the other located in the Eastern European place of business. The local lawyer acts as a resource regarding specific problems and questions pertaining to the domestic law of the country you are involved in. The local lawyer, however, probably will not be able to handle international business negotiations, simply because of a lack of experience. American counsel should handle this; preferably the lawyer should have Eastern Europeans working with him or her. This is the optimal combination. Be careful, however, not to display an attitude of mistrust during negotiations by demanding that your lawyer negotiate every detail of an agreement.

The Agenda

You may find it difficult to get Eastern European negotiators, especially former Communist career negotiators, to focus during a negotiation on issues that are not on their "list of concerns." With this in mind, open up a negotiation by presenting an agenda listing all concerns, both yours and theirs. After negotiations, put down in writing the outcome of the talks and submit it to your counterparts for review. Both sides can then go home, read it, and think about it. When Eastern Europeans see the results of talks moving into print, they tend to resolve misperceptions more quickly.

The Contract

Define your company's points of leverage and those of your counterparts before negotiations open. Maintain an up-to-date list of needs and wants for both sides. Don't negotiate in a piecemeal manner, trying to "close" one clause after another until finished. Discuss all aspects of a deal with all parties who will have some authority over the venture and offer concessions only at the end of these "holistic" discussions. And don't ever agree to use the standard document provided by the Eastern European negotiator. Use your own, or create a hybrid with the partner. The Russian, for example, will frequently pipe up during a negotiation and say, "We've got a standard joint-venture agreement." Five or six different versions of this basic document currently circulate in the Commonwealth of Independent States (C.I.S.), in Russian and English. "It's very simple and you won't have to pay a lot of money to lawyers," they say. These documents are *vague*, and lawyers working in Eastern Europe recommend that contracts there be *very* specific. If the contract is vague and has been negotiated via phone calls between people who don't speak Russian or English well, that vagueness in the contract will prevail and will be interpreted in a way that is advantageous to your partner rather than to you.

If a problem arises, and something in the agreement must be changed, deal with the problem forthrightly and with flexibility. In the United States, when conditions change to the detriment of one of the partners, you follow the letter of the contract, and if the other side hasn't thought of something, well, that's their problem, right? You *can't* do that in Central Europe because everything is new to your partners, and they can't possibly anticipate every unforeseen contingency. Moreover, foreigners who forge "organic" agreements based on performance fare better in the long run than those who seek a watertight, "quick-kill" contract. Last, don't leave loose ends. Issues to be negotiated in a joint-venture agreement include the following; don't sign until all of these issue have been resolved: .

Equity split/share

Valuation of contribution

Management charter

Autonomy of venture from outside

Financing

Pricing

Expatriate pay

Training

Marketing

Local content

Duration of venture

Arbitration procedure

Technology transfer

Contract type

Communicating in Eastern Europe

Everything about you communicates—your words, your gestures, your gender, even your clothes. But communication patterns don't always cross borders. In Bulgaria, a nod of the head means "No," and shaking one's head from side to side means "Yes." Your use of hand, arm, and facial gestures to get your point across may be considered strange and uncouth in eastern Germany. When flagging a bus in Hungary, you might use the word "bus" rather than "autobus" (*awh-tow-boos*), not knowing that the word "bus" is a homonym for *fornication* in Hungarian. A phrase that sounds like "See ya!" means "Hello!" in Hungarian slang, while a phrase that sounds like "Hallo!" means "Good-bye!" in Hungarian slang. One foreign company pitched the idea of selling foreign tours to hunting types who wanted to shoot pheasant in Uzbekistan. The Russian marketing adviser thought the foreigner meant *peasants*. The discussion followed along this line until the distinction was made between an Uzbek pheasant and an Uzbek peasant. There you have it: Many a foreigner has fallen into the communication abyss. Recently, I asked Richard Fischer of General Electric Aircraft Engines in Warsaw to offer a few tips for foreign firms transferring technology to Eastern Europe. Interestingly, all his advice involved problems of *communication*. "The guys with the M.A. degrees forget their audience, writing and speaking loftily, forgetting that they are in a quasi-Third World country without English capabilities. Write and speak *plainly*," Richard advises. "And don't mumble or use a fast, hard-nosed, New York accent. The Poles start nodding with that glassy-eyed look. The Poles like a flat, Midwest accent." The same applies throughout the former Eastern bloc and Soviet Union.

Facilitating Two-Way Discussion

How do you get communication running smoothly in a meeting in Eastern Europe? By *facilitating*. That's a fancy term used by communication experts for "positive feedback." (Another way they describe it is "active listening.") The challenge is to get the two sides talking *with* each other rather than *at* each other. This may sound trite, but remember that both sides have to communicate through an interpreter, which can make any discussion, even one between old friends, awkward and disconcerting for both parties. Ensure the smooth flow of communication with an Eastern European by remembering the following four steps, recommended by consultant Bonnie Best, who has trained Soviet managers in Russia. First, validate the other person after he or she has spoken. ("I understand your situation.") Then *empathize* with what the person has said. ("I can see how difficult your situation here is.") Third, *clarify* what the person has said. ("Your situation here will require a complete overhaul, is that correct?") And last, *summarize* the content of what the person has said. ("Given what you've told me, your factory needs to upgrade its technology, find new markets, and reduce its workforce.")

Facilitate by Interjecting Questions. Because of the language barrier between you and your Eastern European host, the best way for you to encourage the Eastern European side to explain its product needs, technological know-how, or interest in your proposal is to ask questions. Lots of them. You should enter *every* meeting in Eastern Europe, whether formal or informal, with a long mental (if not written) list of inquiries to be answered by your partners. Eastern Europeans may consider it impolite if you interrupt them with a tangential comment or opinion, but *not* if you do so with a relevant question about their presentation; this is perceived as attentive listening on your part and is appreciated. If you do not understand a sentence, stop the interpreter immediately and ask for clarification. A good way to do this is to restate the point made and gauge whether you have received the information correctly. The idea is to break some of the monotony of an interpreted conversation by interjecting relevant questions which turn the one-way presentation into a dialogue. This helps to personalize the meeting and to get the two sides exchanging information and ideas rather than merely taking turns delivering them. Your Eastern European partner may not feel comfortable asking a question purely out of curiosity, as an American might. Your partner may qualify his or her question before asking it. Even when the context for a question seems clear, for example, after a presentation when it's time for Q&A, Eastern Europeans may qualify their questions with preamble. This is important for you to do also. From the Hungarian perspective, for example, Westerners just don't understand Hungarian managerial and social circumstances. In order for us to answer their questions, they've got to explain their conditions so that we understand how to answer. The Hungarians might ask the Westerner how the venture can find a supplier. The American says: "You pick up the phone and call around." But in Hungary it might not be so easy to pick up a phone and call, since a directory of suppliers has never been available there.

Your partner will provide better answers to your questions if you avoid using "closed questions." A closed question is one that can be answered with a Yes or No. ("Are you satisfied with this situation?") An "open question" can be answered without Yes or No; it encourages the respondent to offer an opinion and commentary. ("How did you feel about the situation?" "What happened then?")

Slow Way Down. Westerners often destroy the atmosphere of a meeting by replying too quickly and offhandedly in their attempts to appear forthcoming. The Eastern European has spent a considerable amount of time formulating a complete idea or opinion, which he or she conveys seriously to the Westerner. The Easterner is surprised when the North American comprehends and responds immediately, and rather inarticulately, after formulating a "snap judgment." Eastern Europeans feel let down and irritated when North Americans do not dedicate as much energy and time to their comments as Eastern Europeans do...and while Eastern Europeans have worked out their ideas completely so that they can communicate them clearly and succinctly, Westerners' ideas arrive at their mental doorstep in long, wordy statements that waste Eastern Europeans' time trying to translate, reassemble into logical sequence, and comprehend.

By nature, the Eastern European sometimes feels more comfortable just listening. Deliberate before replying to get your ideas in order. Don't worry that by not responding quickly you will be perceived as not having an answer. Take your time, and you will be considered thoughtful and intelligent, not unprepared or elusive. Don't be afraid of allowing periods of silence, especially after you are asked a question. Taking time to formulate your thoughts does not mean that you haven't got an answer or that you're being evasive. A Bulgarian remarked to writer Peter Laufer: "A Bulgarian does not talk without thinking first, the way an American does." Don't be afraid to think before you speak.

Practicing Humor.   Through humor, Easterners have been able to express much of their pain and their opposition to the political system. A good joke is said to get heard by every Hungarian in the country in 24 hours. Humor is a key part of communicating, and a good sense of humor is greatly admired and appreciated. Jokes and humor in Eastern Europe are generally like those in America—ironic and self-effacing. Hence, you can exercise your sense of humor when doing business in the region without fear of robbing someone of face. Says Richard Fischer of General Electric in Warsaw: "The Poles have a sense of humor. They will blend business and personal [relationships]; they're not like the Germans." Among Poles, finding humor in everyday things, often bawdy humor, is part of conversation. Germans, however, do not make a habit of practicing humor in the context of business discussions. Don't tell jokes to Germans. Only during a purely social event would it be appropriate to crack a joke. Business is a serious matter; do not try to loosen things up with sarcasm or a sardonic quip. Remember that an opening joke during an after-dinner speech might be common in the United States, but it is not as common in Eastern Europe. In fact, in Germany an executive might be asked to give a speech at a luncheon or reception, and he or she would bring a fifteen-page speech and deliver it without one merciful moment of comic relief. The German audience simply expects this. Don't cheat your audience by speaking for only four minutes and opening with a joke.

Dealing with the Language Barrier

Unless the foreigner plans to spend the next five years of his or her life doing business in Eastern Europe, there is little chance of learning an Eastern European language. Luckily, many Eastern European business people have made great strides in learning business English. However, typically they are not yet expert in speaking English; thus, you almost always will need to communicate through an interpreter.

Conveying Your Message through an Interpreter. Building strong business relationships in Eastern Europe may sound relatively easy to do. To achieve these relationships while communicating solely through an interpreter is, however, hardly a simple proposition. I have witnessed few foreigners in Eastern Europe who understand how to be interpreted well; this is unfortunate, since to be clearly understood, you must know how to get your message clearly interpreted. Most people who have problems getting through to Eastern Europeans blame their interpreters; I teach my seminar participants that *they* must take responsibility for getting their message better interpreted.

Choosing an Interpreter. If you have a particular technical focus in your business, choose an interpreter who is acquainted with the terminology or has interpreted for other foreign companies that have dealt with the same industry. At an international trade fair you might wish to hire someone who, with respect to the terms used when discussing your product with potential buyers, can switch from English to the local language and to German at will. All these languages are likely to be represented at a large trade fair. In addition to being versed in the terms of your industry, an interpreter should be able to supply you with inside commercial intelligence about your competition, the local players in the industry, and the state of the industry at any given time. Interpreters always have some inside "dirt" to tell you; of course, picking the interpreter's brain may involve some special entertainment—like a dinner in honor of the interpreter. The perfect interpreter takes a personal interest in educating the American; the worst type interprets "by the book," word for word, without any care about opening the cultural door to the foreigners and without concern that the foreigner's questions about a place and a people get fully answered. They will merely, "vomit out all this pre-learned spiel that he or she had to learn to pass her test to become an interpreter," one executive told me who had been doing business in the former Soviet Union.

In other words, personality is critical. Find a person with whom you can establish good rapport, and who will not be awed by you, or continuously defer to you, just because you are from the United States, or another "rich" Western country. They must understand the purpose, and the mission, of your visit in the country and take some initiative rather than merely follow whatever you say. Sometimes, you will not know where to visit, or whom to see, or what to do while in-country. Your interpreter should know the "lay of the land" up to the minute because the situation is changing so quickly in the region. For example, where should you go to get the cheapest, and most reliable, fax service while in Bucharest? An experienced interpreter will know. Where do the local all-star dealmakers conduct "power lunches" these days in Budapest? Who was here last week from General Motors talking to so and so? A good interpreter will know.

Should you trust an interpreter to be confidential within the context of a sensitive negotiation? No, and that is true when you are doing business anywhere in the world. Do not include your interpreter in pricing strategies or concession-giving tactics. Your interpreter is not a negotiator and certainly not likely to remain your loyal confidant after you've returned to New York or Los Angeles. Plus, you don't want to put your interpreter in the uncomfortable situation of having to remember what he or she is supposed to say and not say. This does not mean that you should not try to glean from the interpreter everything that he or she can find out, overhear, and sense about the pricing strategy and concession-giving tactics of the other side. Interpreters' cultural "feelers" will be more tuned to the local environment than yours; snippets of overheard conversations in the local tongue can be revealing and very helpful to your side.

Where to Hire an Interpreter.   The best way to find an interpreter is through referral. Interpreters can also be hired at a local university. Listings are available from the local American Chamber of Commerce. If that doesn't work, call the American Translators Association (ATA) in Alexandria, Virginia, at (703) 412-1500.

Being Interpreted Well.   Make sure that the interpreter knows that you want every word you utter to be translated, whether or not the interpreter feels that your statement is redundant, or that the other side doesn't need to hear it, or that you have implied the statement already without saying it. You need the interpreter to be your mouthpiece at all times and not a filter. When you want to reiterate a point, you need to know that your statements are being stated again, often for emphasis, but for clear understanding as well.

The following checklist of "rules" for being interpreted well have helped me in negotiating in the New East:

- *Limit Your Sentences to 10 to 15 Words, Max.*   This may seem like too few words, but it's not. The shorter your sentences, the less likely your audience will lose your train of thought and become fatigued. Write out your script, and you'll see what a challenge it is to speak in short sentences.

- *Do Not Speak until Your Interpreter Has Finished.*   Westerners often forget, especially when things get heated during a negotiation, that anything they say that is not heard by their interpreter will not be understood at all on the Eastern European side. They often get angry and cut in before their interpreter has finished the last sentence. Another tip: When speaking through an interpreter, look at the person to whom you are speaking and not at your interpreter, even though looking at the interpreter can be more comfortable than looking at a listener who cannot understand your language.

- *Train Your Interpreter.*   When I say "train" your interpreter, I mean rehearse your presentation with him or her well before your departure for Eastern Europe. No interpreter will be able to translate all of your technical terms without opening a dictionary; this should be done at home and not in front of your Eastern European audience. Moreover, if there is *any* humor, irony, or special verbal twist in your presentation, make sure the interpreter has rehearsed it, found just the right nuance to translate it, and knows the body and facial language with which to deliver it so that your audience gets your message clearly and responds favorably. Some marketers work with their interpreters for two or three weeks before leaving for Eastern Europe.

Don't Take Yes for an Answer

Out of politeness and a sense of formality, Eastern Europeans avoid the direct use of the word No. Russians will go out of their way to protect you from the truth about how bad things really are. "A Russian will never tell you the truth," writes A. Craig Copetas. "He will also never lie to you. He will tell you what you want to hear. Russians do this to live." You have to assume that the first response to an inquiry will either be intentionally in error or modified for your ears. The Eastern European's initial reply may be designed simply to begin a discussion rather than state the truth. "Keep asking until you receive an answer that seems logical in the context of the discussion," advises Jonathan J. Halperin, president and founder of FYI Information, a venture in Russia. "Stay focused and be firm in pursuing what you want." The upshot of this for doing business in Eastern Europe is you can't

take Yes for an answer *anywhere* in the region without thorough verifi-
cation and cross-checking to ensure that the Yes you have heard was
not a "polite yes" that really meant No or Maybe. The polite yes
annoys the foreigner who eschews verbal guessing games. The Eastern
European is equally disturbed when the foreigner can't take a hint or
read common signals.

What Your Gender Communicates: Foreign Women in Eastern Europe

In Eastern Europe, you will find women occupying top positions at
companies with frequency, although in large corporations, men continue to dominate as managers. Most noticeable, you will meet great
numbers of women in Eastern Europe who have become private entrepreneurs and who have single-handedly set up and run their own
companies motivated by the same imperative as men—to increase
their income in order to deal with the mounting price hikes in the cost
of food, clothing, and other basic necessities.

I am not implying that sexism and chauvinism are absent. Women in
Hungary, for example, complain bitterly about unfair treatment on the
part of male-dominated management, though in many cases, they do
not have the vocabulary to describe their feelings of disenfranchisement from the power centers of a company's management. For example, in a seminar run by management consultant Sue Gould, a male
manager spoke about having to hire a person to travel around the
country and represent his company. "It would never dawn on him to
interview a woman for that job," Sue says, "because 'a woman can't do
that.' She's got a husband and children to feed. You don't hire a
woman to do a job that means she is going to be on the road." I asked
Sue if she spoke to Hungarian women in her training sessions about
"discrimination." She said she had, but not using words like "discrimination," because a vocabulary for discussing gender discrimination
has not taken root in Hungary or throughout the region, though
women there are aware of the women's movement in the West.

Eastern European society can be said to be sexist, but the people
there may not realize or recognize it. Laws that have been on the
books for years call for equality of the sexes. But the laws are not
enforced, and it appears that no one expected them to be enforced.
About Hungary, interpreter Pat Austin says: "It is an overtly sexist
society, although the Hungarians themselves don't realize it." Women
in Hungary have been working [as members of dual-income families
for a long time]. Women hold down full-time jobs and manage the

household in a country where it's difficult to manage a household because you can't walk into a supermarket and buy everything you need instantly. Women are paid less, but this does not show up on paper, because the law calls for equal pay. Women don't rise to the positions that men do. They rarely occupy managerial positions, excect in industries that are totally female-operated. Yet, nearly every official delegation from Hungary that visits the United States includes a token woman. Not because Americans might be sensitive to equality issues but because Hungarian law calls for equality. It's cosmetic. In some cases, the woman will be utterly powerless; in others, she may have influence "if she has a big enough mouth," says Pat. "The one exception was a visiting delegation of judges. The majority were women." Why? Because judges occupy the lowest-paid position in the Hungarian legal system. They are paid the least, and they work the hardest. And the job involves the least amount of interpretive activity because the *letter* of the law, not the spirit of the law, must be enforced. Therefore, Hungarian judges are mostly women, while private-practice corporate lawyers are mostly men.

A lack of gender equality in East Europe does not mean that the Westerner can ignore the sensitivities of Eastern European female employees. Sexual harassment, as oppset to gender discrimination, is a problem for Eastern European women, and they a well-developed vocabulary with which to complain about it. Unwelcome male advances, comments about physical attributes, and inappropriate physical contact must be prevented by the foreign manager of a venture. One area where firms have had troble is in having female employees offer customer service in a region that hasn't known customer service for 40 years. In Prague, Kmart passed out pins to be worn by store clerks that read, "I'm Here for You," suggesting the friendly service of the West. "It offends me," a female Kmart employee complained. "People can interpret it any way thay want; it looks as though I'm here not just for business but for the amusement of certain customers." There you have it. Because of the great degree of sexual harassment experienced by women in these societies, you may find that female employees are highly sensitized to the issue, and you need to respect their point of view.

Are foreign women treated differently by Eastern European men than foreign men in the context of doing business? Most of my female interviewees admit discriminatory treatment in all of the former Warsaw Pact countries, but the problem quickly subsides when men realize that their female business counterpart means business, is serious, and has mastered her field of endeavor.

However, the Eastern European man may not be accustomed to the straightforward, aggressive, and (to them) "unfeminine" business behavior of Western women who go to Eastern Europe to conduct business discussions. Call it macho. Women in these countries simply have not behaved in a "capitalist" fashion in the past; few *men* have. Your firm handshake, direct eye contact, and cool, business-oriented conversation may cause discomfort at first among your male counterparts in Eastern Europe. But that discomfort will vanish quickly, as long as you aren't curt, loud, rude, or impersonal. Give something of yourself, and you'll make friends of your business partners as fast as any Western male will. As female business people, you will be considered foreigners first and women second in the eyes of Eastern Europeans. If you bring with you what is needed to enhance your business partner's status, business, and reputation, your partner is not going to care what gender you are.

Proximity Boundaries: How Close Is Too Close?   There's a difference between what experts call *proxemics,* and touching. North Americans stand about 18 inches apart when speaking to one another, whether the person is a stranger or a friend. In Eastern Europe, it's about the same, but for foreign women doing business in the East, you may have to enforce a comfortable proximity boundary with your male counterparts after relations have warmed and the vodka has begun to flow. At that time, the typical Russian, for example, will invade your space. Obviously, one cannot generalize about men in the region, but many of the women that I interviewed for this section, both Western and Eastern European women, report that men frequently become physical and aggressively flirtatious when hosting female business people from the West. Russia expert Barbara Chronowski enforces clearly defined proximity boundaries with all male acquaintances during meetings, sightseeing tours, and drinking parties. It's important because any woman, Western or Eastern European, may be considered "loose" if she participates in physical camaraderie. Such behavior also diminishes a woman's business stature.

Tips for Foreign Women as Delegation Leaders

- Consider taking along a male vice president to conduct initial interfacing with an Eastern European company.

- Arrange and pay for all entertainment beforehand, in order not to offend a male guest who might insist that a man pay.

- Know your skill area and wear it on your sleeve. In Eastern Europe, you will *not* be treated as a woman; you will be associated with your training, skills, and job position. Be able to supply accurate and useful information at the asking; this will earn you instant respect.

- Before meetings take place, send an agenda that includes short biographies of yourself and your team members. Describe yourself as "team leader" or make it apparent from your title that you are the superior-ranking delegate.

- Communicate your leadership role nonverbally, by entering doorways before your team members, for example, and by sitting in the place of honor at the negotiation table, directly across from the head negotiator on the Eastern side. Initiate and conclude all meetings with an opening and closing speech.

- Make sure that your team members defer to you at all times, and ask that questions from the Eastern side, if directed to members of your team, be directed to you instead. If the Eastern negotiators persist in ignoring you or in refusing to acknowledge your leadership, you may find it necessary, as a last resort, to ask to continue the meeting without your team members being present.

The Rites of Gift Giving

Gift giving in Eastern Europe, until the era of glasnost, meant risqué calendars, Scotch whiskey, and—to celebrate the signing of a really big deal—a stereo or an air conditioner. With perestroika came foreign business suitors willing to entice decision makers with free vacation in the United States, automobiles, Concorde tickets, and large amounts of foreign exchange. My advice: Keep business gift giving to a minimum in Eastern Europe: use it to forge bonds of friendship rather than to manipulate people for what usually turns out to be a momentary gain. If you're dealing with someone who is motivated only by such gifts, you're dealing with the wrong person. Bring gifts from the West, but don't worry about bringing expensive gifts.

Observe Five Eastern European Gift-Giving Customs. First, wait until the end of your visit before presenting a gift to a business counterpart whom you are meeting for the first time. Second, do not open your gift in the presence of the giver unless you are asked to do so. Thank the giver and place the gift at your side. Third, on subsequent occasions, always *refer* to a gift you received earlier. This, among other things, helps build continuity in your business relationship. Fourth, never give a gift to a group without alerting your host that you are going to do so. For example, inform your host that you will be bringing a gift to his or her office before leaving for the airport. That way, the whole group will be present, which is important. And fifth, give a gift to an individual only in private; give to a group during a scheduled group gathering when everyone is present. Remember that the worst mistake you can make in Eastern Europe is to rob people of face by giving gifts to their colleagues but not to them.

A note on *corporate logos:* They can appear on small, novelty-type gifts to individuals or on large gifts given by your company to a company in Eastern Europe. Otherwise use your company logo sparingly so that your gifts don't seem promotional. Never give a gift unless it is wrapped and accompanied by a suitable card.

When invited to the home of an Eastern European, don't forget to arrive with a gift. Gourmet-quality foods purchased in the West are your best bet. A basket of fruit is a good gift. (Nice fruit baskets can be bought locally in Eastern Europe.) Boxes of chocolate and other sweets work well, too.

Gift Ideas

American postcards

Calenders

American stamps

Technical and marketing books

Tape recorders and dictaphones

Pen sets

Digital watches

Cigarettes

Scotch whiskey or brandy

Lingerie and panty hose

Picture books of your home state, town, or country

Technical books

This may sound strange, but a wonderful gift is the conference proceedings to an important roundtable or seminar program. Information is scarce in Eastern Europe, and much prestige comes to scholars and scientists who possess important, recently published research.

Catholic Eastern Europeans celebrate their saint's name day; one's name day is more important than one's birthday. Each saint in the Catholic pantheon has a day on which that saint is celebrated. Bring a small gift to a party celebrating a person's name day. Know your secretary's name day and celebrate it by giving flowers, candy, cakes, or some other small gift.

When Gifts Become Graft. A "gift" of Marlboro cigarettes, women's lingerie, or a Milky Way candy bar will open many a bureaucratic door in Eastern Europe. However, an American company must know that giving gifts of value or cash to a goverment official is illigal under the Foreign Corrupt Practices Act. Some companies decide that a policy of giving and receiving no gifts is best. All gifts are sent back to the giver with thanks and an explanation of why gifts cannot be accepted. Whatever your company policy, make sure that it's clear and that you know what it is before forging business relationships in the East.

Dining Etiquette for the East

European table etiquette is generally different from the American. Working as an interpreter in Hungary, American Pat Austin remembers an incident when a waiter refused to take a plate off the table because an American executive had not placed his knife and fork parallel to one another on his plate. The executive complained, the waiter got upset, and snapped: "How should I know if you were finished if you don't put your knife and fork parallel!" And the waiter was right. How should he know? And this is not Hungarian protocol; it's *European* protocol. Similarly, the fork is held in the left hand while the knife is used to push food onto it; you don't have to switch hands to eat with your right hand holding the fork. Simply lift the fork with your left hand to eat. The table setting is similar to that in the West, with an extra spoon for coffee. When you are finished, leave some food on your plate. Cross your fork and knife on the plate to signal that you are resting; setting them parallel indicates that you are finished eating. Don't sit down at the head of the table; sit at the side. The guest of honor is often seated at the head of the table.

You may not find the glass of plain water on the luncheon table that Americans take for granted; you will have to order mineral water instead. At lunch, don't wait to be seated; the seating hostesses common in the United States are rare in Europe. Other people may often sit at your table after asking perfunctorily if the open spaces are free. If crowded conditions make it difficult for you to find a seat, you should feel free to do the same. Business can be discussed at lunch or dinner, but also use the occasion to expand philosophically about the business deal you are involved in. Share some war stories and personal opinions. If you want to invite someone out to dinner but don't know of a great restaurant, take the person to a restaurant located at a fine hotel. If you invite business people to dinner who are also friends, ask their spouses as well. Throughout Eastern Europe, the restaurant, usually in a nice hotel, is the business meeting place of choice. At lower-end eateries, ask the waiter which items on the menu are available. Many items may not be.

Regional Differences

In Poland, a business lunch could take place as late as four in the afternoon. After-hours dinners for core managers are big events—long, multicourse meals hosted by the director. You can drink from a bowl of beet soup; you don't have to use a spoon. Never leave a Polish meal early; feel free to engage in lengthy conversations. At the table in the former Yugoslavia the fork will be on the left and the knife on the right. Indicate that you are finished eating by placing your silverware on your plate, with the tines of the fork and point of knife resting on the plate's edge. In Bulgaria, the guest of honor does not sit "isolated" at the head of the table but sits in a central location. The table setting will look familiar, except that a stirring spoon will be set above the center plate. In the former Soviet Union the typical table will feature bottled water, vodka, caviar, and a plate of vegetables and cold meats. Three glasses confront the diner: one for wine, one for Pepsi, and one for vodka. In Hungary, the guest of honor sits to the right of the hostess. Wait for the hostess to begin each course. Hungarians would not dream of eating before they've said, "Good appetite." They will not begin eating until everyone at the table has been served, unless specifically asked to by the host—say, at a large banquet. Otherwise, they'll let the food get cold, while the American digs in. This is something to be aware of if you are the host; suggest that they begin if the serving process is taking a while. Then it's their choice to wait or not to wait; it will then come down to how hungary they are. Sorry: Bad joke.

Who Pays?

Eastern Europeans may refuse to allow you to pay, even when you have invited them out to a meal, even when they are not expecting to receive your business. You're on their turf, and nothing will deter them from playing the role of host when you are in their country. When in doubt, the one who extends the invitation is the one who pays. Another axiom: Sellers pay, buyers don't.

Business Entertainment: Drinking and Nightlife

Options for entertainment include pub crawling, theater, dance shows, musical concerts, and alas, sex shows. Evard Hiltenkamp, a representative of the Treuhandanstalt, intimated to me in Berlin recently that the type of entertainment German hosts suggest to visiting foreigners depends less on their country of origin than on their industry. "We sound out guests during the first meal," says Evard, "and then decide where to take them." He has found that steel executives, from whatever country, tend to want to eat heartily and drink hard at the pubs. Textile industry people usually want to eat haute cuisine and then go to bed. The hotel industry people want to eat, drink moderately, and then paint the town red. In other words, if your company is being courted, make your entertainment desires subtly clear early on in your stay in Eastern Europe.

With the demise of puritanical communism, business entertainment has become de rigueur for hosting foreign business people in Eastern Europe and invariably involves a trip to the "hot" new dance show at a local club or to the dance lounge at a "foreigner" hotel. You will find that your Hungarian host will take you on the rounds of the new porno-strip show nightclubs as part of entertaining you during your business trip. Warsaw is the same, often on your first night in town. (Even under the old regime, prostitution parlors existed behind the facade as a way to entertain foreigners and state officials in the bureaucracy.) On his first visit to Warsaw as a representative of Arthur D. Little, Karsten Finke got taken out by his Polish partner (whom he had never met before) to a hot new local strip joint near the Marriott. "Warsaw is a naughty place," he informed me the following morning in a surprised German accent. At the reception for the delegates at the trade conference in Moscow recently, "traditional folk dancers" appeared on stage wearing frilly Las Vegas-style dancing outfits. The "folk dance" suddenly turned into a sex show when one of the male dancers, dressed in black leather, cracked a whip.

Leaving spouses at home is normal operating procedure, especially in light of the popularity of sex shows, which cannot be labeled "lewd" in the sense they can be in Thailand or Japan but do feature women dancing chorus-line steps with their tops off. Foreign businesswomen should be prepared for wild dancing on the part of the young male businessmen, especially in the Commonwealth of Independent States (C.I.S.). Most of the dancing is free-form, so you don't have to worry about learning the mazurka.

Toastmasters

"To be drunk was a common feature of Russian hospitality," wrote Russian historian Robert K. Massie. "Unless guests were sent home dead drunk, the evening was considered a failure." In the former Soviet Union, vodka drinking occurs at night, during dinner banquets, but not during a business lunch or breakfast. Be prepared to handle inquiries after drinking has taken place. Once you're drunk, you might be asked questions about how much money you and your company make, for example. The host leads in the toasting ritual, especially in Georgia, where drinking ritual are strictly observed. The toastmaster is called a *tamada*. He toasts everything: You, your wife, your company, your venture, peace, the kitchen help...everything. Whether the toast is with vodka or wine, you have to toss it all back. Don't leave a drop, or you will be compromising the toast. When you want to make a toast yourself, ask the toastmaster before doing so; the tamada will usually permit it. Vodka is served cold, without ice; the local stuff is smooth, with no bite—just a glow inside you that builds. In Poland, one toast at a meal will be made with chilled vodka (no ice) with the words "to your health" or stolat (may you live one hundred years). Empty your vodka glass at such a toast. Schnapps (brandy) or wine will be served before the meal in Hungary. Tokay, a sweet dessert wine, comes after dessert. Be prepared for pear-flavored brandy as well. Hungarians will not pick up their glass and start to drink before a toast has been made. It doesn't matter whether they are drinking wine, beer, or Pepsi. If someone else is present, they must toast the other person before they drink. It's a minor matter of lifting glasses, clinking them together, and just saying, "To your health." But the Hungarian would not dream of drinking without first toasting you. Typically a Bulgarian toast may be made with *rakija*, a plum or grape brandy. Watch it with this stuff; it can sneak up on you. Local Bulgarian drinks include *slivova* (a plum brandy), *mastika* (an anise drink), and vodka. In Romania, toast often by touching glasses and saying: "To your health," or "Good luck." When your host stuffs the cork back into the bottle of wine, dinner is over.

What if you are a nondrinker? Olga Ringo, a consultant and C.I.S. travel specialist in San Francisco, says: "The Russians *drink*. And you have to be able to be one of the fellows who can handle that. I don't drink, so I tell them I have an ulcer." Also, she holds her glass up and sips, without gulping down the contents during a toast, preventing her glass from being constantly refilled. The Russian side won't necessarily drain their glasses during a toast, but they may expect you to. So again, claim that you have a medical condition. "Doctor's orders."

Traveling in Eastern Europe—Fasten Your Seatbelts for a Bumpy Ride

The first rule for Americans east of the Rhine is: Don't be an "Ugly American." In traveling in the region, it is essential that you represent the United States well. Avoid prostitutes and drinking your lungs full. You are dealing with cultured people who have a high standard of conduct. Under communism, the only control they had was over their own behavior; they aspire to a higher notion of *civility* than most Americans. Excessive and/or vulgar behavior on the part of the foreign visitor can have disastrous consequences. Your business partners will have a tendency (and a knack) for knowing what you are doing all the time that you are in-country. People talk. Anything *doesn't* go. You must be most circumspect in your conduct.

Where To Stay—Finding the Best Hotel

You can expect to pay dearly for an adequate hotel room everywhere in Eastern Europe. A top hotel in the former East Berlin—say, the Palast Hotel— runs $204 for a single per night, without meals. Of course, the rooms overlook the Unter Linden, East Berlin's main drag, have working televisions offering CNN and MTV, and are supplied with functional telephone service. In Budapest, Prague, and Warsaw you will find the rates at the top hotels between $150 and $250 per night for a single, depending on the season. In the medium range, you can rent a room for about $60 to $90 per night for a single, but these rooms are harder to find and the accommodations are often substandard. For example, the Stadt Berlin in East Berlin charges $65 per night for a single and the rooms are drab but comfortable. The cost includes a wonderful Western breakfast in the restaurant on the first floor. However, the building itself is Russian made, and one has the uneasy sense that it could fall down at any moment. At midnight one evening, I had the disquieting experience of getting trapped in one of the hotel's elevators between floors. After three phone calls to hotel clerks from the elevator emergency phone, the elevator finally inched up. I had to pry the doors open by hand. I exited the lift into a dark lobby, no one in sight, with a lot of sweat under my collar.

The low end of the hotel market is almost nonexistent in Eastern Europe and consists mainly of small pensions and apartment rooms made available to foreigners for $20 to $35 per night. Business people from the West who want to create the right image won't want to stay in a dilapidated low-end hotel or a person's home for a fee, but the traveler on a budget might consider it. Especially in Prague, the availability of homes and apartments for rent is great, and staying with a local can be a unique experience. Find the best place by talking to the people in the information booth at the train station. In Prague, you will be accosted by people wanting to rent you a room; the central Cedok travel service has reputable room renters on computer.

Don't judge a hotel by its cover; go inside and ask to check the room before registering. Hotels in the former Soviet Union look clean and modern on the outside, but in a hotel guide the rooms would rate low to skid row. Rusty water, used sheets, broken television, you know the score. Be aware that many first-class hotels charge astronomical fees for long-distance and/or international calls placed from the hotel. Pay phones in public places like post offices are a better option. Or go over to another hotel that has private phone booths and doesn't charge exorbitant fees. Communicate with the home office by fax if for no other reason than it costs a lot less. Recently, I paid eight deutsche marks to send a fax from the Stadt Berlin Hotel; the next day I paid 108 deutsche marks ($60) for a fifteen-minute phone call to the States! You can cut hotel costs by renting a car and staying on the outskirts of a capital city or by staying where the locals stay. As in Western Europe, pensiones are springing up everywhere, and in Czechoslovakia tourist agents operate a computer database of homes and apartments in which you can rent a room cheap and get an inside view of the local lifestyle at the same time.

Travel Savvy

Money Tip.   When changing money, don't accept large bills. You need small bills because you won't be able to get change when buying things from small shops.

Time Difference.   Most Eastern European capitals are 6 hours ahead of New York time and 9 hours ahead of Los Angeles. Moscow is 8 hours ahead of New York and 11 hours ahead of Los Angeles.

The Escalator Rule.   Stand on the right, walk on the left.

Sundays.   Don't get caught needing something crucial on Sunday; stores are closed and the streets get rolled up.

Drinking Water.   Always have something bottled to drink with you when in the former Soviet Union. Depending on where you are, the difficulty in finding something safe to imbibe can be frightening. One U.S. engineer got so dehydrated during a business visit that he developed kidney stones! In Russia, citizens pay five kopecks for a drink of water at water vending machines. Everyone uses the same glass, called a "people's glass." There's also the kvass truck that pulls up at a street corner and sells nonalcoholic beer, also out of a common glass. The willingness to share in Russia is an endearing trait, but you may want to bring your own glass to avoid sampling a Russian city's current strain of head cold.

Driving.   To see a country up close and intimately, you have to drive through it. Rent a car in a capital city. Most rental agencies limit you to the country, but not all do. Driving in Eastern Europe requires patience and caution. Highways are rough-surfaced and two-lane, which means that one horse-drawn cart on the road can delay a time-strapped foreign business person for an hour or more. In Germany, if you want to drive under 50 miles an hour, stay in the right lane; I clocked lightning-fast Mercedes, BMWs, and Peugeots in fast lanes moving at 110 miles an hour. When someone coming up behind you flashes their headlights, get over to the right in a hurry.

In some countries you may have to buy coupons to purchase rationed gasoline. Even with coupons, gas station attendants may say Nyet to your request to fill up, because, they say, there is no gas left. Just park your car nearby and wait for the station to clear out of locals. Usually when you return and ask again, there will be gas and you can fill up. The problem is that the gas station owner doesn't want to be seen serving a foreigner gas when gas is rationed. Gasoline runs from three to five dollars a gallon and is tabulated in liters. Don't pass a gas station when you're half-empty expecting another station up around the bend. Keep the tank full; if you run out of gas in a desolate area of Eastern Europe (anywhere outside the capital cities) your game is over. Also, remember to remove your windshield wipers at night, if you are leaving the car on the street. They grow legs.

Taxi Tips.   Don't get in a taxi if it doesn't have a meter. And ask what the approximate fare will be to your destination. Don't leave it up to the driver to decide what you should pay. Recently, I paid 32,000 zlotys (three dollars) to go from the Marriott Hotel in Warsaw to Old Town; the taxi driver who brought me back asked for 85,000 zlotys (eight dollars)! I refused. The driver shrugged and lowered the fare to 40,000 zlotys. "Thank you," I said and grinned victoriously. On another occasion I had twenty minutes to burn in Krakow, so I got a taxi to take me to Wavel Castle, which was a ten-minute walk from my hotel. The taxi took ten minutes to get there, swooping through the outskirts of the city. Twenty dollars later, I arrived at the castle. After looking over the castle, he took me back to the hotel. By a different route, we arrived in about two minutes. Burned again.

Smoking.   A great many Eastern European business people smoke, many incessantly. Smoking at the negotiating table will not offend, but asking before lighting up if others don't smoke is considered polite, as it is elsewhere.

Swimming. Do not go swimming in any body of water—river, sea, or lake. Most rivers in the region are so poisonous that swimming in them might kill you.

Pilferers, Pickpockets, and Black Marketeers. With democracy comes crime. In the past, there was no violence and no crime; now, there is. Everybody has a scam, a game to make a buck or a ruble. Whenever you are on the street, you will immediately become the focus of (generally younger) men trying to sell black market goods like Hard Rock Café shirts or sweatshirts that read: The University of Moscow. Young women sell their bodies. (Male companionship is for sale, too.) To prevent mishap, do not walk alone at night or in train stations or underground walkways.

A Note about Writing Dates and Numbers. When writing, put the day first, then the month, and then the year. Thus, August 11, 1991, would be written 11.08.91. Also, if this date was handwritten, the two number 1's would be handwritten like two uncrossed cursive "t's," which would look like an "M." Very confusing. Also, a handwritten number 9 tends to look very like the number 8.

Visiting Someone at Home

Americans tend to be quick to invite visiting executives to their homes. This is not common in Eastern Europe. The eastern Germans, for instance, will go to great lengths to have everything just right if they do invite foreigners home. It is not a good idea to drop in on people unexpectedly at home. Whenever you are invited to someone's home, bring flowers—on the first and all subsequent visits. To a dinner served at a home, bring a bottle of wine or whiskey, a box of chocolates, or a can of good coffee. To a Bulgarian home, bring candy or flowers, wrapped. Yellow symbolizes hatred, so avoid giving yellow flowers. Also, gladioli or calla lilies are only for weddings or funerals. To a Polish home, you can bring flowers, but be aware that chrysanthemums are used only for funerals. In the former Soviet Union, and elsewhere in Eastern Europe where times are tough, eat the minimum amount of food that you can when dining in someone's home. In the old days (before the fall of communism), Russian hosts would have to apply to the local chapter of the party before hosting foreigners; then the party would send over enough food for the occasion. The meal might be the best meal the host family had eaten in months. "The Russians never seem to be smiling in your photographs," I said to Hecht-Nielsen, amused by his conspicuous grin in each snapshot. "These people are starving," he told me. They were top Soviet scientists and mathematicians, and they were barely scraping by. The sensitive foreign guest would leave as much as possible for the family to enjoy later.

Holidays In Eastern Europe

Plan your business around holidays. Eastern Europeans traditionally take vacations in August, and for most of the month. So don't plan to conduct business negotiations during August. Little business gets done between mid-December and January, either. (See Holidays in Eastern Europe in the appendix for a list of regional holidays.) In general, make appointments in Eastern Europe two months in advance.

What to Bring to Eastern Europe

- Penlight for reading and use during power outages.
- Aspirin.
- City maps in English.
- Inflatable seat pillow, earplugs, blindfold, and sleeping pills.
- 100-watt light bulb (carried in a plastic bag) to use in dimly lit hotel rooms.
- Traveler's dictionary and a dictionary of technical terms, if needed.
- Blood-type identification card. (Know your blood type before leaving for Eastern Europe in case you need a blood transfusion. You don't have to worry about tainted blood, as it is now screened in most of Eastern Europe, with the exception of some of the former Soviet Republics.)
- Voltage converter with assorted plug adapters.
- Water purification tablets.
- Common antibiotic.
- Antidiarrheal medication.
- Funnel (for use with a rental car).
- Vitamin pills.
- Instant tea and coffee.
- Insect repellent. (You could throw a saddle on some of the region's roaches.)
- Rubber stopper, because bath plugs are often stolen.
- All toiletries, including toilet paper.
- Medical kit, including a disposable syringe. (One hospital in Moscow has one syringe for the entire hospital! It often goes uncleaned between patients.)

13

Formulas for Business Success:

Five Corporate Cases

The best way to prepare for doing business in Russia would be to spend a year as a roadie for a rock band. You know, the concert is about to begin, and the microphones are dead, and the amplifiers are dead, and the instruments are lost, and the lights don't work, and the lead singer is in a coma—and you have five minutes to fix everything, and all you've got is a pair of pliers and roll of duct tape. That's what it's like in Russia, all the time....You have to take a step back and say, 'O.K., O.K., this isn't reality as I know it, but I survived Alice Cooper, and I can survive this.'"

KENNY SCHAFFER
The New Yorker

Every company approaches business opportunities in Eastern Europe guided by the nature of its product and industry. You can't, as of yet, generalize about the "right" or "wrong" approach. And you cannot lay out simple-to-follow, "one-minute" solutions to the problems of doing business in a region where the swift tide of change has not yet begun to ebb. I had thought that, if I interviewed a large number of business people who had entered into Eastern European ventures, a list of "commandments" might emerge that the reader could take to Warsaw or Bucharest or Minsk and, by adhering to the list, feel assured of success. International business is never so easy; indeed, its difficulty is one of the unarticulated causes of America's persistent trade imbalances.

In Search of "Formulas" for Success

One "commandment," however, can be followed by everyone doing business in the New East: Thou shalt follow the three P's—patience, persistence, and perseverence. "Take a long-range view," advises Duane Best, who works in Czechoslovakia. "My children will follow through on the work I am doing there now." In short, build a long-term strategy.

The Eastern Europe market is young, and thus pioneers have to respond to opportunities swiftly and deftly even though they may fall outside their intentions in the region. If the Romanians need food at the moment, sell them food and hold off on selling them stereos and VCRs. The point is not to "wait until the market develops," planning to sell the stereos some day in the future, when your company could exploit the real opportunities that exist in the present. As a consultant friend of mine advises, "You have to hover like a butterfly, and sting like a bee," as the market matures. Ultimately, the most successful firms will begin to link up their country-specific activities into regional interrelationships over the course of years. They will obtain raw materials and components from one country, manufacture the products in another, and sell the finished products in yet another. This "bifurcated presence" in all the markets of Eastern Europe has been achieved by a number of German firms and by only a handful of American companies—as of yet. The goal for strategists is to learn to scan for regional opportunities and create synergies between Eastern countries that differ in what they offer in terms of comparative advantage.

We have talked about some of the largest American ventures in the New East, like those of GE, GM, UTA, and USWest. Only one of the corporate cases described in this chapter—that of the Amway Corporation—involves a large American corporation. The stories in this chapter are about enterprising Americans who have responded to opportunities and struggled for Eastern European business success.

After each story follows a set of "lessons," though I suspect readers will glean their own rules, formulas, and advice from them. One thing is certain: The dramas will encourage you to think about how to approach Eastern Europe opportunities in novel and creative ways.

Amway Products Enter the Homes of Hungary

I have mentioned before that the Amway Corporation has made great strides in penetrating the Hungarian consumer market in detergent, soaps, and cleaning products. Thus far, no other American company involved in Eastern Europe has been as successful as Amway (that I know of) in generating brand awareness, sales, and, most important, in setting up an innovative and effective distribution network in Eastern Europe. I obtained the full story in a conversation with Jim Devoss, manager—New Market Development at Amway World Headquarters.

What has been the evolution of Amway's move into Eastern Europe?

Amway in Europe started way back in 1973, when we entered into the market of the United Kingdom. Between 1973 and the late eighties we entered most of the free markets in Europe including Germany, France, Italy, Spain, Portugal, Belgium, Netherlands, Austria...it was a natural extension. In the late eighties we started seeing the Wall come down, and so we looked at middle Europe. Hungary happened to be the first.

Hungary was close to Austria, and our Austrian general manager had an interest in Hungary. We looked at Hungary for about a year, as we normally do with all new markets, to make sure that it would be viable for both the corporation and, even more important, the independent Amway distributors. Once we found out that, legally, Amway could open in Hungary, we made a commitment to do so. In January 1990, we started putting people on the ground in Hungary on an almost-permanent basis—myself being one of them.

The things we had to put together are pretty standard to our operation. First, we had to establish an affiliate headquarters, an office, staffed with the various functions: Finance, distribution, sales, marketing, and so forth. And then we set up our distribution centers. That was a little more chalanging than setting up the office just because of the infrastructure in Hungary. Dealing with the numbers of people we do, communications are extremely important, and the telephone system in Hungary is not so good. We set up "pick-up centers" throughout the country, which are mini-entities of Amway where distributors come to get products. We also utilize the centers to pass communications back and forth. We collect data on orders and who placed tham, and what kind of volumes they have, which is critical to our payment of performance bonuses. Every day, we have someone pick up the data needed to make the Amway Sales and Marketing Plan work properly.

What were the steps Amway took to pull together a number of competent distributors who were Hungarian?

We opened on June 3, 1990, and by the end of June 25,000 distributors had joined us in Hungary. We're well over 60,000 at this point in time. One of the [characteristics] of our sales and marketing plan—a multi-level direct sales plan—is that distributors from anywhere in the world who know an individual in a market authorized for Amway activity need only encourage that person to call us. We don't simply take names out of the phone directory and we don't want to "cold contact" people. We tell distributors to ask new candidates to call or write us, and then we find someone near to them who is already a distributor, and ask that person if they would be willing to see the candidate and talk about the Amway sales and marketing plan. Of course, our people are in business to expand their organizations for profitability, so they are delighted to do it.

Did you find that Amway's success in Hungary—in terms of expanding the number of distributors—was spearheaded by Hungarian-Americans who were working for Amway in the United States and then went to Hungary?

I give credit to three countries. One is Canada, one is Australia, and one is the United States—[all places where large numbers of Hungarians had emigrated].

What cost is there to a Hungarian person who wants to become a distributor?

As everywhere around the world, it is the cost of what we call a sales and product kit. In Hungary that happened to be 5,500 forints, which was about $70(U.S.)—about a week's wages for the average Hungarian. Every kit contains a number of documents on how to own and operate an Anway business, a number of documents explaining the Amway sales and marketing plan and how it works, documents on the products and brochures, pamphlets about the products, price lists, order forms—the things that you need to run the business. The kit also contains sample products. They're very high quality, very high in concentration, and they're environmentally sensitive. We like distributors to take those products and use them so they know how good they are, and can therefore better sell them.

Now, it's a cash business. Distributors can expand according to their own means. They can buy one product and sell it and save some of the money to start building—there are different ways people do it depending on what they have at their disposal with regard to funds for the business.

Did it take a long time to get products approved for distribution in Hungary?

Not any longer than it does anywhere else. The testing does take time, but it went smoothly. The Hungarian officials were very willing to work with us as long as we did what their regulations required and, of course, we always do. It took some time, and it took the money to cover the cost of all of the extensive testing, but we're used to it.

Were there any problems helping Hungarians learn how to use Amway products?

We start with those products which are basic to our line, simple to demonstrate, easy to use, provide a good value for money on a cost-per-use basis. Then you factor in quality, which is an intangible. We first prove that we're effective on a cost per use, and then we teach the intangibles. Because we have to teach this aspect and a whole lot more about the products, we start with the most basic products. Distributors have to learn how to build and grow a business at the same time, so we don't want to overwhelm them. We start in every market with a three-year plan in which we move from a small number of limited products to a very extensive line.

Are the Hungarian distributors producing a high level of gross sales relative to other countries?

At this point, Hungary is on track to producing the biggest first-year market volume in Amway history. A lot of things contribute to that, such as the expertise with which we are now launching markets. We are into a tremendous spurt of international growth. And, of course, the more markets you open and the more often, let's face it, the more you remember the mistakes you made last time, and can preclude them the next time. We've got a broad base of distributors, we've got a lot of excitement in the international areas, and therefore, as we open markets up, they open with the resounding splashes that we saw in Hungary.

Was there any problem with convertibility of currency?

Our Hungarian business is a Hungarian business, so all transactions are done in Hungarian forint. So, within the markets there is no challenge whatsoever. For payment outside the market, there is "internal convertibility," which means you can go to the bank and convert forint to whatever type of currency you need to make outside payments. The only restriction is that if the currency you need isn't available, of course, you can't obtain it.

Do you find a lot of people signing up and finding out that it's harder than they thought and that they drop out? Is there much attrition?

There is no more attrition in Hungary than we see in any other new market—it's somewhere around 40 percent attrition on an annual basis, because we're not for everybody.

Are a lot of people going to Amway as a second or third job in Hungary?

Anywhere in the world we find that. And particularly initially, because Amway is not a "get-rich-quick" scheme. It takes work, it takes effort. We gear the development of our sales marketing plan, and the bonuses that are paid, toward an average middle-management-level position in the firm, knowing that by the time someone makes what we call *direct distributor* in our business, they have sufficient income to sustain their standard of living. That's what we aim for. Again, it takes a while to learn a new business, to learn the products, to get the sales and build the organization. I don't know of anyone really who's joined us with an intention of going full-time immediately. There have been a couple of success stories where people have committed to it and they've done it, but most start out part-time. What we find is that sometimes a distributor starts and goes and goes until all of a sudden he says, "I'm running more money through my Amway business than I am through my regular job. What could I do if I go full time?"

Do you have to work on keeping your public image up and steady in Hungary? Do you do much advertising or company public relations of any sort?

We have a firm public relations plan in place in all markets, and this is especially important in our new markets where Amway brings a unique and unfamiliar concept to the marketplace.

Amway's philosophy is based on being a profitable business. But the company and its cofounders have always had a strong commitment to the community and to contributing to the market over the long term.

In Hungary, for example, we sponsored the "homecoming" concert of Sir Georg Solti and the Chicago Symphony Orchestra. This memorable event took place in Budapest well before the launch of Amway Hungaria, and it was a means of presenting Amway to govermental officials, media, and the public for the first time.

We do little advertising, and when we do, it is "image advertising." Really, our more than two million distributorships around the world are a wonderful form of advertising.

Our commitment to the community and to corporate sponsorships in the areas of culture and the arts, education, sports, the underprivileged, and environment is a major cornerstone for presenting the Amway philisiphy.

Lessons Learned from Amway Corporation

- Expand a multilevel marketing network by offering cash and/or product benefits to Eastern Europeans who are experienced in working at more than one job. Look out for distributors the way you would look out for customers.

- Deal creatively and forthrightly with deficiencies in communication and distribution infrastructure. Find a solution instead of avoiding a market because of these deficiencies.

- Set up an information system that is not dependent on ultra-efficient telecommunications.

- Consider convertibility potential carefully.

- In expanding your market network effort, look for ways to generate synergies between ethnic Eastern Europeans living in the West and those living in Eastern Europe.

- Assist your Eastern European distributors in learning how to form a company, informing them of the risks of doing so and the legal aspects of running it. Educate your independent marketers to help them prosper.

- Make it very inexpensive for independent Eastern European marketers to become members of the network, to purchase samples and sales literature, etc.

- Educate independent marketers using a clear, simple, and basic approach to selling, product usage, and business knowledge.

- Launch a few products at a time, starting with the most basic, so as not to overwhelm your marketers.

- Move into other countries of Eastern Europe before your product does through unorthodox or illegal means.

- Label products in the local language.

- Promote the image of your company in Eastern Europe by sponsoring educational, cultural, and environmental projects at the community level.

Ron Plunkett and Company: An "Expedition" into Soviet Airspace

In searching for the perfect contact with the clout and authority to influence a deal, one runs into all sorts of business personalities in Eastern Europe. Dealing with shenanigans can be extremely frustrating, time-consuming, and expensive. Let Ron Plunkett's experience be a parable.

Ron is a practicing international lawyer whose hobby is studying and searching for vintage World War II aircraft. With three colleagues who have the same avocation, he formed a company which aimed to locate and sell vintage World War II aircraft rusting away in the former Eastern bloc countries and the U.S.S.R. You can buy a MiG fighter jet in the former Soviet Union for $25,000, but the rarest planes in the world—Spitfires, Hurricanes, A-20 Havocs, P-47s, and P-38s—are worth over a million dollars each. The equivalent of a major fleet of vintage aircraft exists somewhere in Eastern Europe, worth zillions. One might be in someone's chicken coup, another might be at the bottom of a lake, another at the end of an abandoned airstrip.

Ron's team knew that planes existed inside the U.S.S.R.; the hard part was finding them and getting them out. To look for them, you had to be invited to the Soviet Union. That was the first step, and as it turned out, the most difficult. As Ron says, "In those years [the mid-1980s] you applied for a visa and they said, 'Why do you want to go?' If you wanted to go in a tour group and look at the paintings in Leningrad, that's fine. But you were never going to get outside the view of the tour guide." The boys needed to get into restricted areas, roam around dilapidated airstrips, poke around in the woods.

The eight partners (among them an airline pilot, a Navy man, a teacher, a guy from military intelligence...average guys) hatched a clever ploy. Earlier in this century, there had been a famous Russian pilot who was thought to have been lost at sea, named Levinesky—Russia's Lindbergh. In 1937, Levinesky decided that he'd fly from Moscow to the continental United States via the North Pole, which nobody had ever done. Levinesky made radio contact during his flight but suddenly vanished and was never heard from again. If the company could find out what happened to Levinesky, there was a chance that someone inside the Soviet Union would be interested in talking to them and in helping them pursue their interests in searching for valuable aircraft. They formed a nonprofit foundation with the objective of finding the lost Soviet pilot.

The foundation went through old newspapers and scoured the Aviation Archives in Washington, D.C., looking for nuggets of information that would lead them to the Levinesky crash site, and they hoped, the wreckage of his plane. *That* would get the interest of the Soviets. They found a map of his proposed route and verbatim transcriptions of transmitted conversations between radio operators on the ground and Levinesky's radio operator. They obtained weather data for the particular days of the Levinesky flight, and using sophisticated computers that were not available to early investigators of the Levinesky crash site, they plotted Levinesky's probable route, and pinpointed his likely crash site, which disagreed with the areas searched by two 1937 expeditions by 500 to 1,000 miles, one of which was sponsored by the National Geographic Society. Their projection suggested that the pilot had gone down in an area well south of the North Pole near Alakanuk, Alaska.

For the next six years starting in the mid-1980s, the foundation focused on conducting interviews with people in that remote area, and conducting anomaly detection (which scans for underground metal). They *found* anomalies. And they found the daughter of a bush pilot who had searched for Levinesky in the thirties. She showed them her father's old scrapbook and expedition notes that mentioned two Eskimos who knew something about Levinesky's crash. They even found Levinesky's personal mechanic, an American, who lives in Riverside, California. You see, Levinesky flew only American airplanes on his famous trips—Lockheed Vegas—except for his last trip, when he flew an enormous four-engine Russian-built plane. Amazingly, the foundation located the two Eskimos, still alive, living near Alakanuk. They were very old (but they couldn't tell the foundation how old) and said that they had *watched* Levinesky's plane go down in 1937. They showed the Americans where; the spot was adjacent to the sight where they had found the underground anomalies. The wreckage had been pushed from its original site by ice floes.

Each August (the only month when the ice melts to expose the tundra) for the next five years, the foundation put together expeditions to search for Levinesky's plane. In August 1991 they found what they believe is the main spar and the engines buried beneath layers of silt. Unfortunately, the state of Alaska got involved, Ron says, "as soon as they figured their might be money in it." The whole process became bogged down in assessments of the environmental impact of digging up the wreckage. Further, Alaskan law provides that any memorabilia, including war planes, found on state soil, become the property of the state of Alaska.

But the foundation had no interest in raising the Levinesky plane. A data plate from one of the engines would prove to the Russians that they had found the right plane. Then they could get invited by the right person to survey the old airfields of Russia in search of valuable vintage planes. A data plate would, as Ron says, "be their ticket into the Soviet Union." And it was. The Russian aviation press picked up the story about a bunch of crazy Americans who were spending hundreds of thousands of dollars of their own money to find a lost Russian pilot. (Arco, it should be mentioned, as a co-sponsor of the expedition, supplied accommodations for the expedition in the Yukon and much of the sophisticated equipment in Alakanuk.) An invitation was forthcoming from the director of the Kiev Air Museum, who had been commissioned by the Soviet government to write the history of aviation in the Soviet Union. He invited two of the foundation partners over in 1986; they visited him four times, and each time they met increasing numbers of people, including retired and active air force generals, ministers of aviation, and the editors of aviation magazines. But their playing card worked. An old Russian general, the museum director, and the minister of aviation offered to hand over three World War II planes if the foundation could, indeed, prove that it had located the Levinesky plane. The offer proved that such planes did, indeed, exist in the Soviet Union, and this would be the first time that any collector had gotten a plane out of Russia. The resale of a P-39, an A-20 Havoc, or a B-25 could mean millions of dollars to the foundation, depending on the condition of the plane. The guys wanted to take a look at them, but the Russians refused. Nor would they reveal the location of the planes.

The foundation sent another expedition to Alakanuk in April 1991 to "prove" the veracity of their claim that they had found Levinesky. The director of the Kiev Museum and an aviation editor from *Pravda* were invited to come and see the crash site for themselves. Then things started to unravel. Ron explains: "These guys showed up in Anchorage, after flying from Russia, with a total of two dollars and thirty-five cents between them. Nowhere to live. Nothing to eat. And no ticket back." The foundation paid their way, reluctantly, with the hope that the Russians would come through with the quid pro quo of Levinesky for three warplanes. In fact, the foundation expected a lot more than that, but would be happy to take three planes to start with. But, strangely, the two Russians acted as though they weren't the least bit interested in the crash site, the anomalies, or Levinesky himself.

"They were only interested in getting into the storeroom," Ron says, "at the Arco complex, and eating." Arco had a 1,500-square-foot warehouse there with shelves from floor to ceiling, separate from the cafeteria. The two Russians, like the Americans, had access to the warehouse and the cafeteria. "The Russians would each eat two breakfasts, two lunches, and two dinners, and then go to the warehouse and load up. In the end, they threw their clothes away and packed their suitcases with food," Ron says. Though they didn't give a damn about Levinesky, they were, however, interested to know when they could come back for another trip. The foundation declined to offer another trip and expressed more interest in going to Russia and seeing the planes that the Russians had talked about. The Russian's reply: "We'll get back to you."

Two months later, they did get back to the foundation and arranged for another visit to Russia in June 1991. But before that time, the Russian consulate contacted the foundation to say that visas would not be issued for the time being because of turmoil in the Soviet Union. The trip was canceled.

Now for the subplot: About two years into these visits a famous Soviet cosmonaut named Grechko became involved with the project. He's Russia's oldest cosmonaut and holds the record for the longest time in space. "Because of his status, he can do whatever he wants to do," says Ron. "Or be whatever he wants to be. In fact, he came over to the United States at one time with the Olympic ski team for practice. What the heck he has to do with the Olympic ski team, we have no idea," says Ron. And he's been to the States many times before, under many pretenses. The members of the foundation met him at a San Diego Aerospace Museum dinner when he was one of the people being honored. They became friends with him. Six months later Grechko showed up in San Diego on the lecture circuit. The Americans told Grechko what they were up to in Russia, and he confirmed that American-made warplanes "were all over the Soviet Union." The Americans also told Grechko who they had been dealing with, and he concluded that they were dealing with nobodies, that the museum director and the others had no real power to do anything. The Americans asked him who in Russia does have the power to get them close to the planes. Grechko said he didn't know, but he'd find out. It was also at this meeting that Grechko mentioned that he held the honorary position of president of the Republic of Russia. He also said, "in terms of power, the position was the equivalent of a maintenance man in a public toilet." It is strictly an honorary position: You do nothing; you get nothing; it's just a title. The Americans asked Grechko how he got the position. Grechko said that a friend, whom he had known all his life, had him appointed. "Who's your friend?" the Americans asked. Grechko answered, "Boris Yeltsin. He's a party member but he's breaking away. And he's a guy to watch." Grechko promised to talk to Boris and get back to the Americans. Which he did.

Grechko talked to Yeltsin, and Yeltsin promised to look around and get some information on warplanes. Grechko would talk to the Americans soon, as he was coming back to San Diego. Which he did. The foundation members didn't know what to do: Should they stay on the course they had been on, or go with Boris and Grechko? Communication lines remained opened. It was now July 1991. Then a letter came from Grechko. He said things were touchy in Russia and that he had resigned his honorary post as president of the Russian Republic. As a national hero, Grechko has a pension for life and all the accoutrements of the good life; the last thing he needed was political risk. Grechko said that Yeltsin had taken over his post of president of the Russian Republic. And the rest is history. The August putsch placed the foundation's project in limbo. "Every fax number, every telephone number that we had, was disconnected or not working," Ron recalls. "None of our communications were answered. And nobody knows what happened to the people we were communicating with. Even Grechko. All of the air force generals and public officials that we were dealing with are totally incognito now. Nobody can reach them."

Then the coup took place, and Yeltsin became an international figure. The Americans watched in amazement as their man in Moscow took the reins of power with Gorbachev. In September, Yeltsin declared Russia to be an independent state. The foundation waited. Then Jeff, a foundation member, called the partners together for a meeting. He said, "You guys aren't going to believe this, but the phone rang last night and my daughter answered. She said that some crazy who can't speak English was on the phone for me. So I got up from the dinner table and said 'Hello' and it was Boris Yeltsin." Yeltsin said that he had been talking to his friend Grechko and apologized for not getting back to the foundation sooner—there had been some matters that had needed his attention. Then Yeltsin asked Jeff to go to Russia as his guest. Jeff asked what for, particularly. Yeltsin told Jeff that he wanted him to give seminars to major businessmen, and future businessmen, in Russia and some of the other republics. (Jeff is an international business consultant.) He said that these people need to learn what a market economy is—that most of these people don't have the slightest idea of what a market economy is or how one works.

Yeltsin invited Jeff to stay at his new dacha in Georgia—Gorbachev's former dacha—the one Gorbachev had been imprisoned in during the coup attempt in August 1991. Two foundation partners were sent with

Jeff to Georgia. Jeff set off teaching seminars in virtually every corner of the continent. Ron and another foundation member discovered that mentioning other business would have been inappropriate. They moved into a hotel and met Grechko for a tour of some military bases. Things became even more surreal. Military commanders took the two Americans around to various bases, showed them aircraft, including MiG-29's, and asked whether they were interested in buying them. "They would have sold the runway if they could roll it up," Ron remembers. "Suddenly everybody was an entrepreneur and nobody was in charge." The Americans, of course, wanted vintage warplanes, but the Russians wouldn't listen. As for Levinesky, when the Americans mentioned his name to officials in Russia during there trip, eyebrows went up. They said Levinesky was a Soviet! Then they found out that the mere mention of their company's name now put them in bad odor because it contained the word "U.S.S.R."

The allure of finding vintage aircraft behind the old Iron Curtain remains, however. Somewhere in Russia there is a person who was once in charge on a quasi-military airfield who has no more job because the state won't subsidize his do-nothing job any more, who answers to no higher authority because there is no higher authority with oversight of "his" airfield, who would gladly sell the rotting hulks of warplanes that sit at the end of his airstrip to supplement his now-nonexistent income. But who could he find to sell them to? Ron dreams of finding this Russian. It would all be so easy if he could just find this person....

Lessons Learned from Ron Plunkett and Company

- Business relationships that you establish now may work against you in the future. Changes in political climate change the business climate; people lose and gain authority overnight. You need to "keep book" on many people to know the right partner at any particular time. Finding out who is in authority at a given time is a challange for Eastern Europeans just as much as it is for foreigners. The problem won't be corrected in the near future.

- You may discover that your priorities are very different from those of your partner in Eastern Europe. That is, your partner may want to *eat*, while you want to pursue a deal. Consider carefully where a partner is coming from before getting involved in a deal. Whatever you are proposing must be in the interest of a potential partner as well as in yours or the deal is not going to work.

- You need to know when you haven't found the perfect contact and how to bail out of the fledgling partnership. Have a list of questions ready to help ascertain whether a person or an organization is legitimate. In a region where almost everyone carries around a gold-embossed business card, it can be almost impossible to gauge the legitimacy of potential business partners. (See Chap. 8 for information on qualifying partners.)

- Hedge your bets in a partner search by pursuing business relations along more than one line. Don't close doors in order to make a commitment to one avenue of partnership. Moreover, your current activities in searching for the perfect contact may not lead where you thought they would, but they may lead somewhere.

- If your gut-level feeling tells you that your partner is insincere, take steps to protect yourself, or do further research about the person to alleviate your concerns.

- Each step of the way in pursuing a deal, assess the worst-case scenario and consider whether you can afford it.

Anne Devero: Finding Diamonds in the Rust

Anne Devero is a former managing consulting partner with Coopers & Lybrand. When she and her husband got the opportunity to live in Eastern Europe, she decided to start an export company. Anne's story is an inspiration to any "mom-and-pop" trading company or crafts manufacturer.

How did your business get started?

When I first went to Poland, I had anticipated doing importing to this country of crystal and porcelain. When I got there, and started spending time in the galleries in Poland, I realized that the other tradition that is very endemic to the society is silver jewelry. Silver is a very rich natural resource of the country. So I approached several of the well-known jewelry designers in Poland, and we agreed that we would design a contemporary line of jewelry to be imported into the United States.

The area where I lived, in south Warsaw, tends to be a kind of haven for several of the artists, and I started networking in the artist community. I visited all the art galleries and told them what I wanted. Many them were very reluctant to [get involved because the] joint-venture laws were still in a state of flux. But I ran into a woman who runs the best gallery in Warsaw, right off of Old Town Square, and we just instantly hit it off. She's been in the business for about twenty years and we sat down with a translator and hashed out a contract. It had been a state-owned gallery that had been privatized about a year before. She is quite entrepreneurial actually. They are really struggling, too, because the center of the tourist trade used to be in Old Town, and a lot of it has moved out toward the Marriott hotel. That, coupled with the fact that we really got along, allowed us to put together an agreement.

What was the nature of the agreement?

The agreement was that for a finder's fee, they would introduce me to artists they had worked with and knew were good and reliable. They would also act as my agent to handle the logistics of getting my orders to the artists and checking quality control. We'd work together to produce some designs, and the artist would produce a sample. They'd prepare a sample, and we'd negotiate price. I also worked with each of the artists to develop a production capacity plan (which is part of my consulting background). A lot of them didn't understand how to cost their work, and so I helped them understand how one typically would go about costing something. Just the idea, for instance, of capitalizing equipment is a new concept to them. And they were open to strategize; they really appreciated it. All of the artists were struggling because the domestic market had dried up, because jewelry is a discretionary item in the household budget. They wanted access to international markets but didn't know how to get it. I gave them access to a market that they didn't have before.

Where do you sell the Polish-made jewelry?

I started setting up the U.S. market in San Francisco. I really have a unique niche. The quality of this jewelry is very, very high, yet it's sterling silver, which is generally a much lower price point than gold jewelry. I've got goldsmiths working in silver, which is quite an unusual combination. Silver jewelry in the United States is not very high quality because you don't have fine jewelers working in it. The designs I've produced are considered designer jewelry. I wasn't quite sure what my niche would be, but it turned out to be the fine jewelry store that wants a product at a lower price point, but is not willing to sacrifice quality. I got a lot of the product into the stores before Christmas, and everyone did very well with it. Next, I went into L.A. and have developed about a half-dozen clients there.

No problems with diminishing or unpredictable quality?

No, because I have two agents in Poland: One for the relationships that

I develop through the gallery, and one for the relationships with the artists that I found on my own. I haven't had any quality problems yet because I'm working with the very finest people. And everybody knows that if there are quality problems, the work won't sell. There is a real pride in the craftsmanship over there. It's just part of their culture.

So how do you see your business expanding in the future?

The jewelry line will continue to expand and grow, but I'm also now getting into a gift line, such as picture frames and small boxes, because I can sell these to the same customer base, as well as to an expanded customer base. I'm dealing with many of the same artists to do the gift line. I also want to work with crystal and porcelain, but that's going to require me going over there and living for another six months because of the redesign that will have to be done in terms of more contemporary designs. The craftsmanship is wonderful, but the designs are very old-fashioned, very ornate, and I would want to come out with some very simple, elegant designs that would be easier to do.

Did you negotiate an exclusive marketing agreement with the Polish concern?

I didn't demand exclusivity in the beginning, but now we are to the point that we're talking exclusivity. I wanted to be able to guarantee enough of a revenue stream. I have an exclusive arrangement with the gallery that they will only work with me in the United States, but with the artists we agreed that we wouldn't talk exclusivity until I guaranteed them enough of a revenue stream to justify it. A few of the artists we have negotiate exclusives, but until I get to a certain volume I don't ask for that. I don't want the burden on me if their stuff's not going to sell here.

How do you handle communicating with your Polish partner?

I don't speak Polish—my agents deal with the artists, except when I'm in Poland. Both of my agents speak English. And both of them are also very good communicators—one is a psychologist—so they are also very good at dealing with the differences in the culture, which are substantial and which can be subtle but very important.

Any problems training people in Poland?

You have to assume that you are training people from scratch. You've got to be tough and consistent. If someone doesn't deliver, they never hear the end of it from me or from the agent. I haven't had very much of that, but you make your expectations known up front. And you work with people, too. I had one artist who had his workshop broken into over Christmas. He had several tools stolen. He needed a little money up front to replace them. The guy was in the process of having twins—it wasn't like his life was not crazy already. So I provided some advances on orders so he could retool, and he delivered on time. I had one guy who got locked out of a workshop and he had to find a new workshop. You work with that kind of thing. If it's beyond their control, you work with them; if they just don't get it done for a reason that doesn't make sense, that's different.

Lessons Learned from Anne Devero

- As an offshore manufacturer, take advantage of Eastern European traditions of high-quality craftsmanship and attention to detail.

- Be willing to change course in your desired plans to take advantage of opportunities that suddenly present themselves.

- Make networking in your relevant business community in Eastern Europe a first and very necessary stage in pursuing your endeavors.

- Deal with a privatized company, as soon after it has been privatized as possible, preferably one owned and managed by one person who can make unilateral decisions.

- Assist your supplier in running his or her business in any way that you can, utilizing your Western background in production planning cost analysis, financial planning, documentation, and labor relations. Actively help them *strategize* for doing business as a private enterprise.

- Help your supplier design and manufacture for a small and select niche of an overseas market, emphasizing quality and originality. Start small and grow, being careful not to overwhelm your Eastern European supplier.

- In the case of specialty goods, sell via the use of samples and buy on a "to-order" basis to cut inventory costs. Develop and depend on a communication system for "just-in-time" production and delivery, utilizing written communications via fax rather than costly verbal communications over the phone.

- Hire an agent to monitor quality and manage relationships if you remain located in the West.

- Pursue the manufacture of product lines that fall under the Generalized System of Preferences (GSP), which grants trade advantages to developing countries, to keep duty costs to a minimum.

- Expand your product offerings, not by expanding your customer base but by selling new product lines to the same customer base.

- Motivate artisans in Eastern Europe by paying for product "up front"; they will not normally be in a financial position to fund their work on consignment.

- Don't forget to expand your network of producers geographically in Eastern Europe; the same craft may have regional (and marketable) variations across a single country in Eastern Europe.

- Retain the services of a consultant to keep you up to date on the laws and regulations relevant to your specific product line.

- Write a contract which guarantees you exclusive marketing rights once you have sold a certain amount of product. Include a mediation clause in all contractual agreements.

Fear and Loathing from Moscow to Minsk: Gale George and People to People

During Communist times and to this day, Russian business people eschew meeting with foreign business counterparts one on one, especially on the first encounter. Thus it is a wise idea to make your first visit to the former Soviet Union (and to Eastern Europe in general) as part of a trade delegation, rather than on your own. Remember that people of the region heard about "evil foreign capitalists" for decades; they may not be prepared for or at ease with meeting independent entrepreneurs from the "capitalist West." Your challenge is to choose a trade mission that will meet its claimed objectives. As part of a delegation, you will have power in numbers, and you will be less vulnerable to the rigors of traveling in the region.

Gale George's interest in the Russian market was not of long standing. It started when an invitation arrived from an organization based in Spokane, Washington, called People to People, in the winter of 1990. People to People has been sending delegations of Westerners overseas for years, and by and large, the paying participants on their tours have reported satisfactory performance on the part of the organization both as a tour coordinator and as a business liaison service. That is, until the organization sent a delegation of business women from the United States to the Soviet Union for commercial meetings and tours of four cities in the then-U.S.S.R. Gale George told me her almost unbelievable story from start to finish.

The delegation was composed of business women, many of whom were attorneys. Gale had been invited because she is the owner of Essential Emergency Packs, which manufactures portable survival kits, and she is a member of the National Association of Female Executives. Her company sold its product in the United States and was keen to jump into the international marketplace.

She did some homework on the Soviet market and discovered that there were many potential obstacles to succeeding in the U.S.S.R. But she thought a research trip there would be more than worth the $4,600 (including airfare) that People to People charged for the two-week trip. She could meet with business counterparts in Moscow, Kiev, and St. Petersburg and, moreover, see the Bolshoi Ballet, the museums, and other tourist sites. The prospect of joint venturing in the U.S.S.R. also seemed viable. Furthermore, Gale believed that she was representing American women in the U.S.S.R., and that, she felt, was an important reason for going to meet business people in the Soviet Union.

The 22-member delegation was led by Jane Foster,* the chair of a New York housing authority, and her assistant, the male member of the team, Robert Gonzales. None of the delegates, who ranged in age from 27 to 63, had been to the Soviet Union before. As the plane approached Moscow, the passengers were told that the airport was fogged in. This was an omen of things to come. They circled in hopes of landing but were finally diverted to Helsinki, Finland. There they sat, unable to leave the aircraft for five hours since they had no visas. Five hours late, however, the plane landed in Moscow at the city's secondary airport on the outskirts of the city.

Oddly, though, the delegation was not met by anyone at the dungeonlike airport terminal. Moreover, for no apparent reason the delegates were put in a holding area, without chairs, for three hours. Dazed, tired, and totally confused, the 22 Americans were finally freed from customs and met by an interpreter hired by the Union of Soviet Lawyers, the delegation's host organization for the visit, which was responsible for where the delegates would stay, what they would do for sightseeing, and planning all meetings with Soviet business counterparts. A sense of relief was felt by all.

Boarded onto a bus, the group was taken into Moscow. The bus arrived at a hotel on the outskirts of Moscow, called the House of Tourism, though People to People had promised that they would stay in the best hotel each city had to offer. The delegates discovered what they would later call "lobby lizards"—males of indeterminate age loitering in the lobbies of hotels frequented by foreigners. The delegates checked in; they were not all on the same floor of the hotel. Reconvening a short time later, they discovered that some of the women had been joined in the elevator by a lobby lizard. (Each dele-

---

*Some names in this account have been changed to protect the privacy of individuals.

gate was an easy mark because of her oversize name tag.) In fact, a few of the women had been followed to their rooms by these frightening men, whose intentions never became clear. By now, however, the men had matched names with room numbers and began calling the women on the phone. All of this took place within the *first hour* of their arrival at the hotel. What did these men who spoke in broken English want? "They didn't know what they wanted," says Gale, "and that's why it was so disconcerting." The women made every effort to be nice and think the best of everything, to be flexible, and go with the flow. They understood that in foreign climes you can't expect things to run smoothly; you have to expect the unexpected.

But the following day, it became common knowledge that some of the women did not have heat or hot water in their rooms. It was October, and the temperature had fallen to the low forties during the night. Group leader Jane Foster called a meeting, at which it came to light that the rooms that had hot water and heating were the rooms also infested with cockroaches! And not just crawling around on the floor, but in the beds, on toothbrushes, *everywhere* in the room. A few of the women had stayed up all night, terrified. And the lobby lizards continued to follow many of them to their rooms and in the hallways.

After a few days in Moscow, the delegation boarded a plane and flew to Kiev, the capital of the Ukraine. There, the group's suspicions that things were not what they should be were greatly reinforced. They were taken to a hotel that was not on their itinerary and not in any guidebook. "We thought the lobby lizards were bad in Moscow," Ms. George recalls, "but they were extremely bad in Kiev." Again, the delegation was not met by a host organization and had to hire a bus to get to the hotel. The group soon realized that no other foreigners were staying at the so-called Tourist Hotel. Ms. Foster tried to phone People to People in Spokane and its representative in Moscow. Her calls were not returned. Ms. Foster became incensed with Natasha, the group's young Russian interpreter, because she had allegedly lied repeatedly. Ms. Foster fired the interpreter and warned her not to get on the bus with the delegation the following morning. But Natasha did board the bus the next morning. Ms. Foster warned Natasha to get off the bus and said that if she didn't get out of the doorway of the bus, she would close the door and crush Natasha's wrist. At this point, two other women in the group, one of whom had been followed to her room by a lobby lizard, took Natasha back into the hotel, formally left the delegation, and set off to "get out of the country from Kiev alone." Meanwhile, tempers mounted, as the situation escalated into an ugly, possibly international, incident.

The two women set out to find out how to get out of the country

(neither spoke any Russian) and to check some of the other hotels in
Kiev, where they thought the delegation should have been lodged by
People to People. While in the lobby of the Kiev Hotel, they ran into a
film crew from CNN. They asked why CNN was in Kiev and were
told that there had been an accident at Chernobyl, which was forty
miles from Kiev. The two women, of course now completely alarmed,
reported back to the delegation at the Tourist Hotel. The group franti-
cally tried to get information on what was happening at the nearby
reactor. "I want a television and I want it now," screamed Jane Foster's
assistant, Robert Gonzales, to the Ukrainians at the front desk.
"There's been an accident at Chernobyl, and I want to know what's
happened. You get me a television set! I want it in my room in fifteen
minutes." The television was procured but did not receive CNN. It
was not until the following afternoon that Natasha, the interpreter,
appeared to confirm that there had, indeed, been an accident at
Chernobyl and that officials described the mishap as ranking 1 on a
scale of 10. No radiation had been released, was the word.
(Interestingly, the group of women from the States knew about the
accident a full 36 hours before the locals did.) To add to the group's
understandable concern, the delegates had given their passports and
visas to the hotel; to ask for them back in order to leave immediately
would mean the loss of their rooms!

Adding insult to injury, the delegation later met a Canadian clothing
salesman who spoke Ukrainian and knew his way around. From him
the delegates learned that the hotel they were staying in, and paying
$115 each per night for (two to a room), charged only 50 cents a night
to nonforeigners. There were holes in the walls, vermin, and roaches,
and phone calls could not be made to the outside. Paranoia set in
among the group members. Faxes did not get sent or received. Nobody
knew where they were. Fear and loathing reached a crescendo. Goons
roamed the hallways, the group had no visas or passports, and no one
could be sure that radioactive clouds were not blowing overhead.

Then the clincher. It had gotten late; the "farewell" banquet had
ended. Everyone boarded the bus, which headed for a subway station.
Suddenly, the driver pulled over, turned off the lights and motor, and
informed the interpreter that he wouldn't go further unless "he received
fifty dollars, American." Robert Gonzales told the interpreter to tell the
driver that if he didn't get the lights back on and the bus on the road
back to the hotel, he'd have "his ass in jail before the night was over."
Anxious minutes passed before the driver fired up the bus and took
them back to the hotel. Though everyone in the group had had something to drink at the banquet, they were all sober and feeling very vulnerable. "I realized how vulnerable I was," Gale recalls. "That being

from the United States didn't mean diddlysquat when you're in a bus on the side of the road and some clown is trying to extort money from you."

Before leaving Kiev for St. Petersburg, the women had a powwow. They decided that once in St. Petersburg, they would check their hotel before deboarding their bus and would not stay at a roach-infested rat-trap again. The group was angry, and many delegates were now sick. They would refuse to get off the bus if the hotel was another rathole like the one they had been staying in and would demand to be taken to a better hotel. With that agreement in mind, the delegation flew to St. Petersburg and then took a bus to the Govan Hotel. In front of the hotel, the bus was besieged by kids hawking trinkets and gum, taunting the group with hard-sell antics. It didn't look good. Jane and Robert went into the hotel to check out the rooms. Valentina, a representative of the Union of Soviet Lawyers, was waiting in the lobby. While Jane and Robert checked the hotel, Valentina went to the bus and told the remaining delegates: "You all are misbehaving terribly! Behave yourselves. Get off this bus and get registered. Your dinner is waiting for you. And if you want to continue to stay in places as nice as this...." Hoots and hollers broke out in the bus. The group told her to wait for their decision as to whether they would agree to stay in the hotel after Jane Foster's tour of the rooms.

"I have fired Jane as delegation leader," intoned Valentina.

"We don't think so," retorted the irate delegates. "Now get off this bus until we have a chance to meet with Jane."

Valentina wouldn't budge.

Finally, Robert and Jane returned and asked for five minutes to debrief the group about the hotel. Valentina wouldn't leave the bus and tried at length to shout down Jane Foster. Faces flushed with anger. At loggerheads with Valentina, Jane Foster suddenly broke into song: "God bless America."

Members of the delegation joined her in singing.

"God Bless America."

Valentina glared at them, red eyes bulging.

"I will not get off this bus!" she screamed.

"That's fine," Jane said. "I'll just tell the group what I need to tell them. You all need to know that this hotel is the worst place yet that they've tried to put us in. I refuse to stay here. If any of you want to stay here, please feel free to get off the bus and check in."

The decision was unanimous. Jane told the bus driver that the group wanted to go to another hotel, one listed in their guidebooks. Valentina jumped in and shouted to the driver, "You're not taking them anywhere!" Another argument exploded between the group and the Russian woman.

Finally, the driver took them to the another hotel where they checked in. The rooms were fine, although they cost $168 a night, per person. Since these were the last days of their nightmare, cash was short. Luckily, a group member offered to put the charges on her Platinum Card. Dinner was held in a wonderful dining room in the hotel where our road-beaten warriors of international business nibbled their caviar and crackers to the romantic strains of the theme from *Dr. Zhivago,* played by a band of Ukrainian musicians.

The consequence for the group's mutiny, however, was that their interpreter and bus services were taken from them. And the group's professional meetings in St. Petersburg were canceled. They were on their own. But they felt safe because they were in a better hotel. ("As long as they stayed away from the second floor after 10 p.m., because that's where the prostitution took place.") The delegation stayed for three pleasant days. Then Brad, another representative for the Union of Soviet Lawyers called to accuse the group of being "a very poorly behaved bunch of women that had been extremely rude, and furthermore...had burnt holes in the seats of our bus at the Govan hotel." (The delegation had never smoked on the bus.) The final blow came 24 hours before leaving the country. They were told that they would not be flying back to Moscow but would be put on an overnight train (rumored to be filled with thieves and drunks in mixed-sex sleeping compartments!) The delegates who had fallen ill were suffering greatly now, vomiting in bags that they were told to throw off the back of the train. The train arrived in Moscow in the morning. The delegates were taken to Moscow Airport, where they waited five hours for their flight. "It was the first time in my life," recalls Gale, "that I had heard a spontaneous cheer inside a plane when the wheels lifted up off the ground, and then again when we landed in New York City. It was just a *Ya-hoo!!* kind of a feeling."

As for People to People, Gale believes that the company will reimburse the delegation $2,000 each. The payoff, however, will involve a gag order prohibiting the delegation from telling the story of what happened on their misguided tour or otherwise tarnishing the reputation of People to People. (I spoke to Gale before this settlement had been reached.) Why had disaster struck the tour while the company's tours to Czechoslovakia and China have elicited satisfactory comments from other delegations I spoke to? "My understanding is that the problem was most likely that People to People had not done their homework in the Soviet Union in terms of who they were dealing with," says Gale.

Incidentally, the business meetings that were arranged for Gale's delegation amounted to showing up at someone's office unannounced and talking about "joint-ventures." The Russians thrust unprepared into these meetings hardly knew what to make of the 22 women from the United States.

Lessons Learned from Gale George

- American executives should perceive Eastern European states and the former Soviet Union as third world countries, in terms of amenities and infrastructure (telephones, transportation systems, and business services). In these respects, the countries of the region remain undeveloped, at least outside the confines of the foreign-owned hotels in capital cities. Lower your expectations, and you'll be less shocked and less frustrated with what you encounter as a business traveler.

- Hundreds of organizations are putting together business liaison trade missions to Eastern Europe and the former Soviet Union. It's your job to find out whether an organization is reputable and whether its counterpart organization in Eastern Europe is reputable. Find out what delegations have been sent over before and what the participants have reported on the outcome of the missions. Explore these issues carefully without simply trusting that the tour organizer will skillfully "handle everything," as the advertisements may claim. In general, stay with large trade organizations on the Eastern European side that have reputations to worry about; a start-up company might be here today and gone tomorrow.

- Find out about your potential business counterparts before you embark on a business trip to the region. This information should be made available by the coordinating organization sponsoring the trade mission. Make contact by mail with the people you plan to see long before the mission takes place. Apprise them of your objectives, services, and product lines at least two months prior to meeting with them in person.

- Think of Eastern Europeans as semi-impoverished people who might view business people from the West as being incredibly affluent. Many are out to make a fast buck off "rich Americans." Moreover, there remains an absence of Western-style fiduciary ethics, to the consternation of many Western travelers to the region.

Shelley Zeiger: Marketing Maven of Moscow

Shelley Zeiger, president and chairman of Zeiger Enterprises, Inc., in New Jersey, was one of the very first crusading American entrepreneurs to enter the Soviet Union. He loves to tell his story about how he *almost* beat PepsiCo in forming a joint-venture deal in Russia involving the barter of Stolichnaya vodka.

How did you get involved in the Eastern European region?

I was born in the Ukraine, went through the Holocaust, and went to the United States in 1950 at the age of 14. In 1960, my father, my brother, and I went into the wholesale wine business. It was a little family business. We didn't have the major lines. We had only private wine labels. I took a leave of absence for one year to turn around another liquor company that had major labels, in exchange for an equity position in the company. In one year's time, I turned a profit and I wound up with 30 percent of the company with an option to buy the whole thing out of profit. I got cocky and bought another liquor company. And then the economy turned, and it [became heavily] leveraged. That's when I had a little research done and I found out the rights to Stolichnaya vodka in the United States were owned by National Distillers. National Distillers was selling only eight to ten thousand cases a year in the whole United States. So, I decided to go to Russia in 1973, and pick up Stoli and piggyback it with Seagrams. I spoke with the president of Seagrams at the time and told him that I was going to Russia and would like to know that, if I come back with a deal with Stoli, Seagrams would distribute it outside the state of New Jersey, since they have a network of wholesalers. He thought it was a nice idea and was interested to see what I came home with. So at least I had a comfort level because he hadn't said No. So I went to Russia, and while in Moscow I had my meeting. They were very cordial. But they couldn't help me; they broke the news to me that about three or four weeks before they had concluded a contract with PepsiCo. They couldn't give me the Stoli deal because they had just signed a contract. So I said, "Well, I guess I go to the museum and to Red Square and then I'll go home." They said, "You should really try to do business here." I said, "What else do you have, or what would you suggest?" And they started enumerating a number of things. One of them was natural essences for perfume. It struck me that they said that they were natural fragrances. If you will remember, in the seventies we were very conscious of natural things rather than synthetic. It was a kick at that time. So I met with a factory director and placed an order for seven thousand dollars for fragrances. I thought I might as well bring it in and see what happened. I really didn't have time so I gave the whole thing to my wife. I said, "Here is seven thousand dollars worth of fragrances. Have fun.' She sold it. There was one called Red Poppy, one was St. Petersburg, one was Black Casket, and one was Blue Casket. The problem was that the damn things leaked! It had a beautiful bottle if you didn't turn it upside down...and the packaging was superb and the fragrance was good. So we opened up a company called Shelmar

Imports, Ltd. This is [a combination of] Shelley and Marian, my wife's name. I went back to Russia and signed a contract for exclusive rights for the United States and broadened the line by bringing in other products like Russian amber and nesting dolls. I kept moving with the Russian thing persistently, going back and forth, buying products for Shelmar Imports, and developing contacts over the course of years.

In 1985, while being very active in the economic development of Trenton, I was elected to become the chairman of the Chamber of Commerce of Trenton. As such, I created a Trenton delegation consisting of political and civic people, and brought them over to Moscow to meet with government and civic people over there, to see how we could bring about a dialogue between Trenton and Moscow. I proposed that Moscow and Trenton create some kind of a relationship between the two cities. They said, Moscow has eleven million people and Trenton only has a hundred thousand people. I said, "Well, but you have thirty-two districts of Moscow; why don't we just select a district that coincides with ours historically?" They organized a meeting between us and the mayor of the Lenin district. Before, you know, we drank so much cognac, toasting peace, freedom, humanity, children, women...and all of that. By the time we closed out, we had created a very warm city-to-city relationship—the first one between the United States and the Soviet Union, between Moscow Lenin district and Trenton, New Jersey. I put into the sister-city document that we would have exchanges, we would have literary exchanges, the publisher on my delegation would send one of his editors to write for *The Moscow News,* and *The Moscow News* would send one of their editors to work for *The Trenton Times*—and it happened! And this was when it was not very popular. It is very difficult to visualize that today when everything is going so great, but we were there during the rough, rough times. To reciprocate on our movement, the Kirov Ballet came— we didn't even have a signed protocol between the United States and Russia on cultural exchanges, but it just so happened that the Kirov was performing in Canada and they came to Trenton and gave us one performance as a gesture of goodwill for what we had done.

How did this all tie in to your commercial interests?

I'm leading to it! So far I'm giving everything away, but you know there is a bottom line somewhere, right? When the mayor came here to sign the document, I had put in a paragraph that we need to not only have medical exchanges, and correspondence exchanges, and educational exchanges, and cultural exchanges, but also *to develop trade.* So when the mayor came to sign this, I took him to a pizza place. And he ate a pizza and said, "Boy, this is great!" I said, "It just so happens that I want to open one up in Moscow." He said, "how do we do it?" I said, "Very simple, let's just sign, and I'll be in Moscow next month. We'll sign a document and I'll have a self-contained unit, a truck running around selling American pizza." He said, "You really mean it?" I said, "Yes." So, to make a long story short, I went to Moscow to sell pizza. The joint-venture laws were not written yet, so we wrote our own laws. We really didn't even know what we were doing, but we signed documents. And a truck and four containers were moving from Helsinki. From Helsinki we shipped our own driver, and our own mechanic, and three containers with food. On the seventeenth of April, 1988, we had a press conference on the Lenin Hills with the quarter-of-a-million-dollar truck, American and Soviet flags, and about two hundred to three hundred people from the press from all over the world, and proclaimed the first Soviet-American joint-venture. The reaction was absolutely mindboggling! It was just unbelievable. We were feeding about a thousand to fifteen hundred people a day.

We forgot a cash register, so the money was being thrown into plastic bags! I was showing people from CNN and ABC and CBS (everybody was there) inside the truck. I tell this young lady working for us that, "In the United States we have a custom that if we take money from a customer we thank him or her." She looked at me with those little blue eyes and she said, "But you don't have to." I said, "I know you don't have to, but this truck is a symbol of American enterprise, so we need to infuse the customs and the traditions that are held in the United States." And she looked at me and she looked at the big shots in back of me—the mayor, and the chairman of the Communist party in Moscow, and the ministers—and she says, "Well, if you insist." She turned around and as she was taking the money, in a quiet way, she would say *Spaséebo* [Thank-you]. The Soviets had never heard anyone thanking them for giving them food, so by the time the sixth or the seventh person came up, they were thanking her for thanking them! And I stood back and I thought, I've brought a little bit of America right here. And it was a fantastic thing.

As a result of that—the success of that—Pizza Hut went into Moscow. Pizza Hut is owned by Pepsi; so they beat me on the vodka, but I beat them on the pizza! And as a result of the pizza, I decided that I don't want to be on wheels alone, and that's what made me create the Tren-Mos (Trenton Moscow) Restaurant in Moscow. It's not a McDonald's. It's a fine restaurant. Right now it's one restaurant, but I'm leaving soon to go to Moscow to open up the second, which is right next to the Kremlin.

Lessons from Shelley Zeiger

- When you discover a product in Eastern Europe that you wish to import to the West, don't dally; meet with the supplier and sign an agreement as soon as possible.

- If in pursuing your desired business in the East, you find yourself in a cul-de-sac, don't be afraid to listen to alternative ideas with an open mind.

- Once you have successfully marketed an indigenous Eastern European product, feel free to request exclusive marketing rights to others. You may get them on the basis of a single good performance on a previous product.

- Build your contacts before hunting the big deal. Network through trade associations and chambers of commerce and participate in government-affiliated delegations to Eastern Europe, the higher level the better. Consider linking up your city with one in Eastern Europe as a sister city.

- Don't wait for the appropriate laws to be written or modified to accommodate your venture. Forge a deal with the right party, with the necessary enthusiasm and clout, and worry about the legalities later, and you'll be the first on a bandwagon.

- If you build a successful, high-profile venture, share some of the wealth with your patrons via philanthropic projects, discounts, and so on.

Epilogue

Predicting the
Unpredictable
in Eastern Europe

Making predictions about Eastern European countries has been shown to be a humbling game in which participants usually eat their words. Those concerned with the evolution of these countries have learned that it is unrealistic to expect miracles, to expect that there will be "dehydrated solutions to which you could just add water and resolve all the problems of Eastern Europe instantly," as Ernst & Young's Gerry Rohan told me. The remaining years of this century will see the painful elimination of Stalin's industrial legacy and, it is hoped, the rise of private sectors that can replace it, reemploy those put out of work, generate the funds to keep social safety nets in place, and create the wealth to bring Eastern European countries into the next century as independent and self-sufficient players in the European Community (EC). That vision remains, at any rate, the dream of those concerned.

Futurescan for the Year 2000

We can do two things in the hope of predicting what the big picture will look like at the turn of the century. First, we can make specific predictions about each country's probable reform achievements in the near term based on the experience of the countries so far and on where their policies seem to be taking them. Second, we can look for "mega-trends" in Europe that will play a role in how the countries of the East participate in the international commercial arena; that is, what Eastern Europe will look like, and act like, as a regional economic area, in the next century.

Poland

Politically fractured in the recent past, Polish leaders will broker a truce between workers and enterprise owners, permitting approval of more deals with large foreign concerns. Poland, along with Hungary and the Czech Republic, has turned the corner economically. Sustained growth due to a fast-expanding private sector will be seen over the next five years. Poland will suffer immigration problems, however, because of an influx of former Soviets seeking a better life. But it will experience none of the violent ethnic strife seen elsewhere in the region, because of its homogeneous population. The total transformation of Poland's still largely state-held sector will not be achieved by the year 2000, but because of a high number of start-ups and foreign joint ventures (many of which will involve members of the large Polish diaspora), the economy will expand even while state enterprises fold. Poland's parliament will eventually succeed in justifying a bill that will set up mutual investment funds in an effort to privatize hundreds of the country's largest state enterprises.

Hungary

Hungary's ultimately successful transformation is assured by its proximity to Austria and its attraction for foreign banking institutions, not to mention its allure for hard-currency-toting tourists. Hungary, Ukraine, and Kazakhstan trade cooperation will add to Hungary's natural entrepôt positioning. Hitches for Hungary will be internal political feuding (including accusations of anti-Semitism), elections that could flare into protests, and external problems—namely, the fate of ethnic Hungarians living in war-torn former Yugoslavia and incoming refugees from that conflict. One can expect another wave of layoffs in Hungary as more enterprises face bankruptcy and liquidation. Growing annual government deficits, possibly exceeding $2 billion in 1993, will lead to increasing tax burdens for new private companies and fledgling entrepreneurs. But Hungarian exports will continue to grow, and foreign investment will continue to fuel real growth.

The Czech and Slovak Republics

Now that the two republics have separated peacefully, investment will flow into both at a faster rate than ever, though the lion's share will be directed to the Czech side. The Czechs will act more swiftly than the Slovaks in taking advantage of their associate status in the EC. Growing inequalities between the two republics will not lead to violence, because the Slovaks will become less and less nationalistic and idiosyncratic and increasingly interested in appearing accommodating in order to receive international aid as well as Czech investment. Conversely, the heavy and still-growing German presence in the Czech economy will be checked in the Slovak Republic. Economic links between the Slovak agricultural sector and Hungary would be advantageous to both countries.

Slovakia's Prime Minister Meciar announced in March 1993 that his country's transition will proceed more slowly and cautiously than that of the Czech Republic. Joblessness will increase in Slovakia from the current 12 percent as the country will begin offering many of its enterprises for sale to foreign companies. Massive privatization in Slovakia through a public offering of vouchers will not be undertaken in the near term.

Romania

The metamorphosis of Romania's state-owned economy will take longer than in northern Central Europe because it lacks experience with Western business practice and is not as well-endowed with resources. Private entrepreneurial activity will fuel growth in trade, retail, and light manufacturing in regional city centers, while the agricultural sector will find itself increasingly hard-pressed to make ends meet. The country's ailing infrastructure will hold down real industrial growth into the 21st century, although low-cost light manufacturing à la the China model will supply the rest of Europe with increasing amounts of Romanian-made apparel, shoes, toys, and fabric: EC countries will respond with quotas and tariffs.

The good economic news is that industrial production as well as exports rose during each month of 1993, surpassing 1991 output levels in seven industrial sectors. The bad news is that over 1 million Romanians have lost their jobs, representing 9.4 percent of the economically active population; and while exports are up, imports are too, causing a deepening trade deficit. Moreover, the cost of subsidizing staple goods and services such as bread, butter, milk, electricity, and transportation has ballooned and now amounts to 10 percent of GDP. Weaning the populace from these fixed-price goods may be impossible without causing the social upheaval seen in the former Soviet Union.

Bulgaria

Bulgaria's future will remain sanguine if it doesn't maroon itself by discriminating against its Turkish population. Because the Bulgarians were targeted by Moscow to build computer electronics, they have highly trained people and some good factories that could build exportable electronic products. Also, the development of Bulgaria's Black Sea tourist resorts and spas by foreign investors will bring in the needed hard currency to upgrade the country's infrastructure. Foreign investment in other sectors will remain light for the next five years, because the country's former Socialist leaders will remain in power under one guise or another at least until the start of the next century. Prime Minister Lyuben Berov will promote reform and privatization with an eye to attracting foreign investment and receiving funds from both the IMF and the World Bank. Both organizations are trying to help Bulgaria stabilize its currency and get its spiraling economy under control. The sanctions against Serbia are felt in Bulgaria in the form of disrupted trade flows; a wider conflict in former Yugoslavia could spell years of economic hardship for Bulgaria. The perceived political risk of doing business in Bulgaria, because of the possibility of a wider Balkan conflict, will keep investors away, in spite of new legislation on copyrights, patents, and taxation expected to be ratified in the near term. Greek investors, who are culturally similar to Bulgarians, will be an exception. Over 400 Greek businesses have already made investments in Bulgaria since 1989.

Former Yugoslavia

World recognition of the genocide under way in Bosnia-Herzegovina has failed to result in covert operations to oust or assassinate Serbian dictator Slobodan Milosevic. The reelection of Milosevic in December 1992 has resulted in loss of power for Milan Panic, the Serbian-American millionaire who was ousted from Parliament in Belgrade by Serbian Nationalists.

A wave of protests and social turmoil in Serbia due to economic hardships brought on by economic embargo in reaction to the prolonging of war by the Serbian leadership will increase the likelihood of a coup or popular rebellion aimed at removing Milosevic. Monthly inflation has already reached 600 percent in Serbia. In 1992 GDP fell 25 percent and industrial production was down 22 percent. How long the former Yugoslavian person will tolerate the disruption and severe hardship created by Serbian misadventures is anyone's guess.

The Slovenes and Croats, once the war has ended in former Yugoslavia, could emerge, with help from Germany and Austria, as strong partners in trade and together constitute a site for low-cost light manufacturing. Like a pair of phoenixes, the two nations could rise again and become surprisingly vital by the year 2000—two economic sparklers in an otherwise slow-growth Southern Europe. At present both Slovenia and Croatia have recently become members of the IMF and the IBRD, or World Bank. In Croatia, the former head of the Croatian INA oil company has formed a new government. Production is off by a third since the outbreak of hostilities in the Balkans, joblessness is up by 30 percent, and inflation runs at 1000 percent. All of these problems are exacerbated by war in the region. If, and when, that war ends, Croatia's potential, in large measure due to its proximity to Germany, will be actualized. The same can be said for Slovenia at this juncture.

The fates of Macedonia, Kosovo, and Montenegro are in the balance as of this writing, depending on Milosevic's next move to hold on to power and consolidate Serbian unity. If a real threat to his dictatorship arises, he will move to crack down on independence-minded Albanians in the region of Kosovo as a diversionary tactic, drawing in little Albania to protect its brethren across the border. Equally alarming, ethnic cleansing has been advocated by some Serbian nationalists against the Hungarian population of former Yugoslavia, approximately 350,000 of whom live north of Vojvodina. Random acts of violence against Hungarians have already occurred. If the Hungarians in former Yugoslavia are threatened with genocide, Budapest would be likely to join Tirana and Athens in intervening to protect their brethren. Any move in Macedonia could bring in the Greeks; American troops have already arrived to form a "trip line" in case Serbian forces invade. It is hoped that the West will move to remove Milosevic—an anachronism of the Fascist era—before it's too late.

Former Soviet Union

By the end of the century, four of the independent states of the commonwealth—Russia, Ukraine, Kazakhstan, and Belarus—will have stable democracies and economies. In the short term, much will depend on what outside help they receive. These nations are naturally resource rich, with well-trained work forces, 99 percent literacy, 97 percent high school graduation, and strong scientific, technical, and military capability that can be converted with cooperation from the West. If they get through the next three or four years without political upheaval or retrenchment, they will be lucrative markets for Western interests. That said, Boris Yeltsin's appointment of a new cabinet and his replacement of reform strategist and prime minister Yegor Gaidar with untested and conservative Viktor Chernomyrdin, in December 1992, spelled disaster for continued shock-therapy-style reform in Russia. It was also a vote of no confidence by the national leadership for the economic pundits from the West who have advised the Russian reformist since the August putsch. Harvard economist Jeffrey Sachs labeled himself as a "dangling" adviser to the Russian government, but his official role as consultant to Russian reformers may end soon. Glumly, after the ouster of Gaidar, Sachs admitted to *The Wall Street Journal:* "I don't know what to do now." The good news is the privatization program architect, Anatoli Chubais, will remain as vice premier. Privatization of state assets will move ahead, and the voucher system will further motivate a segment of Russian society to behave in an increasingly entrepreneurial (conservatives will say "avaricious") manner.

Only about 100 state firms have been successfully transformed; yet thousands have begun the painful process of "corporatization," or conversion to a joint stock company according to one of three procedures outlined by the government in June 1992. In the course of only one year from mid-1992, half of Russia's small businesses (those employing under 200 people), are in private hands. Millions of Russian citizens have obtained tradeable vouchers; 350,000 vouchers are traded daily at the Moscow Commodity Exchange. The original value of the vouchers has been halved, but when the trading system becomes more a part of everyday economic life in Russia, they will rise in value.

In the short term, however, Russia's poor will get even poorer; already, one-third of all Russians, or 50 million people, live below the poverty line. "What are we going to eat?" said an angry woman shopper to Yeltsin on the street. Yeltsin replied: "You can slice me up, but that won't last you for long." Discontent with Yeltsin reached critical mass in early 1993; he will survive politically against hard-liners. Inflation, currently running at over 2000 percent annually, continues without austerity measures proposed by reformers.

Looking ahead at Russia's business scene, one can safely predict that by 1994 there will be roughly 3,500 privatized large enterprises in Russia, with workers and managers retaining 51 percent ownership of the majority of them. Thousands of small start-up businesses will continue to face rampant inflation, sluggish demand from consumers on fixed wages, unexpected changes in business law, "mafia" groups that extort protection payments, and exceedingly high tax rates. Moreover, the unavailability of "cheap" capital loans will keep small business from playing the locomotive role that it could, and should, play in post-Gorbachev Russia.

Megatrends in Eastern Europe: Scenario Shakeout

The major question facing the Eastern European countries at the moment is deciding what place they will assume during the next 20 years within the global economic system. Three major scenarios are possible: In the first, Eastern European countries become integrated into the European economic system. This would require that they be able to perform economic restructuring, adapt to technological, institutional, and juridical standards in force in the European Community; and create well-structured and stable political systems. In the second scenario, Eastern European countries would remain the intermediate sphere between Western Europe and the nations of the former Soviet Union. This scenario assumes that Eastern European countries, in spite of implementing deep changes in their economies, will not be accepted by the EC, or will not be able to fulfill all its requirements for inclusion (or that the EC will fail to unify itself). In the third, fairly far-fetched, scenario, Eastern European countries would become integrated into the emerging economic system of the Commonwealth of Independent States (C.I.S.), as this system may not pose hard-to-meet conditions on Eastern European countries for inclusion. As Russia's economy falters and cross-republic trading arrangements have come about rather slowly, this outcome has grown increasingly improbable, but that is not to suggest that Central European countries and neighboring former Soviet republics will not create trade and investment alliances. They will, but not before one of the other two scenarios becomes the new order in the region.

The first scenario, in which Eastern Europe becomes integrated with Western Europe, is certainly the hope of policymakers in the East, but, given recent ominous developments in the EC, it is not likely to occur overnight, or in three to six years, as observers originally predicted. The EC is a product of World War II and the Cold War that followed, created for the purpose of banding France and Germany together, and thus reducing, it is hoped forever, the chances of another European war. European unity would integrate the continent economically, too, and help it survive the onslaught of American industrial competition. Ultimately, unified Europe succeeded in both of these objectives. However, it remains a creation of the Cold War, conceived in the context of a Europe split into two opposing blocs. Its original imperative of integrating Europe politically and economically is now at odds with an impinging new reality—to assist, reform, and eventually integrate its poor relations in the old East.

While their Eastern neighbors pleaded at its door, hat in hand, wanting to enter the capitalist West, EC members closed ranks. This has divided Europe once again, this time into the rich nations of the EC and the poor nations of the old Eastern bloc. "In the past," says Simone Veil, a French member of the European Parliament, to *The New York Times*, "We lived between the Atlantic and the wall. We would shed a tear for the misery of those in the East, but the situation was frozen. Now we have uncertainty and we don't know where we're going."

"There's a sort of unexpressed feeling," admitted former president of France Valery Giscard d'Estaing, "that we'd be better off if we could ignore Eastern Europe's problems." But that would soon be impossible, again to the chagrin of prognosticators. The East, to everyone's surprise, became a spanner thrown into the European single-market works. With massive layoffs in eastern Germany after unification, thousands of *Ossis* crossed into western Germany looking for work. Unemployed Romanians, Poles, Ukrainians, and Yugoslavian refugees flooded into Western Europe, along with Africans fleeing starvation. Fifty thousand people sought asylum in Germany in the month of October 1992 alone; over 500,000 people sought asylum in Germany in 1992. France became the home of 2 million Muslims, the largest religious minority group in Europe. Fortress Europe had been invaded, not by Japanese industrial *keiretsu*, or Russian tanks, or even American fruit, but by people carrying suitcases from former Communist Europe and North Africa.

The legions of newcomers put a huge drain on EC social systems and created strife within groups of underprivileged locals, who blamed "foreigners" for their troubles. Racism and virulent nationalism made "European unity" sound like a naive fantasy. Right-wing politicos voiced the angst of the underclasses, focusing their anxiety on the immigration dilemma, and thus gained mainstream political legitimacy. Rather than share the burden of dealing with the refugee problem by assisting the countries in need—dealing with the problem at its source—the EC splintered, members blaming one another for not controlling their borders. Now, the European 1992 mandate to open borders is perceived as akin to political suicide by EC leaders.

Then came the economic impact of liberation in the East. Bonn spent over $100 billion attempting to rebuild eastern Germany; the resulting high interest rates sent other EC currencies spiraling out of control in late 1992, rupturing any chance for a currency union in the EC in the near term.

Hungary, Czechoslovakia, and Poland gained associate status in the EC in late 1991, and Romania in 1992. These countries then enjoyed more favorable exporting quotas and lower tariffs, as well as an assortment of special credits and assistance from the EC. However, a protectionist attitude on the part of Western nations against Eastern European producers has stymied their efforts to freely sell to the West. France resists the inclusion of Poland, fearing that French farmers will be injured by cheaper Polish farm goods. The EC Commission reacted recently to complaints from some of its members about inexpensive steel imports from Czechoslovakia by clearing the way for those countries to impose protective measures. It has become clear to the EC, that either it can accept the East's products, and thus generate economic growth in the East, or it will be forced to accept immigrants in vast numbers who seek a better life. This brings us to...

The Most Likely Scenario

In the second scenario described earlier, Eastern Europe learns to go it alone, with help from the West. Intraregional trade between Eastern European countries, in the form of a reformed Comecon trading bloc, may be a practical alternative to immediate inclusion in the EC. Output in these countries has tumbled because of the collapse of ruble-based intraregional commerce, but this trade must be resuscitated if trade is to grow, especially in light of protectionist trade policies currently pursued by the EC. Lacking hard currency, the countries would have to conduct much trade via barter; great synergy seems possible since raw materials from the former Soviet states could be traded for manufactured goods made in Central Europe. Eventually, the commonwealth republics will merge with this community of nations as well, supplying raw materials and inexpensive labor for the production of products sold in the EC.

Sure enough, the Central European countries of Hungary, Poland, and the Czech and Slovak republics created a free-trade zone in December 1992, agreeing to liberalize all trade within a decade, starting with raw materials, followed by industrial products, and finally including agricultural goods. The rebirth of intraregional trade between former Eastern bloc countries will be followed by gradual economic integration of "the Big Three"—Poland, Hungary, and the Czech Republic—into the EC. Acting as entrepôt trading centers, these three countries will then be well positioned to link their non-EC-member trading partners to the EC, much in the way Hong Kong links China to the capitalist West. With well-orchestrated help from the West, new markets will be fostered for Western firms, creating new jobs in the West through exports, and a new Europe will emerge for which the phrase "the Other Europe" will have no meaning except to historians.

Appendix

Sources of Information for Marketers

U.S. Government Sources

U.S. Department of Commerce
14th & Constitution Avenue NW
Washington, DC 20230
Tel: (202) 482-2000

National Technical Information
  Service (NTIS)
Subscriptions Department
5285 Port Royal Road
Springfield, VA 22161
Tel: (703) 487-4600

Eastern Europe Business
  Information Center (EEBIC)
U.S. Department of Commerce
International Trade Administration
Washington, DC 20230
Tel: (202) 482-2645

Business Information Service for the
  Newly Independent States (BISNIS)
U.S. Department of Commerce
  14th Street and Constitution
  Avenue, NW
Washington, DC 20230
Tel: (202) 482-4655
Fax: (202) 482-2293

In Eastern Europe

U.S. Embassy Sofia
1 A, Stamboliiski Blvd.
BG-1040 Sofia
Tel: (359 2) 884 801-5

Mailing Address:
U.S. Embassy Sofia (SOF)
APO NY 09213-5740

U.S. Embassy Prague
Trziste 15
CS-12548 Prague 1
Tel: (42 2) 536 641/9

Mailing Address:
U.S. Embassy Prague (PRG)
AMEMB Box 5630
APO NY 09213-5630

U.S. Consulate General—Bratislava
Hviezdoslavovo Nam. 4
CS-81102 Bratislava
Tel: (42 7) 330 861; 333 597

U.S. Embassy Budapest
V. Szabadsag Ter. 12
H-1054 Budapest
Tel: (36 1) 112 6450; 128 450
Tlx: (861) 18048

Commercial Development Center
Bajza utca 31
H-1062 Budapest
Tel: (36 1) 224 222
Tlx: (861) 227136

Mailing Address:
U.S. Embassy Budapest (BUD)
APO NY 09213

U.S. Embassy Warsaw
Aleje Ujazdowskie 29/31
PL-00540 Warsaw
Tel: (48 22) 283 041

Mailing Address:
U.S. Embassy Warsaw (WAW)
APO NY 90213-5010

U.S. Trade Center (Warsaw)
Ulica Wiejska 20
PL-00490 Warsaw
Tel: (48 22) 214 5156
Tlx: (867) 813934 USTDO POL

U.S. Consulate—Cracow
Ulica Stolarska 9
PL-31043 Cracow
Tel: (48 12) 229 764; 226 040;
  227 793
Tlx: (867) 325350

U.S. Consulate—Poznan
Ulica chopina 4
PL-61700 Poznan
Tel: (48 61) 529 586; 529 874; 529 587

U.S. Embassy Bucharest
Strada Tudor Arghezi 7-9
R-70132 Bucharest
Tel: (40 0) 104 040
Tlx: (864) 11416

Mailing Address:
U.S. Embassy Bucharest
AmConGen (BUCH)
APO NY 03213-5260

U.S. Embassy Moscow
Ulitsa Chaykovskogo 19/21/23
SU-121834 Moscow
Tel: (70 95) 252 2450-9

U.S. Foreign Commercial Service—
  Moscow
Novinsky Bulvar, 15
Moscow, RUSSIAO
Tel: (011-7-502) 224-1105

Mailing Address:
American Embassy Moscow
PSC 77-FCS
APO AE 09721

U.S. Consulate General—Leningrad
Ulitsa Petra Lavroa 15
SU-St. Petersburg
Tel: (7 821) 274 8235

Mailing Address:
St. Petersburg CG—Box L
APO AE 09723

U.S. Consulate General—Kiev
9 Florentsiya St.
Second Floor
SU-Kiev
Tel: 517 9001; 517 9732

Mailing Address:
Box K
APO 09862

U.S. Embassy—Alma Ata
99 Furmanova Street
Tel: (011-7-327) 263-2942

Mailing Address:
American Embassy
APO AE 09721
Alma Ata

U.S. Embassy Belgrade
Kneza Milosa 50
YU-11000 Belgrade
Tel: (38 11) 645 655
Tlx: (862) 11529

Mailing Address:
American Embassy Box 5070
APO NY 09213-5070

U.S. Consulate General—Zagreb
Brace Kavurica 2
YU-41000 Zagreb
Tel: (38 41) 444 800

Mailing Address:
AMCONGEN Box 5080
APO NY 09213-5080

Chambers of Commerce and Economic Councils for Eastern European Marketers

U.S. Chamber of Commerce
1615 H Street, NW
Washington, DC 20062
Tel: (202) 463-5460
Central and Eastern European
Trade and Technical Assistance
Center
International Division
U.S. Chamber of Commerce
1615 H Street, NW
Washington, DC 20062

Chamber of Commerce of the
People's Republic of Albania
Konferenca e Pezes Street
AL-6 Tirana
Tel: (355 42) 7997; 4246; 22934

Bulgaria-U.S. Trade and Economic
Council
c/o U.S. Chamber of Commerce
1615 H Street, NW
Washington, DC 20062
Tel: (202) 463-5473

Bulgarian Chamber of Commerce
and Industry
Stamboliiski Blvd. 11a
BG-1040 Sofia
Tel: (359 2) 872 631

Czechoslovak–U.S. Economic
Council
c/o U.S. Chamber of Commerce
1615 H Street, NW
Washington, DC 20062
Tel: (202) 463-5473

Czechoslovak Chamber of
Commerce and Industry
38 Argentinska Street
CS-12041 Prague 7
Tel: (42 2) 872 4111

Czechoslovak Chamber of
Commerce and Industry
Gorkeho 9
CS-81603 Bratislava
Tel: (42 7) 591 98

Hungarian-U.S. Business Council
c/o U.S. Chamber of Commerce
1615 H Street, NW
Washington, DC 20062
Tel: (202) 463-5482

U.S.—Russian Business Council
1701 Pensylvania Avenue, NW
Suite 650
Washington, DC 20006
Tel:(202) 956-7670

Hungarian Chamber of Commerce
Kossuth Lajos ter. 6/8
H-1055 Budapest

Mailing Address:
P.O. Box 106
H-1389 Budapest
Tel: (36 1) 153 3333; 153 4384

American Chamber of Commerce
in Hungary
Dozsa Gyorgy utca 84/A, Room 412
H-1068 Budapest
Tel: (36 1) 142 8752

Budapest Chamber of Commerce
and Industry
Krisztina krt. 99, VI. 601
H-1016 Budapest
Tel: (36 1) 149 1010

Hungarian-American Chamber of
Commerce
Arany Janos utca 24
H-1051 Budapest
Tel: (36 1) 117 2464

Polish-U.S. Economic Council
c/o U.S. Chamber of Commerce
1615 H Street, NW
Tel: (202) 463-5482

Poland-California Chamber of
Commerce
3111 Camino Del Rio North
Suite 1100
San Diego, CA 92108
Tel: (619) 563-7052

American Chamber of Commerce in
Poland
c/o U.S. Trade Development Center
Ul. Wiejska 20
PL-00490 Warsaw
Tel: (48 22) 214 515

Romanian-U.S. Economic Council
c/o U.S. Chamber of Commerce
1615 H Street, NW
Washington, DC 20062
Tel: (202) 463-5473

Chamber of Commerce and
Industry of Romania
Blvd. Nicolae Balcescu 22, Sector 1
R-70122 Bucharest
Tel: (40 0) 139 883

U.S.–Yugoslav Economic Council
Richard E. Johnson, President
1615 H Street, NW
Washington, DC 20062
Tel: (202) 463-5473

Eastern European Sources

Albania

Mission to the United Nations of
the People's Republic of Albania
320 East 79th Street
New York, NY 10021
Tel: (212) 249-2059

Albanian-American Trade
Association, Inc.
1010 Vermont Avenue, NW
Suite 512
Washington, DC 10005
Tel: (202) 737-0213

Bulgaria

Embassy of the Republic of
Bulgaria
1621 22nd Street, NW
Washington, DC 20008
Tel: (202) 387-7969

Office of the Commercial Counselor
to the Bulgarian Embassy
121 East 62nd Street
New York, NY 10021
Tel: (212) 935-4646

*The Czech and Slovak Federal
Republics*

Embassy of the Czech and Slovak
Federal Republic
3900 Spring of Freedom Avenue,
NW
Washington, DC 20008
Tel: (202) 363-6315

Embassy of the Slovak Republic
3900 Linnean Avenue, NW
Washington, DC 20008
Tel: (202) 363-6315

Hungary

Embassy of the Republic of
  Hungary
3910 Shoemaker Street,
  NW
Washington, DC 20008
Tel: (202) 362-6730

Commercial Offices

Main Office of the Hungarian Trade
  Representation in the United States
2401 Calvert Street, NW
Suite 1021
Washington, DC 20008
Tel: (202) 387-3191

Office of the Commercial Counselor
150 East 58th Street
33rd Floor
New York, NY 10021
Tel: (212) 752-3060

Branch Office of the Commercial
  Counselor
1 Prudential Plaza, Suite 1930
130 East Randolph Street
Chicago, IL 60601
Tel: (312) 856-0274

Poland

Embassy of the Republic of Poland
2640 16th Street, NW
Washington, DC 20009
Tel: (202) 234-3800

Polish Embassy Economic Office
1503 21st Street, NW
Washington, DC 20008
Tel: (202) 467-6690

Office of the Commercial Counselor
  of the Republic of Poland
820 Second Avenue, 17th Floor
New York, NY 10017
Tel: (212) 370-5300

Consulate General of the Republic
  of Poland
Commercial Division
333 East Ontario Street, Suite 3906B
Chicago, IL 60611
Tel: (312) 642-4102

Consulate General of the Republic
  of Poland
Commercial Division
3460 Wilshire Boulevard, Suite 1200
Los Angeles, CA 90010
Tel: (213) 365-7900

Romania

Embassy of Romania
1607 23d Street, NW
Washington, DC 20008
Tel: (202) 332-4846 (4848)

Office of the Romanian Economic
  Minister Counselor
200 East 38th Street
New York, NY 10016
Tel: (212) 682-9120

The Former Soviet Union

Embassy of the Russian Federation
1126 16th Street, NW
Washington DC 20036
Tel: (202) 628-8548

Trade Representative of the C.I.S.
  Economic Counselor's Office
2001 Connecticut Avenue, NW
Washington DC 20008
Tel: (202) 232-5988

AMTORG Trading Corporation
  (representing the Ministry of
  Foreign Trade)
15 W. 26th Street
Sixth Floor
New York, NY 10018
Tel: (212) 956-3010

Consulate General of the Russian
  Federation
2790 Green Street
San Francisco, CA 94123
Tel: (415) 202-9800

Former Yugoslavia
Embassy of the SFR of
  Yugoslavia
2410 California Street, NW
Washington, DC 20008
Tel: (202) 462-6566

Selected Newsletters for Marketers

(weekly)
Business Eastern Europe
The Economist Intelligence Unit
215 Park Avenue South
15th Floor
New York, NY 10003
Tel: (212) 460-0600

(monthly update)
Doing Business with Eastern Europe
The Economist Intelligence Unit
215 Park Avenue South
15th Floor
New York, NY 10003
Tel: (212) 460-0600

East/West Executive Guide
World Trade Executive, Inc.
P.O. Box 761
Concord, MA 01742
Tel: (401) 454- 2005

Eastern Europe Business Bulletin
Eastern Europe Business
  Information Center
U.S. Department of Commerce
Washington, DC 20230
Tel: (202) 482-2000

(biweekly)
PlanEcon Report
PlanEcon, Inc.
1111 14th Street, NW
Suite 801
Washington, DC 20005-5603
Tel: (202) 898-0471

(quarterly)
Romania Economic Newsletter
Cosmos, Inc.
P.O. Box 30437
Bethesda, MD 20814
Tel: (301) 229-5875

(biweekly)
Eye on the East
Pacific-Sierra Research
  Corporation
1401 Wilson Blvd.
Suite 1100
Arlington, VA 22209
Tel: (703) 527-4975

Focus on Central and Eastern Europe
Office of Public Communication
PA/PC Room 6805
2201 C Street, NW
Washington, DC 20520-6810
Tel: (202) 647- 6316

(daily)
*Foreign Broadcast Information
  Service—Eastern Europe/Soviet
  Union*
National Technical Information
  Services
5285 Port Royal Road
Springfield, VA 22161
Tel: (703) 487-4630

Transition
Room N-11003
The World Bank
1818 H Street, NW
Washington, DC 20433
Tel: (202) 473- 6982

Citizens Democracy Corps
2021 K Street, NW, Suite 215
Washington, DC 20006
Tel: (202) 872-0933

Albanian-American Trade Advisory
Albanian-American Trade
  Association
1010 Vermont Avenue, NW
Suite 512
Washington, DC 20005
Tel: (202) 737-0213

Eastern Europe
OECD (Organization for Economic
  Cooperation and Development)
2001 L Street NW
Suite 700
Washington, DC 20036-4910
Tel: (202) 785-6323

BISNIS Bulletin
U.S. Department of Commerce
International Trade Administration
Washington, DC 20230
Tel: (202) 482-4655

Russian for East Update
Russian Market Information
  Services
P.O. Box 22126
Seattle, WA 98122
Tel: (206) 447-2668

Russia and Commonwealth
Business Law Report
1350 Connecticut Avenue, NW
Suite 1000
Washington, DC 20036
Tel: 1 (800) 333-1291

Islamic Marketing Intelligence Report
27 Old Gloucester Street
London WC1N 3XX
Tel: (071) 404-5014

Privatization Organizations in Eastern Europe

Albania
National Agency for Privatization
Veli Mullaraj, General Director
Martin Mata, Assistant
Tirana, Albania
Tel: 355-42-24974

Bulgaria
Ministry of Finance
ul. Rakovski 102
BG-1000 Sofia
Tel: (359 2) 8491

Ministry of Foreign Economic
  Relations
12, Sofiiska Komuna Street
BG-1000 Sofia
Tel: (359 2) 882 011, 872 041

Czech Republic and Slovak Republic
Ministry of Finance
Letenska 15
CS-11810 Prague 1
Tel: (42 2) 514 1111
Tlx: (849) 121868

Federal Foreign Investment Agency
Richard Sumann
Executive Director
Nabrezi Kapitana Jarose 1000
CS-17032 Prague 7
Tel: (42 2) 389 2823

Hungary
Ministry of Privatization
ul. Krucza 36
00-525 Warszawa
Tel: 2/628-02-81

State Property Agency
Roosevelt ter. 7-8
H-1051 Budapest
Mailing Address:
P.O. Box 708
H-1399 Budapest
Tel: (36 1) 111 0200

Poland

Ministry of Finance
ul. Swietokrzyska 12
PL-00916 Warsaw
Tel:(48 22) 200 311

Ministry of Ownership
  Transformation
ul. Mysia 5
PL-00696 Warsaw

Tel:(48 22) 292 010; 283 261

Foreign Investment Agency
Aleje Roz 2
PL-00556 Warsaw
Tel:(48 22) 295 717; 285 061 ext. 694

Romania

Ministry of Finance
Str. Doamnei 80-10
R-79537 Bucharest
Tel: (40 0) 133 063; 132 000

Russia

Ministry of Finance
Kuibysheva St. 9
SU-103097 Moscow
Tel: (70 95) 298 9101

Currencies and Conversion Rates (as of November 1992)

Country	Name of currency	Rate per $1(U.S.; approx.)
Germany	Deutsche mark	1.58
Hungary	Forint	83.13
Poland	Zloty	15,371.0
Czech Republic	Koruna	28.63
Yugoslavia	New Dinar	750.0
Romania	Leu	437.30
Bulgaria	Lev	24.34
Albania	Lek	110.0
C.I.S.	Ruble	447.0
Estonia	Kroon	12.83
Slovenia	Tolar	96.90
Croatia	Dinar	441.0

Holidays in Eastern Europe

Bulgaria
New Year's: January 1
Woman's Day: March 8
Labor Day: May 1 and 2

Day of Bulgarian Culture: May 24
National Day: September 9 and 10
Day of Russian Revolution: November 7

Czech and Slovak Republics
New Year's: January 1
Easter Monday
Labor Day: May 1
National Day: May 9
Christmas: December 25
St. Stephen's Day: September 26

Former Soviet Union
New Year's Day: January 1
Woman's Day: March 8
International Labor Days: May 1 and 2
Victory Day: May 9
Anniversary of the Russian Revolution: November 7 and 8

Germany
New Year's Day: January 1
Easter Friday and Monday
May Day: May 1
Ascension Day: around May
Pentecost: around June
Memorial Day: June 17
Cemetery Day: Third Wednesday in November
Christmas: December 25 and 26

Hungary
New Year's: January 1
Liberation Day: April 4
Easter Monday
Labor Day: May 1
Constitution Day: August 20
Christmas: December 25

Poland
New Year's Day: January 1
Easter Monday

Labor Day: May 1
Corpus Christi: early June
National Day: July 22
All Soul's Day: November 1
Christmas: December 25 and 26

Romania
New Year's: January 1 and 2
Labor Days: May 1 and 2
Liberation Days: August 23 and 24

Yugoslavia
New Year's: January 1 and 2
Labor Day: May 1 and 2
Partisan Day: July 4
Republic Day: November 29 and 30

City Specialties in Eastern Europe

	City	Population	Major industries
East Germany	Berlin	1,270,000	Electrical equipment
	Dresden	520,000	Computer technology, data processing, office equipment
Czech and Slovak Republics	Prague	1,400,000	Tourism, electric energy
	Bratislava	380,000	Chemicals
	Brno	360,000	Heavy machinery
	Ostrava	150,000	Mining, steelworks, rolling mills
	Pardubice	100,000	Chemicals, plastics, electronics, machinery
	Pribam	—	Mining, mine locomotives, mine drilling equpment, control systems for mining processes
	Prievidza		Coal mining, chemicals and rubber, electric power, woodworking, footwear
	Proprad		Machine engineering, chemical and textile manufacturing, agriculture, tourism
Poland	Warsaw	1,641,300	Automobiles, generators, vodka
	Lodz	850,000	Manufacturing, electronics, specialty health, education, science

	City	Population	Major industries
	Poznan	500,000	Machinery, chemicals, food, tele comunications, banking, insur ance, tourism, business services
	Krakow	735,000	Steelworks
	Nowy Sacz	700,000	Light industry, food, tourism
	Gdansk	464,800	Oil refining
	Gorzow Weilkopolski	120,000	Chemicals, machinery, lumber, food processing, celluloid paper
Bulgaria	Sofia	1,120,000	Steelworks, chemicals, metallurgy, mechanical equipment
	Blovdiv	350,000	Nonferrous metal processing
	Varna	300,000	Shipbuilding
	Pazardjik	200,000	Agribusiness
Romania	Bucharest	2,000,000	Aircraft, chemicals, pharmaceuticals, electronics, paper
	Arad	250,000	Machine tools, metallurgy, food processing, railroad cars, wood processing
Russia	Moscow	8,820,000	Aircraft, power and transport engineering, appliances, trucks, electronics
	St. Petersburg	4,950,000	Electrical engineering
Former Yugoslavia	Belgrade	1,090,000	Agribusiness
	Zagreb	650,000	Manufacturing, oil drilling and refining
Hungary	Budapest	2,100,000	Mechanical instruments, pharmaceuticals, oil and gas, automobile manufacturing, plastics
	Szeged	190,000	Oil exploration
	Bekes	70,000	Agriculture, canning, milk processing
	Mako	—	Spas, tourism
	Gyor	130,000	Automotive, tourism
	Ozd	—	Mining, metallurgy, electronics
	Ploiesti	300,000	Oil production and refining, agribusiness, wine

SOURCES: Population figures from U.S. Chamber of Commerce, U.N. Demographic Yearbook, and the U.S. Department of Commerce. Industry data from "Eastern Europe in the Global Market," published by A. T. Kearney, October 1990; and Eastern Europe Business Bulletin (numerous issues), published by the Eastern Europe Business Information Center, U.S. Department of Commerce.

Bibliography

Aganbegyan, Abel: *Inside Perestroika: The Future of the Soviet Economy*. New York: Harper & Row, 1989.

"After 10 Months in Space, Cosmonauts Is in a New Land," *The Los Angeles Times*, March 26, 1992, A4.

"Aid to EE to Reach $30 Billion by 1995," *Business Eastern Europe*, August 26, 1991, p. 267.

"An Opel Takes Hungary Back to the Future," *The New York Times*, March 14, 1992, p. 17.

Anders, George: "Going East: CEOs Are Bullish on Investment in Eastern Europe, but Worries Remain," *The Wall Street Journal*, September 21, 1990 (World Business Survey), p. R24.

Asland, Anders: "The Reform: Some Early Lessons," *World Link*, September/October 1991, Vol. 4; No. 5, p. 12.

A. T. Kearney: "Eastern Europe in the Global Market: A Portrait of Opportunity and Challenge," October 1990.

Banerjee, Neela: "A U.S. Entrepreneur Treads Warily in Georgia," *The Wall Street Journal*, September 30, 1992, p. A13.

Barnathan, Joyce et al.: "'The Soviet Brain Drain Is the U.S. Brain Gain'," *Business Week*, November 4, 1991, p. 94.

Barzini, Luigi: *The Europeans*. New York: Penguin Books, 1983.

Blejer, Mario I., and Alan Gelb: "Persistant Economic Decline in Central and Eastern Europe: What Are the Lessons?" *Transition: The Newsletter About Reforming Economies*, vol. 3, no. 7, July–August 1992, p. 1.

Blunden, Godfrey, and the editors of *Life: Eastern Europe: Czechoslovakia, Hungary, Poland*. New York: Time Incorporated, 1965.

Bobinski, Christopher: "New Era Dawns for Consumers," *Financial Times*, Special Section: Poland, April 28, 1992.

———: "Signs That All Is not Well," *Financial Times*, Special Section: Poland, April 28, 1992.

Bohlen, Celestine: "Corruption Grows Greedy in Russia," *The New York Times*, March 14, 1992, p. A4.

———: "Irate Russians Demonize Traders from Caucusus," *The New York Times*, October 20, 1992, p. A3.

———: "Once-privileged Writer Shares the Russian Pain Now," *The New York Times*, March 22, 1992, p. 6.

_____: "Russians Put Anxiety Aside and Try to Eke Out a Living," *The New York Times,* March 1, 1992, p. A1.

_____: "The Union Is Buried. What's Being Born?" *The New York Times,* December 9, 1991, p. A1.

Braganti, Nancy L., and Elizabeth Devine: *The Traveler's Guide to European Customs and Manners.* Minnesota: Meadowbrook, 1984.

Bremer, Brian: "Fear and Trembling among the Kremlin Watchers," *Business Week,* January 27, 1992, p. 49.

_____, et al.: "This Month's Soviet Technology," *Business Week,* May 4, 1993, pp. 68, 70.

Broad, William J.: "Nuclear Scientists See an Era for East-West Friendships," *The New York Times,* March 19, 1992, p. A6.

_____: "Sale of Plutonium by Russia to U.S. Faces Unseen Snag," *The New York Times,* March 23, 1992, p. A1.

_____: "U.S. Is Shopping as Soviets Offer to Sell Once-Secret Technology," *The New York Times,* November 4, 1991, p. A1.

_____: "U.S. Moves to Bar Americans Buying Soviet Technology," *The New York Times,* March 1, 1992, p. A1.

Broder, Jonathan: "For the Price of a Nice Car, You Can Buy a MiG," *We/MbI,* September 7–20, 1992, p. 4.

Brooks, David: "In Russia, Only a Dollar Buys a Dream," *The Wall Street Journal,* November 17, 1992, A16.

Brown, Priscilla C: "Gary Hart: A Would-Be President Turned International Strategist," *Business Marketing,* October 1990, p. 27.

Browning, E. S., and Eduardo Lachica: "Sales to Soviets of Technology Are Broadened," *The Wall Street Journal,* May 28, 1991, p. A18.

Burns, John F.: "Protesters Urge Leader of Serbia to Quit," *The New York Times,* March 12, 1992, p. A8.

Burstein, Daniel: *Euroquake,* New York: Simon & Schuster, 1991.

Byers, Jacob E.: "Making the Joint Venture Succeed," *Export Today,* May/June 1990, p. 41.

Callen, Kate: "From Russia with Love: Women Place Personal Ads in Catalogs to Fine American Husbands," *We/MbI,* May 1, 1992, p. 9.

Carrier, Capucine: "Treuhand's Task Force: First Stop for Investors," *Business Eastern Europe,* August 5, 1991, p. 244.

Carrington, Tim: "East Bloc Managers Learn Do's, Don'ts of Capitalist Spirit," *The Wall Street Journal,* December 27, 1991, p. A12.

_____: "Eastern Europe's Ills May Defy Usual Cures," *The Wall Street Journal,* December 7, 1992, p. A1.

_____: "Restless Eastern Europeans Working for West Fret Wide Wage Gaps," *The Wall Street Journal,* June 30, 1992, p. A10.

Clines, Francis X.: "It's Not Yet Capitalism, but Ruble Is Healthier," *The New York Times,* February 18, 1992, p. A8.

Cockburn, Alexander: "Russia, The New Latin America of Economics," *The Los Angeles Times,* January 5, 1992.

Cohen, Roger: "Across Europe: A Growing Malaise Undermines a Dream of Economic Unity," *The New York Times,* September 27, 1992, p. F1.

_____: "East Meets West, Dollars Apart," *The New York Times*, February 5, 1992, p. C1.

Coca-Cola Company, *1990 Annual Report: The Coca-Cola Company*, Atlanta, GA 1990.

"Cola Wars: All Noisy on the Eastern Front," *Business Week*, January 27, 1992, p. 94.

Colchester, Nicholas, and David Buchan: *Europower: The Essential Guide to Europe's Economic Transformation in 1992*. London: The Economist Books Ltd., 1990.

Cole, Jeff: "In Quest for Billions, GM's Hughes to Bring Phones to Tartarstan," *The Wall Street Journal*, August 21, 1992, p. A1.

Coles, Waltraud, and Uwe Koreik: *Simple Etiquette in Germany* [East & West]. Sandgate, U.K.: Simple Books, Ltd., 1991.

Copetas, A. Craig: *Bear Hunting with the Politburo: A Gritty First-Hand Account of Russia's Young Entrepreneurs—and Why Soviet-Style Capitalism Can't Work*, New York: Simon & Schuster, 1991.

Craig, Sally: "Teaching Managers How to Manage," *We/MbI*, June 1–14, 1992, p. 6.

"Credo Bank to Issue VISA Cards," *Business Eastern Europe*, October 21, 1991, p. 367.

Crisp, William: "Companies Reevaluate 'Emigre' Sales Persons," *Business Eastern Europe*, July 1, 1991, p. 203.

_____: "Werner A. Korel: EE Business at Dow Corning," *Business Eastern Europe*, October 28, 1991, p. 384.

Daglish, Robert: *Coping with Russia*. Oxford: Basil Blackwell, Ltd., 1985.

Dahlburg, John-Thor: "Great Unknown Awaits Cosmonaut," *The Los Angeles Times*, March 21, 1992, p. A15.

_____: "Gorbachev Steps Down," *The Los Angeles Times*, December 26, 1991, p. A1.

_____: "When the Lights Go Out at the Kremlin," *The Los Angeles Times*, December 10, 1991, p. H1.

_____: "Russia's Neo-Capitalists Learning Art of Rip-Off," *The Los Angeles Times*, March 1, 1992, p. A1.

Darnton, Robert: *Berlin Journal 1989–1990*. New York: Norton, 1991.

Dixon & Company: *East European Monthly*, Country Report Section, February 1992, New York, NY.

Doohan, John: "Investment in Eastern Europe: Poised to Take Off?" *World Link* vol. 4, no. 5, September–October 1991, p. 10.

Dudley, James W.: *1992: Understand the New European Market*. London: Dearborn Financial Publishing, Inc., 1989.

Eastern Europe Business Bulletin (published by the Eastern Europe Business Information Center, U.S. Department of Commerce, International Trade Administration. October/November 1991; January 1992; February 1992.) The author has adapted many sections of public-domain material in these extremely useful publications.

Ebhardt, Horst: "Investing in the CSFR," *East/West Executive Guide*, vol. 2, no. 4, April 1992, p. 2.

Elliot, Stuart: "Figuring Out the Russian Consumer," *The New York Times*, April 1, 1992.

Engelberg, Stephen: "Eager If Uneasy, East Europe Accepts German Investments," *The New York Times*, January 23, 1992, p. A1.

_____: "Polish Premier Urging Flexibility in Criteria on Monetary Fund Aid," *The New York Times,* March 2, 1992, p. A4.

_____: "Polish Tax Agents Learn from I.R.S.," *The New York Times,* March 26, 1992, p. C1.

Erlanger, Stephen: "Russians Getting Share Vouchers but Ruble Falls," *The New York Times,* October 2, 1992, p. A7.

_____: "Tatars Vote on an Issue All Agree Is Confusing," *The New York Times,* March 22, 1992, p. 6.

Ertugrul, Irene: "Sea Land Tries to Establish Land Bridge Across Russia," *We/MbI,* October 5–18, 1992, p. 5.

"Ex-Soviet Summit Called a Success," *The New York Times,* February 16, 1992, p. 6.

Faust, Juergen K.: "Germany's Communications Gap," *World Link,* vol. 4, no. 5, September–October 1991.

Fialka, John J., and Laurie Hays: "U.S. May Be Missing Rare Chance to Obtain Soviet Spy Technology," *The Wall Street Journal,* December 17, 1991, p. A1.

Fisher, Andrew: "Gaping Holes in the Safety Net," *The Financial Times,* April 1, 1992, p. 16.

Flaes, F. Angela: "GM in Hungary: Expanding EE Production Base," *Business Eastern Europe,* July 8, 1991, p. 211.

Flint, Alison: "Crisis Could Dampen Romanian Investment Flows," *Business Eastern Europe,* October 7, 1991, p. 338.

_____: "Foreign Investment in Romania," *Business Eastern Europe,* June 3, 1991, p. 173.

Forman, Craig: "Creeping toward Capitalism," *The Wall Street Journal,* September 21, 1990 (World Business Survey), p. R10.

Fowler, Brenda: "Albania Searches for Stable Future," *The New York Times,* February 16, 1992, p. 7.

Frankland, Mark: *The Sixth Continent: Mikhail Gorbachev and the Soviet Union.* New York: Harper & Row, 1987.

Friedman, Thomas L.: "Nixon Scoffs at Level of Support for Russian Democracy by Bush," *The New York Times,* March 10, 1992, p. A1.

Fund, John H.: "Undoing Communism in Albania," *The Wall Street Journal,* March 18 1992, p. A14.

Gatling, Rene: "Hungary: UT Automotive's New European Plant Site," *Business Eastern Europe,* April 22, 1991, p. 123.

Gelb, Leslie H.: "Nixon's Tricky Crusade," *The New York Times,* March 13, 1992, p. A15.

General Electric Company, *1990 Annual Report: General Electric Company, Fairfield, CN* 1990.

Gold, Jacqueline: "Removing the Dead Hand of State," *Financial World,* March 3, 1992, p. 38.

Goldberg, Carey: "Adventures in Red Tape: Preparing to Open a Moscow Hotel," *The Los Angeles Times,* May 26, 1991, p. D16.

_____: "Industry Failing Under Weight of Russian Reform," *The Los Angeles Times,* July 27, 1992, p. A1.

_____: "Moscow Sex Shop Is a New Plateau in Glasnost," *The Los Angeles Times,* March 3, 1992, p. A4.

_____: "New Slavic Bloc Seen Paving Way for Economic Reform," _The Los Angeles Times_, December 11, 1991, p. A13.

_____: "True Soviet Believers Rally Round Communist 'Truth'," _The Los Angeles Times_, September 11, 1991, p. A1.

Gowers, Andrew: "'Big Bang' Is a Damp Squib," _The Financial Times_, April 28, 1992, Special Section: Poland.

Grebenshikov, Viktor K.: "A Clown That Everyone Is Now Taking Seriously," _The Los Angeles Times_, December 10, 1991, p. H5.

_____: "Conservative Russian Group Waits in Wings," _The Los Angeles Times_, December 9, 1991, p. A11.

_____, and Michael Parks: "Ex-Soviet States at Odds: Group's Future in Doubt," _The Los Angeles Times_, March 21, 1992, p. A1.

Greenhouse, Steven: "In a Failed Hungarian Factory, Jeans Succeed," _The New York Times_, November 10, 1990.

_____: "In Distressed Poland, a Success Story," _The New York Times_, March 5, 1991, p. C1.

_____: "Keeping a Soviet Enterprise Afloat," _The New York Times_, October 22, 1991, p. C1.

_____: "Running on Fast-Forward in Budapest," _The New York Times_, December 16, 1990, Section 3, p. 1.

Gumbel, Peter: "Moscow to Broaden Its Trade with Seoul," _The Wall Street Journal_, May 10, 1990, p. A16.

_____: "Newly Freed Capital Flees Soviet Union," _The Wall Street Journal_, October 3, 1990, p. A18.

_____: "Russians Remember the Gorbachev Years with Mixed Feelings," _The Wall Street Journal_, December 20, 1991, p. A1.

Gurley, John G.: _Soviets at the Edge_, Stanford Alumni Association, Stanford, CA, 1990.

Gutterman, Steven: "Public Wants Food, Not Politics," _The Los Angeles Times_, December 10, 1991, p. A10.

Guyon, Janet, and Michael J. McCarthy: "Coke Wins Early Skirmishes in Its Drive to Take Over Eastern Europe from Pepsi," _The Wall Street Journal_, November 11, 1992, p. B1, B8.

Hahn, Carl: "Revving Up Skoda," _World Link_, vol. 4, no. 5, September–October 1991, p. 18.

Hall, Brian: _Stealing from a Deep Place: Travels in South-Eastern Europe_. London: Heinemann, 1988.

Halperin, Jonathan, J.: "Ten Commandments," _Business in the U.S.S.R._, May 1991, p. 72.

Hanke, Steve H.: "IMF Money Will Buy Trouble for Russia," _The Wall Street Journal_, April 29, 1992, p. A24.

Harrington, Guy: "Privatization: Poland's Fast Track," _World Link_, vol. 4, no. 5, September–October 1991, p. 23.

Hays, Laurie: "Russia Corruption Transcends Communist Era, Tainting Even the 'New Generation' Politicians," _The Wall Street Journal_, October 6, 1992, p. A10.

Heller, Mikhail: _Cogs in the Wheel: The Formation of Soviet Man_. New York: Alfred A. Knopf, 1988.

Henneberger, Melinda: "Well, the Ukraine Girls Really Knock Them Out," *The New York Times,* November 15, 1992, p. E6.

Hewlett-Packard S.A.: "Hewlett-Packard Contributing to Europe," *Switzerland: Public Affairs Europe,* April 1990.

Hofheinz, Paul: "Let's Do Business," *Fortune,* September 23, 1991, p. 62.

_____: "New Light in Eastern Europe?" *Fortune,* July 29, 1991, p. 145.

Holusha, John: "Business Taps the East Bloc's Intellectual Reserves," *The New York Times,* February 20, 1990, p. A1.

Hunyadi, Csilla (ed.): *Hungary Today: Business, Economic and Political Newsletter,* vol. 4, no. 1, January 1992.

Hyland, William G.: "The Case For Pragmatism," *Foreign Affairs,* vol. 71, no. 1, 1992, p. 1.

Ignatieff, Michael: "Can Russia Return to Europe?" *Harper's Magazine,* April 1992, p. 15.

Ignatius, Adi: "Die-Hard Soviets Try Not to Fade Away," *The Wall Street Journal,* March 18, 1992, p. A10.

_____: "In Russian Provinces, Yeltsin's Reformers Fight for His Dream," *The Wall Street Journal,* June 15, 1992, p. A1.

_____ : "Moscow Entrepreneurs in Street Kiosks Point Way to New Economy," *The Wall Street Journal,* March 25, 1992, p. A1.

_____: "Rain, Rain, Go Away, Go Soak Someone Less Willing to Pay," *The Wall Street Journal,* October 2, 1992, p. A1.

_____: Russia Goes Private: It's Fun, It's Now, It's an Ad on TV," *The Wall Street Journal,* September 23, 1992, p. A1.

_____: "Success Story: This Russian Plant Actually Makes Stuff," *The Wall Street Journal,* October 27, 1992, p. A1.

_____: "Yeltsin Keeps Most Reformers in Cabinet Posts," *The Wall Street Journal,* December 24, 1992, p. A4.

Iwanciw, Eugene M.: (letter to the editor) "Don't Favor Russia among Ex-Soviet States," *The New York Times,* March 16, 1992, p. A14.

Jefferson, David J.: "Russian Art, Once Unknown, Is Peddled in America," *The Wall Street Journal,* February 24, 1992, p. B2.

Jehl, Douglas: "U.S. Fears Friction from Closed Club in Commonwealth," *The Los Angeles Times,* December 10, 1991, p. A11.

_____, and Doyle McManus: "The Betting in Washington Is on Yeltsin," *The Los Angeles Times,* December 12, 1991, p. A11.

Jenner, Richard A., and Joseph Gappa: "Learning Under Fire: The Adaptability of Polish Managers to Competitive Market Conditions," *Journal of World Trade,* vol. 25, no. 2, April 1991, p. 81.

Johnson, Robert: "Kazakhstan, Elf Aquitaine Set Oil Pact," *The Wall Street Journal,* February 19, 1992, p. A8.346

_____, and Allena Sullivan: "A Small Joint Venture Is Leading the Way in Getting Russian Oil," *The Wall Street Journal,* January 29, 1992, p. A1.

Johnson, Simon, and Heidi Kroll: "Managerial Strategies for Spontaneous Privatization," *Soviet Economy,* vol. 7, no 4, October–December, 1991, p. 281.

"Joint Ventures in Poland," *Business Eastern Europe,* February 18, 1991, p. 53.

Jones, Tamara: "An American in Estonia: Venture Brings Gain, Grief," *The Los Angeles Times,* April 14, 1992. p. H4.

_____: "Yeltsin Calls Russia a Foreign Investment Opportunity," *The Los Angeles Times, November 23, 1991, p. A4.*

Jonscher, Charles: *"Why So Little Investment?"* World Link, vol. 4, no. 5, September–October 1991, p. 15.

Kamm, Henry: "Ex-Communists Lose in Albania Vote," *The New York Times,* March 23, 1992, p. A3.

_____: "No Food or Jobs or Spirit: Albania Prepares to Vote," *The New York Times,* March 12, 1992, p. A6.

Kaslow, Amy: "U.S. Missing Trade Opportunities in Central and Eastern Europe," *The Christian Science Monitor,* March 11, 1992, p. 1.

Kateraas, Espen: "Eastern Europe: Human Resources Management Tips," *Business Eastern Europe,* July 8, 1991, p. 212.

Keating, Robert: "Changes in Moscow's Political Climate Spread Gloom among Western Advisors," *The Wall Street Journal,* December 18, 1992, p. A7.

"Keeping Russia From Sliding toward Abyss," *The Los Angeles Times,* March 1, 1992, p. M3.

Kelly, Erin: "Business School in Prague Trains Future Capitalists," *The Los Angeles Times,* January 12, 1992, p. D3.

Kemp, Frederick: "Germans Try to Stem Right-Wing Attacks Against Foreigners," *The Wall Street Journal,* December 4, 1991, p. A1.

Kinzer, Stephen: "U.S. Is at Odds with German Backing for Slovenia and Croatia," *The New York Times,* December 8, 1991, p. 7.

Kirkland, Richard I. Jr.: "The Big Japanese Push into Europe," *Fortune,* July 2, 1990, p. 94.

Kiser, John W.: "Eastern Europe's Intellectual Capital," A paper prepared for the Royal Institute of International Affairs, July 1991.

_____: "What U.S. Business Can Learn from Leninism," *The Wall Street Journal,* January 3, 1991 (op. ed. page).

Kiva, Alexei: "War between Republics?" *We/MbI,* March 1992, p. 4.

Klebnikov, Peter: "U.S. Companies Must Offer Extras to Succeed in CIS," *We/MbI,* May 1, 1992, p. 6.

Kobylka, Jari: "Advertising Options Expanding in Czechoslovakia," *Business Eastern Europe,* September 9, 1991, p. 293.

_____: "Changing FTOs in the CSFR Still Good Contacts," *Business Eastern Europe,* October 28, 1991, p. 373.

_____: "Polish Mass Privatization Could Be Disappointing," *Business Eastern Europe,* August 19, 1991, p. 259.

_____: "Suggestions for Doing Business in the New CSFR," *Business Eastern Europe,* July 15, 1991, p. 219.

Knox, Noelle: "He'll Be Premier There, in Arrears Here," *The Los Angeles Times,* July 11, 1992, p. D1.

Kuklinski, Antoni (ed.): *Transformation of Science in Poland.* Warsaw: State Committee for Scientific Research, Republic of Poland, 1991.

Landy, Joanne: "One Step Forward, Two Steps Back: The East Chases the Worst of the West," *The Progressive,* June, 1991, p. 17.

Langenecker, Juliane: "Getting Paid with EE and USSR Licenses," *Business Eastern Europe,* September 23, 1991, p. 317.

_____: "Progress in Treuhand Sell-Off," *Business Eastern Europe,* July 22, 1991, p. 228.

_____: "Survey Highlights German-German Cooperation Woes," *Business Eastern Europe,* April 15, 1991, p. 115.

Laufer, Peter: *Iron Curtain Rising.* San Francisco: Mercury House, 1991.

Lengyel, Jyörgi: "Uncertain Executives," *The Hungarian Observer,* May, 1990, p. 7.

"Lessons in Polish Business," *The Financial Times,* April 28, 1992, Special Section: Poland.

"Let's Make a Deal—But a Smaller One," *Business Week,* January 20, 1992, p. 44.

Levinson, Macha: "The Soviet Union: After the Coup," *World Link,* vol. 4, no. 5, September–October 1991, p. 8.

Lewis, Flora: *Europe: A Tapestry of Nations.* New York: Simon & Schuster, 1987.

Liddell, Bill: "Hold On to the Managers," *World Link,* vol. 4, no. 5, September–October 1991, p. 25.

Lloyd, John, and Martin Wolf: "From Catastrophe to Mere Crisis," *The Financial Times,* April 22, 1992.

_____: "Russian Relaxes Tight Monetary Policy," *The Financial Times,* April 21, 1992, p. 1.

Lohr, Steve: "Goldman's Pitch for Deals in Russia," *The New York Times,* March 12, 1992, p. C1.

"Long Days, Low Pay, and a Moldy Cot," *Business Week,* January 27, 1992, p. 44.

Manasian, David: "Business in Eastern Europe," *The Economist,* Special Survey, September 21, 1991, p. 1.

Mann, Jim: "Russia Parliament Told It Perils Aid Package," *The Los Angeles Times,* April 13, 1992.

Mannick, Catherine et al.: "Interview with Deputy Privatization Minister Dmitri Vassiliev," *East/West Executive Guide,* vol. 2, no. 4, April 1992, p. 5.

Markoff, John: "Russian Computer Scientists Hired by American Company," *The New York Times,* March 3, 1992, p. A1.

Marshall, Tyler: "Last 'Little Stinker' Signals End of an East German Era," *The Los Angeles Times,* April 30, 1991, p. A1.

Martin, Fred: "Heard the One About the Copy Shop in Budapest?" *The New York Times Magazine,* December 16, 1990, p. 43.

Massie, Suzanne: *Land of the Firebird: The Beauty of Old Russia.* New York: Simon & Schuster, 1980.

Matthews, Paul: "A Diamond in the Rust," *World Link,* vol. 4, no 5., September–October 1991, p. 20.

Mayer, Jane: "Moscow Goes Gaga Over Sex, Phantoms and 'Bio-energetics'," *The Wall Street Journal,* December 3, 1991, p. A1.

McCauley, Denis: "Consumer Survey in Eastern Europe," *Business Eastern Europe,* April 8, 1991, p. 108.

McClenahen, John S.: "Light in the East," *Industry Week,* March 2, 1992, p. 14.

McIntosh, Mary: "Poles Support Market Economy—With Caution," *Transition,* vol. 2, no. 9, October 1991, p. 5.

McManus, Doyle: "Ambivalent President Takes Plunge," *The Los Angeles Times,* April 2, 1992, p. A8.

_____ : "Conference May Offer More Hope Than Help to Ex-Soviet Republics," *The Los Angeles Times,* January 20, 1992, p. A4.

Meister, Petra Ines: *Doing Business in East Germany*, Federal Republic of Germany: Frankfurter Allgemeine Zeitung GmbH Informationsdienste, 1990.

Melcher, Richard A.: "Europe, Too, Is Edgy About Imports—From America,"*Business Week*, January 27, 1992, p. 48.

Méras, Phyllis: *Eastern Europe: A Traveler's Companion*. Boston: Houghton Mifflin, 1991.

Meth-Cohn, Delia: "Hungary Spa's Powers Set to Be Reduced," *Business Eastern Europe*, August 12, 1991, p. 249.

_____: "P&G Acquisition in CSFR: Good Precedent For Foreign Investors," *Business Eastern Europe*, July 1, 1991, p. 203.

Meyer, Mark A.: "Managing Political Risk," *East/West Executive Guide*, vol. 2, no. 6, June 1992, p. 11.

Michaelides, Stephen G.: "In the Soviet Union: A New Breed of Entrepreneur," *Restaurant Hospitality*, May 1989, p. 108.

Miller, Leroy, and Maria Von Harpe: "Dealing with a Unified German Market," *Export Today*, May–June, 1990, p. 34.

Morton, John H.: "Case Study: Goldman Sachs Describes Role in Privatization and Natural Resource Development," *East/West Executive Guide*, vol. 2, no. 4, April 1992, p. 3.

Naj, Amal Kumar, and Timothy Aeppel: "GE to Reduce Spending at Plant in Hungary, Citing Soaring Costs," *The Wall Street Journal*, March 27, 1992, p. A11.

Nasar, Sylvia. "Russians Urged to Act Fast," *The New York Times*, January 6, 1992, p. C1.

Nestorovic, Cedomir: "The Automobile Industry in the East," *East European Economics*, Summer 1991, pp. 67–83.

Newman, Barry: "East Europe Faces Biggest Challenge Yet: Privatizing Its Industry," *The Wall Street Journal*, October 1, 1992, p. A1.

_____: "Poland's New Coalition Leaders Defend Shift in Economic Plan," *The Wall Street Journal*, February 19, 1992, p. A9.

_____: "Poland, Stung Twice, Begins to Shed Its Naivete About Wiles of Capitalism," *The Wall Street Journal*, December 3, 1991, p. A11.

_____: "These Days, Bulgaria Longs for Its Old Ties to the Soviet Union," *The Wall Street Journal*, April 30, 1991, p. A1.

Owen, David: "Profiles: Opening Windows," *The New Yorker*, December 2, 1991, pp. 48–115.

Pakula, Hannah: "Elena Ceausescu: The Shaping of an Ogress" *Vanity Fair*, August 1990, p. 121.

Pallay, Steve: "How GE-Tungsram Handles Layoffs in Hungary," *Business Eastern Europe*, July 1, 1991, p. 204.

Papp, Bella: "Hungary as Trade Channel to the Soviet Union?" *Business Eastern Europe*, September 9, 1991, p. 289.

_____, and Joseph Hollos: "Otis JV in Hungary: Reinvesting Profits," *Business Eastern Europe*, July 15, 1991, p. 220.

Parks, Michael: "Doing Business: Bloc-Buster Deal," *The Wall Street Journal*, July 21, 1992, p. H1.

_____: "Former Leader Seeks to Extend His Philosophy," *The Los Angeles Times*, December 26, 1991, p. A1.

_____: "Russia Needs $20 Billion in '92, U.S. Advisor Says," *The Los Angeles Times,* January 16, 1992, p. A9.

_____: "Russia Taking Painful Steps to a Free Market," *The Los Angeles Times,* January 2, 1992, p. A1.

_____: "Russia Wins Pledge of Aid, on Its Terms," *The Los Angeles Times,* July 7, 1992, p. A16.

_____: "Strauss Offers Store of Ideas for Russia," *The Los Angeles Times,* February 20, 1992, p. A8.

_____: "Unprecedented Auction Puts Russians in Business," *The Los Angeles Times,* April 5, 1992, p. A1.

_____: "Western Aid Designed to Save Yeltsin, Reforms," *The Los Angeles Times,* April 2, 1992, p. A9.

_____: "Yeltsin Mystery: True Democrat or Tyrant?" *The Los Angeles Times,* December 27, 1991, p. A1.

Perlez, June: "In East Europe, Kmart Stores Confront an Attitude Problem, "*The New York Times,* July 7, 1993, p. A1.

Petchenkine, Youri: "The Current Economic Situation: A Survey of the Government's Data on 1992 Developments," *East/West Executive Guide,* vol. 2, no. 4, April 1992, p. 19.

_____: "Valuation of Russian Enterprises: Rules and Procedures for Privatization," *East/West Executive Guide,* vol. 2, no. 4, April 1992, p. 11.

Peterson, Jonathan, and Robert A. Rosenblatt: "U.S. Firms Still Face Uncertainty in Former U.S.S.R.," *The Los Angeles Times,* April 2, 1992, p. D1.

Pietrucha, Bill: "High Risk in CIS Operations Can Pay Off If Companies Find Niche Markets," *We/MbI,* May 1, 1992, p. 7.

"Poland: Country Marketing Plan for Year 1991," Commercial section of the American Embassy in Warsaw, March 1991.

Polish-American Enterprise Fund, 1991 Annual Report, 535 Madison Avenue, New York, NY 10022.

Polish Ministry of Privatization, "Poland's Prevatization Program," *The Insider,* Warsaw, Dec. 9, 1991 (special information supplement).

Prokesch, Steven: "Dilemma of a Salesman in Prague," *The New York Times,* December 27, 1990, p. C1.

Protsman, Ferdinand: "German Overhaul Is Led by Phones," *The New York Times,* March 11, 1992, p. C1.

_____: "Miming the Capitalists Is Not Easy," *The New York Times,* January 20, 1991, p. F23.

Rakitinsky, Nikolai: "The Most Expensive Commodity Is Information," *We/MbI,* July–August 9, 1992, p. 7.

Rank Xerox: *Annual Report and Accounts 1990,* Rank Xerox, Buckinghamshire, England.

"Re-awakening: A Market Economy Takes Root in Eastern Europe," *Business Week,* April 15, 1991, p. 46.

"Ready for Business," *The Warsaw Voice,* February 9, 1992, p. B5.

Remnick, David: "Report from Moscow: The Trial of the Old Regime," *The New Yorker,* November 30, 1992, pp. 104–121.

Riding, Alan: "At East-West Crossroad, Western Europe Hesitates," *The New York Times*, March 25, 1992, p. A1.

"R.J. Reynolds to Produce Cigarettes in Russia," *We/MbI*, July 27–August 9, 1992, p. 7.

Robinson, Anthony: "Profile: Henryc Winkler of Katowice—Veteran Capitalist," *The Financial Times*, Special Section: Poland, April 28, 1992.

_____: "Profile: George Bonar—A Hunter of Business Gems," *The Financial Times*, Special Section: Poland, April 28, 1992.

_____: "Profile: Zbigniew Socha of Brodnica—Survivor Prospers," *The Financial Times*, Special Section: Poland, April 28, 1992.

_____, and Christopher Bobinski: "Paradise For Consultants," *The Financial Times*, Special Section: Poland, April 28, 1992.

Roche, David: "Trade and Foreign Capital Are Key," *World Link*, vol. 4, no. 5, September–October 1991, p. 28.

Romanowski, Hubert: "Technology Transfer Opportunities in Poland," Unpublished paper presented at U.S.–Poland Chamber of Commerce briefing, February 18, 1992.

Rosenblatt, Robert A. "Aid Package Like Bailout of Corporation," *The Los Angeles Times*, April 2, 1992, p. A8.

Rubinfien, Elisabeth: "Russia Is Urged to Abandon Income Tax That Threatens to Drive Out Foreigner," *The Wall Street Journal*, April 24, 1992, p. A11.

Schares, Gail E.: "Czechoslovakia: Reluctant Reform," *Business Week*, April 15, 1991, p. 55.

Schecter, Jerrold L.: "Gaidar: Russia's Economic Hope," *We/MbI*, March 1992, p. 4.

Schmemann, Serge: "Ex-Communists Win Lithuania's First Election Since Independence," *The New York Times*, October 27, 1992, p. A5.

_____: "To Each According to His Shares," *The New York Times*, December 14, 1992, p. C1.

_____: "War and Politics Bercking Prosperity for Azerbaijan," *The New York Times*, July 9, 1993, p. A1.

_____: "The World According to Gorbachev Disappears," *The New York Times*, December 8, 1991, p. E3.

Schmieding, Holger: "The Miracle That Remains a Mirage," *The Financial Times*, February 25, 1991.

Schoenberger, Karl: "Taking a Chance on Russia," *The Los Angeles Times*, January 3, 1992, p. A1.

Seib, Gerald F.: "Iran Is Re-emerging as a Mid-East Power as Iraqi Threat Fades," *The Wall Street Journal*, March 18, 1992, p. A1.

_____, and David Wessel: "IMF Approves Russia and 13 Other Republics," *The Wall Street Journal*, April 28, 1992, p. A2.

Shenon, Philip: "Eastern Europe Stymies All but the Hardiest of Western Capitalists," *The New York Times*, March 5, 1992, p. C8.

Shipler, David K.: *Russia: Broken Idols, Solemn Dreams*. New York: Penguin, 1983.

Shogren, Elizabeth: "Beleaguered Gorbachev Insists He Will Not Quit," *The Los Angeles Times*, December 11, 1991, p. A12.

_____: "Ex-Soviets Will Form Peacekeeping Force," *The Los Angeles Times*, July 7, 1992, pg. A 18.

_____: "In the Shadow of 'Big Brother'," *The Los Angeles Times,* May 1, 1992, p. A32.

_____: "SOS for Russian Science," *The Los Angeles Times,* September 29, 1992, p. A1.

_____: "Yeltsin Takes Charge of the 'Nuclear Button'," *The Los Angeles Times,* December 26, 1991, p. A10.

Simms, Milton A., Jr.: "San Diego Connects with Vladivostok," *New Visions Journal,* March 1992, p. 4.

Simon, Stephanie: "Communists Looking for a Capital Ally," *The Los Angeles Times,* July 7, 1992, p. A18.

_____: "It's Make My Day in Moscow," *The Los Angeles Times,* July 20, 1992, p. A1.

_____: "New Words Tongue-Tie Russians," *The Los Angeles Times,* August 29, 1992, p. A1.

_____: "Russian City's Privatization Effort Reaping Wages of Bitterness," *The Los Angeles Times,* September 7, 1992, p. A3.

_____: "Russia's Poor Push Their Luck," *The Los Angeles Times,* November 23, 1992, p. A1.

Slatter, Irene: *Simple Etiquette in Russia.* Sandgate, England: Paul Norbury Publications, 1990.

Smith, Hedrick: *The New Russians.* New York: Random House, 1990.

Sorokin, Evgeny: "Foreigners Learn to Play by New Rules," *We/Mbl,* June 1–14, 1992, p. 6.

Stanley, David: *Eastern Europe on a Shoestring.* Berkeley, CA: Lonely Plant Publications, 1989.

Steinbeck, John: *Russian Journal.* New York: Paragon House, 1989.

Stillman, Edmund, and the editors of *Life: The Balkans.* New York: Time Incorporated, 1964.

Sowinska, Magda: "Data Market Overload," *The Warsaw Voice,* February 9, 1992.

Stankiewicz, Tomasz, and Wladyslaw Jermakowicz: "Privatization through Restructuring: Motivation Is the Key," *The Insider* (Special Information Supplement), December 5, 1991 (unpaginated).

Stark, David: "A Sociologist's Perspective: Can Designer Capitalism Work in Central and Eastern Europe?" *Transition: The Newsletter About Reforming Economies,* vol. 3, no. 5, May 1992, p. 1.

Stewart, Robert W.: "Nixon Urges U.S. to Lead Aid to Commonwealth," *The Los Angeles Times,* March 12, 1992, p. A6.

Tagliabue, John: "When the Best Customer—the Ex-Soviet Union—Is Broke," *The New York Times,* April 5, 1992, p. F11.

The editors of Time-Life Books: *Eastern Europe.* Alexandria, VA: Time-Life Books, 1987.

_____: *The Soviet Union.* Alexandria, VA: Time-Life Books, 1985.

The Europe Review, Economic and Business Report. Essex, England: World of Information, 1991–1992.

"The Latest Russian Expatriate: Hard Cash," *Business Week,* February 10, 1992, p. 41.

Thompson, Jon: "East Europe's Dark Dawn," *National Geographic,* June 1991, p. 36.

Thorniley, Daniel: "Privatization in the USSR Is Still a Long Way Off," *Business Eastern Europe*, July 22, 1991, p. 225.

Thurow, Roger: "Investors Avoid Yugoslavia as Its Supply of Troubles Begins to Seem Inexhaustible," *The Wall Street Journal*, May 22, 1991, p. A14.

Torbert, Preston M.: "Implications for Foreign Corporations," *East/West Executive Guide*, vol. 2, no. 4, April 1992, p. 4.

Toth, Robert C.: "New Ties to the Old Country," *The Los Angeles Times*, May 14, 1991, p. A1.

Treuhandanstalt: "How to Purchase a Company in Eastern Germany: Questions and Answers," Berlin.

Uchitelle, Louis: "A Failed Cliché in Siberia: Rich in Oil, Not 'Oil Rich'," *The New York Times*, February 11, 1992, p. A1.

_____: "Hunting for Riches in Ex-Soviet Lands," *The New York Times*, December 27, 1991, p. A1.

_____: "Now That They Must, Former Soviets Hustle for Money," *The New York Times*, March 15, 1992, p. E3.

_____: "Russia's Central Bank Resists Cuts in Lending," *The New York Times*, February 16, 1992, p. 7.

_____: "U.S. Oilmen Sample Russia's Pitfalls," *The New York Times*, January 30, 1992, p. C1.

U.S. Department of Commerce: Data File: Soviet Union and Baltic States, Hungary, Poland, Romania, Bulgaria, Czechoslovakia, Bulgaria, International Division, Central and Eastern European Trade and Technical Assistance Center, Washington, DC, 1991.

_____: "Defense Conversion Opportunities: 'Red October' Submarine Plant Looks for Western Partner," *BISNIS Bulletin*, September 1992.

_____: Directory of Contacts for Central and Eastern Europe and the Soviet Union, Washington, DC, 1991.

_____: Eastern Europe Business Bulletin, International Trade Administration, Business Information Center, Washington, DC, October 1991–March 1993.

_____: German Trade Fairs: A Handbook for American Exhibitors and Exportors, U.S. and Foreign Commercial Service, American Embassy, Bonn, Washington, DC, May 1986.

_____: "Investing in Hungary," International Trade Administration, Business Information Center, Washington, DC.

_____: Sources for Financing Your Ventures in Eastern Europe, Eastern Europe Business Information Center, Washington, DC, 1992.

U.S. Department of State: Doing Business in the Five New German States, American Embassy, Commercial Section, Berlin.

U.S.–Poland Chamber of Commerce: "Manufacturing in Poland: An American Perspective," U.S.–Poland Connection, vol. 1, no. 3, Spring 1992, p. 5.

"Update on Joint Ventures," *The Soviet Business Review*, vol. 2, no. 9, September 1991, p. 1.

Varga, George: "Market-Share Strategies," *World Link*, vol. 4, no. 5, September–October 1991, p. 27.

Viktorov, Viktor: "Ten Tips for the Accidental Tourist," *Glasnost News & Review*, April 1991.

Wallach, John P.: "Bush Should Get Off the Dime to Help the Ruble," *We/MbI*, March 1992, p. 4.

_____: "Privatization: A Complex, Confusing Process," *We/MbI*, August 24–September 6, 1992, p. 1.

Wartzman, Rick: "Major U.S. Concerns Remain Reluctant to Invest Heavily in Ex-Soviet Regions," *The Wall Street Journal*, May 11, 1992, p. A5C.

Weiss, Stanley A.: "Companies: Watch Your Exports!" *World Link*, vol. 4, no. 5, September–October 1991, p. 7.

West, Rebecca: *Black Lamb and Grey Falcon: A Journey through Yugoslavia*. New York: Viking Press, 1940.

Whitford, Rob: "Private Agents in Bulgaria," *Business Eastern Europe*, November 4, 1991, p. 388.

Williams, Carol J.: "Bulgaria's Lack of Reform Stunts Nation's Rebirth," *The Los Angeles Times*, May 19, 1991, p. D1.

_____: "Cash Is Burden to Hungary's Consumers," *The Los Angeles Times*, May 16, 1991, p. D2.

_____: "Doing business in These Balkans: Rock Bottom Cost...and Quality," *The Los Angeles Times*, June 26, 1990, p. H4.

_____: "No Solutions in View, Serbs Cling to Status Quo," *The Los Angeles Times*, March 11, 1992, p. A6.

Willis, David K.: *Klass: How Russian's Really Live*. New York: St. Martin's Press, 1985.

Wolf, Kenneth: "Programmers Sell Artificial Intelligence Developed in Belarus," *We/MbI*, July 27–August 9, 1992, p. 7.

Woutat, Donald: "General Motors Cuts a Deal to Assemble Autos in Poland," *The Los Angeles Times*, February 29, 1992, p. D1.

Wyden, Peter: *Wall: The Inside Story of Divided Berlin*. New York: Simon & Schuster, 1989.

Yoshihashi, Pauline: "Chevron Signs Initial Pact to Develop the Tengiz Oil Field in Kazakhstan," *The Wall Street Journal*, May 8, 1992, p. A8.

Index

About the Author

Christoper Engholm is currently the director of marketing for Rowland & Associates in San Diego, specializing in international executive training for Eastern Europe, the Middle East, and the Pacific Rim. He is the author of numerous articles and three books on international business, the latest of which is *When Business East Meets Business West*.